Warehouse Management

SECOND EDITION

Warehouse Management

A complete guide to improving efficiency and minimizing costs in the modern warehouse

Gwynne Richards

LONDON PHILADELPHIA NEW DELHI

First published in Great Britain and the United States in 2011 by Kogan Page Limited
Second edition 2014

2nd Floor, 45 Gee Street	1518 Walnut Street, Suite 1100	4737/23 Ansari Road
London EC1V 3RS	Philadelphia PA 19102	Daryaganj
United Kingdom	USA	New Delhi 110002
www.koganpage.com		India

© Gwynne Richards, 2011, 2014

The right of Gwynne Richards to be identified as the author of this work has been asserted by him in accordance with the Copyright, Designs and Patents Act 1988.

ISBN   978 0 7494 6934 4
E-ISBN   978 0 7494 6935 1

British Library Cataloguing-in-Publication Data

A CIP record for this book is available from the British Library.

Library of Congress Cataloging-in-Publication Data

Richards, Gwynne.
   Warehouse management : a complete guide to improving efficiency and minimizing costs in the modern warehouse / Gwynne Richards. – Second edition.
      pages cm
   Includes bibliographical references and index.
   ISBN 978-0-7494-6934-4 – ISBN 978-0-7494-6935-1 (ebk)   1. Warehouses–Management.   2. Business logistics.   3. Materials management.   I. Title.
   HF5485.R53 2014
   658.7'85–dc23

                                                                              2013050663

Typeset by Graphicraft Limited, Hong Kong
Printed and bound in India by Replika Press Pvt Ltd

CONTENTS

LIST OF FIGURES

LIST OF TABLES

ACKNOWLEDGEMENTS

First I need to acknowledge the help and support of my wife Teresa who has provided hours of encouragement and insight, together with bucketfuls of tea and coffee.

Second, I must acknowledge the help of my co-writers:

Mike Hodge

David Cairns of Q Log Consulting;

Chris Sturman of FSDF;

Ruth Waring of Labyrinth Logistics Consulting;

Simon Edwards of Aaron and Partners, Solicitors, and his colleagues Claire Riding, Julie Sillitoe and Tim Culpin.

My thanks also to Kate Vitasek and Bill Dibenedetto for their contribution on outsourcing and for providing some excellent data, and to Peter Baker from Cranfield University.

Thanks also to the Chartered Institute of Logistics and Transport training team who asked me to run their Warehouse Management course from which I have gained further insight into the subject both through the delegates and the need to keep up to date with advances in this area.

My thanks also go to Tim Abraham of Toyota, Mike Allibone of SSI Schäfer, Stephen Cross of ATMS, Ian Davies of LXE, David Hyslop of Vanderlande, David James of Knapp, Keith Washington of System Logistics, Gary Frankham of Atlet, Simon Brown from Bendi, Scott Williams of the Constructor Group, and all other contributors of facts and photographs, all of whose websites are included at the back of the book.

Finally, thanks to Julia Swales of Kogan Page for her patience and resilience through this whole process.

Introduction

What is a warehouse?

" *A warehouse should be viewed as a* temporary *place to store inventory and as a buffer in supply chains.*

It serves, as a static unit – in the main – matching product availability to consumer demand and as such has a primary aim which is to facilitate the movement of goods from suppliers to customers, meeting demand in a timely and cost-effective manner.   **ADAPTED FROM VAN DEN BERG (2013)**

Primarily a warehouse should be a trans-shipment point where all goods received are despatched as quickly, effectively and efficiently as possible.

The basic processes of warehouse management remain the same over time. We receive goods into the warehouse, we process orders, we replenish, we include some value-adding services and then we despatch the product. Advances in warehousing tend to relate to the increased use of technology and automation, improved performance measurement and the effective management of resources.

In the second edition of this book we have retained the core concept of discussing each warehouse process in turn together with putting the role of the warehouse into context within the overall supply chain.

However, in this edition we have increased the number of case studies from companies who have achieved improvements and cost savings through the introduction of new technology and equipment, leaner processes and environmental initiatives.

The saying goes that a picture paints a thousand words, so in this edition we include more photographs of the equipment and also links to videos where you can see the equipment and technology in action.

Where you see the following symbol you will be able to access a video of the equipment or process discussed:

The warehouse continues to play a major role within supply chains and will continue to do so for the foreseeable future, although these warehouses will appear in different guises.

The growth in fulfilment centres for e-commerce, for example, is certainly changing the warehousing landscape. Finished stock needs to be held as close to the point of consumption as possible to reduce ever increasing transportation costs and to meet increasingly demanding customer delivery requirements. This has led to many warehouses transforming into cross-dock and transhipment centres, fulfilment centres, sortation and consolidation points, reverse logistics centres as well as fulfilling their roles as storage facilities.

As a result, managers need to have a greater understanding of the various roles that warehouses can fulfil and how these affect the business and the supply chain as a whole.

No two operations are exactly the same, even within the same company, although the underlying principles remain. This book aims to share these principles and enable managers to get a better understanding of how to achieve best-in-class status.

This book aims to further update readers on current and potential future advances in warehouse management whilst tackling the issues that are challenging today's managers.

These include the pressure on managers to increase productivity, reduce cost, improve customer service at least cost to the environment whilst ensuring the health and safety of staff employed in the warehouse.

The author and contributors have a number of years' experience in managing and consulting on warehouse operations. This book is written from the perspective of hands-on operators and aims to share past experiences and knowledge gathered over recent years.

Having moved into consultancy, the author is continually updating his knowledge in this rapidly changing sector of logistics. This book also draws on the knowledge and experience of colleagues and the results of recent benchmarking studies and surveys from Europe and the United States.

Warehouses evolve. Technology has moved on apace and as a result, opportunities to improve efficiency and effectiveness within the warehouse are constantly being introduced. This, together with increasing demands from customers and internal pressures to reduce costs yet improve service levels, can prove a significant challenge to warehouse and logistics managers everywhere.

The introduction of sophisticated automation, robotics and advanced software systems into warehouse operations can potentially have an effect on logistics operations comparable to the introduction of the wheel millennia ago. These advances in technology are likely to lead to a significant reduction in staff and improved efficiency. This comes at a cost, however.

Not all warehouse operations are likely to benefit from such advances or can afford large investments in technology. This book will examine the basic processes required to manage a warehouse effectively. In fact, these processes need to be in place in all warehouses prior to any thoughts of introducing new technology.

Automating a bad process might make it quicker but certainly doesn't make it more efficient. The author recognizes the huge diversity of warehouse operations globally and although the book discusses current concepts and technologies it concentrates in the main on how all warehouses can become more efficient and effective, irrespective of budget.

Logistics is very much about trade-offs. This book will examine these in detail as they will affect how warehouse and logistics managers approach their jobs and the decisions they take.

Major trade-offs include:

- cost versus service;
- storage capacity versus speed of retrieval;
- speed versus accuracy;
- lower inventory versus availability;
- efficiency versus responsiveness; and
- volume purchases versus storage cost and availability.

These trade-offs appear both within the warehouse itself and also between the warehouse operation and other logistics services.

This book has been written in such a way that it will be a useful reference point for staff involved in the day-to-day operations of a warehouse; senior managers who require a basic understanding of warehouses; designers and planners; external agencies needing a basic understanding; and, finally, those who are considering a career in warehousing and logistics.

Through the use of case studies and examples, the author shares fundamental tools and processes that have been prevalent in the industry over the years and have been instrumental in assisting managers to increase efficiency and reduce costs.

The book concentrates on the areas that challenge today's warehousing and logistics managers. These include:

- improving efficiency and productivity whilst reducing costs;
- improving quality and accuracy;
- reduced lead times from customers;

- technological advancements;
- workforce availability and management;
- health and safety; and
- effects on the environment.

Chapters 1 and 2 of the book discuss the roles of the warehouse and warehouse manager in today's supply chain. Within these chapters we also examine one of the main challenges for warehouse managers – attracting and retaining quality staff.

Chapters 3 to 7 analyse the individual processes within the warehouse, outlining areas where costs can be reduced whilst productivities increase through the use of technology and improved methods.

Chapters 8 to 10 explore in detail equipment utilized within the warehouse, including warehouse management systems, handling and storage equipment.

Chapters 11 and 12 discuss how to resource and calculate the costs of a warehouse.

Chapters 13 and 14 look at performance measurement in detail and also the opportunities afforded by outsourcing.

Chapters 15 and 16 provide an insight into areas that currently take up a significant percentage of a manager's time today. These include health and safety and the continuing pressure on companies to reduce the effects of logistics operations on the environment.

The final chapter looks at current advances in warehousing and attempts to predict the future.

The book has been written by a UK-based author and has contributors from both the United Kingdom and the United States. They have all worked and lectured in many different countries. It is hoped that this book will be read globally and that the information provided will resonate with warehouse operators, students and management teams worldwide.

Books such as this are an excellent resource for today's managers. However, they need to be used in conjunction with other, easily accessible resources. These include your peers, staff on the warehouse floor, the suppliers of warehouse equipment and consultants – all of whom have a wealth of experience to share with today's managers.

A large glossary of terms and acronyms can be downloaded from the following website: **www.appriseconsulting.co.uk/warehousetools**. The password is apprise1234.

There are online resources available for operators, teachers and lecturers. Examples include warehouse audits, space calculations, PowerPoint slides, videos and lists of useful websites.

The role of
the warehouse

01

If I don't have room for an item I put it in warehouses.
URSULA ANDRESS (1936–)

Introduction

Warehouses have, in the past, been constantly referred to as cost centres and rarely adding value. The movement of production to the Far East, the growth of e-commerce and increasing demands from consumers has seen a step change in warehouse operations. Warehouses are now seen as a vital link within today's supply chains. In fact, as stated in a recent survey by Motorola (2013):

> fewer organizations continue to view warehouses and DCs simply as commoditized links between endpoints of the supply chain. Warehouses are no longer necessary evils that are fundamentally cost centers. The movement from linear to complex, multi-node supply chains recognizes this shift in perception, and is being driven by greater volatility, constrained capacity, evolving regulations, major shifts in customer demographics and buying patterns, and increasingly demanding customer and supplier requirements. Warehouses today can drive competitive differentiation and, by doing so, increase profitable growth.

The pressure remains on managers to increase productivity and accuracy, reduce cost and inventory whilst improving customer service.

As an introduction to the main aspects of the book we set the context by examining the role of the warehouse in today's economy and its likely place within future supply chains.

We will also look at the factors involved in choosing a suitable location for a warehouse and how many warehouses might be required.

We have also taken three examples of specialist warehousing and expanded on these. We realize there are other areas such as hazardous goods storage and maintenance stores, but the need to cover all the fundamental areas precludes us from going into these areas in detail.

We believe, however, that the same underlying principles apply, albeit with greater emphasis on both legal and safety aspects. The role of a supply chain is to deliver the right products, in the correct quantity, to the right customer, at the right place, at the right time, in the right condition, at the right price.

The warehouse plays a significant part in this. Delivering the right product in the right quantity relies on the warehouse picking and despatching products accurately. Delivering to the right customer at the right place, on time, requires the product to be labelled correctly and loaded onto the right vehicle with sufficient time to meet the delivery deadline. The warehouse also has to ensure the product leaves the warehouse clean and damage free. Finally, at the right price requires a cost-efficient operation that delivers value for money.

The warehouse is therefore crucial in delivering the perfect order. This can be done in many ways.

In the past, warehouses were seen mainly as stockholding points, attempting to match supply to demand and acting as a buffer between raw material and component suppliers and the manufacturers and between the manufacturers and the wholesalers and retailers and/or consumers. Stock visibility along the supply chain was limited and information flow was very slow, resulting in companies holding more stock than necessary.

Warehouses also fulfilled a major role in storing raw materials. As land and buildings were relatively cheap, the cost of holding significant quantities of raw materials and finished stock was seen as the norm and totally acceptable.

Production runs in those days were very long as it was an expensive process to change models, colours, styles, etc. The economy was also seen as supply driven with manufacturers producing products in the hope that retailers would stock them and consumers would buy them.

As a result there was a large proliferation of warehouses and stockholding increased appreciably.

In today's market with expensive land, buildings, labour and energy costs, together with the introduction of concepts such as just in time (JIT), efficient consumer response (ECR) and quick response (QR), companies are continually looking to minimize the amount of stock held and speed up throughput. The use of tools such as postponement – where products are completed in the warehouse, not at the manufacturing location – are becoming common place.

We have gone from a 'push' to a 'pull' supply chain over recent years. In fact, the phrase 'supply chain' can be a bit of a misnomer and rather it should be called a demand chain, with consumers holding sway.

In the past, manufacturers produced goods and passed them on to the retailers, expecting them to sell as many of their products as possible. The manufacturers operated a large number of local warehouses and delivered product direct to store.

This situation changed in the 1980s when retailers took partial control of their supply chains and began to build national and regional distribution centres. This changed the face of warehousing with a move towards larger, multi-temperature sites owned by the retailers and in many situations operated by third-party logistics companies.

These sites continue to grow, with Tesco recently building a 1.2 million square foot warehouse at Teesport in the United Kingdom, and Marks & Spencer have commissioned a 900,000 square foot distribution centre at London Gateway, the UK's new super port. The location of these warehouses are also part of a movement towards port-centric logistics.

The trend towards outsourcing Western production to India and Asia has resulted in companies having to hold higher levels of finished goods stock than previously. This is to cover the extended lead time between production and final delivery.

Containers from Shanghai to the United Kingdom, for example, can take upwards of 31 days, not including clearance at the port of entry. As can be seen in Figure 1.1, there is a requirement for some form of warehouse operation throughout the supply chain.

Types of warehouse operation

There are many different roles for a warehouse in today's supply chain. As can be seen in Figure 1.1, warehouses can be operated by raw materials suppliers, component and finished goods manufacturers, wholesalers, retailers and companies involved in reverse logistics. The warehouses can be owner operated or subcontracted to third-party logistics providers.

These warehouses fulfil the following roles:

Raw materials storage

These warehouses store raw materials and components either close to the point of extraction or close to the manufacturing point. Raw materials must be held in order to ensure continuous production. These materials include plastics, precious metals, sand, aggregates, etc.

Intermediate, postponement, customization or sub-assembly facilities

These warehouses are used to store products temporarily at different stages in production. These centres are also used to customize products before final delivery to the customer.

FIGURE 1.1 Warehousing in the supply chain

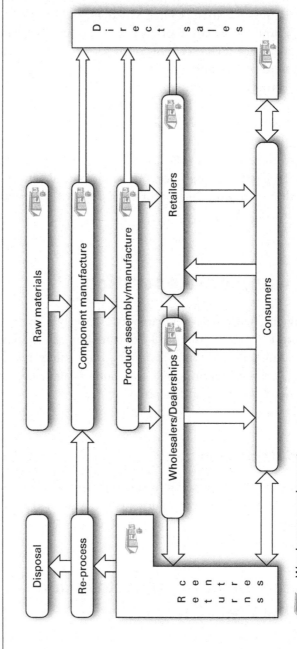

Postponement and sub-assembly activities can include the following:

- specific packaging or labelling being changed or added, eg for store-ready items or printing in different languages;
- computer assembly to include different graphics cards, memory chips, software, etc;
- product bundling for promotional activity;
- country-specific items being added such as electrical plugs; and
- special messages being added, eg stencilling of greetings messages on mobile phones.

Finished goods storage

These warehouses store products ready for sale, on behalf of manufacturers, wholesalers and retailers. They provide a buffer or safety stock for companies, enabling them to build up stock in preparation for new product launches, expected increases in demand and to deal with seasonality.

 www.youtube.com/watch?v=a81z7wkwC7s (the FTA channel)

This video shows how Samsung products are moved through the supply chain via a number of finished goods warehouses including the store's own warehouse.

Consolidation centres and transit warehouses

Consolidation centres receive products from different sources and amalgamate them for onward delivery to the customer or onto a production line. This can include just-in-time centres where automotive parts are delivered to a warehouse where they are brought together and sequenced for delivery onto the production line.

They can also be retail stock consolidation warehouses where products from different suppliers are consolidated for onward delivery to the stores. Rather than deliver part-loads to the Retail Distribution Centres (RDC), manufacturers deliver to these facilities where their stock is consolidated with other suppliers for onward delivery to the RDC. These differ from cross-dock centres in that product can remain in the centre for a period of time awaiting call-off from the final destination. Many of these consolidation centres are operated by third parties.

Transhipment or break-bulk centres

Transhipment centres receive products in large quantities from suppliers and break them down into manageable quantities for onward delivery to various locations.

Cross-dock centres

Cross-dock centres are seen as being the future for warehousing. Efficient consumer response and quick response within retail require operations to be able to move goods quickly through the supply chain. Cross docking requires deliveries into these centres to be already labelled and ready for onward delivery. Here the items are identified and consolidated with other deliveries, ready for despatch. Items should remain in the warehouse for as short a time as possible. Same-day receipt and despatch is the target.

Although companies are beginning to realize the efficiency of cross docking, there are a number of barriers to a successful introduction. These can include warehouse management systems support, quality control systems, reliability and cooperation of suppliers and carriers, warehouse design and uncertain demand. Cross-dock warehouses or transhipment centres are also utilized in outlying geographic areas to transfer products onto local, radial distribution vehicles. This transhipment process can take place either inside or outside the warehouse. Typical cross-dock products are perishable items such as fruit and vegetables, meat and fish, which need to be moved quickly through the supply chain. Motorola's recent study (2013) showed that 31 per cent of companies practised cross docking and this was expected to increase to 45 per cent by 2018.

Sortation centres

Sortation centres are used in the main by letter, parcel and pallet distribution companies. Goods are collected from all parts of the country, delivered into hubs or sortation centres, sorted by zip or post code, consolidated and delivered overnight to their respective distribution areas for onward delivery.

Today's retailers are also moving towards automated sortation centres with pallets being de-layered on entry, the use of mini-load systems for temporary storage and retrieval and finally automated pallet build on exit.

Fulfilment centres

The growth of e-retailing has seen an increase in the number of customer fulfilment centres. These warehouses have been designed and equipped specifically to manage large volumes of small orders. The video shows the fulfilment operation of an internet retailer called i-herb.com.

 www.youtube.com/watch?v=uAsl8-UQJFl (Dematic Corp)

These centres can also double up as returns processing centres as e-commerce has a larger percentage of returns than normal retail activities. This area is covered in greater detail later in this chapter.

Reverse logistics centres

The growth of e-retailing and specific environmental legislation such as the European Union's Waste Electrical and Electronic Equipment (WEEE) Directive (2007) has compelled companies to focus time and energy on reverse logistics. Today, companies recognize that returning product to stock or disposing of it quickly can positively affect cash flow.

As a result, a number of warehouses have been set up specifically to deal with returned items. Third-party contractors are providing a service to retailers where customers return unwanted or defective items to the stores; the items are then consolidated and sent to the returns centre, where they are checked and either repackaged, repaired, recycled or disposed of.

Waste legislation has also resulted in large quantities of returned packaging having to be disposed of in an environmentally friendly manner. This includes sortation by type and use as fuel or recycled material. There are case studies in the environmental section that go into more detail on this subject.

Other reverse logistics processes include the return of reusable transit packaging equipment such as roll cages, barrels, kegs, pallets, tote boxes and trays. When used in the food industry added services include washing and sanitizing the items before they re-enter the supply chain.

For example, Norbert Dentressangle, a 3PL, service and maintain more than a million roll cages, as well as 230 million trays and flower buckets and dollies for Tesco.

Public sector warehousing

Outside the commercial world there are also warehouse operations which support the public sector, armed forces and the third sector.

The increasing number of natural disasters such as earthquakes, droughts and tsunamis is resulting in third-sector organizations opening up warehouses in strategic locations across the globe. This ensures that they are closer to the disaster areas and thus able to react quicker.

Other public sector warehouses will store supplies for local government facilities such as schools and offices. Products will include stationery, uniforms, furniture, computer hardware and software, etc.

All the warehouse operations mentioned above can be owned, leased or operated by third-party companies on behalf of a principal.

Warehouses operated by third-party logistics providers are either dedicated operations on behalf of a single customer or can be shared-user or public warehouses where a number of different customers share resources and are accommodated under one roof.

These include:

- companies with different products but with common customers such as retailers or automotive manufacturers;
- companies with the same or similar products delivering to common customers, eg tyre manufacturers; bicycle manufacturers, pharmaceutical companies and multimedia companies (a typical example is where Sony, Universal and Warner share a warehouse in the United Kingdom);
- companies needing similar types of service, eg fulfilment or returns processing; and
- companies requiring the same environmental conditions, eg hazardous goods, explosives or temperature controlled.

Users of shared-user warehouses are, in the main, companies looking for economies of scale through sharing facilities, equipment and labour costs.

Why do we hold stock?

A supply chain with the minimum amount of stock within its pipeline is utopia. Unfortunately this happens very rarely. Our society and our markets are not predictable and therefore we need to hold stock at various stages within the supply chain. Increased consumer demand for greater choice has resulted in a proliferation of product ranges and sizes leading to unprecedented demands on storage capacity.

Reasons for holding stock are as follows.

Uncertain and erratic demand patterns

Suppliers of ice cream, suntan lotion, umbrellas and the like will potentially experience erratic demand patterns based on the changeability of the weather. Other unpredictable sales can revolve around the launch of a new product and the progress of a team in a major competition such as football's World Cup or baseball's World Series events.

Trade-off between transport and shipping costs, justifying larger shipments

The ability to move product in large quantities tends to attract lower costs per unit. The trade-off here is between the cost of storing additional units compared with the higher cost of transport for smaller, groupage-type deliveries. If the transport cost is very attractive then additional storage space will be required. There also has to be a strong conviction that all the items purchased will be sold.

Discounts via bulk buying

The possibility of reducing the unit rate through buying in greater quantities is always an attractive proposition for buyers. This can, however, have a negative effect overall if the company fails to sell all of the additional units purchased or has to sell at a loss to clear the warehouse. In this situation it is our contention that the whole-life cost of the item is calculated before the decision is made to purchase additional quantities. These costs will include additional storage and handling costs, working capital interest, possible discounted sales and disposal costs. A trade-off exists between lower unit purchase costs and increased storage costs per unit. I'm sure there are many warehouses out there holding obsolete stock due to the overenthusiasm of procurement and sales staff!

Distance between manufacturer and the end consumer

As mentioned earlier, the distance finished stock has to travel today requires a greater amount of stock to be held in the warehouse. Lead times can be anything between four and eight weeks depending on the manufacturer's location. The trade-off here is between more expensive local suppliers and producers and increased costs in transport and inventory holding costs.

Cover for production shutdowns

Many manufacturing companies and sectors continue to shut down their operations for vacations, machine maintenance and stock counts. As a result retailers and wholesalers need to build up stock prior to the shutdown period to ensure stock availability for their customers. Manufacturers will also build up a stock of components to ensure that their production lines are not brought to a standstill as a result of supplier shutdowns.

Ability to increase production runs

Changing or adjusting production lines in order to accommodate changes in models, colour, design features, etc is expensive. The longer the production run, the lower the cost per unit to produce. However, the trade-off here is between the lower cost per unit versus the additional cost per unit for storage.

To manage seasonal production

Certain food and drink products are produced at specific times of the year and therefore need to be stored until required.

High seasonality

Seasonality can be a period of time such as summer and winter or a specific date in the calendar such as Easter, Valentine's Day, Independence Day or the Chinese New Year. Figure 1.2 shows the stock build-up for a chocolate manufacturer in the run-up to Easter. As can be seen, pallet storage ranges from 500 pallets to a staggering 10,000 pallets at peak.

Large sporting events can also have an impact on the requirement for additional storage. This includes the World Cup, the Olympics, Super Bowl final and World Series baseball, etc. Figure 1.3 shows the activity of a clothing manufacturer leading up to the two distinct seasons of summer and winter collections.

Spare parts storage

To ensure an uninterrupted production line operation, manufacturers need to hold stock of spare parts just in case an item becomes defective. This can be expensive but the trade-off here is between the cost of the part together with its holding cost and the potential breakdown of the production line and the consequences that brings with it. This doesn't mean, however, that these items should not be reviewed regularly and decisions taken as to whether to stock them or not. Things to take into account include supplier lead time and machine failure rate.

Work-in-progress storage

Many companies will part-build products in anticipation of orders. The chocolate manufacturer mentioned above produces the two halves of the Easter egg

FIGURE 1.2   Seasonality: chocolate

FIGURE 1.3   Seasonality: apparel and equipment

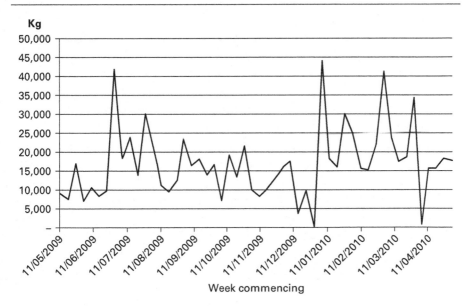

prior to receiving any firm orders. This enables them to complete the process at a later date, once they know the type of packaging, style and insertions required.

Investment stocks

A number of products can increase in value the longer they are held in storage. These include fine wines and spirits, cigars, precious metals and stones, antiques and fine art.

Document storage

Both public bodies and private companies have an obligation to store documents over a period of time. These can include correspondence, invoices, accounts, etc. This can be a legal requirement. Other examples include evidence storage and patient records by the emergency services.

Warehouse location

Locating a warehouse strategically and in the most cost-effective geographic location is one of the most important decisions a company will make. For example, in terms of fulfilment centres, because of the nature of deliveries, an important criteria is the need to be located near to the motorway network to delay the latest collection time from the parcel companies and therefore enable companies to introduce a later order cut-off time for next day delivery. Grocery retailers with online sales will have a requirement to be much closer to their customers due to the different temperature regimes of the products being delivered.

The selection of a warehouse location requires multiple criteria to be assessed, including both quantitative and qualitative data.

Many companies will look at the location and size of customers which, although relevant, is not as important as it would be when locating a retail outlet. Other factors include land cost, labour availability, travel minimization and total cost. The environment will also play a part in the decision-making process. The following are specific factors that need to be taken into account when deciding on a warehouse location:

- cost of land, rent and rates;
- access to transport networks;
- availability of affordable skilled labour;
- transport links for staff;

- availability of funding, grants, etc;

- availability of existing buildings;

- availability and cost of utilities including telecoms;

- availability of finance and resources;

- goods traffic flows;

- proximity to ports and airports;

- location of suppliers and manufacturing points; and

- the potential neighbours (eg proximity to oil storage depots can be a negative factor).

A recent report by DTZ (2013) stated that the global top five least expensive markets for warehousing are dominated by the Chinese Tier II cities of Wuhan, Shenyang and Chengdu, with Atlanta and Marseille completing the top five. Costs in all these markets are below US $70 per square metre per annum. Meanwhile, London Heathrow remains the most expensive area globally – at US $313 per square metre per annum, followed by Hong Kong, Zurich, Singapore and Oslo. Hong Kong is projected to see the biggest cost decline in the next five years, with occupiers continuing their migration to more affordable premises in mainland China.

In the Savills (2013) survey, the top nine requirements for e-retailing operations in terms of location were as follows:

- land/rent/lease costs;

- access to affordable labour;

- expansion space available;

- close proximity to parcel hub;

- close to motorway network;

- central location (covering all United Kingdom);

- close proximity to consumers;

- government incentive; and

- close proximity to higher skilled labour.

Fortunately the decision on where to site a warehouse does not have to be totally manual as there are a number of software programs available which will take the majority of these criteria into account and produce a number of viable alternatives.

Many of these systems work on the basis of volume centre of gravity calculations which locate the warehouse at the centre of supply and demand by minimizing distances to customers and from suppliers.

A more accurate method is to utilize the cost centre of gravity calculation which locates the warehouse at the centre of supply and demand by minimizing transport costs to customers and from suppliers.

Route planning and optimization software will produce a viable location; however, supply chain optimization tools will further enhance this decision.

FIGURE 1.4   Warehouse costs globally (courtesy of DTZ)

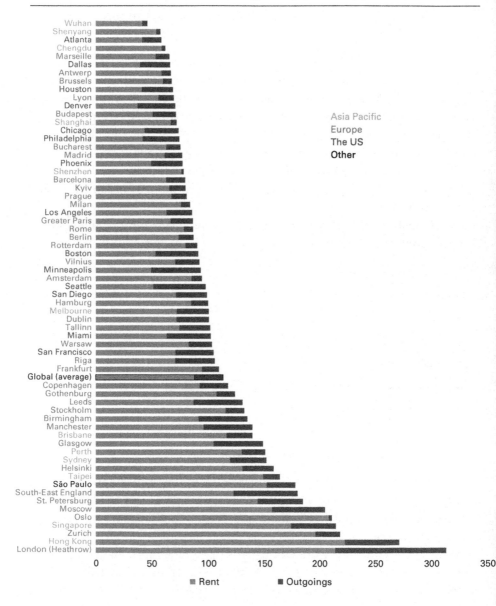

FIGURE 1.5 Factors determining the location of a warehouse

Adapted and reprinted from Expert Systems with Applications, Multi-criteria warehouse location selection using Choquet integral, Tufan Demirel, Nihan Çetin Demirel, Cengiz Kahraman, May 2010, with permission from Elsevier

Number of warehouses

There is an ongoing debate as to whether companies are going to increase or reduce the number of warehouse operated within the supply chain. A recent survey by Motorola showed that 35 per cent of the respondents planned to increase the number of warehouses operated whilst 36 per cent looked to increase the size of their existing facilities.

A survey by Savills (2013) in the UK showed that warehouse take-up by retailers only, will total 50 million square feet over the next five years and that is 21 per cent up on take-up in the last five years. Some 13 million square feet of this future take-up will be within e-tailing specific property, driven by online sales. There is no doubt that the move to multichannel retailing is having an effect on the number and size of locations operated.

The increasing cost of fuel, a move towards near-shoring and a requirement to be nearer the customer could see the number of local warehouses and distribution centres increasing with cross-dock operations being favoured by more companies.

As with most areas of the supply chain there is a trade-off here. We can see from Table 1.1 that most costs are higher if multiple warehouses are chosen; however, all of these costs can be off-set by a significant reduction in local transportation costs and improved service.

In terms of inventory we need to be able to calculate by how much we will increase or reduce our safety stockholding when we change the number of warehouses operated.

TABLE 1.1   Comparison between many and fewer warehouses

Criteria	Many warehouses	Fewer warehouses
Inventory costs	Higher	Lower
Customer reaction time	Quicker	Slower
Facility costs	Higher	Lower
Inbound transport cost	Higher	Lower
Outbound transport cost	Lower	Higher
Systems cost	Higher	Lower

One way of doing this is by using the Square Root Rule which was first introduced by David Maister in 1976. Maister's rule enables companies to quickly calculate the reduction or increase in safety stock required when the number of warehouses is changed.

It states that the total safety stock in a supply chain is proportional to the square root of the number of locations at which a product is stored. The calculation is as follows:

$$\text{Reduction in stockholding (\%)} = [1 - (\sqrt{x} \div \sqrt{y})] \times 100$$

Where 'y' is the original number of warehouses and 'x' is the proposed number of warehouses.

This calculation cannot be used in isolation. Other factors, such as supplier and customer lead times, the product itself (different types of electrical plug for example), transport costs and distribution centre costs also have to be taken into account.

The rule is based on the assumption that the amount of safety stock in each existing warehouse in the system is approximately the same.

Supply chain trends affecting warehouses

This section examines current trends within today's supply chain and how these are likely to affect warehouse operations.

The e-commerce phenomenon will continue to grow both for business-to-business (B2B) and business-to-consumer (B2C) sectors. From a convenience point of view and under greater environmental pressure, grocery home shopping and delivery will also grow significantly.

This will necessitate more fulfilment centres and returns processing facilities.

Retailers and manufacturers will continue to look for further cost savings as markets become even more competitive. Warehouses will be expected to be more efficient and cost-effective, with the likely closure of inflexible buildings and inefficient operations.

Retailers will continue to take stock out of the supply chain, leading to increases in stockless depots, transhipment and consolidation centres and cross-dock operations.

The cost of transport and stock-reduction targets could potentially bring manufacturing closer to the consumer. Eastern Europe has recently become a centre for manufacturing within automotive and electronics and near-shoring is becoming a distinct possibility with US and European companies bringing some production back to their shores.

The increase in port-centric logistics has resulted in companies building large warehouses as close to the ports of entry as possible. As mentioned, Tesco's 1.2 million square foot warehouse at Teesport UK is a typical example.

The miniaturization of products such as mobile phones, DVD players and computers, together with the increasing use of electronic media for listening to music and reading books via downloads, is likely to result in less space required for these types of products.

The sustainability agenda will also play its part within the supply chain. This will result in the development of further brown field sites, linkages to rail and potentially canal and river networks, and self-sufficiency in terms of energy use.

Future warehouses will be expected to be carbon positive which will be backed up by legislation in the future. UK retailer John Lewis built a new distribution centre in the UK with a view to significantly reducing its carbon footprint. Early results showed savings of 18 per cent in energy costs, 45 per cent in water usage, an overall reduction of 40 per cent in CO_2 emissions and a cost saving of circa £250,000 per annum.

It is expected that new warehouses will be targeted with having their own means of power generation, be it solar or wind, and may also convert waste into power. See page 360 on the environment for further information.

Greater collaboration within the supply chain both vertically and horizontally will lead to greater consolidation and an increase in shared-user operations. This is likely to lead to a reduction in the number of warehouses and the construction of purpose-built centres.

The ability for companies to work closely with each other and trust each other will be a major factor as to how quickly this collaboration takes place.

The growth of e-fulfilment and its effect on the warehouse

According to Forrester (2013) online retail sales in the United States in 2013 will reach $262 billion – a rise of 13 per cent over 2012's $231 billion representing 8 per cent of the total retail market and will reach $370 billion by 2017. In the United Kingdom online retail sales accounts for approximately 10 per cent of overall sales and is likely to grow between 10 and 15 per cent over the next few years. The growth in countries such as China is closer to 75 per cent.

Internet retailing is still in its infancy and there are no signs of this rapid growth slowing. According to Goldman Sachs, the global e-commerce market could be worth around $1 trillion by the end of 2013.

With regard to warehousing, pure internet traders have had an advantage in developing purpose-built facilities according to a recent TI report for Savills (2013) whereas existing retailers and manufacturers who are selling online need to adapt existing logistics systems and facilities to meet these new demands or create new ones to accommodate the move to multichannel retailing.

The report suggests that the tipping point for dedicated e-commerce fulfilment centres is approximately 200,000 orders and that warehouses are in the region of 20–60,000 square feet.

There are significant challenges for warehouse managers when operating an e-fulfilment warehouse.

These warehouses are significantly impacted by seasonality. The demand on staff and equipment varies tremendously with the seasons: large, bulky items such as barbecues and garden furniture during spring and summer and much smaller electrical products during the run-up to Christmas. These have very different impacts on handling and storage equipment.

Second, the wide range of products stored requires warehouse managers to efficiently process low-value, single-item orders. This is one of the main challenges facing all warehouses today but in particular those dealing with internet orders. Picking and packing low-cost items utilize the same amount of labour and equipment as for high-cost items but the margin is going to be significantly different.

Third, as consumers flex their muscles in the market, accuracy and on-time delivery become paramount if companies are to retain the loyalty of their customers.

Inventory management is another challenge for the warehouse manager. The increase in the number of product lines will put pressure on the number of pick locations whilst slow-moving and obsolete lines can take up much-needed space in the warehouse. From a picking point of view the proliferation of product lines will result in warehouse managers having to look at alternatives to ground-floor pick locations such as mezzanine floors, flow racking and carousels.

In order to release vital space to the warehouse operation, stock turnover has to be managed well and decisions made quickly regarding the disposal of non-moving stock.

As discussed earlier, one of the main by-products of e-commerce is a large percentage of returns. This can be between 30 and 40 per cent of outward volume. Significantly, many of the returns are good stock which can be resold but have to go through a thorough quality check.

Mark Hewitt, ex-chief executive of iForce in the United Kingdom, sees this developing interest in returns:

There will be a growing demand for outsourcing e-fulfilment to companies that can also offer returns processing from the same facility, as this will drive down costs by enabling a more efficient process for putting returned goods straight back into stock.

(*Supply Chain Standard*)

A number of the third-party providers are now assisting their clients with the disposal of the returned goods through having their own eBay stores.

Next-day delivery is seen as the norm, which puts further pressure on the warehouse manager to balance speed with accuracy. Allied to this is the requirement to be able to integrate systems with couriers and customer services to be able to track and trace the progress of each order.

According to Savills (2013) there is no current 'blue-print' for the optimum e-fulfilment centre design. Different retailers adopt very different strategies.

Companies such as Amazon have developed unique systems that are capable of handling extremely large volumes of different types of products (ranging from relatively small in size to larger goods).

Smaller businesses will carry out fulfilment in their retail premises until the volume makes this unmanageable. Many small logistics providers and mail fulfilment firms now offer e-fulfilment, typically in general warehouse premises used for other aspects of the business.

A number of multichannel operators have developed dedicated e-fulfilment centres, once online sales volumes have become large enough.

Others have adopted a strategy of keeping e-retail volumes and traditional store volumes together, either as an opportunity to utilize spare capacity or due to minimal advantage in separating channels.

To summarize, there are three types of fulfilment centre:

- integrated fulfilment, where internet sales are carried out alongside existing retail operations;
- dedicated fulfilment, carried out in a purpose-built facility; and
- store fulfilment, which involves picking online orders from existing retail shelves for separate delivery ex store. A same-day courier service provided by Shutl boasts a record delivery time of 13 minutes 57 seconds for an online order using this channel!

The third option has been favoured in the past for launching the service and establishment of e-fulfillment but is least favoured for a substantive operation.

In this section we briefly discuss three specialist types of warehousing, customs warehousing, refrigerated storage and fashion logistics.

Specialized warehousing

Customs warehousing by Mike Hodge and Gwynne Richards

This section is written specifically for the United Kingdom. However, most countries will have some form of customs warehousing.

The operation of running a customs warehouse can bring huge benefits to an international trade business by delaying the payment of import duty and VAT and avoiding the payment of these taxes altogether if the imported merchandise is exported outside the EU. This is particularly useful if the company is unsure of the ultimate destination of the product. This section deals only with customs warehousing, which is a regime for the importation and storage of products imported from outside the EU which are liable to customs duty, VAT, anti-dumping duty, etc. It does not deal with excise duty products – beer, wines, spirits, tobacco, which are covered by other specific regulations.

In the customs 'area', there are basically two types of warehouse. There is a Type A warehouse which is operated by a warehouse keeper who has goods belonging to a number of companies in the warehouse. All customs responsibilities lie with the warehouse keeper. There is also a Type C approval which is granted for one importer to store his own goods in his own warehouse. No special security measures (eg barred windows, separate areas, etc) are required. There is also a Type E approval whereby a number of warehouse sites are included in the same authorization.

As an example of a Type C operation, consider a business importing forklift trucks that are manufactured in China. The rate of import duty at importation would be 4.5 per cent of the landed cost, insurance and freight (CIF) value. If the annual import value is £20 million, the duty cost will be £900,000 and the VAT impact, £4.18 million – a not inconsiderable sum. By obtaining an approval to operate a customs warehouse (on the importer's own site), the duty and VAT payments are delayed until such time as the forklift trucks are sold into the UK market. At that stage an import declaration is made and the duty and VAT is paid. By using the duty and VAT deferment scheme, a further six weeks of cash flow benefit can be obtained. If the trucks are sold into the EU, only the customs duty is payable as long as the EU customer can provide an EU VAT registration number. If the forklift trucks are exported outside the EU, no duty or VAT is payable. The cash flow savings and duty saving opportunities are obvious and significant.

It is true to say, however, that obtaining approval to operate a customs warehouse is not without its difficulties. The EU is in the process of re-writing the legislation (known as the Union Customs Code), which covers all customs matters. In 2016 or so, when the new legislation takes effect, it is highly likely that a customs warehouse operator will require a financial guarantee to cover the potential duty and VAT on all products stored in the warehouse. There is a way to avoid this requirement and that is for the applicant to obtain a different (safety and security) approval called authorized economic operator (AEO). An AEO is an economic operator who, by satisfying certain criteria, is considered to be reliable in their customs related operations throughout the European Community. The introduction of AEO status is the EC's response to the need to secure international supply chains and the introduction of Customs-Trade Partnership Against Terrorism (C-TPAT) in the United States and the development of the Safe framework of standards in the World Customs Organization.

The aim is to provide businesses with an internationally recognized quality mark which will indicate that their role in the international supply chain is secure and their customs controls and procedures are efficient and compliant. An operator with AEO security and safety status implies that apart from being reliable in the traditional financial and customs terms, they are also compliant in respect of security and safety standards and can therefore be considered as a 'secure' trader and thus a reliable trading partner.

Effectively, to obtain approval to operate a customs warehouse, the applicant *has* to reach the AEO standards so that achievement automatically grants a waiver from the need for a financial guarantee.

The customs warehouse operator will have to invest in a duty management system which interfaces directly with the HMRC's computer system known as CHIEF (Customs Handling of Import and Export Freight).

Customs warehousing can bring substantial benefits both in controlling the flow of merchandise and savings in tax. A first step is to look at the business case where the costs and benefits can be established. The use of a customs expert in this area is strongly advised.

Refrigerated warehouses (by Chris Sturman)

The growth in the refrigeration market, due to demand for food that can retain its freshness as opposed to produce with a shelf life, has placed increasing pressure on cold-store operators.

The key function of a refrigerated warehouse is to maintain the temperature of products at the level at which they were received. Blast freezing and tempering chambers are used for managing any change of temperature required and these activities should take place away from the main storage areas to minimize the risk of temperature deviation (+/–) to goods being held in stock. Cold chain management and maintenance of food quality and safety whilst managing significant energy and materials handling cost levels are priorities.

At the same time, boards of directors and management need to assess the risks which relate to fire and business continuity, these being major issues facing both the food processing and storage and distribution industries in the United Kingdom. A business continuity and disaster recovery plan should be a core requirement of the business regime, with staff involvement and training being prerequisites.

Materials handling and storage in a temperature-controlled environment

A wide range of storage media is used, all with the intention of optimizing storage capacity with accessibility, given the high fixed and variable costs prevalent in the sector. The most popular are:

- Wide, narrow and very narrow aisle racking. Used in faster-moving operations, particularly in order picking by case and by unit. These suit secondary distribution layouts, where access to a wide range of stock-keeping units (SKUs) is required, and delivery lead times are short. Often reserve stock is held in a national or primary distribution centre (NDC or PDC).

- Drive-in racking. Used for bulk pallet storage and more frequently for longer-term storage, to suit seasonal production and supply peaks or production/packaging operations to meet different packing formats.

- Mobile racking. Buildings must first be constructed with mobility in mind, as the building needs substantial steel runners set flush into the insulated cold-store floor surface. Popular with smaller companies that have higher volumes to store but also need accessibility for range and stock rotation.

- Automated storage. More common in continental Europe, although recent developments on behalf of multinational food processors in the United Kingdom have seen two further high bay stores built and commissioned for primary/national pallet storage and distribution. These are very economical for customers if volume related, and best attached or contracted to a high-volume production plant. However, they are totally dependent on design and WMS software for operational capability and capacity/speed, and these demand high standards of presentation within the design pallet gauge. Reliability is key, with benefits in low manpower and energy costs.

The most recently constructed frozen food facilities are highly automated sites, with high-density storage areas. These types of storage media result in less air circulation and as a result reduced energy usage.

CASE STUDY   Fredericks Dairies

Fredericks Dairies are the UK's leading manufacturer of ice cream. Fredericks has a reputation of excellence, providing the highest quality products and services possible in the industry.

When business expansion necessitated they expand their warehousing facility, Fredericks looked to pallet racking industry leaders to create a solution that would be ecologically friendly, efficient, cost-effective and fit within strict building guidelines. Fredericks knew what they wanted; at least 13,000 pallet spaces in a building with imposed size limitations that could move 600 pallets within an eight-hour shift, all in a freezing −28 °C environment.

RediRack developed a revolutionary automated pallet storage, retrieval and sequencing solution using a pallet buffer and sequencing system. Using this technology, RediRack were able to increase the storage density by up to 90 per cent whilst reducing annual running costs by a similar amount. In new build situations, the same storage capacity can be provided with a 45 per cent reduction in the building footprint giving substantial savings in construction costs.

This solution produced a storage capacity of 13,500 pallets. Terry Haigh, Operations Director, said: 'Traditional solutions such as VNA, crane systems and mobile racking just couldn't achieve what Fredericks needed.'

 www.reditechnix.com/solutions/RediLogX/

The UK's largest frozen food logistics facility to date was opened in Wisbech, Cambridgeshire in 2010. The store, operated by Partner Logistics, has space for 77,000 pallets, operates at temperatures of −27 degrees centigrade, and measures 175 metres by 88 metres by 36 metres high.

The density of storage is achieved by drive-in racking. This uses the cube of the building efficiently and is important in terms of economies for energy usage.

All these cold stores require specific types of MHE equipment, which have to be specially adapted by the manufacturer to be able to operate efficiently in chilled and sub-zero environments. Key aspects include:

- heavy-duty batteries designed for a minimum eight-hour shift life;
- special hydraulic oils to withstand sub-zero temperature levels; and

FIGURE 1.6 Bendi articulated truck for use in a refrigerated environment

- electronic and electrical systems encased or coated to prevent moisture ingress.

In some cases, trucks are fitted with heated cabs to avoid driving staff having to wear special temperature-controlled clothing. This enables them to work longer since they no longer need the in-shift warming breaks (see Figure 1.6, courtesy of Bendi).

Energy management and plant maintenance

Energy is a large proportion of operating costs, ranging from 12 to 30 per cent on average. The actual amount will depend first on the age and condition of the building, relative thermographic integrity and the age and management of refrigeration plant, and second on equipment management and maintenance.

Buildings flex naturally, but cold stores more so, because of the temperature and humidity range between the inside and outside environments. The most important area of focus is the avoidance of heat ingress into the cold space through panel joints, door frames and structures. An annual thermographic scan with immediate attention to panels and joints is essential. The second priority is to ensure that no condensation is allowed to settle on top of cold boxes which, depending on the time of year, can repeatedly freeze and melt, with potential ingress through surrounding joints into the panel structure, thereby allowing delamination and subsequent structural strength decay.

The shifting of energy loads to more suitable and cost-effective periods, thereby reducing the tariff rate or alternatively agreeing to be cut off at peak load periods, are methods of energy-cost reduction. An alternative and latest version of this is to be paid to agree to have supply curtailed for a fixed period on a timed basis.

The focus on energy and carbon reduction has resulted in significant research in techniques by which to generate even greater improvement. These include:

- a reduction in cooling demand by ensuring that product enters at the correct temperature;
- improved plant design;
- improved operational management and maintenance;
- recovery of heat to use elsewhere in the business – hot water, space heating, etc;
- examination of the use of CHP (combined heat and power) – tri-generation; and
- consideration of low carbon electricity – wind, wave or hydro-electric.

In addition, there are more radical approaches; with more positive and closer store management attention. These are as follows:

- carefully review the cold-store room layout and thereby change the temperature flows;
- raise refrigeration evaporating temperature for a potential 11 per cent or more cost saving;
- reduce refrigeration condensing temperature;
- seasonally adjust refrigeration to take account of external ambient temperature;
- where fitted, split cold-store and blast-freezer refrigeration systems;
- install and use variable-speed drive fans; and
- focus on and manage more closely door opening design and operations.

Safety and risk assessment:

There are two different types of refrigerants used in temperature-controlled stores. These are either Hydro Chloro Carbon (HFC/HCFC) or ammonia based, with sometimes a brine or Freon secondary refrigerant, to minimize the ammonia charge.

HFC based refrigerants are currently being phased out, as a consequence of legislation following the adoption of the Montreal Protocol, to reduce Ozone Depleting Substances (ODS) or those with high Global Warming Potential (GWP).

The only economically realistic alternative is ammonia, a naturally available chemical. However, ammonia has dangerous and explosive attributes that require specific risk assessment and management (EU/UK ATEX/DSEAR Regulations 2002 or equivalent in other countries).

Additionally, legionella risk assessment and management of condensers are required to ensure the safety of workers and occupiers of adjacent properties.

Stock management and housekeeping

In addition to the normal stock-management processes found in conventional warehouses, the following specific processes can be found in the temperature-controlled sector:

- *Traceability*. EU 178/2002 sets out specific requirements for food safety, traceability and recall of unsafe foods. Warehouse operators should carefully consider whether they can be classed as food business operators (most public cold-store operators are) and register accordingly. Food Standards Agency Guidance Notes are available, which should be considered along with the Food Safety Act 1990 (Amendment) Regulations 2004 and the General Food Regulations 2004, along with requirements for marks and labels which differ depending on whether the product has been prepared for final consumption. Food Labelling Regulations 1996 (Regulation 35) also need to be considered.

  Subsequently, EU Regulations 852 on the hygiene of foodstuffs and Regulation 853 laying down specific hygiene rules for food of animal origin require (inter alia) the maintenance of cold chain, implementation of procedures based on HACCP principles, consultation of good practice guides, and establishment of microbacterial and temperature-controlled requirements based on scientific risk assessment, albeit that this requirement applies to storage and transport but not to retail establishments.

- *Temperature checks*. All stores need to be fitted with temperature-monitoring equipment that is checked on a shift or am/pm basis and records kept for regulatory and operational analysis.

- *Product checks*. All products should be checked on intake to ensure that the product is sound and to specification. They should then be checked outbound to demonstrate to the collecting company and final receiver that they were at the specified temperature level on despatch. Care should be taken not to damage product at any time.

- *Segregation*. All damaged or unfit product should be labelled or marked and removed to ensure it cannot move further down the food chain.

- *Date codes*. Particularly with fast-moving chilled products, codes need particular attention to ensure correct rotation and 100 per cent acceptance at retail RDC or other final delivery point.

- *Product spills*. Need quick response, to avoid crushed product and packaging from spreading across the working space, and ingestion into the working parts of equipment.

Health and safety issues

Additional hazards are particularly harsh at zero degrees or below, but can still apply in certain cases to the chilled chain.

Specific issues surround the effect of cold temperature and the cold environment on people, and will also vary by type and size of facility and operations being undertaken.

Specific hazards:

- accidental lock-in risk, requiring alarms and quick-release equipment;

- the effect of cold on people and use of PPE require specific advice and training for staff to wear appropriate thermal clothing, drink lots of water, protect bare skin (particularly fingers, noses and ears), taking greater care if smokers or drinkers;

- accidental release of refrigerant, particularly ammonia;

- use of materials-handling equipment in slippery floor areas where ice build-up may occur, particularly around door openings. Slip and trip hazards are ever present along with the risk of skidding and overturning;

- ice build-up on panels present an ice-fall hazard, and can, if left, cause roof panels to fall, risking injury to operators below;

- product falls from pallet racks, due to displaced product;

- working at heights: the use of non-integrated platforms using forklift trucks has effectively been eliminated from all stores other than in sub-zero temperatures, and the use of mechanized elevating working platforms (MEWPs) is obligatory. However, these items of equipment are not equipped for sub-zero temperatures. Here the practice is closely scrutinized as agreed between the industry and the Health and Safety Executive.

- The Food Storage and Distribution Federation, British Frozen Foods Federation and Health and Safety Executive have worked together to deliver a Supplementary Guidance (PM 28) during 2010 to help manage these risks.

Transportation issues

These revolve around the loading dock, where operational regimes need to ensure the maintenance of the cold chain, preventing temperature migration between the cold store, the outside temperature and the open vehicle whilst loading and unloading.

Solutions include the use of dock ports and shelters, with close-fitting seals around the door apertures of the vehicle, and air curtains to prevent the ingress of warm air.

Summary

Overall housekeeping regimes in any environment require the provision of a safe, clean, clear, unobstructed floor or work space to allow for the safe movement of goods, vehicle equipment and people. The temperature-controlled environment requires that extra care is taken to address condensation and ice build-up on equipment, floors and walls, and that operational processes are designed with the care of people and product in mind.

Risk assessments and operational methods and instructions need to be developed with that as the first priority.

Fashion logistics

With large and fast-changing product ranges, as well as dramatic seasonal fluctuations, the fashion industry has demanding logistics requirements.

The need to balance distribution capacity between replenishing retail stores, fulfilling online orders and dealing efficiently with returns is making warehouse automation an increasingly attractive option for the fashion industry.

Fashion products are either boxed or travel as hanging garments. This mix of items requires different handling capabilities and ensuring that expensive items of clothing are not creased or crushed in transit through the supply chain provides supply chain and warehouse managers with some interesting challenges.

FIGURE 1.7 Sorter bag system (courtesy of Knapp)

Companies are able to store coats and dresses on moveable rails within the warehouse; however, a more efficient and space effective method is to use some form of automation.

Product profile fashion logistics

With e-commerce presenting the challenge of large numbers of orders that each have a small quantity of items, KNAPP has developed a new concept that looks to bridge the gap between hanging and boxed product. Pick-it-Easy Pocket is a solution that allows flat-packed goods and hanging garments to be processed together, for the first time, on the same system. The system consists of hanging pockets – suitable for flat-packed clothes, shoes, accessories, books, DVDs or toys – that are conveyed to a matrix sorter so that they arrive at the packing stations in the correct sequence to collate each customer's order. The pockets can be fitted with RFID tags and the solution can process up to 10,000 items an hour.

The utilization of a hanging garment sorter means that the cube of the building can be fully utilized with rails travelling above the work and storage areas.

Summary and conclusion

There are many types of warehouses operating within very different supply chains. No longer are they simply stockholding points.

The transfer of supply chain control from manufacturers to retailers in the 1980s and 1990s has seen a significant change in the operation of storage facilities worldwide. Warehouses are, in the main, no longer seen as static storage units. Concepts such as consolidation, cross docking and postponement have become commonplace with the ultimate goal of stock reduction and increased throughput within the whole supply chain.

Retailers are continually looking to move stock back through the supply chain thus releasing more sales space in store. This requires more control over the supply chain, improved forecasting and accurate and timely information flow.

The advent of e-commerce has also changed the warehouse landscape appreciably, as has the necessity for cost reduction and the growing pressure to reduce the impact of logistics operations on the environment.

Companies are continually striving to reduce inventory within the supply chain and the continuing use of offshore manufacturing, increasing consumer choice and a predilection for instant gratification ensure that stockholding remains a necessity even in these days of just-in-time, efficient consumer response and quick response.

Warehouses remain a crucial link within today's supply chains. As a result, warehouse managers and their colleagues need to be better equipped to manage a constantly changing environment and also need to work closely with their counterparts in their wider supply chains.

Role of the warehouse manager

02

> *Managers today have to do more with less, and get better results from limited resources, more than ever before... A manager's job is to provide the environment where individuals are internally motivated to do the very best job possible, in the very best spirit possible, to make the very best contribution possible.*
>
> **(BRIAN TRACY)**

Introduction

Today's warehouse managers no longer patrol the warehouse in brown coats clutching a clipboard and pencil. They are more likely to be in a suit or corporate uniform, use a personal digital assistant (PDA) and more often than not are seen hunched over a laptop deciphering the latest cost and productivity figures.

This chapter examines the challenges facing today's warehouse manager and the attributes required to deal with them. Each challenge is introduced to the reader and is further examined in detail in the remaining sections of the book.

One of the main challenges for the warehouse manager before we begin to look at the warehouse itself is whether they and their colleagues see themselves as the right person for the job.

Nick Weetman, commenting in *Retail Week* (2009), said:

> It is a neglected area. The effort expended on developing warehouse management is not proportionate to the importance of the warehouse as a business... We see a lot of warehouse management where people have just been promoted and don't really understand how to run warehouses. Those (retailers) that do have it in-house need to understand it's a critical part, and retail is just the end of the supply chain.

A recent job description for a distribution centre manager required the following key skills and outlined core accountabilities which are typically sought from today's senior warehouse managers: these included an ability to negotiate, information technology skills, basic finance and business acumen, people management skills and an ability to motivate and lead large numbers of employees through communication and engagement.

These are very much people skills and as Lee Iacocca (1984) said, 'Management is nothing more than motivating other people.'

The job description and the core accountabilities were as follows:

- the provision of a responsive and cost-efficient warehouse that is aligned with the current and long-term requirements of the global business strategy;
- responsibility for the leadership and direction of the warehouse team;
- to ensure that the warehouse is capable of delivering the volume requirements of the business;
- to drive continuous improvement in the cost-efficiency of the operations;
- to set the long-term vision for the warehouse in line with the strategic plan and to ensure that future volumes and customer service requirements can be met;
- to safeguard the human and physical assets employed in the warehouse;
- the management of projects and introduction of new initiatives;
- to maintain strong relationships with suppliers; and
- the development and management of industrial relations within the warehouse environment.

The people aspect is very important and a job description for a distribution centre manager produced by WERC suggested that the manager needs an ability to:

- develop and maintain a productive work team by creating programmes for hiring, training and professional development;
- match the skill and background of personnel to the work required;
- apply sound communication and motivational techniques, create programmes to supervise, counsel and discipline associates; and
- implement an appropriate performance evaluation system for recommending promotions, wage increases and terminations.

The warehouse manager has a number of operational challenges and is also expected to understand and implement company strategy in relation to warehouse activity.

Again we see the trade-offs that the warehouse manager has to deal with. These include cost versus responsiveness, and cost-efficiency versus volume throughput.

It is good to see that safeguarding human assets is included in the list of core accountabilities as this is a common worry for warehouse managers.

Today's manager has to maximize the effective use of his/her operational resources whilst satisfying customer requirements. This can be done effectively through motivating and managing staff effectively. People are a warehouse's most valuable assets and should be used appropriately.

The above job description is reasonably typical of the requirements of a warehouse manager in today's fast-moving economic environment. The expectation is that the manager will achieve high customer service levels but also reduce cost through improved productivity and performance. Added to this is the constraint of lower inventory, reduced customer lead time and the pressure to ensure the safety and security of staff, equipment and stock.

The six basic tenets of warehouse management can be summed up as follows:

- accuracy;
- cost control;
- cleanliness;
- efficiency;
- safety; and
- security.

Warehouse trade-offs

Managing trade-offs within the warehouse is fundamental to the role of warehouse manager.

The main trade-offs are shown in Figure 2.1.

Warehouse managers are also expected to recognize and balance other trade-offs within the warehouse, examples of which are as follows:

- increased throughput versus reduction in labour costs;
- storage density versus quicker pallet extraction;
- manual versus automated processes;
- increased pick rates versus accuracy;
- inventory holding costs versus cost of stock outs; and
- speed versus safety.

FIGURE 2.1   Warehouse trade-offs

Today's challenges are many and varied and require additional skills from the warehouse manager.

The next section examines these specific challenges.

The warehouse manager's challenges

Pressure on today's warehouse manager comes from many different directions. These are both internal and external pressures.

A recent survey carried out by Intermec suggested the following:

- Nearly 3,000 hours per year are lost in warehouses and DCs through inefficient processes.
- 80 per cent of managers have been tasked with finding cost savings in existing operations.
- On average managers have been tasked with finding nearly 20 per cent cost savings across their organizations.
- The majority of managers suggested the following areas were most inefficient:
  - inventory control (53 per cent);
  - picking (47 per cent);
  - putaway and replenishment (45 per cent).

One surprising fact that came out of the survey was that one in six managers will not review their workflow processes until they receive a customer complaint (Intermec 2012).

The main pressures and challenges are as follows:

Pressure to reduce operating costs

Companies are targeting the supply chain as an area where costs can be reduced further and as a result pressure is increasing on transport and warehouse managers to reduce costs whilst also increasing customer service.

This has resulted in companies evaluating outsourcing options as well as reviewing their own logistics operations.

Achieving the perfect order

A recent key performance indicator (KPI) introduced into the supply chain is the perfect order metric. A perfect order is deemed to be one that has been delivered on time, in full, in perfect condition and accompanied with the correct paperwork. This metric includes many of the current supply chain performance measures, and providing everybody uses the same parameters it can be adopted as one of the leading supply chain measures and a differentiator between companies and supply chains. If we ever get to a paperless transaction we may need to replace the fourth metric.

Shorter order lead times and stock availability

Order lead time is the length of time between the placing of an order and the receipt of the item by the customer. Order lead time can be a significant differentiator between competitors. For example, if your favourite cereal is not on the shelf of the supermarket, you are unlikely to wait for the next delivery but will look for it in another store or choose the closest alternative, whether from the same brand or a different brand. Online consumers are likely to choose the quickest delivery method providing the quality and costs are alike.

The quality of products is such that competitive advantage is gained through fast, timely and accurate delivery. With the internet providing price transparency through a proliferation of price comparison websites, competitive advantage is now gained through offering the best service by whatever channel the consumer decides.

The most effective warehouses are those that have reduced lead times whilst maintaining quality at a reduced cost.

Delivery through multiple channels

Companies are increasingly delivering via multiple channels to reach customers more effectively. The pressure on the warehouse is brought about through having to present goods in a variety of different ways.

These include direct delivery of single items to the end user, multiple SKU orders direct to store and bulk orders to retail distribution centres. Each has its own different pick requirement and is likely to rely on different equipment. Order lead times will also vary, as will the method of delivery.

Steve Smith of Manhattan Associates (*Supply Chain Standard*) summed this up when he said: 'Moving from a comparatively uncomplicated process of supplying and replenishing high street stores – with some added complexity around special promotions – to an online presence with fulfilment from either a store or a warehouse, be that dedicated or part of an existing facility, creates complexities associated with "singles" picking, small order volume, the number of deliveries, time limits, availability issues, and so on.'

Smaller, more frequent orders

Manufacturers and retailers are continually striving to reduce inventory whilst retail stores are looking to increase floor sales space and thus reduce the amount of inventory held in stock rooms. Just-in-time methods, increasing internet sales and initiatives such as efficient consumer response (ECR) and quick response (QR) are resulting in smaller, more frequent orders. This again necessitates changes in warehouse operations, with a move away from full-pallet picking to carton and individual-item picks.

Greater fluctuations in demand

The days of predictable sales are long gone, with consumers rather than manufacturers flexing their muscles in the marketplace. Seasonality remains a factor in terms of market sectors such as fashion, while pre- and post-Christmas sales are now stretching warehouse resources to the limit as the rush to get product to stores intensifies.

Companies have to be able to ramp up resources during the peak periods and have a much leaner operation during slower, quieter periods.

The clothing manufacturer shown in Figure 1.3 on page 15 operates with a core team of seven warehouse staff, which can increase to over 40 during busy periods.

Increases in stock-keeping units

The proliferation of product lines gives the consumer choice; however, it is a major challenge for warehouse managers in terms of having sufficient, cost-effective pick locations. Once operators have to pick items at height, productivity rates reduce significantly.

Retailers continue to seek differentiation and as a result are continually looking to introduce product variants, not only in terms of the product itself but also in pack size, the type of packaging, labelling and product combinations. Retailers are also introducing more of their own-brand labels to provide consumers with even greater choice.

This has led to a number of companies introducing postponement into the warehouse. This entails holding stock of the basic product and only adding the 'extras' once orders have been received. Examples include loading specific software onto personal computers, adding additional memory or including extras such as monitors and keyboards – known as bundling.

Labour cost and availability

During periods of high employment many countries are seeing labour rates steadily increasing and coupled with the fact that a number of countries have an ageing population it is becoming harder to source experienced warehouse operatives. Additionally, working in a warehouse is not seen as being the most glamorous of occupations and this deters a number of young people from entering the industry.

Warehouse managers need to come up with ways to attract new staff.

Many workforces have been supplemented with the introduction of staff from abroad. In these circumstances companies need to look at employing bilingual supervisors and contemplate the use of new technology such as voice-directed processes. There is also the added challenge of health and safety, ensuring that foreign staff are able to read and understand instructions.

Another way to attract staff is to be flexible on working hours. This can include shifts that coincide with school hours or with spouses' work hours, such as twilight shifts. The length of shift can also be varied to coincide with worker preferences. This can also attract student workers. Although potentially difficult to organize, this can prove beneficial in the long run.

Parkinson's Law suggests that work expands to fill the time allowed. This can be a problem in many warehouses when volumes are low. The introduction of annualized hours or even zero hour contracts allow companies to match resource to demand as and when required.

Environmental issues

Warehouse managers are not only tasked with cost savings but also the reduction of the warehouse's impact on the environment.

This includes areas such as energy consumption, affecting areas such as lighting, mechanical handling equipment (MHE), cooling and heating.

Managers need to set examples by switching off lights and heaters when they are not in use and ensuring that MHE is operating optimally.

The issue of waste is also high on the environmental agenda. The warehouse can generate a great deal of waste in its daily operation. This includes stretch-wrap, cardboard, tape, pallets, etc. These need to be closely controlled and, where cost effective, recycled, reused or turned into energy.

Data and information transfer

One of the warehouse manager's greatest challenges is how to manage data. Today's supply chain produces vast amounts of data and it is up to the warehouse manager among others to analyse this data and use it effectively.

A further challenge is ensuring that data is transferred to the correct location. It has been said that supply chains are all about the transfer of information and products are a secondary thought. The ability to track items throughout the supply chain is paramount, especially in the food and pharmaceutical market sectors.

As can be seen from this list and Figure 2.2, the role of warehouse manager has expanded significantly over the years and, as a result, the warehouse manager has become an important link within the supply chain.

Lean warehousing

One way of overcoming some of the above challenges is the introduction of 'lean' concepts into the warehouse operation.

The concept of 'lean' comes from the manufacturing sector, more specifically the automotive industry, and is very much associated with Toyota and the Toyota Way.

'Lean' is now being applied not only in manufacturing but also within the public sector and the supply chain. The idea behind lean is to remove any activity that uses resources but doesn't create any additional value.

In this short section we will look at how lean principles are likely to be applied within a warehouse operation.

According to Wild (2010), warehousing operations by definition are not lean. However, cross-dock centres and fulfilment centres can be, provided stock is moved quickly through the facility.

This is where lean techniques can be used within a warehouse environment. The idea is to identify the activities within the warehouse that absorb resources but don't create additional value.

FIGURE 2.2 Warehouse challenges (adapted from Dematic Corporation 2009)

Challenge		Operational Requirements
Cost reduction		Increase productivity, improve utilization of space, staff and equipment
Achieve the Perfect Order		Improve productivity, increase accuracy, improve handling and invest in systems
Shorter order lead times		Improve processes and increase productivity
Sales via multiple channels and increase in smaller orders		Improved picking strategies such as bulk picking and greater use of technology
Fluctuations in demand		Flexible working hours and improved forecasting
Proliferation of SKU		Improved use of equipment such as carousels, A-frames and flow racks
Labour cost and availability		Staff retention through excellent working conditions, flexible hours, training and improved productivity
Increasing cost of energy and environmental challenges		Manage energy more efficiently, better use of waste
Data accuracy and speed of transfer		Introduce Warehouse management system and real-time data transfer

Waste can be found in many areas of the warehouse, none more so than in the use of space. Many managers will say they are running out of space and require additional storage facilities, yet when you walk around the warehouse you may see obvious signs of waste. During a recent warehouse audit we were told that space was at a premium, yet there were many examples of wasted space. These included:

- half-height and quarter-height pallets taking up space in two-metre-high locations;
- part pallets of the same product spread over a number of different locations;
- over 10 per cent of the stock was obsolete.

In the first case there were opportunities to move the smaller pallets to other locations or alternatively invest in more rack beams to increase the number of available locations.

In the second, providing there weren't issues with FIFO, batch numbers or best before dates, the pallets could have been consolidated. Although there is a labour cost involved it would have been more than compensated by the availability of more empty pallet locations.

In the third case, the warehouse was storing software products that had been superseded by new versions and were very unlikely to be sold. Decisions have to be made in conjunction with the finance department to dispose of obsolete product as soon as it is identified.

Other potential areas of waste in terms of both space and time are at the receiving and despatch bays. If companies are confident about the service received from their suppliers and confident in the picking accuracy of their staff there should not be a requirement for product to be staged and checked before put away or despatch.

Gooley (2013) talks about the seven wastes or muda that lean management seeks to eliminate.

Examples in the warehouse include the following:

- transportation (driving an empty forklift);
- defects (time spent correcting errors such as misspicks);
- inventories (congestion at the inbound and outbound areas);
- motion (interrupting movement such as staging product before put-away);
- waiting time (bottlenecks at pick locations);
- overproduction (holding too much inventory); and
- overprocessing (performing unnecessary steps such as labelling and checking).

Other wastes include ignoring employee creativity and knowledge and over-engineering a process.

Lean thinking revolves around having a clean and streamlined operation and removing non-value-adding processes. Waiting time is one of the biggest and most expensive wastes.

The 5S concept that underpins lean thinking can be easily applied to the warehouse as follows: The first S (Sort or Seiri or Clear out) concentrates on removing any unnecessary items from the work area. This can include obsolete and damaged stock, over stocks, defective equipment, broken pallets, waste packaging, etc. It can also refer to unnecessary movement within the warehouse. For example, the introduction of a cross aisle within the picking area will reduce the amount of travel undertaken by the operators.

You can also look to replace manual paper picking systems with radio frequency technology such as scanning, voice or pick to light.

Items marked for disposal can be put into a holding area until a consensus is reached as to what should be done with them.

The second S (Straighten or Seiton or Configure) focuses on efficient and effective placement of items, eg location labelling and putting frequently used items in easy to access locations. Directional signs in the warehouse are also part of this as it should reduce the amount of time taken to find items.

Items such as empty pallets and packaging should be placed in easily accessible areas close to the point of need.

Finally parking areas for handling equipment need to be set up with reminders to staff to put the equipment on charge if required.

The third S (Shine or Seiso or Clean) comes after you have cleared the area of any unnecessary items. Thoroughly clean the area and produce a timetable for cleaning. This can be done at the end of each shift with defects to equipment reported immediately.

Staff take pride in a clean work area; they work better and from experience clean warehouses tend to be more efficient!

Suggestions include putting bins at the front of each aisle to capture waste paper, packaging and broken pallets and making brooms and dust pans easily accessible.

The fourth S (Standardize or Seiketsu or Conform) is all about creating standards for each work area. Walk through each process with the relevant staff and then produce, document and display best practice procedures within the warehouse.

Make them simple to read and understand. A photograph displaying the process with minimal text works well in this situation.

The fifth S (Sustain or Shitsuke or Custom) ensures continuous improvement. Staff are encouraged not to return to previous work practices but to accept change and take things to a new level.

Regular checks and audits need to be carried out with the potential for bonus payments on achieving high performance scores.

More recently companies have introduced a sixth S which covers safety. It can be argued that safety is at the heart of the operation and therefore is a valuable addition to the 5S mentality.

5S needs to be carried out in the correct order. You need to give individuals responsibility for each task and for their respective work areas within the warehouse.

People management

During the past few years as I've been running warehouse management courses, one of the main topics of discussion has been how to attract, manage and motivate staff.

This section concentrates on what we believe to be the lynchpin of the warehouse operation: the people. Technological advancements have brought increased productivity and higher accuracy into the warehouse operation; however, warehouse managers still rely heavily on their staff to ensure a cost-effective and efficient operation.

In all industries, companies face identical workforce management challenges. These include:

- identifying, attracting and retaining good supervisors, first line managers and team leaders;
- retaining and attracting new employees;
- an ageing and constantly changing workforce, including the introduction of foreign staff;
- identifying training needs;
- the need to provide safe, comfortable working conditions;
- employment contract negotiations;
- compliance with employment and health and safety legislation; and
- staff discipline.

People challenges

Warehouse supervisors are seen as the cornerstone of warehouse operations. They can be in charge of large numbers of staff within a warehouse depending on the type of work carried out, the size of the warehouse and the capabilities of the supervisors and their staff.

In our experience, a ratio of one supervisor to 12–15 staff members is the optimum. Any higher and supervision becomes less effective, whilst any lower and costs increase and there is more onus on the supervisor to assist in the tasks. This is not always a bad thing as it provides the supervisor with a greater insight into the job at hand and facilitates progression. However, it can reduce overall effectiveness.

A survey carried out by Cranfield University (Baker and Perotti 2008) showed the average number of operators per supervisor were as follows:

- small warehouse (< 10,000 square metres): 1 supervisor per 8 operators; and

- large warehouse (> 10,000 square metres): 1 supervisor per 15 operators.

As discussed previously, the role of the warehouse and that of its staff has changed appreciably over the last 10 years. Warehouse staff roles are changing to include more tasks that were once undertaken by staff in administration, inventory control and customer service.

McMahon *et al* (2007) undertook research into the various logistics functions and found that warehouse supervisors work in the difficult middle. They must understand and often do the work of operators and clerical staff but also perform management tasks. These jobs are complex, calling for frequent decisions and almost constant activity.

In today's warehouse, supervisors need a comprehensive knowledge of the operation along with significant management skills.

These changes have altered the way companies hire, train and develop warehouse supervisors. They require higher education standards, better training and ongoing personal development.

Supervisors are the people at the sharp end as the warehouse managers are usually found at their desks in front of computer screens evaluating reports and planning future activity.

Warehouse supervisors therefore need high-level supervisory, training and interpersonal skills. They also need to know about supplier and customer procedures that affect warehouse operations.

Supervisors also need to manage by example. A previous director of mine was often seen picking up litter within the warehouse, setting an example to the rest of the staff. This simple task shows how important housekeeping is within a modern warehouse. Having been around warehouses all my working life, I have yet to find an untidy warehouse that is likely to figure within the top 10 best-performing warehouses in the country.

Taking pride in the way the warehouse looks tends to mean that staff take a pride in their work, leading to an efficient warehouse.

According to Ackerman (2000), effective supervisors and managers encourage an open exchange of ideas and have frequent discussions with their staff and peers. They should have nine critical attributes:

1 *Excellent communication skills*
The ability to receive and convey messages clearly and explicitly. Miscommunication leads to confusion, wasted effort and a missed opportunity.

2 *An ability to delegate effectively*
This is a hard skill to master but very effective when achieved. Once a task is delegated, managers and supervisors must not oversee the task too closely but neither should they abrogate responsibility. They need to monitor how the task is progressing and give feedback on performance.

3 *Motivational skills*
Supervisors and managers need to understand their staff and adapt their approach to motivation and feedback according to each person's needs. Providing staff with consistent feedback, even when they are performing well, is as important as the feedback to less well-performing staff.

According to Gavin Chappell, supply chain director at Asda Walmart in the United Kingdom, 'if you get the culture right and the atmosphere, structure and progression right it's not that difficult to get a motivated team' (*Retail Week* 2009).

4 *Problem-solving skills*
Problem-solving and decision-making skills are closely aligned and each requires a person to identify and develop options, and having done so, act decisively.

One example provided by Gagnon (1988) is that 'hidden lost time accounts for about 80 per cent of lost time, yet attracts only about 20 per cent of management's problem-solving attention'.

He said that 'it's easy to see operators standing around because they have no work to do; much harder is to see delays in operations that are the result of system issues, poor data, bad processes, etc – but that time can really add up'. Supervisors should be alert to these situations.

When walking around your warehouse, look for staff who are waiting for something to happen before they can do their own job – find out what's causing the bottleneck and change the process.

According to Goldratt (1984) every operation has some kind of constraint that stops it from operating optimally – the weakest link in the chain. You need to identify the constraint and change the way you work to overcome it.

The five steps in the process are as follows:

- identify the constraint;
- exploit the constraint (get the most that you can out of the current situation);
- subordinate everything to the constraint (avoid producing more than the constraint can handle);
- elevate the constraint (focus on eliminating it); and
- identify the next constraint.

Congestion at a pick face can be an example of a bottleneck:

- identified by people waiting in turn to pick items;
- try to maximize productivity under the current situation;
- don't overload the system by sending too many pickers to the same location;
- increase the number of pick locations for that product.

If cured, return to step 1.

5 *Flexibility*
Supervisors in today's fast-moving warehouse environment need to be flexible, react quickly to urgent requests and shift priorities easily. They are asked to oversee and undertake many different tasks and they need to be able to handle stress caused by the pressure to meet deadlines.

6 *A comprehensive knowledge of company processes and procedures*
Warehouse supervisors need to have a comprehensive understanding of the company's policies and procedures in order that they can effectively train warehouse operatives and coordinate their work. Supervisors are likely to be called upon to oversee and undertake many different tasks within the warehouse. As such, they need to spend time in all sections to get a working knowledge of all operations within the warehouse.

Supervisors need to be involved in and be party to the compilation of warehouse procedures and processes. They need to know both the administrative and operating procedures.

7 *Ability to train others*
Supervisors need to be able to pass on their knowledge effectively to their staff to ensure consistency and continuity. Well-trained staff are more likely to stay and provide the supervisors of the future.

8 *Be customer oriented*
Today supervisors need to be fully aware of customer requirements and manage the operation in such a way that customer satisfaction is

achieved within the parameters set. However, they also need to be mindful of costs and the potential trade-offs involved.

9 *Teamwork skills*

Supervisors need to be able to set out the goals of the company to their team and outline how the team is going to contribute to these goals.

Team-working skills and capabilities include:

- ability to work in a group;
- ability to build relationships;
- ability to cope under pressure;
- negotiating skills;
- ability to cooperate;
- coordination and allocation of tasks;
- influencing skills;
- ability to compromise where necessary;
- ability to make decisions.

Supervisors are paramount to the success of any warehouse operation. They are the liaison between employees and management. Needless to say, they also need to receive suitable, ongoing training.

One pitfall to avoid is not to promote your best operative without assessing their supervisory abilities. Many companies use promotion to award ability; however, the best person in a particular job is not always management material. This is sometimes called the Peter Principle, where staff are promoted as a result of their capability in particular job aspects. This can have a number of consequences. For example, by promoting your best picker not only are you taking them away from the shop floor but you may also be promoting them to a position at which they are no longer competent (they have reached their 'level of incompetence'). Here they stay – or may leave, being unable to earn further promotions and potentially harming the company's operations.

Attracting and retaining warehouse employees

Competition between companies in high-density warehouse areas can be fierce with staff moving between companies for very little increase in hourly rates. This puts a great deal of pressure on management.

Although many firms see monetary incentives as being key to staff recruitment and retention, a number of surveys – including one by Min (2004) in the United States – suggests otherwise with active employee involvement in productivity improvement, management commitment to staff, job security and a sense of community being seen as high on the list.

Flexible hours, recognition of a job well done, clean and safe working conditions, access to training and open communication are all seen as crucial to attracting and retaining staff. Other areas include staff benefits and bonus payments. The opportunity to follow jobs through to their conclusion can also give staff a sense of ownership and a greater understanding of the business.

Surveys (eg Gooley 2001) have shown that the primary reasons for staff leaving their employment isn't pay but employee discomfort with, or misunderstanding of, the corporate culture and the general lack of a sense of belonging.

As Chappell (*Retail Week* 2009) puts it:

> Having motivated, engaged individuals working in warehouses is a must if you want to be cost effective. However, it's also about service. If you need the warehouse to work above and beyond in times of peak or change, would you want a team who is just doing it for the extra overtime or one who is doing it because they want the business to succeed?

An ageing and constantly changing workforce

This is a challenge faced by many warehouses throughout Western Europe and the United States and is beginning to emerge in China also. Experienced staff are nearing retirement age with fewer trained staff to replace them as the position of warehouse operative is not seen as attractive for today's youth.

In order to overcome the challenge of staff shortages, organizations are visiting schools to teach pupils about the role of logistics in today's society and trying to burst the myth that warehouses are cold, dirty, noisy places in which to work. As warehouses become more technically advanced this will also attract a new breed of warehouse employee – those with an interest in technology and automation.

Attracting younger workers and increasing their job satisfaction early on can be key to early integration into the organization, which in turn can lead to improved attitude and job performance. Apprentice schemes are ideal in this situation.

Companies are also utilizing agency workers in greater numbers; this provides cover not only during seasonal peaks but also during periods of absence and holiday cover. The use of agency staff can also provide flexibility during new contract start-up.

As discussed previously, the use of flexible working hours and annualized hours will attract staff who would not normally consider working in this environment.

Operating hours

The legislation that surrounds working hours within the warehouse will vary country by country. This section outlines some of the options available to the warehouse manager in terms of working hours. However, these need to be checked against local legislation.

The operating hours of the warehouse will very much depend on the throughput and customer requirements.

The classic three-shift system is still used widely; however, with the increasing requirement for 24/7 working, many warehouses have adopted different shift patterns.

The classic shift pattern is as follows:

Shift 1: 0600–1400 hours;

Shift 2: 1400–2200 hours;

Shift 3: 2200–0600 hours; and

Shift 4: 0900–1700 hours.

This shift pattern works on an eight-hour day with 24-hour coverage. However, one of the drawbacks is that there is no overlapping shift for the handover of information.

Within these shift patterns we also see staff taking breaks at the same time. Studies differ on the effect of group breaks on productivity. Some suggest that staff interaction at break times is positive and leads to increased productivity whereas others will argue that having equipment inactive and orders stacking up can be detrimental to overall performance and adds increased pressure on the staff. I tend to lean towards the latter.

With the introduction of 24/7 working, a number of companies have adopted a four-day working week for staff based on a 12-hour day on a rotating basis. See Table 2.1.

Other companies have utilized part-time workers with flexible shifts, working around school hours with staff working between 0930 and 1430 hours, for example, in order to supplement full-time staff.

TABLE 2.1   Warehouse shift patterns (adapted from Ackerman 2000)

	Team 1	Team 2	Team 3	Team 4
Monday week 1	0600–1800	1800–0600		
Tuesday	0600–1800	1800–0600		
Wednesday	0600–1800	1800–0600		
Thursday	0600–1800	1800–0600		
Friday			0600–1800	1800–0600
Saturday			0600–1800	1800–0600
Sunday			0600–1800	1800–0600
Monday week 2			0600–1800	1800–0600
Tuesday week 2	0600–1800	1800–0600		

Where 24/7 coverage is not required, typical shift patterns are as follows:

Shift 1: 0600–1400 hours;

Shift 2: 0900– 1700 hours;

Shift 3: 1400–2200 hours.

There can be variations on the above theme. The ideal situation is to ensure that peaks in activity are covered as much as possible. This can include the arrival of inbound trucks in the morning and the normally busy period of picking and despatch during late afternoon and early evening.

When shift working is adopted, public transport and catering facilities need to be available for the staff.

Other considerations include potential congestion during shift changeovers and the effect on nearby residential housing of vehicle movements, noise and light pollution. In a seasonal business the system of annualized hours can be used to cover periods of unpredictable demand. Staff are paid the same amount each month but their hours will vary depending on the work content within the warehouse operation. This can include working longer shifts during periods of increased activity and being sent home when things become quieter.

The adoption of this system provides increased flexibility, reduces the need for agency staff and temporary labour and ensures sufficient labour cover when demand is high, as a result providing better customer service. Through its flexibility and by working with staff it can also contribute to higher levels of employee retention.

Rather than pay overtime during periods of high activity, the company can 'call in' these hours without making additional payments.

This system can work efficiently with the cooperation of staff. Whereas overtime relies on the goodwill of the employee and their commitments at the time, a system of annualized hours should benefit both parties equally. Costs are also reduced as there is no additional cost for each hour.

Temporary labour is expensive, not only in terms of the hourly rate but also in terms of training, supervision and the likelihood of lower productivity. Where temporary workers are utilized it is always a good idea to strike up a relationship with a local agency that can provide staff who have received training specific to your company's requirements and have also received some form of induction.

Training

A whole book can be written on this topic. However, in this section we will cover the basics of warehouse staff training.

First, managers need to ensure that all staff receive an induction. For example: 'At Boots we set up a three-day induction programme for colleagues joining the warehouse, the highlight of which was a day's stint working in store, seeing a delivery being made and working the stock to shelf. It really helped colleagues connect what they do with the store operation' (Chappell 2009). A simple process flow map showing the end-to-end supply chain and how each step impacts the final customer will engage warehouse staff and make them feel part of the bigger process.

Second, the manager needs to undertake a training needs analysis to identify which staff require specific types of training. There are always areas in which staff need to be trained – the trick is in identifying them.

Effective training helps to engage staff and should be an ongoing process. Training across disciplines not only provides the operator with a sense of progression but builds flexibility into the operation.

From a productivity, but more importantly a safety, point of view, all staff operating mechanical handling equipment must be trained on each individual piece of equipment and obtain a licence from the authorities.

Staff must also be shown how to lift heavy items without causing injury as back injuries tend to be one of the most common reasons for absence from work.

Warehouse audit

In order to assist the warehouse manager to improve processes we have produced a warehouse audit which can be found in Appendix I.

These lists of questions are not exhaustive and can be added to by the user to mirror their own operations. Audits should be undertaken by an independent person either from within the company or an outside consultant.

The purpose of the audit should be explained to staff and a timescale agreed to introduce the improvements. Results need to be shared with all the staff and staff need to take ownership of the results and the improvements necessary.

The audits which are concerned with the internal processes are based on what the authors see as best practice in a warehouse.

These audit forms can also be downloaded from **www.appriseconsulting. co.uk/warehousetools** (password – apprise1234).

Quality systems

Finally, in this section we have provided a list of quality standards that warehouse managers may deem necessary or advantageous for their operations.

These are as follows:

- ISO 9001 – a standard of requirements against which your Quality Management System can be evaluated;
- ISO 14001 – a standard of requirements that defines and establishes controls to reduce your company's impact on the environment;
- ISO 50001 – a standard of requirements that deals with the energy impact of your warehouse operation;
- OHSAS – a standard of requirements against which your Health and Safety Management System can be evaluated; and
- ISO 27001 – a standard of requirements which deals with all aspects of information security (this is particularly useful in the case of outsourced warehousing).

Summary and conclusion

If a warehouse is going to operate effectively and efficiently it needs an experienced, knowledgeable, well-trained manager and a motivated team of supervisors and operators.

An ageing population and difficulty in attracting new staff pose more challenges for today's manager, together with increased environmental pressures.

The warehouse manager's challenges are therefore many and varied, not least the requirement to reduce costs and inventory levels whilst increasing customer service.

A comprehensive and ongoing training programme is essential for both managers and supervisors. The warehouse should not be seen as a black hole but as an essential part of the supply chain, and the role of its staff in this chain needs to be recognized and understood.

Quality of service is what sets companies apart these days and the introduction of audits and quality systems into the operation will enable managers to continually assess, evaluate and improve their service both internally and externally.

The next section of the book examines in detail the processes within the warehouse and suggests where the manager can increase productivity and look to reduce costs.

Warehouse processes: receiving and put-away

Introduction

As Peters says, improvement comes from simplifying processes and procedures. These processes need to be aligned and working optimally if we are to improve efficiency and, as a result, reduce cost within the warehouse operation.

Detailed process documents need to be produced and made available to all employees. These need to be continually reviewed and updated. According to WERC (2010) companies who exhibit good to best practice processes define and publish process descriptions and assign ownership of the processes to responsible individuals. Supplementing written instructions with photographs also improves understanding.

In the next five chapters we examine in detail each of the processes associated with a warehouse operation. Although warehouses differ in terms of size, type, function, ownership and location the fundamental processes remain.

These processes include pre-receipt, receiving, put-away, storage, picking, replenishment, value-adding services and despatch. We also include a section on cross docking where products are moved across the warehouse without actually going through the put-away process. Other warehouse processes such as stock counting and inventory control, although undertaken as part of the mainstream day-to-day processes, are included in the section on housekeeping.

By ensuring that the correct processes are in place and operating optimally, companies can not only improve accuracy and efficiency but also take advantage of the new technology available.

Many books on the subject of warehousing will concentrate on the picking process as this is the most labour and cost-intensive process and has a direct impact on customer service.

This section is no exception; however, we also recognize the importance of pre-receipt and the receiving process. Receiving the wrong products or putting products in incorrect locations can result in errors just as easily as picking the wrong item.

Figure 3.1 shows each main warehouse activity as a percentage of cost, emphasizing the importance of the pick, pack and despatch operation. These figures will vary significantly depending on the type of operation.

For example, companies which are under pressure to speed up throughput are likely to use concepts such as cross docking, thus reducing the amount of time spent on put-away, picking and retrieval.

The main activities mentioned above are shown in Figure 3.2 together with their relationships.

FIGURE 3.1   Warehouse activities as a percentage of total cost

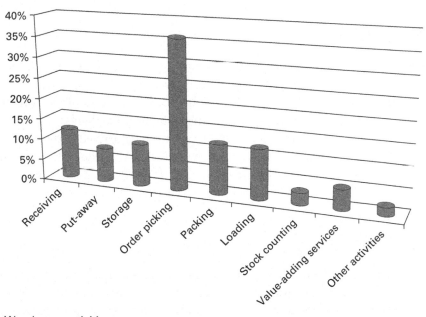

■ Warehouse activities as
  a percentage of total cost

FIGURE 3.2   Warehouse processes

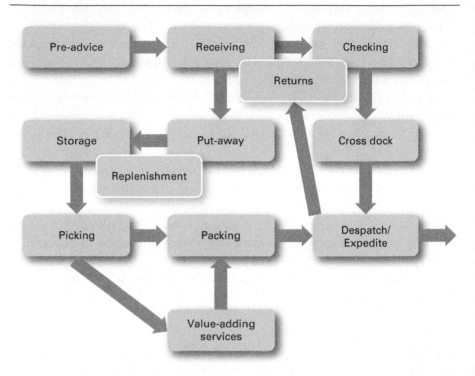

Receiving

Receiving, goods-in or in-handling is a crucial process within the warehouse. Ensuring that the correct product has been received in the right quantity and in the right condition at the right time is one of the mainstays of the warehouse operation. These elements are often termed supplier compliance.

However, it is our contention that once goods have arrived at the warehouse it is usually too late to rectify most receiving issues. We believe there are many steps that need to be taken before the actual act of receiving takes place.

Pre-receipt

First we need to ensure that the supplier presents the products to the warehouse in the most appropriate way. It is normally the buyer who specifies the product and therefore may not have knowledge of the goods-receiving operation.

Our suggestion here is that the warehouse manager is also involved in specifying and agreeing the packaging, items per carton, cartons per pallet,

TiHi (cases per layer, layers per pallet) and any specific labelling required, together with the mode of transport to ensure that the products ordered are compatible with the storage facility.

All too often we see items arriving at warehouses in unsuitable packaging that overhangs pallets, has incorrect or badly positioned labels and with the goods packed in quantities that do not relate to selling-pack quantities. Our proposal here is that samples are ordered and despatched in their transit packaging to ensure full compliance.

All these problems take time to resolve and are better handled at the supplier prior to delivery.

Areas that need to be discussed both internally and externally prior to the order being placed should include:

- size and type of cartons;
- type of transit packaging – cardboard, plastic, totes, metal stillages, roll cages, pallets;
- palletized or non-palletized delivery of product;
- size (length, width and height) and type of pallets, eg euro pallet, four-way entry;
- specific labelling such as product description, barcode and quantities;
- position of label on carton and pallet;
- carton quantities (inner and outer carton quantities, for example); and
- mode of transport, delivery quantity and frequency of delivery.

Delivery in the standard selling quantity is also crucial in assisting the manager to increase the speed of throughput and simplify picking. For example, many companies still place orders on their suppliers in multiples of 12 yet most customers order in multiples of 10 thus causing considerable extra work in computing quantities, opening cartons and re-packaging.

The method of delivery needs to be compatible with the unloading equipment available at the warehouse. The lack of loading bays, for example, will necessitate the use of tail-lift-equipped or side-(un)loading vehicles.

The transfer of much production offshore has resulted in a significant increase in container traffic. The decision here is whether to loose load or palletize the cargo. Another option is to use slip sheets.

The benefits of palletizing product include protection from loss or damage during handling and transportation and a reduction in the number of people required to load and unload containers. The process of loading and unloading is speeded up whilst space required at the loading and despatch bays is also reduced.

The trade-off is the reduction of space utilization in the containers. Depending on the number of pallets used, this can be up to 10 per cent of the space for the pallets alone. Couple that with the clearance height for the pallet and the possibility that pallets cannot be stacked and space utilization is significantly reduced.

One potential method of reducing the trade-off effect is the use of slip sheets in place of pallets. Slip sheets are constructed from fibreboard, thick cardboard or thin plastic in the shape and size of the unit load. The thickness of the sheet is approximately 2 centimetres.

The load is placed on the slip sheet within the container and on arrival at the final destination the slip sheet together with its load is removed by means of a specialist forklift attachment and placed on a pallet for storage.

The increasing legislation (FAO ISPM 15) on the use of wooden pallets makes slip sheets a viable option for the transport of goods in containers. They increase the loading cube within the container, reduce the time taken to offload containers and are easier to clean. They do, however, require both despatch and receiving warehouses to purchase a special attachment for the forklift truck.

Depending on the load configuration, shipping costs can increase between 15 and 33 per cent when using pallets. However, there are notable savings made at the point of delivery plus the reduction in potential damage to products and injury to staff.

The introduction of high cube containers has provided additional internal height and therefore the double stacking of pallets becomes more feasible, providing the products are not easily crushed.

Finally, containers with large numbers of product lines will still need to be sorted at the receiving bay whether they are palletized or loose loaded. In order to reduce in-handling time the supplier needs to be instructed to keep the same product lines together in the container.

If products arrive loose loaded in a container they will need to be palletized prior to being put away in the racking. Where possible these cartons need to be constructed in such a way that there is no overhang and no potential for crushing when they are arranged on the pallet and that as many cartons as possible can be accommodated within the cubic capacity of the pallet space.

For example, for a 1200 mm × 1000 mm (48″ × 40″) approx pallet with a clearance height within the pallet location of 2000 mm (80″), the cartons might measure 300 mm × 200 mm × 250 mm, for example, giving a total potential pallet capacity of 140 cartons if we allow 15 centimetres for the height of the pallet and 10 centimetres clearance between the top of the pallet and the underside of the beam. Each layer will have 20 cartons and will be stacked seven high. There is no overhang on the pallet on either side and cartons are not turned on their sides. The following website provides a tool to calculate TiHi: **http://onpallet.com/**

FIGURE 3.3   Example of incorrectly sized cartons

As can be seen in Figure 3.3, the size of the outer cartons does not allow the warehouse operation to optimally stack the pallet and can result in increased damage.

Utilizing off-the-shelf software can potentially further improve the load-building capability where the carton dimensions are not so straightforward, both on a pallet and within a trailer or container. Not only do the pallets look neat and tidy but the products are less prone to damage.

Currently there is no universally accepted standard for pallet dimensions. Different market sectors and organizations utilize many different pallet sizes around the globe.

The International Organization for Standardization (ISO) sanctions six pallet dimensions, detailed in ISO Standard 6780: Flat pallets for intercontinental materials handling – principal dimensions and tolerances. These are shown in Table 3.1.

Other pallet sizes are seen in the chemicals and printing industries to accommodate drums and printer reels, etc. We are currently working with a client who receives stock on single use American pallets which they have to 'slave' (put on top of another pallet) to enable them to place them in their racking safely. This not only requires additional labour but also reduces the cubic capacity of the storage location. Another client has two different pallet sizes: 1200 mm × 1000 mm and 900 mm × 650 mm. This makes it very difficult to configure storage racks and decide on optimum locations within the warehouse. This required the use of decking in the racking to safely stow the pallets.

The size of pallet to be stored determines the rack configuration. Where companies store different sizes of pallet the configuration needs to be suitably

TABLE 3.1   Pallet dimensions (ISO)

Dimensions in mm (W × L)	Dimensions in inches (W × L)	Country of use
1219 × 1016	48.00 × 40.00	North America
1000 × 1200	39.37 × 47.24	UK and Asia; pallet commonly referred to as a UK or industrial pallet
1165 × 1165	44.88 × 44.88	Australia
1067 × 1067	42.00 × 42.00	Most countries
1100 × 1100	43.30 × 43.30	Asia
800 × 1200	31.50 × 47.24	Europe; pallet commonly known as a euro pallet

flexible. For example, UK companies needing to store both UK and euro pallets will be forced down the route of having their racking set at 1100 mm deep with each 2.7 metre bay accommodating either two UK pallets or three euro pallets.

Companies can utilize timber or mesh decking to accommodate different sizes of pallets but this can prove expensive and reduces the load capacity of the racking.

Other factors to take into account when specifying pallets include whether they are two-way (stringer) or four-way entry (block), the type of timber used (certain countries have restrictions, such as Australia where wood is required to be treated) and the type of nails used.

Certain types of MHE are not able to operate with block pallets, reducing warehouse flexibility. These include pallet stackers.

Plastic pallets are also becoming more widely used whilst the automotive industry has tended to use metal stillages to transport and store automotive parts.

Recent innovations in the pallet sector have included iGPS's plastic pallets that are said to be 100 per cent recyclable as well as being 30 per cent lighter than wooden pallets.

iGPS also claim that their pallets are 'vastly better for the environment' and 'do not absorb fluids that can cross-contaminate food'. One concern that has worried food manufacturers is the treatment of wood pallets with pesticides and fungicides. iGPS's plastic pallets do not need treatment, so they claim they are more suitable for moving foodstuffs in the warehouse.

They have also embedded RFID tags into the pallets to enable tracking to take place and there are also barcode and alphanumeric identifiers. The pallets measure approx. 48″ × 40″ (1200 mm × 1000 mm) and are four-way entry (logistics.about.com).

Products delivered in outer cartons need to be labelled in such a way that they can be easily identified. Information can include barcodes, which need to be compatible with your radio frequency (RF) equipment and which hold data such as product code, description and pack quantity. Ease of identification speeds up the in-handling process.

With regard to carton quantities, many suppliers continue to supply in multiples of 12, yet customers who have grown up with the metric system tend to order in multiples of 5 and 10. There needs to be consistency within the supply chain in terms of pack quantities supplied, pack quantities stored and pack quantities sold.

The pack quantities will depend on the value, weight and volume of the product and, although there is no legal limit, outer cartons should not weigh in excess of 20 kilograms (44 lbs) from a health and safety point of view.

Individual unit sales will always necessitate opening cases to satisfy orders; however, the fewer times this occurs the more productive the warehouse.

There also needs to be consistency by product line to ensure accuracy during stock counts and reduce picking errors. I have come across many instances where different suppliers of the same generic product pack in different quantities. This leads to inaccuracies and delays both on receipt, picking and despatch.

Discussions between the warehouse, procurement, customer services and the supplier should alleviate many of these problems.

The premise is to discuss requirements with the supplier and if you need them to do things differently then you need to take the initiative. There may be an additional cost. However, this needs to be weighed against the additional costs incurred within the warehouse. The supplier may surprise you by changing the way they present things to you. In fact, there may be occasions when this is also advantageous to the supplier. The old adage of 'If you don't ask, you don't get' is very true.

Another truism to bear in mind is the 80/20 rule as it applies to suppliers. Not only is it likely that 20 per cent of your suppliers provide 80 per cent of your stock but it is likely that 20 per cent of your suppliers cause 80 per cent of your goods-in problems.

You need to put measures in place to identify the suppliers who are not performing to standard and work with them to introduce improvements. You can be reasonably sure that your suppliers aren't deliberately causing you problems. The issues arise because they are not aware of the effects of their actions on your operation. You will benefit more from a hands-on approach to the problem and work with the supplier to improve the situation.

In-handling

One of the main challenges for a warehouse manager is to match labour hours with work content. Handling a product the least amount of time possible (labour touch points) leads to reduced labour hours and as a consequence, reduced cost.

Depending on the operation, labour can be the single biggest cost within a warehouse. It can be between 48 and 60 per cent of the total warehouse cost depending on the amount of automation utilized. It is also the most difficult cost to control.

In-handling makes up approximately 20 per cent of the total direct labour cost within a retail warehouse.

Preparation

Prior to the actual receipt a number of processes need to take place. The first step is to ensure that suppliers deliver into the warehouse when you decide, not when it suits them. There will be exceptions to this. For example, it is difficult for parcel delivery companies to adhere to booking times because of the nature of their deliveries; however, pallet and full-load delivery companies expect to be given specific delivery times, albeit this is not their preferred option.

By providing delivery times for each supplier or their subcontractors, you are in control and able to match your work hours to work content. A booking-in or dock scheduling system needs to be introduced. Many of today's WMS have a dock scheduling module these days however an Excel spreadsheet will suffice.

Initially you need to decide on when you are going to receive products into the warehouse. Are you going to have deliveries throughout the day or limit them to a morning shift, for example?

You then need to match the length of the time slots to the time estimated to fulfil the task. Standard time slots do not work as each delivery is likely to be different. For example, it could take 30 minutes to offload a 13.6 metre (45 foot) palletized trailer and a further 15 minutes to check and move the pallets to the storage area, whereas a loose-loaded 20 foot container could take up to three hours depending on the number of SKUs and staff deployed.

You need to keep records of the time it takes for each type of delivery and share this information with your booking-in team. This will give you the amount of labour and equipment required to undertake the task, thus making planning a great deal easier.

By introducing a dock scheduling system you are able to allocate accurate time slots, measure productivity, organize labour and also check demurrage and penalty charges.

Warehouse staff need to be aware of the products being delivered, the type of vehicle and the equipment required to offload. Once this has been ascertained and the time calculated, a suitable booking slot is allocated and a booking reference given to the supplier.

Details of any pallet exchange agreements also need to be ascertained. The use of pallets within a rental system such as Chep, IPP Logipal, LPR and others requires both parties to accurately record movements within the system.

Pre-advice of the products being delivered is also advisable so that the details can be entered in the warehouse management system (WMS). This is normally in the form of an Advanced Shipping Notice (ASN). An ideal method of receipt is to accept the contents of the ASN as correct into the system as soon as possible through the use of RFID or barcode scanning. Some WMSs will use this information to pre-allocate pallet locations for the products prior to arrival. The information is also used to check the delivery.

Offloading

On arrival, the vehicle details need to be checked against the booking reference and the vehicle allocated a loading bay or location in the yard. Any vehicle seals need to be checked against the delivery paperwork.

Prior to offloading temperature-controlled vehicles, the temperature history of the vehicle whilst in transit needs to be checked, together with the current temperature of the goods.

Once the vehicle has backed onto the appropriate bay or has been positioned in the yard for offloading from the sides, the in-handling team should have appropriate labour and equipment to hand, to efficiently manage the offloading process.

Where vehicles are unloaded in the yard this usually necessitates the use of two lift trucks, one to unload the trailer and another to put the product away within the warehouse.

The introduction of articulated forklift trucks which can work both inside and outside the warehouse is going some way to reducing the requirement for two different types of truck for the latter operation.

The most common method of unloading palletized vehicles onto a loading bay is with a powered pallet truck, hand pallet truck or pallet jack. Some companies utilize counterbalance forklift trucks; however, the weight of the truck, driver and load on potentially weak or damaged container or trailer floors can be an accident waiting to happen.

Unloading times will vary depending on the equipment used and whether the load needs to be staged prior to put-away.

FIGURE 3.4   Automated unloading (courtesy of Joloda)

In order to speed up this process, equipment companies have introduced automatic unloading systems, which means that a 26-pallet trailer can be unloaded within five minutes of arriving at the dock. Unloading methods include the use of rollers, tracks (see Figure 3.4) and slip chains whilst others use loading plates or giant slip sheets. These tend to be operated in high volume situations between production plants and off-site storage locations.

Combine these with conveyors or automated guided vehicles (AGV) and the requirement for labour within the receiving operation reduces significantly.

Unloading loose-loaded containers has always been a time-consuming operation. This normally necessitates having at least two people unloading within the container and placing the items onto a pallet. A third person is usually waiting for the pallet to be stacked before taking it to the checking area before put away. This is very unproductive as the staff within the container wait for full pallets to be replaced with empty ones whilst the forklift driver is waiting for the pallet to be built.

There is no guarantee that the same product is together within the container, therefore more sortation needs to take place on the unloading dock. This is very inefficient and can be hazardous to the staff, who are continually bending and stretching within the container and are in close proximity to the MHE. Lighting is usually poor and conditions are not conducive to fast, accurate work.

Added problems arise if the warehouse is not equipped with loading bays and is dependent on a container ramp or worst still a forklift truck with an operator standing on a pallet, which can slow the process even further and has its safety issues.

Figure 3.5 shows a boom conveyor unloading cartons from a container. These can be static or can be moved between loading doors as required.

FIGURE 3.5   Boom conveyor unloading cartons
(courtesy of Best Conveyors)

Placing cartons onto a conveyor means that sortation can take place outside the container, there is less bending and twisting involved as the conveyor is at a manageable height and it provides a continuous, uninterrupted flow.

The person within the container can also utilize a vacuum lift to prevent injury through bending, stretching and lifting heavy cartons.

Pallets or stillages can be laid out either side of the conveyor and can be stacked with the correct item. These pallets can be placed on platforms that rise and fall according to the build height of the pallet, thus reducing the amount of bending and stretching by the operators.

In order for this operation to run smoothly, the supplier needs to be instructed to load the same items together in the container. There is the potential of increasing productivity by up to 50 per cent using this process.

With the increase in automation, there is a greater emphasis on uniform cartons as robots are now utilized for building pallets both on intake and for despatch (see Figure 3.6 below).

In certain operations robots have replaced the manual unloading of containers as can be seen in Figure 3.7 below.

Other equipment includes forklift trucks with clamp attachments for offloading items such as white goods and de-layering pallets, rams or poles for offloading

FIGURE 3.6   Robotic palletiser (courtesy of Bastian Solutions)

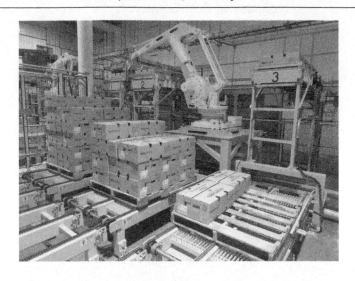

FIGURE 3.7   Robotic unloading of container with boom conveyor (courtesy of Bastian Solutions)

carpets and similar items, rotating clamps for barrels and tyres and forklift trucks with slip sheet attachments for unloading containers.

Checking

Once the goods are offloaded, you need to decide whether they need to be checked before put-away. The ideal scenario is to move inbound goods directly from the loading bay to the storage area or despatch area if goods are cross docked.

However, trust is an issue here and unless you are 100 per cent certain that your suppliers are totally accurate with their deliveries on every occasion, some form of checking will need to take place.

This can, however, take the form of a random check of certain product lines rather than checking the whole consignment. A count of total pallets may be sufficient.

A number of retailers have introduced GFR (good faith receiving) where products are accepted into the distribution centre or store without checking on arrival. Random checks are undertaken and any discrepancies found are charged to the supplier on a pro rata basis. This enables drivers to continue with their deliveries and pressurizes suppliers to increase the accuracy of their shipments.

This can be extended to other operations, providing agreements can be made with the suppliers.

Even if GFR is not introduced, by measuring supplier performance a warehouse manager can decide on the regularity and comprehensiveness of inbound product checks. The rate of checking can be based on the accuracy of recent deliveries.

A client we worked with checks 10 per cent of the lines on each incoming shipment. If they find a discrepancy they will check a further 10 per cent. Further discrepancies result in the whole load being checked.

Where new suppliers are concerned it is likely that you will want to check the whole of the consignment initially until you are confident of the accuracy of the supplier.

There is a trade-off here between the time it takes to check inbound deliveries, the delay in the product being entered onto the system and available for sale, the number of discrepancies found and the time it takes to deal with them.

Another decision to be made is whether the delivery notes are used to check off the delivery or whether a 'blind' count is made (in which operators are not made aware of the quantities expected until the count has been completed) and the actual delivery cross checked against the paperwork once the whole load has been received into the warehouse.

From experience, although it is likely to take longer, it is more accurate to count the product and then compare it with the delivery paperwork than use the paperwork as a checklist.

The utilization of barcode scanners has speeded up the process significantly and improved accuracy. Products can be scanned and the details compared in real time (if wireless enabled) with the expected quantities to determine any discrepancies. Once scanned, the goods can be moved directly to the next staging point, be this quality control, a forward pick face, reserve storage or the despatch bay for cross docking.

The introduction of RFID will further reduce checking time at the receiving bay. Products that have tags fitted can be recognized and counted immediately on entry to the warehouse and details passed in real time to the WMS.

Other equipment can include weighing scales for products that are not easy to check or are stored and sold by weight.

Aberdeen Group (2009b) has reported that 70 per cent of best-in-class companies are more likely than all other companies to receive goods without using paper documents. All have migrated to the use of barcodes, RFID or voice technology.

Recording and reporting discrepancies both internally and externally are a fundamental part of the receiving process.

Table 3.2 shows an example of a goods received non-compliance report.

TABLE 3.2 Goods received non-compliance report

Date received	Supplier	Product code	Purchase order no	Booking reference	Non-compliance
03/04/13	ACS	48145	266460	11228	Barcode does not scan
03/04/13	ACS	104658	266460	11228	Outer carton is > 20 kg. No warning on box
10/04/13	BFP	113144	261688	11317	Barcode on outer, not inner
10/04/13	QRS	102258	267456	11319	Inner quantity = 6 not 12 as expected
14/04/13	QRS	115119	267456	11424	Barcode does not scan
21/04/13	Tco Deli	110002	287547	11563	No price sticker as requested

Cross docking

The goal of most warehouses is to increase throughput rates and reduce the amount of stock held. Cross docking is a process where products are moved directly from goods-in to the despatch bays. This replaces the need to place the product into store and any subsequent picking operation.

Cross docking needs the full support of suppliers as to how they present the product. This includes clear labelling and advance notice of arrival together with accurate, on-time delivery.

Cross docking requires systems to identify the product that needs to be cross docked and a process needs to be in place to recognize and alert the staff.

Once checked in, the products should be taken directly to the despatch area and their floor or temporary rack location recorded on the system, alerting staff that the product is now awaiting despatch. The details must be recorded in order to provide an audit trail.

Other points to take into account include the amount of space available at the inbound and outbound areas. Sufficient space is key to moving products quickly and safely. Any congestion in these areas will slow up the process appreciably and lead to tension between teams. There also needs to be a well-marked staging area where the products can be placed prior to despatch. An area of drive-in racking can assist in marshalling loads for particular collections.

FIGURE 3.8 Example of cross docking

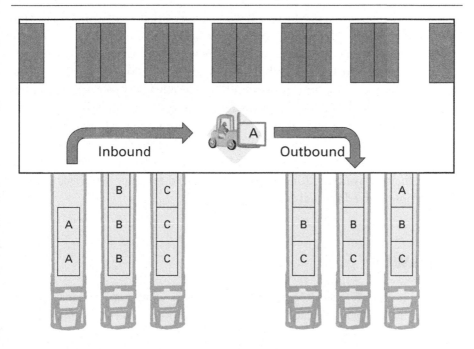

Cross docking is used significantly in the movement of perishable goods through the supply chain and retailers use this system in their distribution centres where they receive products from multiple suppliers and sort and consolidate them for onward shipment to different stores. It has been said that Walmart in the United States delivers approximately 85 per cent of its merchandise using a cross-docking system. This system is prevalent in many retail operations today.

Just-in-time systems also rely on cross docking whereby manufacturers deliver parts to a cross-dock or sequencing centre where they are consolidated and delivered line-side in sequence.

Recording

Depending on the product, there could be a requirement to record more than just the standard data such as product code, description and quantity on arrival. Other information could include batch or lot numbers and serial numbers. Barcode scanning, which we will look at in the following chapters, is ideal for this type of data capture.

Quality control

It is accepted that certain products will require more stringent checking on receipt. These include high-value items, food, hazardous goods, temperature-sensitive product and pharmaceuticals. New suppliers will also fall into this category.

An area close to the receiving bay should be set aside to spot check items on arrival. This needs to be done as promptly and as efficiently as possible so as to avoid congestion and to get the products onto the system quickly. If there are issues, the items need to be taken to a specific quarantine area or, if space is an issue, to the storage area – but must be identified as defective or awaiting the results of tests. Most WMSs are able to block access to products on the system, making them unavailable for picking until cleared for sale. A physical sign at the location is an additional failsafe.

Put-away

Many of today's WMSs allocate product locations in advance and instruct the operator as to where to place the goods. This can be directly to the despatch area if the product is to be cross docked as discussed above, to the pick face as a form of replenishment or to a reserve or bulk-storage location.

In order for this system to work effectively, a great deal of information needs to be programmed into the system. This includes the following:

- size, weight and height of palletized goods;
- results of an ABC analysis or slotting, where fast-moving goods are placed closest to the despatch area (an area we will cover later);
- current order data;
- family product groups;
- actual sales combinations;
- current status of pick face for each product;
- size of pallet locations; and
- weight capacity of racking.

Distance of the locations from the receiving and despatch areas

In circumstances where there is an absence of such a system, the warehouse manager needs to calculate the optimum location for the goods and instruct the operators accordingly.

Another decision to take is whether products are placed into fixed or random locations. In utilizing fixed locations you are designating a specific location for a particular product. A random location is, as it states, where the pallet is placed in the most efficient slot available.

Fixed positions enable the picker to memorize the actual location and speed up the picking process. However, if there is no stock for that particular product at any time, the slot remains empty and pallet storage utilization reduces significantly.

Factors to bear in mind when locating product include their specific characteristics. For example, hazardous items need to be stored in an appropriate area. Items of high value will also require special storage conditions, which might mean a lockable cage or the use of a secure carousel.

When locating cartons, the fastest-moving items should be placed in the middle row of shelving so that the order picker doesn't have to spend time bending and stretching. Slower-moving items should occupy the lowest and highest shelves.

The warehouse manager also needs to take into account that items should be stored in groups by similarity. For example, within an automotive environment gearbox parts should be stored together in the same area. Added to this, products that often appear together on a pick list should be located side by side. For example, a ½-inch bolt needs to be stored next to a ½-inch nut rather than the bolts stored together in one area and the nuts in another.

Finally, some warehouse systems will combine put-away with pallet retrieval. This is termed task interleaving. The system will instruct the operator to put away a pallet en route to collecting a picked full pallet or one that is required for replenishment.

Summary and conclusion

The receiving process is crucial to the efficient and effective operation of the warehouse.

The following five quick steps should help to improve productivity in the receiving and put-away area:

- Ensure that you have booked arrival slots for the majority of your suppliers.
- Reduce the amount of checking required on inbound deliveries.
- Have a system in place to prioritize inbound goods, eg prioritize low-stock items and promotional items.
- Plan your put-away meticulously and ensure product is located accurately and efficiently.
- Cross dock as much as possible.

Warehouse processes: pick preparation

04

Spectacular achievement is always preceded by unspectacular preparation.

(ROBERT H SCHULLER)

Introduction

Order picking is the most costly activity within today's warehouses. Not only is it labour intensive, but it is challenging to automate, can be difficult to plan, is prone to error and crucially has a direct impact on customer service. Typical errors include omitting items from the order, sending the wrong item and sending the wrong number of items.

Companies target the picking operation as the area in which productivity improvements can make a significant difference to overall costs.

The trade-off in this instance is between speed, cost and accuracy. Managers are looking for quick response times, high accuracy rates and high productivity but at least cost.

Satisfying these factors will determine the types of picking systems and processes chosen.

The picking operation has changed significantly over the past 20 years. Previously, full-case and pallet picks tended to be the norm. Today, concepts such as just in time, the growth in online shopping and significant reductions in order lead times have resulted in smaller order quantities and more frequent deliveries.

This type of picking is referred to as item, eaches, broken-case or split-case picking.

In a 2012 benchmarking survey, WERC used the key performance measures shown in Table 4.1 to distinguish best-in-class picking operations.

The imperative here is to ensure that picking accuracy is measured before the order leaves the warehouse in order that operatives can be informed of their performance and additional training instigated if required.

So how does the warehouse of today achieve best-in-class standards? As can be appreciated, there are many interrelated decisions that need to be made and aligned for companies to be effective in this area. Figure 4.1 shows the inter-relationship between labour, technology, equipment and warehouse layout.

TABLE 4.1   Best in class: picking (WERC)

	Best in class	Median	Laggards
Percentage of orders picked accurately	≥ 99.9%	99.5%	≤ 98.0%
Percentage of orders shipped on time and complete to customer request; or on time, in full (OTIF)	≥ 99.05%	95.0%	≤ 84.1%

FIGURE 4.1   Picking interrelationships

Preparation

As with any logistics process, preparation is a key element.

According to Frazelle (2002), less than 15 per cent of SKUs within a warehouse are assigned to the most efficient location, resulting in a 10 to 30 per cent cost increase in travel time and underutilized locations.

Prior to laying out a warehouse, deciding on the most appropriate handling equipment, installing storage systems and deciding on which form of picking system to introduce, a full ABC analysis of stock movements and stock held should take place.

Understanding ABC classification begins by understanding Pareto's Law or the 80/20 rule.

This states that roughly 80 per cent of effects come from 20 per cent of causes. This rule is not universal but it is surprising how often it can apply. The idea therefore is to concentrate time and resources on the important 20 per cent or the 'vital few'.

Examples of the 80/20 rule in relation to the warehouse include the following:

- 80 per cent of sales come from the top 20 per cent of the product lines;

- 80 per cent of sales come from 20 per cent of the customers;

- 80 per cent of profits come from 20 per cent of the customers – not necessarily the same customers as above;

- 80 per cent of profits come from the top 20 per cent of products;

- 80 per cent of the cube usage within the warehouse comes from 20 per cent of the products;

- 80 per cent of the inventory value is in 20 per cent of the products;

- 80 per cent of problems come from 20 per cent of your suppliers;

- 80 per cent of complaints come from 20 per cent of the customers; and

- 80 per cent of staff problems come from 20 per cent of your workforce.

An 80/20 split isn't always the case, however. One current client's profile showed that based on our calculations 80 per cent of the total units sold came from only 5.9 per cent (144) of the total SKUs sold this year (2,443 product lines). A further 202 SKUs (8.3 per cent) provided another 10 per cent of the units sold whilst the remaining 86 per cent of lines made up the remaining 10 per cent of sales.

These analyses allow you to identify not only the highest-selling products but also items that are not selling and may be prime candidates for disposal.

As can be seen in Figure 4.2, this rule can be used to identify relationships between sales and product lines, sales and weight or cube and sales and the number of units sold.

FIGURE 4.2   Pareto's Law or the 80/20 rule (courtesy of Vanderlande)

Pareto's Law is widely used in logistics and is an excellent method for categorizing items. This is normally termed ABC classification.

In terms of sales, under this classification, 'A' is the most important, with 20 per cent of products producing 80 per cent of sales, 'B' is of medium importance with say 35 per cent of items producing 15 per cent of sales, and the remaining 45 per cent being 'C' items producing only 5 per cent of sales.

The precise classification of items will vary between companies and market sectors. However, in broad terms they are very similar.

Many companies will use an ABC analysis to produce an effective warehouse layout. However, the traditional single ABC analysis will only provide a snapshot of the current situation based on one parameter – the level of sales by product, the idea being that the A items, as the highest sellers, are placed at the front of the warehouse, closest to the despatch area.

Unfortunately, using this analysis alone can lead to a reduction in productivity. For example, compare the following two products in Table 4.2.

Although product A is the highest-selling item, it is only picked four times during the period, whereas product B appears on 200 orders, necessitating 200 visits to the pick face. Under these circumstances, in order to reduce travel distances and time, it is product B that should be closest to the despatch bay.

Returning to our client the next analysis we carried out was based on frequency of pick per product line. Here we found that 80 per cent of picks

TABLE 4.2   ABC comparison

	Sales	Number of orders
Product A	10,000 units	4
Product B	1,000 units	200

FIGURE 4.3   Pareto analysis of orders and SKU

% of orders completed by % SKU

10% of sku complete 75% of orders

% of total SKU

came from 15 per cent of the product lines. In fact the top 20 most popular lines by order frequency made up 35 per cent of the total picks.

It is our contention that the picking area layout should be based on the number of pick-face visits taking into account size and weight of the product and any special circumstances such as high security items.

For those who want to take quantity into account as well as pick face visits a double ABC categorization allows you to combine these two factors into one – in this case volume and frequency. This can be done by producing a nine-box grid as shown in Figure 4.4.

In this example, AA products are those that generate the most sales and are sold most frequently. CC products on the other hand are defined as slow movers in that they sell the least and move less frequently.

FIGURE 4.4   ABC analysis: quantity and frequency of sales (courtesy of ABC Softwork)

	High frequency ←		Low frequency
Higher sales	AA	AB	AC
↑	BA	BB	BC
Lower sales	CA	CB	CC

In terms of picking, the more frequently you visit a pick location the more labour intensive it is likely to be. Products in position AA will generate, on average, 50 per cent of your sales yet will only be 8 per cent of your product range.

Figure 4.5 shows the relationship between the frequency of sales and the value of the product. As can be seen, different strategies can be introduced for each of the sectors. These can include factors such as the service level provided, stock-ordering frequency and method, stock-counting frequency and customer and supplier relationships.

There are sophisticated software programs available to enable you to produce these results. However, if you are looking for a quick analysis, the following method, utilizing the 'sort' feature within Excel, will give you reasonable results.

In Table 4.3, the annual demand is multiplied by the number of times the product appears on a pick list to give a weighted volume. If we had used the volume figures alone the top two products in terms of pick-list frequency would have ended up much further away from the despatch area, thus increasing travel time appreciably.

It is likely, for example, that product codes 85866, 77577 and 77212 are sold in full-pallet quantities and can be stored in and picked directly from the pallet racking away from the forward pick faces.

This also reduces the requirement for replenishment for these particular products.

The more times you visit a pick face the higher your labour costs are likely to be. Travel time within a pick operation can account for up to 50 per cent of the total picking time.

Another part of the preparation process is slotting. This is a tool that calculates the optimum location for products within a warehouse. The tool is used to reduce the amount of travel time for operators by not only placing fast-moving products close to despatch but also places items that frequently ship together next to each other in the pick-face area.

For example, in a maintenance stores environment the natural storage method for nuts and bolts is likely to be by family and product code: all the nuts in one area and the bolts together in another area, although reasonably

FIGURE 4.5 ABC analysis: product value and frequency of sales

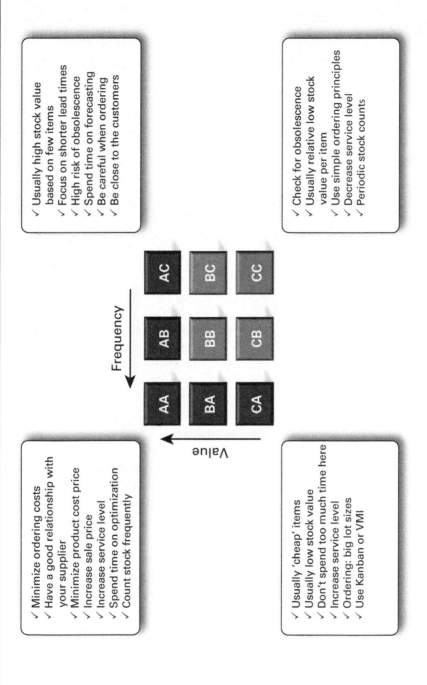

✓ Usually high stock value based on few items
✓ Focus on shorter lead times
✓ High risk of obsolescence
✓ Spend time on forecasting
✓ Be careful when ordering
✓ Be close to the customers

✓ Check for obsolescence
✓ Usually relative low stock value per item
✓ Use simple ordering principles
✓ Decrease service level
✓ Periodic stock counts

Frequency

Value

AC
BC
CC

AB
BB
CB

AA
BA
CA

✓ Minimize ordering costs
✓ Have a good relationship with your supplier
✓ Minimize product cost price
✓ Increase sale price
✓ Increase service level
✓ Spend time on optimization
✓ Count stock frequently

✓ Usually 'cheap' items
✓ Usually low stock value
✓ Don't spend too much time here
✓ Increase service level
✓ Ordering: big lot sizes
✓ Use Kanban or VMI

TABLE 4.3   ABC analysis using Excel

Product code	Annual demand 000	Pick list frequency	Weighted volume	Weighted percentage	Cumulative weighted percentage	ABC categor
85058	200	20,000	4,000,000	41.2	41.2	A
79001	250	15,000	3,750,000	38.6	79.9	A
67553	400	2,000	800,000	8.2	88.1	B
12865	600	1,000	600,000	6.2	94.3	B
13866	800	500	400,000	4.1	98.4	C
13700	1,000	100	100,000	1.0	99.4	C
85866	1,000	40	40,000	0.4	99.9	C
72333	100	80	8,000	0.1	99.9	C
77577	500	10	5,000	0.1	100.0	C
77212	1,000	1	1,000	0.0	100.0	C
	5,850		9,704,000			

close by. Our suggestion is that the same-size nuts and bolts are stored next to each other. This is for two reasons: one, they are normally sold together and two, it provides a separation between two similar-sized products, eg 3/8-inch nut from a 1/2-inch nut. This should lead to a reduction in travel time *and* potential errors.

Table 4.4 is an example of a simple slotting analysis carried out for a client recently which shows how often the same products appear on a pick list. This only looked at pairs of items. More sophisticated software can look at multiple items.

The system can also identify small groups of products that can complete a large number of orders. By examining the popularity of the items combined with the orders that they complete, these items can be identified and stored within a specific area in the warehouse.

TABLE 4.4 Example of product slotting tool (courtesy of John Bartholdi, **www.warehouse-science.com**)

Product code 1	Product code 2	No of orders containing same products
888058	970327	164
10222	970327	158
970327	888075	148
10232	970327	146
970327	375566	133
10222	888075	124
10232	888075	109
316781	970327	107
888058	375566	103
888058	888075	102
888058	10222	90

Slotting can also determine how many and what size of pick face is required for each product line. Very fast-moving lines will require multiple faces to avoid a bottleneck at a single location. These need to be spread efficiently across the front of the racking nearest the start and finish of the picking run.

Slotting will also take into account seasonality and suggest product transfers such as moving garden furniture from the front of the warehouse, where it is stored during spring and summer, to the rear of the warehouse during winter. Although there is likely to be a reasonable amount of additional handling involved, this should be outweighed by an overall reduction in travel, having moved the more popular winter products to the front of the warehouse.

The system can also take into account other parameters such as value, cube, weight and crushability. Retailers can also set up the system to pick in sequence tailored to store layout, thus minimizing the time spent handling the product at store.

This software is integrated within many of today's WMSs but can also be sourced separately; payback is normally less than one year.

By profiling the activity of items and orders received into the warehouse, we can determine which pick method to use, how much space to allocate and therefore where and how to store the product.

The idea is to place the most popular items in terms of pick frequency in the most accessible warehouse locations.

We can analyse orders in a number of different ways. One of the most common is lines per order. This examines how many different product codes make up an order, and as a result we can calculate how many pick locations we will visit for each order.

Table 4.5 shows the number of lines (SKUs) per order on average for different family groups and also the average number of units per line for a manufacturer in the fast-moving consumer goods (FMCG) sector.

As can be seen in Table 4.5, the family groups of products have different profiles. Family groups 8 and 9 have full-carton picks; however, the other family groups are predominantly item picks.

TABLE 4.5 Order analysis: FMCG manufacturer

	No of orders	No of units	No of SKUs	Units per order	Units per SKU	SKU per order
Family group 1	4,783	65,552	29,501	13.7	2.2	6.2
Family group 2	6,955	81,857	34,386	11.8	2.4	4.9
Family group 3	1,892	25,596	12,165	13.5	2.1	6.4
Family group 4	52	817	110	15.7	7.4	2.1
Family group 5	2,555	13,654	4,287	5.3	3.2	1.7
Family group 6	12,974	667,558	189,898	51.5	3.5	14.6
Family group 7	6,067	112,218	55,704	18.5	2.0	9.2
Family group 8	949	1,590,870	40,135	1,676.4	39.6	42.3
Family group 9	62	23,459	643	378.4	36.5	10.4
Overall	36,289	2,581,581	366,829	71.1	7.0	10.1

FIGURE 4.6 FMCG manufacturer: order analysis

This information can help in determining the type of pick operation and also the type of storage medium to be used.

We can also drill down further into this information to determine the number of lines per order by family group.

If we take family group 6 as an example, we can see in Figure 4.6 that there are a larger number of single-line orders together with some large orders with multiple lines. Using averages in these circumstances can therefore be misleading.

With such a large number of single-line orders we also need to determine whether these are standard orders or possibly back orders.

If they are standard orders then a batch pick (discussed later) is probably the most suitable method of picking. Examples of this type of order profile include internet sales, small-parts distribution and engineering spares.

Where items are picked from cases, this suggests that the items could potentially be decanted into smaller receptacles and placed in a specific area within the warehouse where picking operations can be consolidated.

Allied to the lines-per-order calculation is the 'cube per order index' (COI), which calculates the ratio of a product line's space requirement at the pick face to the number of picks per day.

This ratio enables you to decide on which position in the pick run a particular item should be placed. The lower the COI, the better the space utilization of the product and therefore, it should be placed nearer to the despatch bay at the front of each run of racking.

By combining the two measures we are able to determine the method of picking. Multiple orders with a small overall cube can be picked by means of a roll cage or trolley whilst larger cube orders will require pallet trucks or pallet jacks, for example.

FIGURE 4.7   Product cube picked and despatched per month

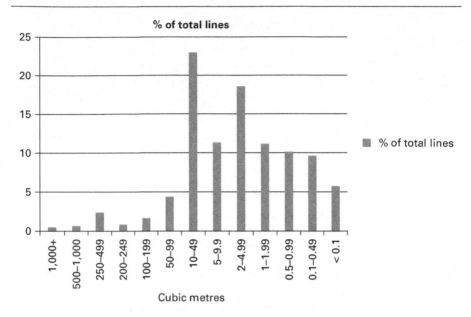

In order to decide on the method of storage for individual product lines we need to examine the cube movement distribution. By detailing the items that fall into specific cube movement ranges we can decide on the most appropriate storage mode.

Figure 4.7 shows an example of cube movement distribution. Approximately 15 per cent of the total items ship less than 0.5 cubic metres per month, which suggests bin, shelf, flow rack or carousel storage, whereas 12 per cent of the items ship in excess of 50 cubic metres per month. This would point in the direction of some form of pallet storage.

Demand variation distribution enables you to determine the size of the pick face and the quantity held for each type of product, the idea being to limit the number of replenishments that take place during a day. The ideal is not to replenish but have sufficient stock in situ to cover demand over a shift. An approximate figure can be derived by calculating the average daily demand and the standard deviation for each item.

Table 4.6 is an example of a client's pick operation that utilizes flow racking and has a mixture of full carton and item picks from carton.

As can be seen from this example, the number of cartons stored in the pick faces is nearly optimum providing there is no significant deviation from the average.

The issue arises when there is a significant daily deviation in the number of items picked. For example, if we take product code 989533 with daily pick

TABLE 4.6 Example of pick-face analysis

Product code	Units picked per day	Equivalent carton pick	Average number of visits to pick face per day	Cartons per flow rack location	Minimum number of locations
989533	886.1	11.1	13.3	6	2
989133	942.3	10.5	16.2	6	2
881043	522.2	8.7	6.4	6	2
978003	5,804.3	7.3	14.4	6	2
989333	309.8	6.2	13.4	6	2
881033	405.7	5.8	4.3	6	2
881053	141.8	4.7	3.7	6	1
989122	554.1	3.7	12.0	6	1
812833	158.8	3.5	11.6	6	1
989144	194.6	3.2	8.8	6	1
989322	277.7	3.1	9.1	6	1

quantities of 11, 13, 19, 5 and 7, although the average pick per day is 11 there is a wide variation across the week.

In order to accommodate an average day's demand with a low possibility of replenishment, we need to store the average number of cartons picked plus two standard deviations for a 5 per cent chance of replenishment and three standard deviations of demand for a 1 per cent chance of replenishment during the day. This suggests the pick face should contain either 21 or 26 cases for this product.

The issue will be whether there is sufficient space available to accommodate this amount of stock in the picking area.

The amount of space made available to the pick operation will very much depend on the total available cubic capacity of the warehouse, the floor space and the amount of reserve stock needing to be stored.

This takes us into the next section, which examines the pick area layout.

Warehouse pick area layout

Having produced a comprehensive profile of the products and orders, we are ready to tackle the layout.

Figure 4.8 depicts a very basic layout that has used an ABC analysis based on the frequency of pick-face visits. The next step is to minimize the amount of travel through the warehouse when picking an order.

The route followed by the picker when assembling the order needs to take into account the following:

- The pick instruction will have each pick sequenced as per the most effective route beginning at the front of the racking nearest the despatch bays.

- Heaviest items are picked first.

- The picker should be able to pick from both sides when moving up and down the aisles. See Figure 4.9 below. In this example the aisles are numbered, not the rows of racking which means that the picker can

FIGURE 4.8   Basic warehouse layout based on ABC classification

FIGURE 4.9 Rack and shelf layout (adapted from and reproduced by kind permission of J B van den Berg)

Adapted from van den Berg P 2012

move from side to side as opposed to travelling up the length of the racking and back down the other side.

- Shortcuts are programmed into the system to minimize travel. For example, a break in a long length of racking (as shown in Figure 4.8) enables the picker to shorten the travel distance but allows the storage of reserve product above the pathway.

- The picker ends up as close to the despatch area as possible. If the picker is not operating in real time the picker may need to return to the start point to pick up a new assignment. This is not ideal.

- Multiple pick locations for the most popular items need to be set up to avoid congestion at the pick bays.

A typical warehouse layout will operate with a reserve pallet storage area (racked or free standing) which may or may not be above the individual pick faces. Whether the storage area is separated from the pick area or not will depend on the number of SKUs and the amount of floor space available for both reserve and pick locations.

This enables the picker to pick full pallets of a product if the order demands it. The picker must not be directed to pick a full pallet from the pick location as this will increase the amount of work required, as that pallet will have to be replaced by another through replenishment immediately.

The worst scenario is where the picker takes 30 cartons from the pick face and a further 30 cartons from the reserve stock to complete a full pallet order of 60 cartons of the same SKU. Unfortunately, some WMSs still work on the principle of emptying the pick face first, irrespective of the size of order. A manual intervention by the picker normally takes place to overcome this situation.

If during the item and order profiling we see that families of items regularly appear on orders together and fulfil a large percentage of these orders, it may be cost effective to establish a separate area within the warehouse for these products. Examples are large customers who only order a specific number of products or customers who have bespoke products with their own labelling and packaging. A mezzanine floor may be constructed to increase the number of pick locations, specifically for smaller, slower moving items.

Third-party shared-user warehousing is a typical example where a number of clients share the building but the picking activities are typically segregated.

Where small quantities of items are picked, the warehouse will also have an area of shelving where the product may be held in bins or totes to make individual-item picking easier. Gravity-fed shelving or flow rack further enhances the picking process, where product is fed in at the back of the shelf and as the carton, bin or tote is emptied another slides into its place. The key to this type of storage is to ensure maximum utilization of the flow rack and timely replenishment.

Depending on the height of the building, these may be situated on a mezzanine floor, thus increasing the cubic utilization of the building and minimizing contact between MHE and the pickers. Although there is a tendency to use mezzanine floors for slow-moving items the floors can be linked by conveyors to quicken up the pick process by using a pick by zone method.

An alternative to shelf locations are carousels, which are described in greater detail in Chapter 5.

When determining the pick layout, you also need to take into account the requirement for space to undertake value-adding services such as labelling, kitting, packing, shrink wrapping, promotional packing, etc. This area needs to be close to both the picking and despatch areas to avoid excessive travelling and handling. It also needs to be segregated from MHE movements to safeguard the staff. Again, a mezzanine floor is ideal for this type of work. Constructed above the inbound and outbound doors not only ensures proximity to the despatch area but also utilizes 'dead' space.

As picking is a labour-intensive operation, the welfare of the operator has to be taken into account when choosing the most appropriate method of picking. This includes safe and comfortable MHE, ergonomically designed storage modules, work stations and equipment.

We will discuss how to approach warehouse layout and the choice of equipment in greater detail later.

In the next chapter we determine the most appropriate picking system based on the data we have compiled. Information required to determine the most effective picking system includes:

- dimensions and weight of the product (item, inner carton, outer carton, pallet);
- product group (hazardous, temperature sensitive, high value, etc);
- total number of SKUs by category (ABC);
- total number of orders in a period;
- total number of deliveries (there is a difference – orders can be consolidated into fewer deliveries);
- mode and average number of lines per order;
- mode and average number of units per line;
- pick-face visits per SKU;
- item, case or full-pallet picks by SKU;
- typical family groupings; and
- items sold together frequently.

This data should be gathered during the profiling exercise. Having compiled the data, we can now proceed to determine the most effective picking systems.

Summary and conclusion

In order to be productive and efficient in the picking process, a great deal of preparation needs to take place. This includes having a comprehensive understanding of the products and their sales patterns and the data available to produce ABC analyses.

Placing products in the most appropriate location reduces travel distances and strain on operatives and as a consequence leads to improved productivity and overall cost reduction.

According to OPS (2009) the 'Ten Commandments of picking' are as follows:

1 Design for flexibility and scalability – things change – build for today, design for the future.

2 Keep pickers picking... not waiting or undertaking other tasks such as carton erection, packing, labelling, etc.

3 Minimize travel.

4 Minimize product touches. If you have expert pickers you shouldn't need to check their work.

5 Never let pickers arrive at an empty location.

6 Measure, measure, measure (productivity and accuracy but also product dimensions).

7 Pick logically, slot intelligently.

8 Pick accurately – get it right first time.

9 Continue to learn and explore.

10 Advocate continuous improvement.

I will add one more to this list: ensure that you make it easy and comfortable for the operator. Provide:

- good lighting;
- ergonomic equipment;
- equipment aids (scanners, voice, RFID);
- assistance with heavy items;
- placement of product – easy-to-reach shelf locations; and
- clear and unambiguous labels.

In the next sections we will look at the different picking strategies and the equipment utilized. We will also examine the use of automation in today's warehouses which requires a different kind of preparation.

Picking strategies and equipment

05

> *Strategy is about making choices, trade-offs; it's about deliberately choosing to be different.*
>
> **(MICHAEL PORTER (1947–))**

Introduction

In this chapter we examine the different types of picking strategies available to warehouse managers and the types of equipment used for storage and picking.

One of the main cost areas within the picking operation is the movement between pick locations. Depending on the operation, this can account for up to 50 per cent of a picker's time. The aim is to reduce the amount of travel. Congestion at the pick face is also an issue as it can convert travel time into waiting time. This section examines the different methods of picking and the equipment utilized to attain these goals of reduced travel and waiting time.

There are a number of dimensions to the picking process. These include how and when the orders are presented, how the actual items are picked and the equipment required. These dimensions are shown in Figure 5.1.

What we can see from Figure 5.1 is that there are many interrelationships and many options. For example, if we decide on a picker-to-goods operation this can either be done by, for example, picking individual orders, batch or cluster picking, utilizing trolleys or pallet trucks and a choice of paper, voice or scanning.

The first point to mention here is that in terms of picking there is no 'silver bullet' or 'one size fits all' solution.

FIGURE 5.1 Picking strategies and equipment

Picker	Orders	Handling equipment	Storage methods	Picking operations	Hardware and software

• Picker to goods
• Goods to picker
• Automated picking
• Robotics
	• Pick by order
	• Cluster picking
	• Batch picking
	• Zone picking
	• Wave picking
	• Compact picking
	• Order Distribution system
		• Pallet jacks
		• Powered pallet trucks
		• Cage/trolley
		• Forklift trucks
		• Order pickers
		• Conveyors
		• AS/RS and Mini-load systems
		• Ergonomic work stations
			• Bulk/floor storage
			• Conventional racking
			• Very narrow aisle racking
			• Carton flow racks
			• Shelving
			• Mobile storage
			• Carousels
			  – Horizontal
			  – Vertical
			• A-frames
				• Paper pick
				• Pick by label
				• Scanning
				• Voice picking
				• RFID
				  – Automatic
				  – Scanning
				• Pick to light
				• Put to light
					• WMS
					• Slotting software
					• Barcode scanners
					  – Hand held
					  – Wearable
					• RFID scanners
					• Voice units

According to an Aberdeen Group report (2009), 46 per cent of best-in-class companies are more likely than all others to use advanced pick methodologies such as batch, zone and cluster picking as opposed to individual-order picks. However, each company has different requirements and these strategies may not suit everyone.

A picking operation may require full-pallet picks, pallet-layer picks, outer-carton picks, inner-carton picks or individual-item picks. In most cases the warehouse will be required to pick a combination of the above and, at times, these combinations on the same order.

Many managers see advanced technology and automation as the silver bullet where picking is concerned; however, they may well be overlooking basic improvements that can be introduced to enhance order picking efficiency and also the potential lack of flexibility that accompanies automation in certain operations.

During many of the warehouse management courses I run I tend to find that the majority of attendees do not use ABC analysis and order profiling. There are many opportunities therefore to improve basic pick operations before introducing automation.

Basic techniques such as profiling, slotting, pick-route planning, pick-face sizing, accurate and timely replenishment, proper equipment selection and documented processes will all help to enhance pick efficiency without having to introduce technology and automation in the short term.

Companies are likely to operate a number of different order-picking strategies and techniques depending on the nature of the product, the quantity of items to be picked and the size of order.

There are usually four types of pick requirement within a warehouse. However, they do not always occur individually and can be included on the same order. These are as follows:

- piece, each, unit, item or broken-case pick;
- full-case or carton pick;
- layer pick; and
- full-pallet pick.

In the following sections we will look at each of the pick strategies in turn and discuss their interrelationships.

Pick strategies can be split into three categories. These are:

- picker to goods;
- goods to picker; and
- automated picking.

Picker to goods

The majority of warehouses continue to operate with minimal automation and picker-to-goods operations prevail.

Pick to order (individual order pick or discreet order pick)

Here the picker takes one order or part of an order (assignment) and travels through the warehouse either on foot with a cage or trolley or with a pallet using a pallet jack or fork lift truck, collecting items until the whole order or assignment is completed.

Orders can be for individual items, full cartons, full pallets or even a combination of these.

The picker follows a route or pick path designated by reading a paper pick list, reading instructions on a radio data terminal or following voice commands.

All order lines are picked in sequence for a specific customer order. Depending on the size of the items, piece pick items are likely to be stored on shelf locations, in carousels or on flow racks for example. Full cartons can be stored on pallets in pick locations, on shelving or in flow racking.

The advantage of picking individual orders is the minimum amount of handling involved as the product moves from store to dispatch in one handling movement.

This remains the most common method of picking. However, orders with multiple SKUs and long distances between picks can be very labour intensive.

There can also be a requirement for a second person to check the order before it is despatched. This requirement for checking is discussed in greater detail in the chapter on despatch.

Cluster picking (sort whilst picking)

In order to reduce overall travel time, operators can take a number of orders out into the warehouse at the same time and pick into individual compartments on their trolleys or cages. Some operations will utilize powered pallet trucks that can carry two pallets at a time or utilize tugs or tractors that can move multiple pallets through the picking aisles as can be seen in Figures 5.11 and 5.12.

Figure 5.2 shows a pick cart with pick-to-light technology used for cluster picking.

FIGURE 5.2   Cluster pick cart (courtesy of Inther)

CASE STUDY   Consumer Electronics – cluster pick to cart

The client is a global leader and technology innovator in consumer electronics, mobile communications and home appliances.

When it set up its new European central parts operation it installed a mezzanine floor with shelving, a conveyor system and the Inther LC Pick to Cart system to manage over 70,000 spare parts.

To increase productivity and reliability a total of 10 pick carts were introduced initially. These carts are used to cluster pick orders both on and below the mezzanine floor. Once picked the orders are transported to the packaging and shipping department via a conveyor system.

When an operator logs on to a pick cart the Inther LC system will generate a batch of picking instructions from all the available orders in the database. When generating the instructions the system will use logic to provide the picker with orders in the same area and produce the most efficient picking route through the warehouse. It will also instruct the picker to pick the highest priority orders first.

The operator is instructed to load the pick cart with empty totes. Each tote must be scanned for the system to register the tote against the pick cart. After loading the totes the operator can start picking. The central display on the pick cart will show the location to pick from. After the operator confirms the location by scanning its barcode, the corresponding pick lights light up with the requested quantities to pick. The operator must pick the articles and confirm the pick by pressing a button. Omitting and shortage functionalities are also available. After the products from the first location are allocated to the totes, the next location is shown on the central display.

When all orders are picked the operator unloads the totes from the pick cart onto a conveyor that transports the totes to the packing workstations. When the pick cart is empty, it is ready to start a new cluster of picks.

Each pick cart can be used, without recharging, during a full eight-hour shift. A battery is installed on the pick cart to provide power for the pick lights, hand scanner and wireless controllers.

In the above example plastic totes are utilized. These may or may not be the final shipping containers. The totes can be replaced by cartons thus reducing the number of touch points by not having to decant the totes. A check weigh system can be used at the shipping area to ensure accuracy.

Although having the advantage of being able to pick several orders at the same time and reducing overall travel, it does need experienced pickers if a put-to-light system is not utilized. There is a possibility of putting the wrong product or wrong quantity of product into a container and therefore a check system needs to be in place to ensure picker accuracy.

Cluster picking can also be used with conveyors, where a tote containing multiple orders diverts into a pick zone. As the tote passes a barcode reader its unique ID is read and all the picks for the current tote are displayed on the individual pick-to-light terminals.

Each terminal indicates both the quantity to be picked and the tote location where it is to be placed. A pick of eight pieces into the B compartment would be displayed as B8. When all picks for all compartments in the current zone are complete, the tote is returned to the conveyer belt and it proceeds to the next zone, where additional picks for any compartment are required (elogistics101.com).

The number of orders per cluster will depend on the number of lines, units per order, total cube and the capacity of the totes, cages or trolleys.

As seen above we have a combination of technologies and pick strategies.

Batch picking

Batch picking is where operators pick products for a number of orders at the same time. This is similar to cluster picking however rather than have a cluster of separate orders, these orders are consolidated into one pick list and once picked are later broken down into their constituent orders. Pickers can be sent to the reserve storage area to pick full pallets or layers of pallets to satisfy the order quantities.

There are two alternatives: pick by line and pick to zero. Pick by line may result in excess items being returned to stock where full pallets or cartons have been picked. For example, a batch of 10 orders may require 100 units to be picked in total. A full pallet holds 120 units and is brought to the order consolidation area. Once the 100 units have been picked the additional 20 units are returned to the reserve storage area or possibly transferred to the forward pick area. In the case of pick to zero the correct number of items (the 100 units in this case) are picked and allocated to customer orders until the lines and units are exhausted. This is also termed bulk picking.

Advantages include less travel and potentially increased accuracy as two people are involved in the pick and allocation process. The disadvantage is that it is a two-stage process and cannot easily manage time-sensitive orders.

Batch picking can significantly increase the number of lines picked per hour; however, you also have to take into account the collation of the items.

The system can be utilized within a cross-dock operation where products can be picked and allocated on arrival at the warehouse. This removes the put-away and replenishment aspects of the operation and increases throughput and accuracy.

Orders can be batched in a number of different ways. For example, mail order or e-commerce operations may well batch by single order lines or single items. A typical usage is in televised home shopping such as the QVC channel. Different products are promoted at certain times of the day and orders are placed for them. This results in a large number of orders for a single product. Each order is likely to be for potentially one or two units. It makes sense to consolidate these orders into one pick list and pick large quantities of the product in one pass. It is then simply a case of attaching a shipping label onto each item for despatch.

Orders containing similar items can also be batched together. Finally orders can be split, based on where the products are in the warehouse.

Batching orders together can be done manually; however, most warehouse management systems (WMSs) today have this capability.

Technology such as put-to-light systems can be used to help ensure accuracy. As the bulk picked products are brought to the sorting or consolidation area each product line is scanned in turn and lights will indicate how many of each product should be placed into a tote or container for shipment. This can be used successfully for multiple retail store delivery with each store having its own cage, tote or despatch area.

Zone picking

In zone picking, products are picked from defined areas in the warehouse and each picker is assigned to a specific zone or zones and only picks items from within those zones. The level of activity will determine the number of zones/pick locations allocated to each picker.

Orders are moved from one zone to the next as each zone completes its pick. This movement can be undertaken by a cage, trolley or pallet being passed from one operator to another but is more commonly done by conveyor. The conveyors may be powered or use rollers or gravity to move the cartons or totes between the zones.

Orders can be picked simultaneously within the zones and consolidated later or they can be picked sequentially. Separate pick instructions are produced by the WMS for each zone for simultaneous picking. A single pick list travels with each order for sequential picking.

The volume of orders sent to each zone needs to be controlled so that each sector has an equivalent amount of picks. The potential for bottlenecks can be high with staff having to wait for orders to arrive.

Zones are usually sized to accommodate enough picks for one or two order pickers. A picker may look after two zones or more if the volumes are reduced on a particular day.

Zone picking can be effective in operations with large numbers of SKUs, multiple orders and low to moderate picks per order. DVD and computer games retailers are typical examples.

The most popular picking method utilized in the zones is pick by light. As an operator scans the next order to arrive in the zone, a number of lights illuminate in the section. A digital display denotes the number of items to be picked. Once the pick is completed the light is turned off and the picker goes to the next illuminated location.

Some companies will also scan the barcode on the product prior to placing it in the tote to ensure that the correct item has been picked.

Advantages include the reduction in travel and an increase in the speed of pick as multiple lines can be picked at the same time compared with pick by order.

This system can be used by companies where there are different zones for product families such as pharmaceuticals, hazardous items and food items.

Wave picking

In wave picking, orders are combined and released at specific times during the day or to associate them with vehicle departures, replenishment cycles, shift changes, product locations, product commonality, value-adding service requirements and priorities. The use of wave picking can also balance workload by time or by area by logically grouping and releasing orders.

Orders can be released at different times to different zones based on how long it takes to pick the orders. The drawback is the requirement for a further step in the process, having to bring the partial orders back together. However, as discussed with batch and zone picking, it does allow for a second check on product codes and quantities.

Goods to picker

Significant benefits can be realized with the use of a goods-to-person system. Even though there are many variations on how a system can be configured, most of the designs allow the following benefits, according to Dematic (2009):

Eliminate picker travel time, use less labour. Order pickers do not need to roam the warehouse walking to and from the dedicated pick faces. Travel time is the largest time component of a traditional order picker in a person-to-goods arrangement. By minimizing this time component, productivity is increased and labour to operate the facility is reduced.

Omit the dedicated pick face. Typically, a goods-to-person system involves storing the inventory in very narrow aisle racking or an AS/RS system. Each SKU is retrieved when it is required. The system dictates when the item is picked and it is less important where it is in the warehouse, although having the fastest-moving items closer to the workstation will further improve efficiencies.

Reduce system footprint. The space required for a goods-to-person design is much less than conventional person-to-goods. If the storage medium is high density, significant space savings can be achieved. A typical footprint may be 30 to 50 per cent less than conventional storage.

Product security. When the product is placed into a high-density automated system (AS/RS), it is secure and not available for access by staff. Product security is important to maintain inventory accuracy, reduce theft, and assure first in, first out principles.

Ergonomic workstations. The pick stations can be designed for employee comfort. Working heights, range of motion and environment (lighting, temperature) can be optimized for the employee. Some designs omit the requirement to move and lift totes/cartons. Furthermore, workstations can be outfitted to support special needs employees, thereby allowing universal access.

Speed in order selection. The pick station design allows high worker productivity. Since there is little or no travel time and the item to be picked is ergonomically served to the worker, high rates of order selection are achieved. Most operations obtain rates of 500 to 1,000 lines picked per hour per operator. The goods-to-person system allows fast- and slow-moving SKUs to be treated equally, which removes the need for separate pick areas based on SKU velocity. This is important for applications where SKU velocity changes on a daily basis.

Accuracy. Order picking using a goods-to-person station tends to be more accurate because operators are typically handling one SKU at a time, making errors less likely. Most goods-to-person stations utilize put-to-light technology to indicate quantity and location to place the item, further enhancing accuracy. The picking process is performed by one person, thereby improving traceability. Accuracy during the inbound process is paramount.

Decoupled workstations. Staff can work in parallel, unaffected by each other. Stations can be opened and closed according to business volume on a particular shift of operation. There is redundancy in this configuration since items can be processed at any location as the workstations are completely decoupled.

High-utilization workstations. Work flows into the pick station smoothly and consistently. Order pickers are highly utilized, since they do not need to wait for work. Worker productivity is not affected by the structure typical of a traditional pick module (high activity in one zone, little activity in another zone, pace issues in a pick-and-pass environment, etc).

Sequencing. When building a customer order, a precise sequence of SKUs can be achieved. For example, items can be presented to the order selector by weight (heavy to light). Or, in another example, orders can be built in sequence by family group.

Order profile. The system is not affected by changes in order profile. For example, single-item orders and multi-item orders are accommodated with equal efficiency. This means that trends such as more orders with fewer order lines do not compromise productivity. This feature adds to the ability of goods-to-person systems to accommodate change as order profiles change in the future.

Efficiently accommodates SKU growth. If more SKUs are added, the storage system can absorb the new loads (if sized for growth) or the system can be expanded with additional automated storage modules, or existing modules can be extended.

Types of automated picking

The requirement for increased speed, accuracy and productivity has pointed managers towards automation as a realistic option in today's competitive automated equipment market. A high-volume item pick operation is an area where automation can have a high impact. An operation where the despatch of upwards of 3,000 cartons per day is worth consideration in terms of automation.

The advantages of automation include the following:

- increased space utilization and reduced space requirement;
- high bay, narrow aisle systems (up to 30 metres high);
- random storage;
- higher density storage for refrigerated products, leading to cost reduction through lower energy requirements;
- improved control;
- pallet tracking through enhanced WMS;
- labour and energy savings;
- no heat and light requirement unless required for product integrity;
- minimum supervision required;
- continuity;
- 24 hours, 7 days per week operation;
- product security;
- high bay areas, use of first in, first out principles;
- less human intervention;
- safety;
- elimination of manual handling;
- reduction in accidents;
- ability to cope with hazardous/harsh environments such as refrigerated storage;
- integration;
- coordination of product flows, avoiding bottlenecks;
- constant performance levels; and
- continuous review.

Examples of automated picking systems

Compact picking system

The goods-to-picker-based compact picking system by Vanderlande is ideal for slow-moving products in retail and wholesale warehouses. It is also cost effective for warehouses handling parts and components for sectors such as the automotive industry which have a large range of SKUs and very high service levels.

For example, in a manufacturing warehouse product is retrieved from the automated storage and retrieval area and taken by conveyor to the operator's workstation. There it is consolidated with other items that do not fit the profile such as exhaust systems, gearboxes, body panels, etc. They are then placed in a shipping carton, a crate or on a pallet for despatch. The use of ergonomic workstations enables operators to achieve a constant high order picking performance (up to 1,000 order lines per operator per hour) over a prolonged period of time, without risk of work-related injury.

 www.youtube.com/watch?v=vMAC0b1MlmY#t=41

Order distribution system

An order distribution system is ideal for business processes where a large number of order lines are fulfilled from a relatively small number of SKUs. Totes or cartons of single-line products are transported to operators who distribute goods into order totes controlled by put-to-light displays. This concept works efficiently in mail order and e-commerce sectors.

In both the above operations the workstation plays a major part in the overall system. The main features include:

- optimal ergonomics because of horizontal order picking (one level);
- ideal height for the operator using a movable platform;
- operator learning curve of only 15 minutes;
- constant productivity level through fatigue-free working; and
- high accuracy and safety by pick-to-light displays, detection light grids and a touch screen.

Mini-load AS/RS systems

A mini-load automatic storage and retrieval system handles loads that are contained in small containers or totes, with load weights typically falling in a range of 40 to 250 kilograms. The capacity range can go to 350 to 1,000 kilograms at the high end. The system is ideal for storing small quantities of large numbers of SKUs. 'Slave' trays can also be used to transport shipping cartons to reduce the amount of decanting within the warehouse.

One key feature of a mini-load system is that it maximizes the cube of the warehouse, saving space whilst increasing throughput. Recent innovations include double-deep locations thus further increasing space utilization.

Product is put away in random locations and the system manages the put-away and retrieval of the product. Dynamic slotting enables fast-moving products to be located in the most accessible locations. When a part is required, the system will identify the location and the tote or tray will be transferred to the operator, who is standing at a pick station located in front of the rows and columns of storage bins.

Once the item has been picked from the tote, it is returned to a position in the racks. Different SKUs can be stored in each tote providing the operator has the ability to distinguish one part from another. Picking is normally managed by put-to-light systems which denote the quantity and into which outgoing tote to place the item. Some systems can provide a photograph of the item on screen to ensure further accuracy.

Each pick station can have multiple totes arriving and leaving at the same time, ensuring an effective flow of goods and increasing productivity. This is similar to batch picking by line (350 to 700+ lines per hour). See Figure 5.3.

3D shuttle technology

Although an AS/RS system, the Cimcorp 3D shuttle™ uses gantry robot technology, combined with an innovative shuttle device integrated into the gantry,

FIGURE 5.3 Mini-load system (courtesy of Vanderlande)

to store and retrieve goods in plastic crates, totes, bins and containers required for order fulfilment. The system creates stacks on entry to the storage area. These stacks are then collected by one of the gantry robots and deposited somewhere within the robot's working envelope.

When a particular SKU is required to fulfil an order, a robot retrieves the corresponding tote and deposits it on the shuttle device. The shuttle travels along the gantry and transfers the tote to the outfeed conveyor, which then transports it to a conveyor line that feeds the picking stations.

Once picking from a tote is complete, it is conveyed back to the entry point to the storage area.

The system's advantages are as follows:

- Up to six times more efficient than a manual solution.
- Productivity of up to 1000 totes/hour.
- Low investment cost.
- Excellent cost/storage capacity ratio.
- No racking required resulting in significant cost savings.
- Optimum space utilization with no space wasting aisles.
- Exceptionally high storage density.

Example 3D shuttle cell (two robots)

Throughput capacity: up to 5,000 totes in or 1,000 totes out per one hour by one cell/two shuttle robots (stacks in/single totes out). Average throughput 500 totes in and out/hour.

Storage capacity of 31 totes per m², tote size (L × W × H) = 600 × 400 × 250 mm, storage size 25,000 totes per cell.

SKU quantity enables thousands of SKUs (31 SKUs per m²).

The advantage of this system is that it doesn't require any racking or grid structure with 80 per cent of the operational time feeding the pick stations.

 www.cimcorp.com/CIMCORP_3D_Shuttle_for_automatic_storage_and_ retrieval

Autostore

Autostore is an AS/RS system which stores goods in bins that are stacked directly on top of one another in a self-supporting aluminium grid. The grid not only guides the bins but also serve as rails for the robots to travel on. The battery operated robots are controlled using a wireless system and manoeuvre the bins within the grid. They also transport the bins to and from workstations for goods to be decanted or picked. Bins containing fast-moving products are stored at the top of the storage system whilst slow-moving stock is stored in the

FIGURE 5.4   Cimcorp 3D Shuttle

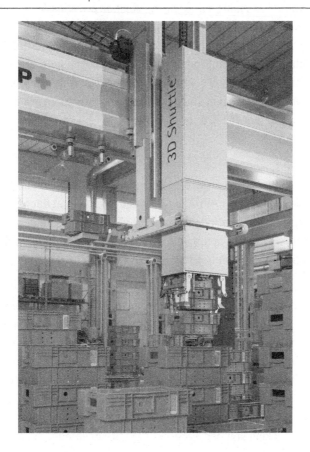

lower sections. Once the goods are placed in the bins they are ready for picking and despatch.

The system uses less energy than a mini-load system and is scalable.

CASE STUDY   Asda Stores

Founded in the 1960s, Asda is one of Britain's leading retailers with over 180,000 dedicated Asda colleagues serving 18 million customers. The second largest supermarket chain in the United Kingdom, holding around 18 per cent market share, Asda is part of the Walmart group, the world's largest retail chain.

Asda is unsurprisingly a leading proponent of warehousing innovation. The business is constantly looking at ways to improve the use of space within its existing distribution centres. Asda selected Swisslog's AutoStore solution to handle a range of its products in a more space efficient and productive way. An intelligent storage and retrieval system for small case lines, the solution provides Asda with flexibility for its future expansion. Swisslog worked with Asda at each phase of the project from the initial design to the installation and ongoing support. Work started on-site in 2012. Before installation of the AutoStore system could commence a robust mezzanine level was built on which the new solution would be constructed. Once the preparation work was completed, installation and commissioning took place in a matter of months, as the rest of the IDC was in full operation.

The operation:

1 Decant

Pallet loads of inbound goods are conveyed automatically to one of six ergonomic decant stations. An Asda colleague working at each station transfers products from a pallet into AutoStore bins, whilst lift tables eliminate the need for bending, thereby making the whole process highly ergonomic. Each station also has a chute for colleagues to dispose of waste.

2 Picking

The AutoStore robots always work ahead of colleagues to ensure a constant stream of bins are presented at the picking port. Reaching required bins usually involves a digging process, which temporarily stores those above the required bin on top of nearby stacks.

The solution includes carousel picking ports, designed for high throughput operations. These ports have three rotating arms which are able to carry three bins simultaneously in order to provide seamless delivery to colleagues. With 10 ergonomic picking stations, where orders are collated for store delivery, the site is able to process a large quantity of orders. They're also aided by the robots delivering the bins in sequence. Each colleague has a touch-screen computer instructing on how many of each product line to pick for particular orders, moving them from the captive AutoStore bin into the store consolidation tote. Once all items for a store are picked, colleagues push the tote onto the conveyor for shipping.

3 The benefits

From the outset, the system enables Asda to manage several thousand different product lines, whilst allowing further phased investments to accommodate more bins, in line with the retailer's developing requirements. AutoStore's key benefit is that of space efficiency, allowing for maximum utilization of the area, in this case bolstered by its installation on a mezzanine level. This leaves the ground level available for other operations.

4 Factfile

- Number of robots: 140
- Number of bins: 44,860
- Number of pick stations (ports): 10
- Number of decant stations (ports): 6

- Bin presentations 335/hr per pick station
- Length of grid 48.8 m
- Width of grid 29 m

- Height of grid 6.8 m
- Height of mezzanine approx. 6.5 m from ground level

 www.youtube.com/watch?v=M5T1VPyzVM0

Ergonomic workstations

As with all goods-to-person systems the comfort and safety of staff are paramount. Ergonomic workstations are therefore used in conjunction with goods-to-picker solutions.

FIGURE 5.5 Autostore robot

The workstations are designed to enable continuous, sustainable performance. The goal is to counter the risk of repetitive strain injury (RSI) and fatigue, thus increasing effective operator time.

These ergonomic workstations are also important from a disability worker point of view. Many warehouse and distribution centres such as those operated by M&S in the United Kingdom and Walgreens in the United States are designing their warehouses with disabled staff in mind.

 www.dcvelocity.com/dcvtv/news/2057658540001/

PRODUCT PROFILE   RapidPick workstation

Dematic has introduced a workstation (RapidPick), which can be fully tailored to match the individual requirements of the operator. As a first step, operator platforms and work tables are adjustable for height. This allows the stations to be optimally adapted to different body sizes, whilst also providing flexibility in terms of the volume of totes or cartons to be processed. Moreover, the picking stations feature optimal workplace lighting, large and comfortable operating controls and acknowledge buttons. Height- and rake-adjustable human–machine interaction (HMI) screens are also part of the ergonomic equipment package.

The HMI display provides the visual management of the pick processes. Its multicolour, high-resolution screen displays simple, intuitively understood symbols for article volumes, photos of the products to be picked and a 3D description of the positioning of the picks in the order carton. All these features contribute to accurate, safe order picking with virtually no error rates. As optional additional verification, volume weighing can be integrated into each picking station.

A further distinctive feature adding to the high throughput capacity of RapidPick is the possible configuration of the automated sequences in the picking process. In addition to the empty tote/carton management for the order cartons, the station can be equipped with two conveyor tracks – one behind for the donor totes, one in front for the order cartons. The donor totes are automatically presented at a frequency that is optimal for the packing sequence of order fulfilment and transferred to the picking station by the conveyor system. The totes/cartons are presented ergonomically to the operator to ensure that picking access is comfortable. Picking to the order carton is directed by the visual parameters shown on the display screen. Each placement in the order carton is confirmed via a terminal or an acknowledge button. Once the order is consolidated, the superimposed IT system triggers the automatic removal of the donor totes and order cartons. If totes become empty during picking, they are buffered in the station and used in the ongoing process as order cartons when directed to do so by the IT system.

The expectation is that these workstations will pick up to 1,800 units per hour at full capacity.

 www.youtube.com/watch?v=9DJcQG4u0Jg

There is still a low take-up of fully automated warehouses. As can be seen in Figure 5.7, automation does not figure highly in this sample of warehouse operators. Automation is a big step to take and it is a decision that should not be taken lightly. A recent survey undertaken by Peerless Research Group showed that 70 per cent of the respondents in the United States were planning on spending less than $250,000 dollars on warehouse equipment this year (2013) with only 11 per cent contemplating the purchase or evaluation of automated systems.

You should not under any circumstances automate a bad or broken process. Always ensure that your warehouse operation is working as efficiently as it can without the use of technology. It is only when you are at this stage that you should contemplate using technology to further improve the operation.

FIGURE 5.6   Ergonomic workstation (courtesy of Dematic)

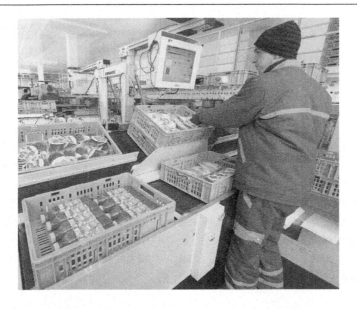

FIGURE 5.7   Use of equipment for picking (Baker and Perotti 2008)

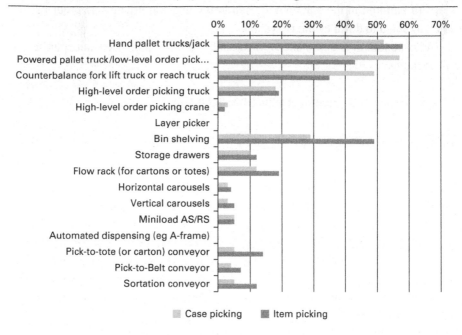

Case picking   Item picking

Processes need to be as streamlined as possible and any unnecessary steps eliminated.

The following case study is an example of how a company has fully embraced automation to improve efficiency and reduce the total footprint of their warehousing.

CASE STUDY   Automated storage Maspex Wadowice, Poland

Maspex Wadowice Group is amongst the leading Polish companies in the food industry, being the market leader in the production of juices, nectars and soft drinks in Poland, Czech Republic and Slovakia, and a main player in Hungary, Bulgaria and Romania.

Their challenge was to amalgamate operations from different regions in Poland, requiring a warehouse with large storage and handling capabilities, mixed pallet picking and assembly, full traceability and error-free inventory and deliveries.

Amongst many options evaluated, a highly automated solution proposed by System Logistics was selected, as it fulfilled all the requirements and achieves a reasonable payback of the investment.

A storage capacity of 54,000 pallets has been obtained within an area of nearly 9,000 square metres, installing a self-cladding rack, 35 metres high, within which operate 15 stacker cranes, each one of them able to handle two pallets at a time. In front of the rack is a four-floor building. The shipment area is on the ground floor, adjacent to the receiving area, and is designed to load over 10 trailers every single hour.

The first floor is connected by a pallet conveyor to the factory located on the other side of a public road. Situated on both the first and second floors are the case-picking activities, based on the goods-to-man principle, producing double the productivity of staff through the use of ergonomically designed workstations.

Layer-picking activity is carried out on the third floor, by means of two automated robots which are able to fulfil more than 60 per cent of the total picking volume. To cope with the high flow of pallets required, the handling system on each floor uses the system vehicle loop (SVL) monorail steering shuttle technology. The result is therefore a particularly compact installation.

Data

- warehouse dimensions: 140 metres × 66 metres × 35 metres;
- 54,000 pallet capacity;
- 15 stacker cranes with telescopic forks;
- 4 SVL loops;
- 41 SVL shuttles;
- 2 layer pickers.

Productivity

- 125,000 cases per day;
- 340 pallets shipped per hour.

Automation requires a great deal of preparation and time spent on design, evaluation and implementation. Automation can provide significant improvements in productivity and accuracy – but it can also prove to be the wrong solution.

In 2004 a major supermarket chain in the United Kingdom had to write off over a quarter of a million pounds' worth of automated equipment and IT systems due to the failure of the system to improve on-shelf availability.

Continuing to do what you've always done but more quickly and potentially with less paper is not going to improve your overall performance. As Drucker (nd) said, 'Do not believe that it is very much of an advance to do the unnecessary three times as fast.'

FIGURE 5.8   Highly automated solutions (courtesy of System Logistics)

Automation has its place; however, there are a number of disadvantages. These include:

- High opportunity cost: could the investment have been spent more effectively elsewhere?
- High investment costs: building, equipment, information technology.
- System failure: operations are entirely reliant on technology.
- Standardized unit loads are required.
- Anomalies are not accepted and need to be handled separately.
- More quality control is required on intake.
- High cost of disposal of equipment.
- Lack of flexibility.

Robotics

Robots are a common sight in manufacturing operations and on automotive production lines. However, they are rarely seen operating in warehouses.

Robots in the form of automated guided vehicles utilized for transferring pallets within the warehouse have been in use for a number of years, but they have been a rarity within picking operations.

However, things are beginning to change and robots have been adapted to pack items into boxes and stack those boxes onto pallets in the most efficient way.

The use of robots in the pick process is also beginning to increase. These are in areas where labour is scarce or very expensive, where the tasks are reasonably straightforward or where the operation is undertaken in hazardous conditions where manual handling is deemed dangerous.

Examples of the use of robotic arms fitted with suction pads and an optical reader being used to pick items from a conveyor and deposit the items into their respective containers are beginning to appear.

PRODUCT PROFILE   Schäfer Robo-Pick

Schäfer Robo-Pick is the first fully automatic picking cell that can be smoothly integrated into existing warehouse architectures. It is neither necessary to enter article characteristics into the system nor to place the articles in special positions in the storage tote. An innovative two-step image-processing system automatically recognizes the position of the products on the tray and controls the universal picking robot. Schäfer Robo-Pick achieves up to 2,400 picks per hour in continuous operation. According to SSI Schäfer, the Schäfer Robo-Pick cell is a particularly economic system, the investment costs being far below the costs for corresponding conventional goods-to-person stations with equivalent picking performance. See Figure 5.9.

 www.vimeo.com/29425533

Another recent innovation has been the introduction by Kiva Systems of a pick operation where mini AGVs or robotic drive units move free-standing shelving (pods), arranged in rows and columns in a memory-chip-like grid, from a storage area to pick stations. When a consumer submits an order, the robotic drive units deliver the relevant shelving units to workers who pack the requested items in a box and

FIGURE 5.9   Robot picking (courtesy of SSI Schäfer)

ship them off, utilizing other drive units, to the despatch bay, allowing workers to fill orders two to three times faster than they could with conventional methods. Each pick station is equipped with a pick-to-light and put-to-light system. The drive units can work in parallel, allowing dozens of workers to fill dozens of orders simultaneously.

The robotic system is also faster because the entire warehouse can adapt, in real time, to changes in demand by having the robots move shelves with popular items closer to the workers, where the shelves can be quickly retrieved while items that aren't selling are gradually moved farther away. This becomes a very sophisticated slotting system. This is all controlled by radio frequency with floor labels providing the drive units with the location coordinate information they require to navigate the warehouse.

According to Kiva, the system is capable of up to 750 picks per hour, per worker. The system is modular and scalable but very system dependent and unless a mezzanine floor is utilized does not use the cubic space of a building efficiently. See Figure 5.10.

 www.dcvelocity.com/dcvtv/viewercontributed/590136746001/

FIGURE 5.10   Robotic systems (courtesy of Kiva Systems)

These systems remain expensive and at present require reasonably uniform items. A fully equipped 100,000 square foot warehouse reportedly costs between £3 and £5 million to fit out. Depending on the operation, payback has been estimated at anything from three to five years or beyond.

Since the first edition of this book was published, the company has been purchased by Amazon who had installed the system into some of their DCs.

Handling equipment

Warehouses have a number of different types of handling equipment at their disposal to undertake the picking process. These range from relatively cheap trolleys through mechanical equipment to large conveyor and automated systems. Figure 5.7 shows the results of a survey undertaken by Cranfield University into the types of equipment utilized in UK warehouses. As we can see, there remains a heavy reliance on picker-to-goods systems with the use of pallet trucks, lift trucks and the utilization of shelving and racking as storage media.

In this section we examine some of the equipment used in picking operations. A point to note here is that companies utilize a combination of equipment to handle different types of products and order profiles.

Manual and mechanical handling equipment

This equipment is the least capital intensive and the most labour intensive.

Trolleys/cages/carts/garment rails

These are pushed along picking aisles or shelving by pickers and have shelves or compartments or slots into which the picked items are placed or hung. They are used in both item and full-carton picking. The aisles are usually a minimum of one metre wide.

Productivity is relatively low (50–80 lines per hour) with pickers spending over half their time propelling the equipment rather than picking. Tiredness also becomes an issue later in the shift.

Roll cages can also be utilized for transportation, thus reducing the need for double handling.

Hand pallet truck, pallet jack, powered pallet truck, manual stacker truck

Hand pallet trucks have hydraulic pumps to enable the operator to lift a pallet sufficiently to be able to move it across the warehouse floor. They are cost effective for transferring pallets across short distances.

Powered pallet trucks are used for loading, unloading and picking full cartons (although item picking is possible) and for pallet-transfer duties to and from the receiving and despatch areas. They can be supplied as pedestrian, stand-on or seated versions.

The choice of truck will depend on pallet throughput per hour and distances travelled within the warehouse.

Advances in this area include pallet trucks which have a lift ability up to 800 mm in height.

Manual stacker trucks have a 1,000 kg lift capacity up to 3 metres, depending on the model.

Forklift trucks

In the absence of pallet trucks both counterbalance and reach trucks can be utilized in the picking process and each has the advantage over pallet trucks of being able to lift a pallet to a height such that the operator doesn't have to bend down to place cartons onto the pallet. This will of course depend on the width of the aisle and the number of orders picked per day. These trucks are also utilized to pick full pallets from the racking.

Low-level order pickers (LLOP) and towing tractors

Low-level order-picking trucks are electrically powered and have the facility of moving two pallets or up to three roll cages at a time along picking aisles. These trucks are able to operate at first and second levels with the operator being lifted upwards on a platform as can be seen in Figure 5.11.

The towing tractors are ideal for horizontal transport and low-level order picking. These can move or 'tram' multiple pallets and cages, long distances from the reserve storage and picking areas to despatch. See Figure 5.12.

High-level order pickers (HLOP)

In operations where there is a high number of product lines and insufficient floor space to provide enough pallet pick faces, there is a requirement to pick from the storage slots that are high above ground level. In these circumstances we need to operate high-level order pickers as shown in Figure 5.13.

The advantages of this system are that we end up with a high density of pick faces by utilizing narrow aisle racking and trucks; it can also eliminate replenishment if a random storage system is utilized.

FIGURE 5.11   Low-level order picker (courtesy of Toyota)

FIGURE 5.12 Tow tractor (courtesy of Crown)

FIGURE 5.13 High-level order picker (courtesy of Toyota)

However, disadvantages include a much slower retrieval process (< 30 picks per hour) and a potential for bottlenecks in the aisles, together with the inflexibility of narrow aisle racking. Other issues include the requirement for harnesses for staff (in the United States) and the ergonomic issues of reaching to the far side of a pallet to retrieve stock.

The system is mainly suited for operations with a large number of slow-moving items and low numbers of lines per order.

A recent entry into the market is an articulated forklift truck with the ability to lift the operator up to 6 metres. This truck, introduced by Translift Bendi, has the ability to not only put-away, retrieve and replenish full pallets but is also able to pick product from level three in the racking. The truck has the ability to work in 1.8-metre aisles and can put-away pallets up to 12 metres. Whilst most picking operations are carried out with great efficiency, there remains a sticking point when an order picker, picking at ground level reaches an empty pallet location. The operator will put out a call for the replenishment truck to get another full pallet of stock, which interrupts the picking process and causes unnecessary delays or missed picks that are both a waste of space and time – both of which cost money. It was here that the idea for an articulated order picking truck was born.

FIGURE 5.14   Translift Bendi order picker

Conveyors

Conveyors carry goods by power or gravity. They are an integral part of zone picking and goods-to-picker systems as they transfer cartons and totes between zones and to the operator workstations.

Powered conveyors tend to be used for transferring goods over longer distances and utilize belts, chains, slats and rollers.

Gravity conveyors can be used to transfer picked items from a mezzanine floor to the despatch area for consolidation with other picked items or along short distances within zones.

Conveyors can have non-powered or powered rollers or belts. The latter tend to be less expensive than powered rollers and have the advantage of being able to move all types of boxes and bags without fear of jamming up the conveyor.

The disadvantages of conveyor systems include high capital cost, less flexibility, regular maintenance requirements and they are an obstruction to both pedestrians and trucks.

Sortation systems

In situations where there is a high degree of commonality in terms of orders with a known number of delivery locations such as retail stores, a pick to belt system can be used effectively. Here products are picked in bulk using the batch picking method and the items are placed on a conveyor belt. As each item passes a barcode reader it is identified and diverted to a particular location on route. The items can either drop into a bin or slide down a chute. Here the items are consolidated and packed into a shipping carton, a cage or loaded

FIGURE 5.15 Conveyor systems (courtesy of Dematic Corporation)

directly onto a vehicle. Examples are cross belt, narrow belt, bomb bay and tilt tray sorters. Productivity can range from 6,000 to 20,000 units per hour.

    www.youtube.com/watch?v=s3U5ihEJALo

Storage equipment

The type of storage equipment utilized within the warehouse for pick operations will vary substantially depending on the type and size of product, the throughput envisaged and available capital.

We also have to take into account the requirement for reserve storage and how product is transferred from the reserve storage area to the pick face; this is termed replenishment.

Floor/bulk storage

In situations where capital is at a premium and goods are of a low value with very few SKUs, the use of the floor area for storage and picking is totally acceptable.

The disadvantages, however, are the low utilization of the cubic capacity of the building, operators having to bend down to pick from the floor and the inability to replace picked pallets without compromising the FIFO rule. This leads to what is commonly termed the 'honeycomb effect'.

Standard and narrow aisle pallet racking

Definitions in this area can be rather confusing. In these examples we see wide aisle racking as being used in conjunction with counterbalance trucks or reach trucks, narrow aisle with reach trucks and very narrow aisle racking with very narrow aisle trucks, articulated forklift trucks and cranes.

Standard or wide aisle (> 3.5 m – 4 m) and narrow aisle (≥ 2.5 m) adjustable pallet racking (APR) is used to provide ground-floor pick locations and reserve storage for full-carton picks. The racking can also be used with high-level order picking trucks if there are insufficient ground-floor pick locations.

Pallet locations can also be reduced in height through the use of steel, wooden or mesh decking and can also be segmented into bins providing less than full pallet locations and enabling companies to have more SKU in a smaller cubic space.

There are issues with picking in racked areas. One is the fact that having a 1,000 mm or 1,200 mm deep location makes it more difficult to pick as the operator has to stretch in to pick the cartons. There is the potential issue of trucks and people operating in the same aisle at the same time and finally there is the possibility of congestion at the pick face with a number of operators arriving at the pick face at the same time.

Very narrow aisle pallet racking (≥ 1.6–1.8 m) metres

This racking can be utilized for the storage of reserve pallets and for pick operations. There are a number of issues to bear in mind, however, if picking from this area. Along with similar challenges to those mentioned above there is also the issue of rail guided narrow aisle trucks which preclude the use of pallet trucks or pallet jacks to manoeuvre pallets in and out of the pick locations within the racking. This makes picking much more difficult and less productive. Some countries require aisles to be wide enough to allow staff to be able to pass between the trucks and the racking safely. Another safety concern is when narrow aisle truck operators are high up in the racking it is more difficult to see the pickers at ground floor level.

The use of automatic cranes in very narrow aisle racked areas precludes the picking of individual cartons. Full-pallet, single-SKU picks are however undertaken.

Carton flow racking

Carton live storage operates by means of gravity-fed rollers on adjustable shelving. Cartons are loaded at the upper end of sloping lanes, in the rear aisle and move down under the force of gravity when a carton is removed from the picking face. The rollers can be adjusted to take different sizes of cartons and can also be fitted with a braking system to protect the more fragile items.

As can be seen by comparing Table 5.1 and Figure 5.16, the occupancy rate is high, travel time is reduced and the system is fully FIFO compliant.

FIGURE 5.16   Carton flow rack (courtesy of Knapp)

TABLE 5.1 Shelf storage versus carton flow storage (courtesy of Cisco Eagle)

Factor	Gravity/carton flow	Static shelving	Gravity flow gain
If total available floor space is	equal	equal	–
Then items stored (0.03 cbm) =	155	122	29%
Shelves high	5	3	2
Cases per opening/face	15	12	3
	2,325	1,440	61%

If space is an issue, and a second aisle cannot be accommodated, companies can use a push-back system, which loads from the front as opposed to the rear. However, this will mean a last in, first out (LIFO) as opposed to first in, first out (FIFO) system of stock control.

Full pallets of stock can be stored above the carton live storage, thus utilizing the cube of the area.

Shelving

Shelving is used to store less than pallet quantities of product. The items can be stored in their original cartons or in totes or bins. There are many different types of shelving, most of which are adjustable with different widths and heights.

Bin or tote storage makes it possible to present a large variety of items on a very compact face. These bins or containers are of different sizes, colours and shapes, and most have semi-open fronts.

Static shelving is reasonably inexpensive. The hidden cost, according to Cisco Eagle, is the cost of labour: the amount of time operators spend picking and restocking. Cisco Eagle reports that pickers spend only 15 per cent of their time doing productive work using static shelving. By using gravity-flow shelving, pickers are a lot more productive.

FIGURE 5.17 Static shelving versus carton flow (courtesy of Cisco Eagle)

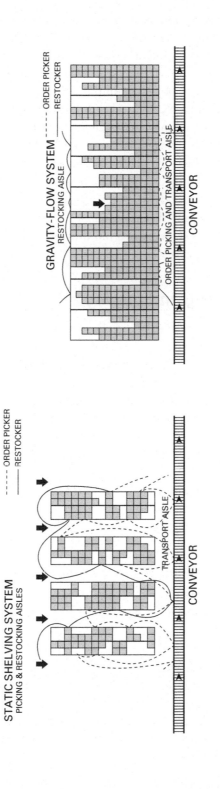

Gravity-flow shelving does cost more than static shelving; however, this is more than made up for by the labour cost savings. Travel time is reduced significantly, as is the time spent locating and replenishing products.

Gravity-flow racking uses floor space more efficiently. Fewer aisles are required and more product can be stored in the same amount of floor space, as shown in Table 5.1. This system can also be retro-fitted into existing racking. One area to take into account is the length of run for gravity shelving. Too long a run can result in wasted space as each lane can only hold one product line. The option is to have one product line across a number of lanes rather than have a long run. Two further points to bear in mind are the need for ongoing maintenance for the rollers and secondly the fact that different products will have different weights and will require different inclines to propel them down to the front.

An alternative to shelving are bin drawers, which provide greater security and high-density storage.

Mobile shelving and racking

Where space is at a premium and access to items is intermittent, as in the case of archive material and very slow-moving items, mobile shelving and racking, which runs on guides or rails and is either manually operated or powered, is a potential alternative to static shelving.

Access to each run of shelving is gained by either turning a wheel at the end of the run or by accessing it electronically at the touch of a button. This type of racking can be utilized in cold-store operations – for long-duration product – where its use can effectively eliminate aisles that otherwise have to be cooled.

 www.youtube.com/watch?v=Ewf1MpqPcxw

Carousels

Carousels are designed for medium- to high-throughput environments. They are also ideal for small, high-value items. There are two types of carousel: horizontal and vertical.

Horizontal carousels

Horizontal carousels work on a similar principle to a merry-go-round. The carousel can be made up of shelves, bins or garment holders. These rotate and are controlled by an operator who uses a computer keypad to type in the location, product code or order number, depending on how the software has been set up. If an order number is keyed in, the carousel will stop at the operator station in pick sequence.

An operator may look after more than one carousel (pods) in order to limit the amount of down time waiting for each carousel to rotate. Goods-to-operator systems are designed to keep the operator working as much as possible and reduce the amount of travel time.

Horizontal carousels vary significantly in length depending on the nature of the product to be stored. They can also range in height from 2 to 8 metres, necessitating the use of a platform to access the product or the introduction of automatic extractors.

Horizontal carousels are ideal for storing and picking high numbers of SKU, small individual items, medium to large cartons and products including hanging garments. They are especially effective in low-headroom areas.

According to OPS (2009) a multiple pod (three or more) can be used to pick between 200 and 400 lines per hour.

Horizontal carousels are expensive and are limited by the amount of time they take to rotate. Cubic space utilization can also be an issue, as can safety if the carousel is not enclosed. It is difficult to replenish when picking and they are limited in terms of the number of operators. They are also very system driven.

 www.youtube.com/watch?v=rDdDulwsCDo&feature=c4-overview-vl&list =PLDJ8Kavy9h6c8rPBUMCYYiW5ULXJ_0xir

FIGURE 5.18　Horizontal carousel

Vertical carousels

Vertical carousels are enclosures which have shelves that rotate in either direction similar to a Ferris or big wheel at a fun fair, bringing a requested item to the operator at a suitable working height. They allow you to use the maximum height available within the building, providing the best use of space within a very small footprint. Vertical carousels are ideal for small- to medium-size parts. The carousel takes up a much smaller footprint than a horizontal carousel. The shelving can be adjusted and sub-divided to handle different sizes and weights.

Vertical carousels provide added security. However, their effectiveness is tempered by the speed of movement. Here the trade-off is between the height of the system and therefore its greater storage capacity and the length of time it takes the shelves to rotate.

Some carousels will operate with a lift system as opposed to rotating shelves. These can handle heavier items.

The software provided with vertical carousels can manage the stock within the carousel, pick in sequence, work with pick-to-light systems and provide accurate reporting. The system can also work with scanners to confirm the correct item is picked every time.

In both examples operators may look after more than one carousel, thus reducing downtime. Vertical carousels can also operate with two or more openings so that staff at different levels can access the parts stored.

Pick rates vary from 100 to 300 lines per hour. As in the horizontal carousel it requires ongoing maintenance and is very system reliant.

 www.youtube.com/watch?v=_ty1gxxAv9U

Vertical lift module (VLM)

Similar to a vertical carousel a VLM is an enclosed storage system consisting of two columns of extractable 'trays' each able to hold multiple cartons, totes or bins. A computer-controlled insertion/extraction device between the two columns automatically locates and retrieves the tray containing the item to be picked. Trays are delivered to an access window for the picker. A pick-to-light system will normally indicate the quantity and the item to be picked, whilst slotting software controls the location and number and size of items per tray. As with the VC multiple VLMs or pods reduce the amount of dwell time by the operator. (OPS/WERC 2009)

FIGURE 5.19 Vertical carousel (courtesy of System Logistics)

A-frames

These machines are similar to vending machines but on a much bigger scale. They are ideal for high-volume items of uniform size and weight. This sorting and picking equipment operates most efficiently in an environment where these two characteristics are present. Typical products include CDs, DVDs, cosmetics and pharmaceuticals.

The products are placed in magazines on a frame resembling a letter A and are automatically dispensed via a computer controlled trigger system into a tote or directly onto a conveyor as it passes through the tunnel created by the frame. A section of the conveyor is allocated to each order. As the order reaches the end of the A-frame it drops into a tote or carton and is then conveyed via conveyor to another picking area if the order is incomplete or to the packing area. While the machine is operating, manual replenishment activities can be performed with no impact on the dispensing operations.

A-frame systems are capable of filling orders quickly: up to 750,000 units per day, 3,000 lines per hour, depending on capacity and the replenishment capability. They can be highly accurate, with operations recording over 99.95 per cent accuracy.

However, this system does require manual replenishment and inaccuracies can occur when filling the channels.

 www.youtube.com/watch?v=IQDtp7d7cnA

Summary and conclusion

There are many different picking strategies that can be utilized within a warehouse operation. Each one will depend on the nature of the product, the velocity of throughput and the company budget.

Picker-to-goods strategies remain the most utilized method within today's warehouse operations. However, goods-to-picker methods are gaining ground as automation becomes more sophisticated and also more affordable.

It is likely that multiple strategies will be used in today's warehouses as they look to cope with multichannel distribution requirements.

Figure 5.20 provides some guidelines to the type of picking and storage equipment to use, based on product size, number of orders, speed of throughput and size of inventory.

Table 5.2 provides a comparison between the different picking strategies.

TABLE 5.2 Comparison chart – order pick strategies

Pick method	Typical Applications	Benefits	Disadvantages
Pick by individual order	Most operations	• Single stage operation • Flexible • Quick implementation • Ability to isolate urgent orders • Picker able to decide pick path • Utilize manual or technology systems	• Low pick rate • Very labour intensive • Can result in bottlenecks at the pick face • Training can take some time depending on the tools used
Cluster picking	Most operations	• Multiple orders picked at the same time • Reduce travel in the warehouse • Reduce overall pick time	• Training can take some time • Accuracy can be an issue • Urgent orders cannot be separated easily • Requires equipment to hold multiple orders • Requires low cube items in the main • Requires system assistance to combine orders • Can result in bottlenecks • May require second stage to pack orders

TABLE 5.2 *Continued*

Pick method	Typical Applications	Benefits	Disadvantages
Batch pick to zero	e-commerce Retail store orders	• Multiple orders picked at the same time • Very effective for e-commerce orders where 100s of orders for single line • Reduced travel • Increased accuracy • Can be used successfully in a cross dock operation	• Urgent orders cannot be separated easily • Requires system assistance to combine orders • Bulk pick will take longer than with pick to line • Requires sortation area and additional staff • Re-packaging required
Batch pick by line	e-commerce Retail store orders	• Multiple orders picked at the same time • Increased accuracy • Very effective for e-commerce orders where 100s of orders for single line • Reduced travel	• Urgent orders cannot be separated easily • Need to return unallocated items to stock • Requires sortation area and additional staff • Re-packaging required
Zone pick	Situations where there are large numbers of SKUs and low number of items per order line	• Less travel for operator • Orders can be picked simultaneously or sequentially • Can accommodate different families of items on orders such as hazardous, temperature controlled, etc.	• Normally requires conveyors • Cost of equipment • Normally combined with pick/put-to-light systems • Can lead to idle time if work is not balanced between zones

TABLE 5.2 *Continued*

Pick method	Typical Applications	Benefits	Disadvantages
Wave pick	When orders are released on a timed basis or to meet departing trucks	• Ability to schedule work efficiently • Orders are picked in time for a production run or vehicle departure	• Urgent orders cannot be separated easily • Requires a WMS to manage the allocation
Goods to picker	High intensity pick operations	• High pick rates • High accuracy • Equipment moves, operators stay in the same place • Reduced space requirement • Product security • Ergonomic workstations • Training is less intensive	• High equipment costs • High energy costs • Potential system failure • High opportunity cost • Standardized unit loads required • Limited to smaller items in the main

FIGURE 5.20 Pick module selection matrix (courtesy of OPS Design)

PICK MODULE SELECTION MATRIX

	Manual – Conventional					
OPS DESIGN CONSULTING	High-Density Drawers	Bin Shelving	Decked Rack	Carton Flow Rack	Pallet Rack Position	Pallet Flow Rack
Picking Type						
Piece	◆	◆	◇	◆	◇	
Inner Pack	◇	◆	◆	◆	◇	◇
Full Case		◇	◇	◇	◆	◆
Full Pallet					◇	◆
Security						
High	◇					
Medium	◆	◆				
Low	◆	◆	◆	◆	◆	◆
Pick Unit Size						
<0.0005 Cubic Ft.	◆	◇	◇	◇	◇	◇
0.0005–0.015 Cubic Ft.	◇	◆	◇	◆	◇	◇
0.015–0.125 Cubic Ft.		◇	◆	◆	◆	◆
0.125–1 Cubic Ft.			◆	◇	◆	◆
1–5 Cubic Ft.			◇		◆	◆
5–10 Cubic Ft.					◆	◆
>10 Cubic Ft.					◆	◆
Daily Hits						
<0.05	◆	◆	◆		◆	
0.05–0.2	◆	◆	◆		◆	
0.2–1	◆	◆	◆	◇	◆	◇
1–5	◇	◆	◆	◆	◆	◆
5–10		◆	◆	◆	◆	◆
10–50		◆	◆	◆	◆	◆
>50		◆	◇	◆	◆	◆
Daily Cubic Velocity						
<0.005 Cubic Ft.	◆	◆	◆		◇	
0.005–0.1 Cubic Ft.		◆	◆	◇	◇	
0.1–0.5 Cubic Ft.		◇	◆	◆	◆	
0.5–5 Cubic Ft.			◆	◆	◆	◇
5–10 Cubic Ft.			◇	◇	◆	◇
10–25 Cubic Ft.					◇	◆
25–100						◆
>100						◆
Average Inventory Cube						
<0.125 Cubic Ft.	◆	◆				
0.125–2 Cubic Ft.		◆	◇	◇		
2–5 Cubic Ft.		◇	◆	◆		
5–10 Cubic Ft.			◆	◆		
10–25 Cubic Ft.			◇	◆	◇	
25–250 Cubic Ft.				◆	◆	◇
>250 Cubic Ft.				◆	◆	◆

◆ OPTIMAL
◇ FEASIBLE

© Operations Design, Inc. 2006

FIGURE 5.20 *continued*

	Mechanized – Automated				
	Automated Dispensing System	Vertical Lift Module or Carousel	Horizontal Carousel	Mini-Load AS/RS	Pallet Load AS/RS
Picking Type					
Piece	◆	◆	◆	◆	◇
Inner Pack	◆	◆	◆	◆	◇
Full Case	◇	◇	◇	◆	◆
Full Pallet					◆
Security					
High		◆	◇	◆	◆
Medium	◆	◆	◆	◆	◆
Low	◆	◆	◆	◆	◆
Pick Unit Size					
<0.0005 Cubic Ft.	◆	◆	◇	◆	◇
0.0005–0.015 Cubic Ft.	◆	◆	◆	◆	◇
0.015–0.125 Cubic Ft.	◇	◇	◇	◆	◆
0.125–1 Cubic Ft.				◆	◆
1–5 Cubic Ft.				◇	◆
5–10 Cubic Ft.					◆
>10 Cubic Ft.					◆
Daily Hits					
<0.05		◇	◇	◇	◇
0.05–0.2		◇	◇	◇	◇
0.2–1		◆	◆	◆	◆
1–5		◇	◇	◆	◆
5–10				◇	◇
10–50	◇				
>50	◆				
Daily Cubic Velocity					
<0.005 Cubic Ft.		◆	◆	◇	
0.005–0.1 Cubic Ft.	◇	◆	◆	◇	
0.1–0.5 Cubic Ft.	◇	◇	◇	◆	
0.5–5 Cubic Ft.	◆			◆	
5–10 Cubic Ft.	◆			◇	◇
10–25 Cubic Ft.	◆				◇
25–100	◇				◆
>100					◆
Average Inventory Cube					
<0.125 Cubic Ft.		◆	◆	◇	
0.125–2 Cubic Ft.	◇	◆	◆	◆	
2–5 Cubic Ft.	◆	◇	◇	◆	
5–10 Cubic Ft.	◆			◆	
10–25 Cubic Ft.	◆			◇	
25–250 Cubic Ft.	◆				◆
>250 Cubic Ft.	◆				◆

◆ OPTIMAL
◇ FEASIBLE

© Operations Design, Inc. 2006

Order-picking methods

06

" *Fast is fine but accuracy is everything.*

(WYATT EARP (1848–1929))

Introduction

This is the area in which advances in technology have transformed the picking operation and improved accuracy and productivity significantly. The introduction of barcoding, voice technology and pick-by-light systems is not only improving warehouse picking operations but also producing an acceptable return on investment.

The following picking methods are currently in use in today's warehouses:

- paper pick lists;
- pick by label;
- pick by voice;
- barcode scanning;
- radio frequency identification;
- pick by light/pick to light;
- put to light;
- automated picking.

Paper pick lists

A paper pick list will normally detail the order number, location, product code, description and quantity to be picked. If utilizing a WMS, each product line will be shown in sequence, enabling the picker to travel the most efficient way around the warehouse and ending up as close to the despatch bay as possible.

The operator is however at liberty to choose a different route if it is felt that it is more direct. The fastest-moving items should be placed close to the despatch area to minimize travel. Stock control systems and manual applications may not have this ability and therefore some form of manual intervention is required to reduce the amount of pick travel undertaken.

The picker will utilize a trolley, cage, pallet truck or possibly a forklift truck. The advantage of using a forklift truck is that the pallet can be lifted to a suitable height as the picker continues along the route.

Any discrepancies are written onto the pick list. When the pick list is returned to the supervisor, the discrepancies should be checked immediately and alternative locations provided if there are shortages. Details of the pick are entered manually into the system. This can lead to errors if the writing is illegible or there is confusion over the way a number is written. This all adds time to the operation. Paper picking requires little investment; however, it can have low accuracy and may require order validation.

Once an order has been picked the operator has to return to the office for further pick lists or instructions. It is not a real-time system.

Pick by label

In this system, pick lists are a series of labels on a sheet, which are printed in pick order. The picker attaches a label to each item picked and returns any unused labels to the supervisor's office. Any discrepancies are checked immediately and additional labels printed if the stock is available elsewhere in the warehouse. This can eliminate a step at the despatch area as address labels are already attached. It's also more accurate than paper picking as you can soon tell if there has been a mis-pick in terms of quantity.

These are both very manual operations and rely on the operator, supervisor and administration clerk all playing their part to ensure accurate information is recorded.

These manual forms of operation and low levels of productivity and accuracy have led to an increase in the use of technology within the warehouse.

Pick by voice

The use of voice technology is gaining ground in warehouses globally, particularly for order picking, although other processes such as cycle counting, put-away and replenishment also utilize the system. Many companies are moving directly from paper picking to voice and bypassing barcode scanning.

Operators are issued with a headset and a microphone together with a small terminal that is attached to a belt or can be worn on the wrist. The WMS sends messages to the computer via radio frequency (RF) transmissions, utilizing transmitters installed throughout the warehouse, and these messages are converted into voice commands. The operator also uses voice to communicate back to the system.

Voice was first employed about 20 years ago for cold-storage applications where gloves and extreme temperatures made it difficult to use scanners and paper based systems.

The list of benefits are stated as being very comprehensive. They include:

- increased accuracy;
- increased productivity;
- reduction in paper usage;
- reduction in errors through elimination of re-keying data;
- improved safety through hands- and eyes-free operation;
- reduction in damage;
- real-time stock updates leading to fast and accurate replenishment;
- real-time updates regarding potential shortages;
- increased operator time on the warehouse floor;
- reduced training times;
- multilingual, accommodating a diverse workforce;
- easy to integrate with other systems;
- potential reduction in employee turnover; and
- normally a quick ROI.

In a survey by ARC Advisory Group and *Modern Materials Handling* magazine, nearly 60 per cent of respondents saw productivity gains greater than 8 per cent in their picking operations when they adopted voice, whilst another 26 per cent saw productivity gains of between 4 and 8 per cent.

More than 83 per cent of the companies who had implemented voice reported that their investment had met their financial hurdle goals.

 www.youtube.com/watch?v=KkADR5P37Is

Figure 6.1 shows other benefits identified by the survey.

This system has become prevalent in the food service and grocery retail sector. It is particularly suitable for both chilled and frozen environments where

FIGURE 6.1 Benefits of voice picking
(courtesy of ARC Advisory Group)

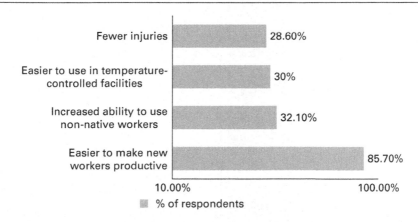

gloves hamper the use of radio data terminals (RDTs) and paper, whilst the hands-free aspect of the system has major advantages over paper pick lists, labels and barcode scanning.

Increased accuracy can negate the need for additional checks at despatch. The reduction in picking errors is significant in most of the companies who have adopted this technology. Some companies have, however, introduced a failsafe by scanning the item once picked.

For high-volume operations, even small improvements in accuracy can produce a substantial payback. For example, a warehouse that picks half a million cases per week with a 99.8 per cent accuracy level (two errors per thousand) incurs 52,000 errors per annum. Increasing accuracy to 99.96 per cent or 0.4 per thousand, for example, will reduce errors by 41,600 per annum.

If we accept that the cost of a mis-pick is approximately £25 ($39), this can be an overall saving of £1,040,000. ($1,627,000)

When UK retailer Waitrose introduced voice into its picking operation it recorded an increase in accuracy from 98.68 per cent to 98.88 per cent based on sample audits.

Companies that have invested in voice systems are seeing increases in accuracy rates of up to 99.9 per cent and a number are recording reduced staff turnover and training time.

Perhaps most importantly, voice solutions demonstrate direct benefits to the bottom line: payback is typically less than one year. This can be achieved through accuracy alone.

As can be seen in Figure 6.2, voice can eliminate a number of steps in the pick process, leading to increased productivity and accuracy.

FIGURE 6.2 Why voice outperforms scanning

Scanning

| Read next location | Travel to location | Scan location | Read qty on screen | Free hands place device elsewhere | Perform task | Locate device | Press buttons to confirm |

Voice

| Hear next location; travel | Speak check digits, hear instructions, perform task | Hear next location, travel |

Elapsed time

CASE STUDY   Waitrose

Waitrose was founded in London in 1904. It has since been acquired by the John Lewis Partnership, who opened the first Waitrose supermarket in 1955. Today there are 280 branches, dedicated to offering quality, value and customer service.

Waitrose combines the convenience of a supermarket with the expertise and service of a specialist shop.

Locations range from high streets to edge-of-town sites and vary in size from just 7,000 square feet to approximately 56,000 square feet.

Waitrose services its stores from four regional distribution centres across four sites at Bracknell, Aylesford, Leyland and Brinklow. Having recognized potential productivity improvements through the use of voice technology, the Waitrose supply chain team decided to research the technology by visiting other UK retailers and testing different systems.

Prior to the introduction of voice-picking technology, Waitrose operated with a variety of picking methods including pick sheets, pick labels and RDTs.

Having chosen a supplier, the team introduced voice for the pick operations only, although there are plans to utilize voice for other operations in the warehouse in future. The implementation began at Bracknell and was subsequently rolled out to the other sites. The fresh foods department was excluded from this implementation phase.

One reason for the partial implementation was the fact that the existing WMS was a bespoke system, didn't operate in real time and therefore would have required greater functionality to be written into the voice software system.

Waitrose utilized their productivity systems team to measure productivities within each department prior to the implementation to enable them to compare the different methods of picking.

The voice-picking operation was measured after a three-month settling-in period.

In order to introduce voice technology, a business case was produced which, based on discussions with other companies who had introduced voice, predicted a 7.5 per cent increase in productivity.

Having operated the technology across a number of sites and for a reasonable period of time, Waitrose has calculated that the overall productivity improvement is on average 8 per cent. As the staff become more experienced, the productivity rate is likely to improve further. Staff are also able to monitor their own productivity through the voice system in terms of cases picked per hour, for example.

In terms of pick accuracy, independent auditors recorded an increase from 98.68 per cent to 98.88 per cent accuracy based on sample audits. The system only operates with check digits for the location and doesn't include product confirmation. There is pressure therefore on the put-away team to ensure accurate placement.

The team at Waitrose has been very happy with the implementation to date even though the process didn't run smoothly throughout.

When considering the introduction of voice technology, the Waitrose team came up with a list of Dos and Don'ts as follows:

Do:

- visit other operations to assess impact of introduction;
- work in partnership with these companies where possible;
- get a full understanding of the potential technology issues;
- ensure sufficient RF coverage throughout the warehouse;
- ensure the management team fully understands the benefits and has a full understanding of the system;
- consult and gain full acceptance from your staff;
- explain fully the advantages of voice and allay fears regarding safety and any 'Big Brother' issues;
- appoint super users to respond to and react quickly to issues;
- ensure training standards and procedures are maintained at a high level;
- provide choice to the users in terms of headsets and voices;
- provide opportunities for staff feedback;
- measure productivities before and after implementation and ongoing;
- continually assess and review the processes.

Don't:

- think it's easy to implement and manage;
- assume staff will accept it unconditionally;
- implement other systems at the same time.

The main advantages to date include:

- improved health and safety as a result of the hands-free operation;
- a safer working environment as staff are able to concentrate fully on the job in hand;
- improved productivity;
- greater accuracy;
- quicker staff training compared with paper- and RDT-based picking;
- ability to use many nationalities in the same operation.

The Waitrose case study shows an initial average productivity improvement of 8 per cent across all the operations.

In order to calculate the benefits you need to measure productivity levels before and after implementation.

Increases in productivity can be measured in terms of the average cases per hour picked by each worker. Take the cases picked per day divided by hours per day worked (eg 7.5 actual hours) divided by number of pickers (in this case 35):

36,000 cases ÷ 7.5 hours per day ÷ 35 operators = 137 cases

per hour per operator. A 10 per cent productivity gain would raise the cases per hour to 151.

To calculate the reduction in operators, take the same equation and solve for X as the number of operators:

36,000 cases ÷ 7.5 hours per day ÷ (x) operators = 151 OR
x = 36,000 ÷ 7.5 ÷ 151 = 32 operators

In this example that means three fewer operators are needed with the switch to voice-directed selection based on a 10 per cent improvement in productivity.

Further savings can be made in terms of stationery, the labour involved in administrative tasks, the training of personnel, improved safety, reduced sickness levels and potential compensation claims and quicker, more accurate stock checks.

Time to full productivity for a new worker using scanning methods is typically two to three weeks; with voice it can be as little as three to four days.

In terms of expected return on investment, this will vary significantly from company to company. It will depend on:

- the current level of productivity and scope for improvement;
- the current method of picking;
- the amount of checking within the system;
- the number of picking shifts within the system;
- the current level of RF infrastructure; and
- whether the WMS can support voice.

Voice on its own may not work in all environments. Where companies require the capture of data such as serial numbers or batch codes, voice needs to be supplemented by some form of scanning or image-capture technology.

Voice technology, unless used in conjunction with scanning, may not be 100 per cent accurate. It does rely on the correct product being in the right location. Some companies have supplemented voice confirmation of quantity with product recognition by repeating the last four digits of the barcode, for example.

Even if hands-free picking is a requirement there are other systems on the market that can be as appropriate, if not more so.

Overall, voice technology can provide a reasonable return on investment by improving accuracy, increasing productivity and improving ergonomics, thus reducing staff illness and, as a consequence, improving customer service.

Taking things a step further, a number of manufacturers have introduced a combined voice and automated guided vehicle (AGV) or laser-guided forklift truck system.

The AGVs feature a laser navigation steering system which charts the picker's route. At the first location the voice system instructs the picker as to which item should be loaded onto the empty pallet. The picker informs the system as to what has been picked and loaded and the truck continues to the next location without the operator having to control it.

Once the truck is fully loaded it transfers to the loading bay while the picker moves on to the next order, arriving at the first location where another AGV with an empty pallet has just arrived. See Figure 6.3.

By implementing both systems simultaneously, the Swedish Co-op reported that it had improved productivity by up to 70 per cent.

Barcode scanning

A barcode consists of a series of vertical bars of varying widths that represent letters, numbers and other symbols. Barcodes are used to identify products, locations in the warehouse, containers (totes, cartons, pallets), serial and batch numbers.

FIGURE 6.3   Laser-guided AGV with voice (courtesy of Toyota)

FIGURE 6.4   One-dimensional and two-dimensional barcodes

ADDR0010C62620AE

As with many areas of logistics, there is no conformity and thus no universal barcode. This can make it difficult to transfer products between companies and countries. The main barcode standards include EAN-8, EAN-13 and Code 128. Appendix 2 has a comprehensive guide to all the barcode options.

Recent developments include two-dimensional barcodes, the advantage being that you can store a greater amount of data within a much smaller space. See Figure 6.4.

A current debate is whether the pharmaceutical industry should be investing in 2D technology or radio frequency identification (RFID) tags. Both are able to hold more information than a standard linear barcode; however, certain types of RFID tags are rewritable. Currently there is a significant difference in price between barcodes and RFID tags.

Barcode readers come in many different forms. They can be hand held, static, truck-mounted or wearable.

The hand-held scanner has a screen and a trigger. It scans the barcode, deciphers it and stores or transmits it to a computer. These scanners have the ability to read a number of different types of barcode, although this will depend on the manufacturer, model and cost. Some PDAs and mobile phones also have scanners and cameras able to read one-dimensional and two-dimensional barcodes.

Data can be read, stored in the scanner and then downloaded by attaching the scanner to the computer via a USB connection. Information can also be transferred in real time via RF.

A pen or wand scanner swipes the barcode through contact and reads and deciphers the information.

Barcode scanning, utilizing hand-held scanners with real-time data transmission has made data collection faster and more accurate in today's warehouse environment. It has also increased productivity by ensuring that operators don't have to return to the office for instructions each time they complete a task. The instructions are on screen in the form of text which the operator scrolls through and advances by choosing specific commands.

However, barcode scanning with hand-held devices does have drawbacks. These include having to set down the reader whilst tasks are carried out or struggling to hold the unit and carry out the task at the same time. Errors tend to occur when using hand-held scanners if they are holstered or put down on a surface. This movement can cause the picker to pick from the wrong location or miscount the items. There is potential for greater damage if scanners are dropped or mishandled. Safety is also an issue as operators try to read the instructions whilst in motion.

A stationary scanner will read the barcode as it passes by on a conveyor, for example. This requires the barcode to be easily visible, intact and in a uniform position on the item. Static readers tend to be used with belt sorters and conveyors for example.

Recent advances in this area include the introduction of hands-free, wearable computers that enable the operator to handle product with both hands as opposed to having to hold a barcode scanner, paper pick list or roll of labels.

A wireless-enabled, wearable computer allows operators to receive instructions in real time, scan barcodes, enter data and transmit in real time. Wearable computers are typically worn on the wrist or lower arm and feature a screen and a small keyboard or touch screen, with the option of a finger-mounted scanner that either plugs into the unit or communicates via Bluetooth technology. These have gained in popularity within warehouses where heavy items require both hands free to execute a task.

Companies choose wearable solutions for a variety of reasons. Wearable computers require very little change to existing warehouse operations that currently use hand-held computers.

Wearable computers also require little re-training of staff and usually no software modification. The existing applications designed for hand-held or forklift-mounted units can usually run on a wearable device with no modification.

Workers simply need to adjust to putting the wearable components on, to the feel of the computer on their wrist, and if chosen, to the use of a ring scanner. Today's wearable units typically weigh just a few ounces, so fatigue and comfort are typically not an issue. Power is usually supplied from a battery pack worn on the arm or at the small of the back. See Figure 6.5.

By using wearable computers, one task is eliminated, thus making the pick process quicker and potentially reducing errors. Productivity and accuracy improvements can quickly add up to substantial savings.

To put things into context, imagine a warehouse with 20 order pickers, that pick 100 cases per hour (based on an eight-hour day, 253 days per annum). An accuracy rate of 99.5 per cent incurs 20,240 errors per annum. An increase in accuracy to 99.8 per cent reduces the errors to 8,096 errors. If each error costs a conservative £25 ($39) that amounts to an annual saving of £303,600 ($475,000).

The computers can also be supplied with easy-to-read touch screens and two-dimensional imagers. They can be configured to be voice enabled, allowing pick operations to be even more accurate as items can be scanned to ensure the correct item has been picked from the location.

Other advantages include less damage to equipment and less strain on the user. Figure 6.6 shows an operator carrying both a scanner and a box. Not all

FIGURE 6.5   Wearable RDT with finger scanner
(courtesy of Vanderlande)

FIGURE 6.6   Picking with hand-held barcode scanner
(courtesy of LXE)

his fingers are around the box, making it more difficult to grip. This compares with the operator in Figure 6.7, who is using both hands to hold the box.

These systems are also providing benefits in other areas including improved customer service, decreased training time, a reduction in damages and accidents, increased employee satisfaction and increased compliance.

One of the main disadvantages of barcodes is their potential to be damaged, thus making reading difficult and/or potentially inaccurate.

A recent advance in hand-held units by companies such as Tecsys is visual logistics whereby instead of lines and lines of text operators are being presented with a visual warehouse location map to quickly guide them to the assigned pick location and a visual guide as to the exact carton or tote into which to put the selected products, eliminating the wasteful and time-consuming process of searching for the pick slot. They are also being presented with product-specific images to enable a visual validation and to ensure that the appropriate quality assurance checks are performed.

FIGURE 6.7 Picking with finger scanner (courtesy of LXE)

According to Tecsys the time to pick a product line can be reduced by up to 30 seconds. Workers are empowered to access critical information to make faster decisions and accelerate their workflows, particularly in environments where literacy is an issue. It also reduces training time.

Radio frequency identification

RFID is a means of uniquely identifying an item using radio waves. Data is exchanged between tags and readers and depending on the frequency, may or may not require line of sight. Common uses in today's world include library books, toll passes and access ID cards.

Its use in the supply chain has been limited until recently. However, high-profile projects within the US military, Asda, Walmart and Tesco have increased awareness.

The system enables the simultaneous reading of multiple items as opposed to barcodes, which need to be read individually.

There are two types of RFID tags: those that are passive, have no power source, limited data storage capacity, are read only and have a limited read range, and those that are active, have their own power source, have a larger data-storage capacity, have a read/write capability and are readable from a greater distance.

Passive tags hold little actual data but are able to identify an item to a database where more comprehensive data is stored. For example, a conveyor-based sortation system can identify the item and interrogate the database to receive routing instructions.

Active tags have a higher capacity and can have their item's status updated once a task has been completed. They have a shorter writing range than reading range and the internal power source is likely to burn out within 5 to 10 years.

Frequency is an important factor in transmission range and speed and not all frequencies are available for use globally, which can cause issues from a supply chain perspective.

Individual-item-level tracking for the majority of products is unlikely to happen during the next 10 years or so due to the cost of implementation; however, unit-load identification is possible and potentially cost effective. The tracking of roll cages, pallets and returnable packaging such as totes, kegs, barrels and trays can be made simpler and cost effective through the use of RFID.

The difficulty faced by proponents of RFID is that barcodes are so cheap to produce and remain an accurate and cost-effective method of identification.

The cost of operating an RFID system will vary tremendously depending on the application, the size of installation, the frequencies used and the quantity of tags purchased. As take-up increases, the costs will reduce.

The following items are required to introduce an RFID application:

- RFID readers (from £300 to £1,500);
- RFID tags (from £0.05 to £0.10 upwards depending on the frequency and method of application to the item);
- middleware;
- systems upgrades; and
- RF network within the warehouse.

Current disadvantages of RFID include:

- reading issues when in close proximity to liquids and metal;
- dead areas in the warehouse where signals are weak;
- tags can be damaged by liquids, static discharges and magnetic surges; and
- intermittent data capture, with the possibility of some tags not being read.

Pick by light/pick to light

Light travels at a speed of 186,000 miles per second (299,792,458 metres per second) whereas sound travels at 0.2 miles per second (343 metres per second), therefore the human eye can see a light faster than it takes for the brain to interpret a voice command.

Pick to light or pick by light uses light-indicator, LED or LCD modules mounted to shelving, flow racks, pallet racks or other storage locations.

This system tends to be used in conjunction with zone picking.

To begin the process an operator scans a barcode on an arriving pick tote or shipping carton which denotes the next order number to be picked. This communicates to the system that the operator is ready to pick. The system then sends a message to the zone in which the operator is stationed and all the pick locations for that particular order light up at once.

A digital display tells the operator the quantity to pick; once this has been picked the operator turns the light off to confirm the pick. The operator can then move on to the next location indicated. The pickers continue until the pick in their area is completed. Some systems allow the operator to scan the item before placing it in the shipping carton to ensure accuracy. This does however slow down the process but is a check on the accuracy of the put-away process. Other systems provide an image of the product to be picked to increase accuracy. The tote is then passed to the next zone for the rest of the order to be picked. This is a typical pick-and-pass method of picking.

All information is exchanged in real time with the enterprise resource planning (ERP) or WMS system.

Unlike scanning and voice picking, which are sequential in nature, all locations are indicated to the operator at the same time. This means that the operator can choose the best pick path.

Pick by light necessitates operators being stationed in zones looking after a certain quantity of SKUs. The order tote moves between zones on a conveyor, cart or other transportation method.

As operators are based in a specific area, this reduces the amount of walking required within the warehouse.

At the end of the pick an operator will check the order number, possibly check the weight of the consignment, attach an address label, add the delivery documentation and signify the carrier if multiple carriers are used.

By getting the operator to the right location each time, the picking process is greatly improved and productivity increased. Training is relatively simple and is conducive to the use of temporary labour and seasonal employees. Some companies have introduced portable pick-by-light systems that can be moved around the warehouse as required or to a temporary warehouse to cover peaks in business.

As with voice, there is very little upheaval when implementing the system. The lights can be retro fitted onto shelving and racking. The system can also be used in conjunction with carousels.

In terms of systems integration, pick to light is relatively simple. It requires the downloading of a file with the order number, product codes, locations and quantities. It can easily deal with part cases and individual items.

A further enhancement of the pick-to-light system is the SpeasTech system where indicator lights are automatically deactivated by the motion of the picker's hand through an infrared window in and out of the bin. One less step is required of each pick, so pickers can work faster. And if a hand reaches into the wrong bin, an audible alarm is sounded.

 www.speastech.com/product-overview_5111_ct.aspx

CASE STUDY   SSI Schäfer and Yankee Candle

Picking efficiency has improved by 50 per cent and picking errors have significantly reduced at Yankee Candle's European distribution centre in Bristol as a result of SSI Schäfer's paperless pick-to-light system installation.

Yankee Candle are distributors of the world's largest selection of scented candles and home fragrance product scents to retail stores, export organizations and the consumer via the internet. They wanted to improve overall picking accuracy and efficiency by building upon the existing KDR (push-through conduit shelving) flow-racking system previously installed by SSI Schäfer.

The original KDR flow racking, designed to hold forward-picking stock in over 1,800 locations, is divided into pick zones in a U-shaped layout with a conveyor running through the centre. Originally supporting paper-based picking, the KDR flow racking has been significantly enhanced by the addition of SSI Schäfer's pick-to-light system.

Yankee Candle is already reaping the benefits of the new paperless system which uses the latest in Schäfer's software technology by providing the advantage of flexible zone picking to balance out workload, contributing to increased picking efficiency, meaning fewer labour hours and reduced picking errors, resulting in fewer missed or low-level product shipments.

Mike Alibone, business development manager, SSI Schäfer, says: 'As well as improving picking efficiency the system is designed to provide enhanced volumetric packing, multiple order consolidation, order progress optimization and shipping detail transfer to third-party carriers, taking Yankee Candle to a new level in operational excellence.'

Bruce Mitchell, operations manager at Yankee Candle, is delighted with the new system. He says: 'The system has lifted picking efficiency by 50 per cent whilst significantly increasing the accuracy of the pick. In fact, shipping volumes are up by more than 40 per cent on this time last year while the number of errors is down by over 50 per cent of last year's figure.'

In terms of packing, the system calculates the sizes and number of cartons required and prints labels in advance with the content. The system is reliant on using a database of carton volumetrics/packing parameters and is enabled when the operator scans the barcode on the carton label. Multiple orders can be consolidated for a single shipment to a customer.

For order progress optimization, all defined pick zones are able to commence order picking simultaneously, even when a single large order is split across different zones. It relies on operators in each zone picking in the printing sequence of the labels, which have been issued to synchronize order progression. For each pick wave the system looks at the distribution of the picks and calculates a zone size for each operator to work in, thereby spreading the number of picks evenly across a maximum of 12 operators.

Shipping detail transfer to third-party carriers allows cartons to be scanned and the details of the shipment to be transferred electronically via an interface between the SSI Schäfer system to any one of five carrier systems in order for the latter to generate their own despatch documentation.

Having installed the original, highly customized 'flexible zone' pick-to-light system, to improve picking efficiency and reduce picking errors, SSI Schaefer were contracted back in to support and work with Yankee Candle® Europe in their move to a new 175,000 square foot warehouse ensuring the necessary alterations and extension to the system within the new site.

In just one month, SSI Schaefer dismantled the existing zone picking system made up of carton live storage, pick-by-light picking and conveyor-based carton sortation, transported it to the new DC and reinstalled it in conjunction with a complete reconfiguration and extension. At 175,000 square feet, this new DC is almost three times the size of the old facility and the addition of extra pallet positions has significantly increased storage capacity.

There are now more picking locations in the carton live storage, an additional full-case 'pick to belt conveyor', additional 'sort-to-route' sortation lanes for completed orders and separate shipping carton feeds from two zone picking areas. The whole system has also been given a complete software overhaul including additional interfaces to contract carriers' systems.

The extended automated system, which includes additional sortation capability and a new automated full-case picking area, has and will enable Yankee Candle® Europe to continue increasing its throughput efficiency of the picking operation and accommodate with ease, future requirements of its growing internet business.

FIGURE 6.8   Yankee Candle pick to light (courtesy of SSI Schäfer)

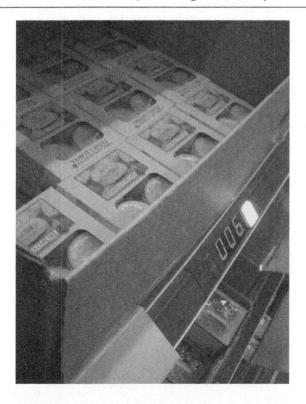

Put to light

This system is particularly prevalent in retail store replenishment operations.

The WMS will consolidate all the store orders for a particular group of stores. This might be done by region or despatch times from the distribution centre (DC). The system needs to ensure that each group of stores has similar volumes where possible.

Depending on daily volumes, staff can increase or decrease the number of locations (stores) that they look after. Large-volume stores may be situated in a number of different zones with the totes/containers being consolidated at the despatch area.

Individual product lines required by the stores will be picked in bulk and transferred to the correct operator station by cart, pallet truck or via a conveyor. Each store will have a tote or totes assigned to it.

Once the SKU has arrived at the 'put' station the operator scans each item and a flashing light displays at each location indicating which containers (relating to a particular store) require that product and how many items are required.

Confirmed 'put' results are uploaded to the system in real time to update the WMS.

With pack-to-light or put-to-light systems there is a requirement to set up a central processing area, which can result in the design of a new layout and the introduction of further equipment.

In terms of systems, put-to-light technology requires order consolidation and a batch pick of products. Part pallets or cases will need to be returned to stock if stores do not order in complete cases or the total number of units ordered does not equate to full case quantities.

Pack or put to light can be more dynamic and works well with cross-dock operations where product can be received, allocated, picked and despatched on the same day if required.

One further note to add here, which is also relevant to other picking strategies, is the introduction by retailers of pick sequences that duplicate store layouts, enabling retail staff to replenish shelves efficiently.

CASE STUDY   Put to light

A UK clothing retailer installed a put-to-light system at one of its DCs. Twenty stations were installed, each with a capacity of up to 24 stores. Product is automatically delivered to each station, utilizing an automated storage and retrieval system.

The light display at each location indicates how many items must be placed into each of the order totes, which means that a single operator can look after 24 store orders at the same time.

Once an order tote is full, the display instructs the operator to push the tote onto a conveyor system, which takes it to the despatch area.

The high-rate put stations (up to 1,000 items per hour, depending on order profile) significantly reduce the time taken by staff travelling between store orders.

Operators are fed with a continuous supply of products and each workstation is ergonomically designed.

A leading sporting goods manufacturer introduced a put-to-light system at a UK operation in 2008, investing over £20 million in the project. The company says: 'Automation allows us to handle a lot of volume in a relatively small amount of space, which keeps overheads down... automation allows us to flex the volume up and down accordingly. High-rate put stations enable operators to achieve an average of 500 units per hour, with a potential capability of 1,500 picks per hour. With over 70,000 SKUs the pick face for a manual operation would have been massive and given the seasonal nature of our business we would have been continually changing it – automation improves efficiency fivefold.'

Comparisons

Table 6.1 shows the various methods of picking utilized within today's warehouse. These show a combination of picker to goods and goods to picker. In section one we tend to have a single-pick operation where the picker collects all the items for a particular order and then takes it to despatch prior to picking the next order. Picks can be made from a floor-level pick face or, if there are significant numbers of SKUs and too few floor locations, from a higher-level pick face. In this situation the productivity reduces significantly as soon as the operator has to go up into the air.

FIGURE 6.9 Pick rate comparison for the various pick technologies (Wulfratt 2013)

Velocity in order lines selected per paid person hour

SKU velocity Category	0	100	200	300	400	500	600	700	800	900	1000	1100	1200
A							Automated/semi-automated pick technologies						
A				Horizontal carousels									
A & B			Pick to light										
ABC		Voice picking											
ABC			Visual picking										
C & D	RF picking												
C & D	Paper pick												
	Rack and static shelving			Pick to belt carton and pallet flow			Carousels and semi-automated systems						

Movement category

TABLE 6.1 Pick method comparison (adapted from CILT Warehouse Management course)

	Method	Equipment	Speed	Accuracy	Order size (lines)	Cost
Pick faces in aisles	Picker to goods	Low level with hand pallet truck, jack or roll cage	Medium	Paper: low RDTs: med–high Voice: high	Large	Low Medium Medium
	Picker to goods	Low level with PPT/CBT	Fast	Paper: low RDTs: med–high Voice: high	Large	Low Medium Medium
	Picker to goods	High-level order-picking truck	Slow	Paper: low RDTs: med–high Voice: high	Small	Medium Medium Medium
	Zone pick	Pick to light	Fast	High	Medium–low	Medium–high
Bulk pre-pick (batch)	Pallet to picker followed by picker to tote/pallet	By RT/CBT	Medium–fast	Paper: medium RDTs: high Voice: high	Low–medium	Low Medium Medium
	Put to light	Cart, pallet truck or conveyor	Medium–fast	High	Medium–high	Medium
Mainly automated	Goods to picker	Carousel	Medium–fast	High	Low–medium	High
	Picker to goods or goods to picker	Conveyor or sorter (A-frame)	Fast	High	Medium–high	High
	Goods to picker	AS/RS to pick station	Medium–fast	High	High	High

PPT – Powered Pallet Truck; CBT – Counterbalance Truck; RT – Reach Truck; AS/RS – Automated Storage and Retrieval System; RDT – Radio data terminal.

In section two we have a two-stage process where product is picked in bulk, for example by batch, followed by a sortation process into individual orders. Although in two stages, the pick rates are reasonably high and it also includes a double check of items and quantities, thus improving accuracy. Put-to-light systems use batching to collect all the items for specific orders.

In section three we have the use of carousels, conveyors, flow racks and fully automated AS/RS systems.

Utilizing this form of picking, we see pick accuracy rates increasing together with the ability to handle large numbers of SKUs and items.

Table 6.2 provides a comparison between the different pick methods in terms of advantages and disadvantages.

Marc Wulfratt of MWPVL provides the following (Table 6.3) in terms of cost and accuracy comparisons. Costs are based on 2013 prices.

The costs are approximate and are based on a 100,000 square foot warehouse with 25 operators and 2,500 SKU.

Cost of errors

It is an accepted fact that increased errors lead to increased costs.

There are many calculations for the cost of a mis-pick. The elements involved in an incorrect pick include:

- cost of recovering the item;
- labour cost of in-handling and checking the item on its return;
- cost of picking the replacement item;
- cost of re-packing;
- cost of re-delivery;
- administration costs of handling credit claims, etc;
- cash flow with reference to non-payment of invoice;
- potential loss of sale for the product incorrectly despatched;
- cost of re-training staff; and
- possible stock write-off if the returned product is outside an acceptable shelf life or has been damaged in transit.

In addition, if the error is an under-pick then it could result in a lost sale and the associated margin. If it's an over-pick and is reported, there is the cost of transport to collect the item and labour costs as above or potentially a loss of margin in persuading the customer to keep the item. If not reported, the cost becomes the loss of the product and margin.

TABLE 6.2 Pick system advantages and disadvantages

	Applications and pick rate	Benefits	Drawbacks
Paper picking	• Most operations • Where there is very little systems support • Low-cost areas • < 100 lines per hour	• Low cost • Single stage picking operation although two stage update operation • Flexible • Quick implementation • Ability to use in other areas of the warehouse such as receiving • Ability to isolate urgent orders • Picker able to decide pick path • Low maintenance • Suitable as part of a contingency plan	• Low pick rate • Not hands free • Low accuracy • Duplicated tasks • Not real time • Training can take some time • Requires manual update of system from written instructions • Requires return to desk for further instructions
Pick by label	• Most operations • Where there s very little systems support • Low-cost areas • < 100 lines per hour	• Low cost • Reasonably accurate • Single stage picking operation although two stage update operation • Flexible • Quick implementation • Low maintenance	• Low pick rate • Not hands free • Duplicated tasks • Need to print labels • Not real time • Training can take some time • Label information may be difficult to read • Can damage product • Requires return to desk for further instructions

TABLE 6.2 *Continued*

	Applications and pick rate	Benefits	Drawbacks
Barcode scanning with gun	• Most operations • < 100 lines per hour	• Improved accuracy • Paperless • Flexible • Real time stock update** • Ability to deal with multi-sku locations	• Low/medium pick rate • Not hands free • Can take longer than paper picking • Cost of hardware • Requires barcode on product • Issues with international standards • Requires system interface • Requires maintenance
Wearable scanners	• Most operations • < 150 lines per hour	• Paperless • Flexible • Improved accuracy • Improved productivity • Hands free • Less strain on operators • Damage reduction • Real time stock update • Ability to deal with multi-sku locations	• Cost of hardware • Requires barcodes on product • Issues with international standards • Requires system interface • Requires maintenance

TABLE 6.2 *Continued*

	Applications and pick rate	Benefits	Drawbacks
Voice picking	• Most operations • Ideal for temperature-controlled areas • Heavy, awkward items • 100–250 lines per hour	• Paperless • Flexible • Fewer processes • Improved accuracy* • Improved productivity • Quick training • Hands free/eyes free • Improved safety • Less strain on operators • Damage reduction • Real time stock update	• Cost of hardware • Difficult in noisy environments • Requires system interface • Requires maintenance • Problem with multi-sku location • Serial number capture is an issue • Unsure of long term health issues
Voice picking plus finger scanning	• Most operations • Ideal for temperature-controlled areas • 125–250 lines per hour	• Paperless • High accuracy • Good productivity • Hands free • Less strain on operators • Damage reduction • Real time stock update • Ability to deal with multi-sku location	• Cost of hardware and software • Requires barcode • Requires system interface • Requires international standards • Unsure of long term health issues

TABLE 6.2 Continued

	Applications and pick rate	Benefits	Drawbacks
Pick to light	• Low/medium no. skus high volumes per individual item • mail order/e-commerce • (approx. 250–450 lines per hour)	• High accuracy* • High productivity • High pick rate • Easy to train staff • Staff can choose pick sequence • Real time stock update • Hands free • Improved safety • Damage reduction • Simultaneous or sequential picking • Can be used for goods-to-person and person-to-goods picking (zone)	• Cost of hardware • Requires system interface • System failure • Cost of maintenance • Low flexibility • Long implementation time • Limited in terms of product types • Problem with multi-sku locations • Difficulty with batched or clustered orders
Put to light	• Retail store operations • Cluster picking	• High accuracy • High productivity • Damage reduction • High pick rate • Easy to train • Real time stock update • Can be used for goods-to-person and person-to-goods picking (zone)	• Cost of hardware • System failure • Limited in terms of product types • Cost of maintenance • Two stage operation
RFID	• High value goods • Items requiring accurate traceability • 200–300 lines per hour	• Very high accuracy • Real time stock update	• Cost of hardware • Read distances very short • Requires international standards • Requires system interface • Cost of maintenance

* High accuracy is dependent on accurate put-away. Can be supplemented by reading out last four digits of barcode.

TABLE 6.3 Cost and accuracy comparison of the various pick technologies (Wulfratt (2013))

Equipment type	Accuracy	Approximate Cost
Radio frequency hand held terminal	99.3–99.5%	$108,000
Radio frequency visual hand held unit	99.4–99.6%	$120,000
Pick to light	99.5%–99.7%	$300,000–$425,000
Voice technology	99.7–99.97%	$188,000–$280,000

If this happens too often then it is the likely loss of a customer.

Estimations of the cost of mis-picks range from £25 to £40 with £25 being seen as a significant underestimation. This will, of course, depend on the type of product and market sector.

Deciding on type of picking system and equipment

This is quite a dilemma for warehouse managers today as they grapple with labour shortages and pressure to reduce costs yet increase accuracy, productivity and service levels.

The following factors must be taken into account before you make your final decision:

The return on investment and payback periods for major capital investments will greatly influence the decision as to whether or not to choose automation over more manual processes. A three- to five-year payback or better is considered a reasonable period when investing in warehouse operations.

Ergonomic and green issues are also playing their part in decision making within this arena. A greater concern over energy usage and potential taxation on environmentally unfriendly equipment is a factor that needs to be taken into account.

The long-term strategy of the company will have a bearing on the decision to invest in new equipment. Any potential relocation of the business, changes in product profile or distribution channel suggests that any investment in hard automation needs to be carefully considered. The dismantling and re-installation cost of this equipment is likely to be prohibitive.

High volume due to seasonal peaks such as the pre-Christmas period is not a signal to fully automate the processes. iForce, a UK-based fulfilment centre, has decided against large-scale investment in automation. In a recent article, ex-CEO Mark Hewitt said that peak issues may negate the use of technologies such as hand-held data terminals because it would mean a large number of units sitting redundant for the majority of the year.

The availability of labour is also a major factor in determining the level of automation. The availability of a large and stable workforce of skilled and non-skilled operators at reasonable wages enables you to be more flexible, saves on investment and improves cash flow significantly.

Flexibility and automation tend not to go hand in hand and therefore a thorough review of your pick operations and a discussion regarding future operations are paramount.

Computer simulations can assist in this review. Different types of pick operation can be evaluated and both soft and hard automation can be compared quickly and without disrupting the existing operation.

Simulating different types of pick operation enables you to determine which one is best suited to the operation. It is cost effective and provides instant results.

By comparing picking solutions, such as pick to light and voice picking, for example, the simulation software is able to determine performance indicators such as operator pick rates and overall order throughput and, based on the results, suggest the most cost-effective method. Each of the scenarios is undertaken in the risk-free environment of a computer screen.

Suppliers include Class, Logistics Simulation Ltd and many of the mechanical handling and equipment suppliers.

Finally it is not always a case of having one method per warehouse. Most companies will use a combination of pick technologies to further increase accuracy and productivity. A typical example is the use of voice technology together with finger scanning. This combines hands free picking with accurate data collection.

Summary and conclusion

You should not under any circumstances automate a bad or broken process. Always ensure that your warehouse operation is working as efficiently as it can without the use of technology. It is only when you are at this stage that you should contemplate using technology to further enhance the operation. Processes need to be as streamlined as possible and any unnecessary steps eliminated.

Continuing to do what you've always done but more quickly and with less paper is not going to improve your overall performance.

There are a plethora of suppliers in this market and all are capable of assisting you in making the right decision for your company. They want a sale but they also want a satisfied customer – take advantage of their expertise.

Finally, staff resistance to change is a potential barrier to the successful implementation of any new system and therefore all parties need to be on board before major decisions are taken.

Warehouse processes from replenishment to despatch and beyond

07

Introduction

In this chapter we examine the remaining processes within the warehouse. These include replenishment, value-adding services and despatch, together with the peripheral but essential tasks of stock counting and housekeeping.

We also look at security measures that can be taken within the warehouse.

Replenishment

In order to ensure a smooth and efficient picking process we need to ensure that the right products and quantities are in the correct pick location. This is replenishment.

As in the case of replenishing overall inventory to ensure customer satisfaction, the warehouse also has to replenish its pick faces regularly to ensure picker satisfaction. An empty picking slot, just like an empty shelf location in store can mean a lost sale. The result of a poor replenishment process is order shortages, increased picking times and therefore increased cost per pick and an overall reduction in service level.

Real-time WMSs will recognize the need to replenish pick locations through real-time data transfer. These systems are also able to identify the total actual order quantities and therefore replenish before the next wave of orders arrive on the warehouse floor.

Other systems will rely on a trigger that denotes when the stock level within a pick face falls to a certain level. This will rely heavily on timing as orders that have generated pick lists may not actually have been picked and therefore replenishment has been triggered early. Late replenishment can result where staff have picked out of sequence, for example, and emptied the pick bays before the replenishment team have had an opportunity to top up the location.

Timing is crucial. An early instruction to replenish can cause as many problems as late replenishment, with potentially overfull pick faces and issues with FIFO.

If product can be moved directly to the pick face from the inbound section this cuts out a number of processes. This will require a certain amount of pre-planning to ensure that pick faces are not overfilled. Pallets can be de-layered to correspond with expected pick quantities.

In the absence of a warehouse management system the warehouse manager will need to first ensure that the pick faces are designed to take the optimum quantity of product based on predicted sales per day or per shift and cubic volume, and staff need to be trained to identify replenishment requirements and inform either the supervisor or the forklift truck driver, depending on how the process has been set up.

One other point to note here is that although real time dictates that replenishment and picking can occur simultaneously, there are issues of worker safety if forklift trucks and pedestrian pickers are working together in the same aisle.

This can be alleviated by incorporating multiple picking locations for the same SKU, the utilization of flow racking where product is replenished from a separate aisle and by carrying out the two activities at different times of the day if feasible. For example, receiving and replenishment can take place in the morning whilst picking takes place in the afternoon.

Alternatively, replenishment can take place during breaks or after picking has been completed for the day. This mirrors what happens at retail stores where shelf replenishment takes place when stores are closed overnight. Bendi's introduction of their combined articulated truck and picker will also go some way to alleviate the problem of empty pick faces whilst picking.

Value-adding services

Many warehouses have introduced areas where value-adding services can be carried out. These are common in both dedicated and shared-user or public warehouses where third-party logistics companies are providing an all-encompassing service to their customers.

These value-adding services include the following:

- (re)labelling;
- pricing;
- tagging and kimballing;
- (re)packing;
- bundling, as in 'buy one, get one free' (BOGOF) offers;
- reconfiguration;
- sub-assembly;
- repair and refurbishment.

Undertaking shop-floor-ready labelling, tagging, bundling and pricing in the warehouse removes the task from the retail assistants who can spend more of their time selling.

More sophisticated services include some form of production as in the case of postponement where items are added once the customer's order is known. This can include the inclusion of graphics cards and the loading of software in the case of personal computers and laptops. It can also include the fitment or inclusion of a particular part for a specific market. The UK electrical plug is a typical example as it differs from the rest of Europe.

Postponement can be described as a delay in the completion of an item until an actual order is received from a customer. Postponement not only saves time but reduces inventory holding by reducing the total number of SKUs held in stock.

Value-adding services can also include returns processing and a repair service. This area is covered in more detail at the end of this chapter.

Sufficient space needs to be made available for these tasks, with access to power and being close to the despatch area, thus reducing any unnecessary movement. An ideal location, if the height of the warehouse allows it, is above the despatch bays on a mezzanine floor.

Indirect activities

There are many support activities that occur in warehouses and are crucial to the efficient operation of the warehouse. These are, in the main, undertaken by supervisory staff, specialist teams and the housekeeping team. These activities include:

- ensuring optimum staffing levels and providing a pool of suitably trained staff for peak periods;

- managing the allocation of labour for value-adding services;
- ensuring optimum space utilization;
- monitoring work flow and congestion;
- provision, allocation and maintenance of equipment;
- identification and replenishment of fast-moving items;
- identification of non-moving stock;
- stock integrity and dealing promptly with non-conforming, lost or found stock;
- managing cycle counts and organizing full stock checks;
- security of high-value or hazardous stock; and
- ensuring the cleanliness of the warehouse and the safety of both staff and visitors.

The above tasks can be separated into three distinct sections:

- the management of labour, space and equipment;
- the control of stock; and
- the security and safety of stock and people.

Stock management

Inventory or stock management and warehouse management tend to be two very distinct roles.

Warehouse managers are in a position to advise their inventory colleagues on levels of safety stock and the specific movements and characteristics of particular stock items. However, they tend to stop short of determining stock levels.

This function is a major part of a company's operation and the theories and practices are covered in many books on the subject of inventory management.

Although the majority of warehouse managers are not involved directly in the choice, purchase and replenishment of stock, they can play a role in the identification of fast-, medium-, slow-, non-moving and obsolete stock.

This can be done using one of the mainstays of a warehouse manager's armoury – an ABC classification. The information can normally be obtained from the WMS and as mentioned in Chapter 4 a simple spreadsheet can categorize stock items by volume and frequency of sales.

A warehouse manager can extend the normal classification to include non-moving and obsolete stock together with identifying stock that may not require storage in the warehouse but can be despatched direct from the supplier to the end customer where the lead-time is in line with the customer's requirement.

The classification might look something like that shown in Table 7.1.

TABLE 7.1   Stock classification

Classification	Description	% of stock items
A	Fast-moving stock	20%
B	Medium-moving items	35%
C1	Slow-moving items	
C2	Very slow-moving but required for cover	45%
O	Obsolete or non-moving stock	
S	Special or one-off purchases	
X	Non-stock or non-standard items	

The percentages will vary significantly by company and by market sector. Maintenance stores are likely to have a high proportion of their stock in the C to X categories.

The goal is to identify the items in the C to X categories and act accordingly. Obsolete or non-moving stock needs to be analysed and one of the following tasks undertaken:

- Return to seller if the contract allows.
- Sell to staff at a discount.
- Sell the item at a highly discounted rate either through normal channels or via companies who specialize in selling overstocks and obsolete items.
- Assess whether it is cost effective to break the item down into its constituent parts.
- Donate to charities.
- Dispose of the product as cheaply as possible. This may incur charges but it will release space to store other faster-moving product in its place.

A quick and easy way of ascertaining whether there is an excess of slow-moving stock in the warehouse is to calculate the stock turn:

Stock turn = cost of goods sold ÷ average cost of goods stored

or:

Annual throughput in units ÷ average number of units held in stock

For example, an annual throughput of 1,200,000 units with an average stock-holding of 100,000 units gives a stock turn of 12. That is, the stock turns over once per month.

A low turn in most operations suggests that stock sits in a warehouse for far too long, implying that the safety stock level has been set too high.

Typical examples of stock turn within companies are as follows:

150 +: world class using just-in-time techniques;

120 +: chilled foods;

18 +: retail;

10–30: European manufacturing;

<3: maintenance stores.

The higher the figure, the better the company is performing in terms of inventory management. Maintenance stores will always have low stock turns through having to hold stock in case of breakdown.

Stock or inventory counting

All warehouses are obligated to undertake some form of stock count. It depends on the law of the country and accounting requirements as to how frequent and comprehensive the count is.

We have seen over recent years a move towards cycle counting or perpetual inventory counts as a replacement for an all-encompassing annual count of stock in the warehouse.

A full stock count usually necessitates the closure of the warehouse for a period of time when all inbound and outbound movements are suspended. A significant drawback of a single annual count is the difficulty in reconciling the discrepancy as it could have occurred over 11 months ago.

The count is normally carried out at the company's year-end. Some companies will carry out quarterly or possibly half-yearly checks depending on the stipulations laid down by the auditors.

More recently, providing the company can prove that its cycle counting is accurate, auditors have agreed in some cases that if each stock line is counted and audited at least once per annum that will be sufficient for their needs.

Providing the cycle counts are considered to be accurate, the year-end stock figures will be taken from the WMS.

Cycle counting or perpetual inventory counts

When undertaking cycle counts it is prudent to use an ABC analysis to ensure that your fast-moving and high-value items are counted more frequently than your slow-moving, inexpensive items.

Mis-picks are more likely with fast-moving goods, and high-value items are prone to shrinkage.

It is suggested therefore that fast-moving and high-value items are counted monthly, medium sellers are counted quarterly and slow-moving items either once or twice a year. The following percentages can be used to ensure a comprehensive count:

- 8 per cent of A items counted weekly (ensures each SKU is counted approximately once per quarter);
- 4 per cent of B items counted weekly (counted twice per annum); and
- 2 per cent of C items counted weekly (counted at least once per annum).

The accuracy of the counts will also determine the frequency. A high error rate should result in more frequent counts until the accuracy improves. Each discrepancy needs to be investigated and procedures put in place to ensure that there is no repeat of the problem.

Increasing the frequency to daily ensures a more accurate count; however, this will depend on the number of product lines, available resource and the cost of that resource.

The trade-off here is the cost of the error against the cost of discovering it in the first place.

As mentioned previously, a number of auditors will be happy (or as happy as they can be) if stock in the warehouse is counted at least once during the year.

The count itself

All stock counts require organizing. You need to know who will undertake the stock count, what you are planning to count, when you plan to undertake the stock count, what tools and equipment you need and the timescale allotted. For example, if you are counting at height you will need to ensure the safety of the warehouse staff. If you are using forklift trucks a suitable safety cage needs to be provided. Under certain health and safety legislation and company rules the use of cages on forklift trucks are deemed unacceptable and therefore specialist equipment is required such as elevated work platforms (cherry pickers).

Prior to the start of the count ensure that all items have been put away in their correct location and try to despatch as many items as possible prior to the stock take. Secondly, ensure that any obsolete units are disposed of before the start of the count. There is no point in counting stock that shouldn't be in the warehouse.

Some companies will affix a different coloured label on pallets during each year's count. One way of identifying non-moving or slow-moving stock is to look for the labels from the earliest stock count. In the past we have identified stock items that have gone through a significant number of counts and the pallets or cartons have never moved.

It is normal to have a counter and a checker for each section if you are using a paper-based system. If you are scanning locations and products, one person per section should be sufficient. An auditor is likely to be present during a full count to make random checks of locations to verify the count is accurate.

In order to complete a full stock count in the shortest possible time to minimize disruption to sales, companies will inevitably use staff who are unfamiliar with the products. As these counts normally take place at weekends or over the Christmas and New Year vacations, their motivation to do a thorough job might also be suspect.

Where there are a significant number of locations and a number of open cartons and individual items to be counted, it is likely that additional staff will need to be employed from agencies to assist in the count to ensure it is completed in time. However, completion on time is rarely the case as the number of discrepancies can take days to resolve. As a result, operations resume so as not to let customers down but this tends to compound the problems. This is why a number of companies are turning to cycle counts as opposed to full-blown stock counts.

Outside agencies who are experienced in stock counts can be employed as an alternative but can be expensive and the issue of product familiarity is also a factor.

Any discrepancies between the system figures and the count figures should be checked immediately by a supervisor and this continues until you arrive at two matching figures, be they the last two counts or the count and the system figures.

The likelihood of finding the reasons for a discrepancy are low as a year's transactions have passed through the warehouse since the last count. The root cause of discrepancy is seldom discovered and as a result cannot be eliminated.

With a paper system it is usual to provide staff with details of locations and product codes but with the quantities removed. Quantities are written on the sheets together with any changes to the product codes and other comments such as damages are recorded.

This can lead to further inaccuracies as the administration staff try to decipher each person's writing whilst typing the results into a spreadsheet or database.

This system of counting is fraught with problems and if agreed by auditors a perpetual inventory counting system should be introduced to replace the single annual count.

In terms of performance measures companies need to record the number of errors found, not the difference in monetary value as this can hide a number of problems. A difference of a few hundred dollars may seem acceptable; however, there could be hundreds of errors within the system such as the following:

- products in incorrect locations;
- too many items of one product; and
- too few items of another product.

These may balance out but they need to be logged, measured and corrected before operations recommence.

Security

Security of product within the warehouse is paramount. The warehouse manager is responsible for the integrity of all the products under his or her care, whether they are owned or stored on behalf of other companies as a third-party contractor.

This can be achieved through good housekeeping, the use of security cages and carousels for storage, and through vigilance by staff.

Poor security costs companies in lost inventory, higher insurance premiums and personnel turnover.

Loading docks and platforms tend to be the most vulnerable areas – they're very easy places for a thief to remove stolen property, often in partnership with an outsider, a delivery driver for example. Security systems tend to be designed to protect your facility from people breaking in – but many thefts are perpetrated from within.

Closed-circuit television at strategic points throughout the warehouse is a significant deterrent; however, unannounced inspections and walkabouts are also effective and much cheaper.

With regard to the loading bays, one common-sense recommendation is that you separate them from employee parking areas, making it much more difficult to remove items from the warehouse. Searches on entry and exit, whether instigated by staff or by a random system of lights, is also very effective.

Not only is product security important but also the protection of data. WMSs hold a large amount of sensitive data that needs to be protected. Internally this can be done through the use of password protection for different access levels and firewalls for external protection. The data needs to be backed up daily and the backup files stored offsite.

Protecting data from being stolen or copied is also paramount. Equipment such as servers, computers and laptops need to be protected. These items need to be locked with key or code access, and personal computers need to be password protected and those passwords changed regularly.

The core attributes of security within a warehouse are as follows:

- appropriate recording of inbound and outbound products;
- authorizations for all despatches;
- accurate audit trails;
- regular stock checks;
- the use of appropriate storage equipment; and
- vigilance.

Returns processing

Returns processing, or reverse logistics as it has become known, involves the handling of product returns, transit packaging and surplus items. The processes associated with this operation include repair, reuse, refurbishment, recycling and disposal. See Figure 7.1.

The processing of returns has gained increasing importance in the warehouse over the past few years. There is now an increasing awareness of the economic value of reusing products and the effect on cash flow of perfectly serviceable items that can be repackaged and made available for sale. There is also the possibility of fines if products and packaging are not disposed of in an environmentally friendly way.

Doing nothing about returns costs money. They take up space, are difficult to count during stock takes, difficult to value and, more importantly, could be back on sale rather than taking up much-needed space within the warehouse. The alternative is ordering further stock with all its inherent costs.

There has also been a greater environmental awareness backed up by legislation such as the Waste Electrical and Electronic Equipment Directive (WEEE), hazardous waste disposal legislation and more stringent waste packaging directives.

The Waste Electrical and Electronic Equipment Directive came into force in January 2007 in the EU. Its aim is to both reduce the amount of electrical and electronic equipment being produced and to encourage everyone to reuse, recycle and recover.

The WEEE Directive also aims to improve the environmental performance of businesses that manufacture, supply, use, recycle and recover electrical and electronic equipment.

The increase in e-retailing has also seen a significant increase in the level of returns into the warehouse. Catalogue retailing has always had significant amounts of returns, especially in terms of textiles and clothing. These retailers have, in the past, set up returns-processing areas to not only receive the items but also clean them, iron them and pack them for resale.

Other such returns include products despatched on a sale-or-return basis and those where customers are given the option of a 14-day returns policy. These items are likely to be good stock and can be returned to stock almost immediately.

Other groups of returns include reusable packaging such as barrels, kegs, bins, cages, trays, totes and pallets.

Product recalls are also a significant area, needing to be handled carefully. These products need to be quarantined on return so that the company can

FIGURE 7.1 The returns cycle (courtesy of University of Huddersfield)

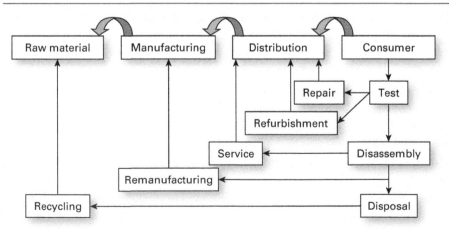

ensure, firstly, that all items have been received and are no longer a potential danger to the public – which is normally one of the main reasons for recall – and secondly, that they are not mixed with good product and sent out in error.

Recently introduced legislation, the cost of landfill both in money and environmental terms and the realization that returns can be an expensive area to neglect have triggered the growth of reverse logistics programmes and the establishment of warehouses built specifically to handle the returns process.

This type of warehouse needs to be set up very differently from a stock-holding facility. Space needs to be set aside for sortation, inspection, repair, refurbishment and disposal. The idea behind returns processing is to either return stock into the supply chain as quickly as possible in whatever format, be it finished goods or spares, or dispose of it efficiently.

Returned items shouldn't remain in the facility for too long.

Should you decide to operate the returns function within an existing warehouse operation then you are likely to set up a warehouse within a warehouse. This needs to be carefully planned to avoid cross contamination – for example, when dealing with damaged or defective items, chemicals and hazardous products.

Prior to making any decision regarding a reverse logistics operation you need to calculate the following:

- percentage and value of goods returned directly to stock and to vendor;
- percentage of goods refurbished and returned to stock;
- percentage of goods dismantled and used for spares;
- percentage of goods destroyed or given away to charity, etc;
- percentage of goods returned due to manufacturing defects; and
- percentage of goods returned due to sales department, warehouse or consumer error.

With regard to the last two points above you need to look at the causes in more detail before putting processes in place. For example, with consumer error it could be that the operating instructions are not clear enough.

In order to justify a returns processing operation the following needs to be calculated:

Total cost of returns processing + cash flow impact versus purchasing/ manufacturing new + cost of disposal and cash flow impact

A final decision to make with regard to reverse logistics is whether to operate the function in-house or subcontract to a third-party specialist. This decision very much depends on the following factors:

- level of returns;
- available space;
- available expertise;
- cost;
- control and efficacy;
- capacity and capability of third parties; and
- lead time from return to available to ship.

You need to determine how many hours per week you are likely to expend on returns processing and how much space you require. You need to calculate the amount of space required at peak, which is more than likely the period after Christmas.

With regard to disposal, companies will need to produce the relevant certification to prove that products and packaging, if not recyclable, have been disposed of properly.

Reverse logistics has gained momentum recently and has gone from being driven by environmental concern to becoming a corporate cost-reduction programme.

According to Stock/WERC (2004) 'the keys to any successful product returns program are having the right combination of people, policies, procedures and priorities'.

They go on to say that best practice in terms of returns management requires the following:

- decision-making process before product is physically returned;
- the use of returns authorization notes;
- ongoing measurement of product return cycle time;
- training of employees in returns handling;
- cross training of staff in warehouse operations and reverse logistics;
- use of software to monitor and evaluate product returns;
- time slots allocated for receipt of returns;
- two-stage approach for returns handling – initial processing to identify quick wins followed by in-depth examination;
- use of detailed product return process maps;
- availability of packaging material to re-box product;
- undertake regular audits; and
- achievement of higher recovery rates (> 80%).

Despatch

The order cycle time or lead time from order receipt to despatch is continually shortening and there is increased pressure on the warehouse manager to coordinate all activities to ensure that product is despatched on time and complete.

Packing – pieces/items/eaches

Once product has been picked there is the question of how it is packaged for despatch. As previously discussed, with individual order picks the operator may well package the product immediately, attach shipping labels and where required insert despatch documentation and invoices.

This reduces the number of touch points in the warehouse but does take the operator away from the prime task of picking.

Where there is the possibility of damage in transit, material can be added to the carton such as polystyrene and foam pellets, shredded paper, corrugated paper, air-filled bags, etc. This again increases time at despatch and puts the onus on the customer to dispose of the excess packaging on receipt. Where possible this material needs to be recyclable. The use of carton erectors which cut the cardboard to fit the contents is one way of overcoming this problem. The trade-off here is the cost of the machine versus the labour and material cost of doing it manually and the cost to the customer.

If orders are required to be checked on despatch this is an ideal time to add the paperwork and affix labels. In terms of checking, items can be removed from the pick container, checked against the order and returned to the original carton or if the order was picked into a tote it can be transferred to a shipping carton. Other methods of checking include weighing the carton and comparing this weight with a system generated weight. This is preferable, providing the information held in the system is 100 per cent accurate. This also reduces the labour required in this area and assists with load planning.

The need to check every order before it leaves the warehouse may well be a requirement for very high value products and products such as pharmaceuticals but I have to question the need to check every despatch order when it comes to other products.

Companies need to measure the accuracy performance of their pickers and base the amount of checking on this figure. A picking team that is constantly achieving > 99.9 per cent accuracy requires minimum checking. Random checks will suffice. Where there is a drop in accuracy the amount of checking can be increased for a time but so should the training of the operators until the accuracy is restored.

There is a trade-off here between the cost of the operators who are checking every order and the overall cost of mis-picks. There is no point in spending £20,000 ($31,400) on a checker per annum to save £3,000 ($4,710).

The introduction of automation into this area of the warehouse enables companies to use equipment to automatically insert paperwork into a shipping container, attach a lid and label it correctly.

Packing – cartons

Full carton despatch is somewhat easier to manage. Individual cartons may require the attachment of a shipping label which may be generated from the WMS or from a carrier system such as those operated by UPS, Fed Ex, USPS and the Royal Mail. In terms of multiple carton dispatch, firstly there is a need to establish whether it is more cost effective to despatch via a parcel network or a pallet distribution or LTL carrier.

This will decide the means of shipment – loose cartons or a palletized load.

If palletized, the decision here is how to stabilize the cartons on a pallet for despatch. Many companies will use stretchwrap to do this. Some companies will stretchwrap manually whilst others utilize an automatic stretchwrap machine. The trade-off here is the cost of the machine versus the cost of labour and the reduction in the use of stretchwrap material.

Velcro has introduced pallet straps to secure cargo. These are more environmentally friendly than stretchwrap but there is the added complication of tracking and returning the straps for reuse.

The use of returnable packaging is also growing under environmental pressure. The use of plastic totes and pallets, slipsheets and collapsible cages is growing; however, there is a trade-off here between the initial cost of these items and the cost of returning them to the shipper versus the cost in money and environmental terms of cardboard packaging and one-way pallets.

Loading

The efficient loading of containers and trailers is crucial in today's environment of rising fuel prices. Unused space is inefficient and can cost a company a great deal of money.

Efficient loading of vehicles and containers begins with the initial packaging of the products.

Companies need to ensure that the outer packaging of their products is designed to fit perfectly onto the pallets used for both transportation and storage. The ideal is to ensure no overhang whatsoever with a reduction in unused space. It also needs to be robust enough to travel.

Pallet loads need to be configured to ensure that product damage is minimized, cubic capacity is fully utilized, load stability is ensured and the configuration is acceptable to the receiving location.

Fortunately there is software available to not only assist with pallet configuration but also container and trailer loading. The software can optimize packing within a container and trailer, on a pallet and even within an individual carton.

This sophisticated software optimization not only takes into account the cube of the products but also their load bearing strength and location within the container.

The latter ensures ease of off-loading at the receiver with all the cartons from the same product line being located together. The software also ensures that lighter items are packed on top of the heavier items. Examples include Cubemaster and CubeDesigner.

Shipping

Many operations are now taking orders late into the evening and despatching that same night for next-day delivery. Next, a retailer in the United Kingdom, has a cut-off time for internet orders of 10 pm for next-day delivery.

Work plans are now centred around the latest despatch time for orders, and managers work backwards from this ensuring that all processes are completed and both labour and equipment are made available at the right time to meet these deadlines.

The despatch process has to be managed precisely and be aligned with most other activities within the warehouse. If, for example, receiving and despatch share the same doors, a daily schedule needs to be drawn up to ensure that labour and equipment are utilized as efficiently as possible, the work content is matched to the number of doors available and congestion is avoided in the dock area.

In many operations receiving tends to take place in the morning whilst picking and despatch occur during the afternoon and evening as order cut-off times continue to be stretched later into the evening.

Depending on the method of picking and the company's procedures regarding checking product before it leaves the building, sufficient space needs to be available at the loading bays to stage the loads and allow for whichever checking method is applied – be it full-carton checks or random checks.

If coordinated correctly, the picked orders should arrive at the loading bay in the sequence in which they will be delivered. That is, the last delivery on the vehicle will be the first order to be loaded.

Collecting vehicles should be assigned a bay closest to where the orders have been accumulated. This requires close coordination between the gatehouse and the despatch supervisor.

Many companies have grids marked out on the warehouse floor at the despatch area to replicate the floor area of the largest vehicle. For example, a UK warehouse handling industrial pallets solely will currently have a grid equivalent to 26 pallets. The introduction of longer vehicles in the future with greater cubic capacity will necessitate an increase in the amount of floor space set aside for marshalling outbound orders. Warehouses handling euro pallets will extend this to 36 pallets. Where vehicles are delivering multiple orders, a system needs to be in place to segregate these orders and make them easily identifiable to the loading team. This can be a simple handwritten pallet label or a barcode label.

Companies with sufficient yard space and available trailers can load product directly into them and park them up, awaiting collection.

As discussed in the section on inbound, companies need to manage the arrival and departure of trucks for outbound goods. A yard management system (YMS) can improve inbound and outbound scheduling, increase visibility of trucks and trailers, manage cross-docking, reduce congestion and delays and ensure the safety and security of both vehicles and operators.

There are both standalone and modular versions of yard management systems.

Where full pallet loads are despatched it may be that pallets are pulled directly from the bulk or racked area and immediately loaded onto the vehicle. This minimizes the amount of double handling and requires precise coordination.

Once the despatch team is ready, vehicles can be called forward onto the despatch bay. This can be done either by the driver of the load or a shunt driver who is loading trailers in readiness for collection by drivers returning from earlier deliveries.

As with the receiving process, the driver's paperwork needs to be checked to ensure that he is collecting the correct load. Loading a vehicle with goods bound for Alaska on a truck scheduled to deliver in Florida will be a very costly mistake.

The trailer should also be checked to ensure that it is fit for purpose, ie clean and watertight, doesn't have any odours which could contaminate the product, is at the correct temperature if loading refrigerated product, and finally that the floor is damage free.

Where products are loose loaded onto a container or trailer, the use of telescopic boom conveyors will assist the loading process significantly.

A tyre manufacturer recognized a number of advantages after introducing three telescopic booms into the operation. These conveyors can also be moved sideways to cover a number of dock doors. The advantages are as follows:

- safer working conditions;
- cleaner working area with better visibility;
- separation of forklifts and operators;
- improved ergonomics: no more rolling of the tyres, no more lifting of the tyres;
- improved quality of the tyres;
- fewer claims, having introduced a counting and video system on the conveyor; and
- improved productivity: 42 per cent increase on tyre loading, 32 per cent increase on tyre unloading.

ROI and payback can be significant in terms of labour saving, increased accuracy and less damage. A fully installed static conveyor will cost in the region of £34,000 in the United Kingdom.

Other companies will use automatic pallet loaders as discussed on page 68, whilst the majority of companies will use hand pallet jacks or powered pallet trucks if loading from a despatch bay. Counterbalance or articulated forklift trucks are normally used if loading outside the warehouse.

The increasing use of double-deck trailers presents its own challenge to warehouse operations, with some loading bays having to be adapted to accommodate the variable heights.

Where loading bays cannot be adapted there are products such as Transdek's double-deck lifts that can be retro-fitted. The product operates with a hinged lift platform that doubles as a dock leveller in order to provide a direct run-through for product from the warehouse to both single deckers and the bottom deck of double deck vehicles.

The lift platform also raises up to 3,000 mm to carry product to/from the top deck of double deckers.

Documentation

Finally, despatch documentation and labelling needs to be completed to ensure compliance with customer requirements and government legislation. Different countries will have different requirements and these will also differ if shipments are within country or for export.

Any errors in the export paperwork can result in non-shipment, seizure, fines or delays.

When shipping hazardous material it is essential that products are labelled accurately and have the correct documentation.

Typical despatch paperwork depending on ultimate destination includes the following:

- advanced shipping notice;
- manifest;
- shipping labels;
- Bill of Lading;
- commercial invoice;
- shipper's export declaration;
- export packing list;
- certificate of origin;
- export licence;
- inspection certificate; and
- insurance certificate.

As mentioned above each country will have its own requirements in respect of the documentation needed.

Role of the driver

In situations where companies operate with their own transportation there are no issues with what the driver's role is in the actual loading process. However, when third-party contractors are used there is the age-old dilemma of what to do with the driver whilst the loading process takes place.

Some companies insist on the driver assisting with the loading and checking the contents of the load, whilst other companies have health and safety issues with external staff being on the loading bay. If the latter is the case then the driver has to be accommodated elsewhere, preferably not in his cab. The possibility of the driver moving off the despatch bay whilst the vehicle is still being loaded is just as real.

There is also the question of what the driver should sign for once the vehicle has been loaded. If he has not seen the products loaded onto the vehicle and the vehicle has been sealed prior to leaving the despatch bay, then it is reasonable to suggest that he is at liberty to sign the document and preface it with the word 'unchecked'. A time limit needs to be agreed in terms of how long the collecting company has to report any discrepancies.

If the vehicle is sealed, the seal number needs to be recorded on the delivery paperwork and any other relevant documentation such as hazardous data sheets handed to the driver.

Summary and conclusion

This chapter has examined replenishment, value-adding services, support functions and despatch.

We have already suggested that both receiving and picking are crucial roles; however, within the warehouse, the above operations are no less important.

Well-timed replenishment will ensure an efficient pick operation whilst a timely and accurate despatch ensures that customer lead times are achieved or at times surpassed.

The warehouse's ability to undertake value-adding services enables the manufacturer to postpone certain activities until the order arrives, resulting in fewer stock codes, and it enables retailers to transfer activities from the retail store back to the warehouse, freeing up valuable sales time.

Stock counting and security are fundamental to the integrity of products stored in the warehouse and are crucial to maintaining credibility whether an in-house or outsourced operation.

Warehouse management systems

Trade isn't about goods. Trade is about information. Goods sit in the warehouse until information moves them.

(C J CHERRYH)

Introduction

As we have seen in earlier chapters, the introduction of technology can significantly improve warehouse productivity, increase utilization, reduce costs and increase customer satisfaction.

As customers become more sophisticated, requiring accurate, secure, fast data exchange, and as the competition becomes more intense, companies need to have the information-technology tools to support the business and build reliability, speed, control and flexibility into the warehouse operation. The ability to communicate in real time is crucial in today's fast-moving technological world.

Paper-based warehouse management systems or even spreadsheets can fulfil a need and manage stock accurately if managed well. However, I still find it incredible that companies can operate a warehouse without a location system, relying on staff knowing where the items are located in the warehouse.

Other warehouses have stock control systems that tell you where the stock is and how much there is of it, but don't provide optimum pick paths or slotting functionality.

If a company is going to compete effectively it needs to introduce a real-time warehouse management system.

The cost of these systems has reduced significantly over the past few years and today companies are able to rent systems on a month-by-month basis using software as a service (SaaS) and cloud computing, in which you can pay as you go, share resources and only use the functionality you require.

Warehouse management systems (WMSs) can be stand alone or can be part of enterprise resource planning (ERP) systems supporting the latest technological advances within the warehouse including automation, RFID and voice recognition.

Although there has been some consolidation within the WMS marketplace, there continues to be a myriad of systems to choose from.

This chapter looks at the process of choosing a WMS and the functionalities that assist companies in improving productivity and reducing costs.

Why does a company need a WMS?

Although companies operating with paper-based systems are able to introduce best practice into the warehouse such as improving warehouse layout and minimizing travel time by having the fastest-selling items closest to despatch, they can improve even further and become more productive by introducing software technology into the warehouse.

Customers are becoming increasingly demanding and the ability to communicate via electronic data interchange, have online visibility and receive instant replies to queries is more of an expectation than a need. A WMS can be part of this solution.

Sales and marketing teams are also desperate for real-time information, whilst finance departments are chasing data constantly.

Before we discuss the advantages of a WMS we need to point out that a stock-control system is not the same as a WMS. We have come across many companies who have purchased an inventory management system in the belief that it will operate the warehouse efficiently. Stock-control systems will manage the inventory at stock location and quantity level, but the majority of these systems will not manage productivity within the warehouse.

In our opinion, in order to be productive, warehouse systems need to be able to work in real time, manage all the processes within the warehouse and have the ability to communicate with other company systems. We will go into more detail as to the minimum requirements of the system later in this chapter.

A WMS can process data quickly and coordinate movements within the warehouse. It can produce reports and handle large volumes of transactions as experienced in e-commerce operations.

The introduction of new technologies into your operation not only improves your competitiveness in a challenging market but can also be instrumental in meeting ever-increasing customer demands.

The potential benefits of having a WMS in place include the following:

- real-time stock visibility and traceability;
- improved productivity;
- accurate stock;
- reduction in mis-picks;
- automatic replenishments;
- reductions in returns;
- accurate reporting;
- improved responsiveness;
- remote data visibility;
- improved customer service; and
- minimized paperwork.

The diagram from Tompkins in Figure 8.1 illustrates how the quality of information can lead to increased sales and cost reduction.

FIGURE 8.1   Advantages of quality information (used with permission of Tompkins Associates)

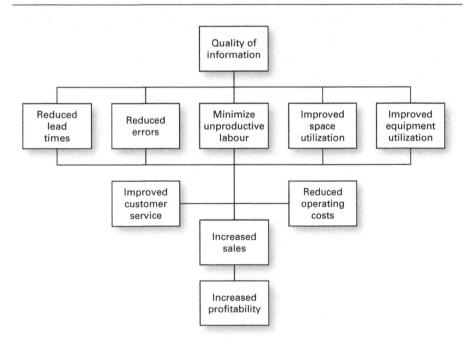

There is an adage that says that any IT system costs twice as much as quoted, takes twice as long to implement and produces half the benefits. In order to avoid this, there are a number of simple steps that need to be followed when choosing a WMS.

Choosing a WMS

When choosing the right WMS for a company you first need to fully understand the needs of the company and the key business requirements, not only today but some time into the future.

You need to understand your company strategy, ensure that your specific needs are met by selecting the solution that best matches your business objectives.

The solution can either be sourced internally by writing your own software or you need to ensure that you choose the right business partner to work with to develop the most effective solution.

A final step will be to calculate the return on investment (ROI) on the purchase and ongoing support of the WMS.

The process

It may be argued that not everyone needs a WMS. In fact, one of the greatest challenges to introducing a WMS is not choosing the right system but convincing the management team that one is required in the first place.

During a project to improve the space utilization and productivity within a client's warehouse we were surprised to learn that the warehouse manager had not been fully involved in discussions regarding the new ERP system that was going to be introduced in the near future.

The vendor was asked whether their system could run the warehouse operation and they replied in the affirmative. Unfortunately the system being introduced could manage the inventory but was not a warehouse management system.

When the new system had been implemented, the finance, sales and marketing teams were very happy with it but the warehouse manager was left to operate a manual system to manage the workflow through the warehouse. As a result, stock visibility improved on the system but productivity didn't change. When we suggested that the warehouse required a WMS to integrate with the ERP system we were told that no further investment would be made in the IT system as the system was able to manage inventory perfectly well.

Selecting the right WMS

To ensure that the system you choose is the right one for your operation, here are some best-practice guidelines courtesy of Business Application Software Developers Association (BASDA) (2009) and Sage Accpac (2005):

- Form a project team.
- Define, record, review and improve current processes. Don't automate redundant or poor processes
- Create a list of key functions required of the new system.
- Incorporate any future growth plans in your specification.
- List the benefits to your company of a WMS.
- Research and approach a select number of vendors and select a small number with experience of providing solutions for your market sector.
- Visit reference sites to look at operational effectiveness and discuss the benefits the WMS system has brought about since implementation.
- Produce a return on investment (ROI) report.

We will now look at each stage in more detail.

Form a project team

Assemble a team of people capable of logical thinking who will decide what your company needs from a WMS and what functionalities it must have and those it will be nice to have. The team should include members from finance, sales, production (if applicable), IT and of course the warehouse.

Appoint a project leader and define each person's role, responsibilities and their level of involvement in terms of time and decision making during this process. Ensure that all participants are able to make available the time and resources to ensure the success of the project.

Define, record, review and improve current processes

The first stage of the design process is to collect and collate as much information as possible about current processes and procedures. Once this is done you need to go through each process to decide whether it is actually required. There is no point in specifying an IT solution for a defunct process.

Do not make the error of automating poor processes. You need to get the processes within the company right before contemplating introducing a WMS. Use a project team and your warehouse staff to identify which processes they find frustrating, redundant and inefficient.

You need to understand which processes are going to be improved by the introduction of technology, by how much and whether it is cost effective.

Understand how the warehouse communicates both internally with other departments and externally with customers, suppliers and transport companies.

Create a list of key functions

Each project team member needs to compile a list of the key functions required of a system and rank them by importance, eg 1, 2 or 3; or essential, greatly desired or nice to have.

Produce an agreed list of the essential requirements from the ideas produced by the individual team members and document them ready to be included in a request for information (RFI).

This list should only have the essential, 'must have' functions. This will enable you to quickly discard systems that do not meet your fundamental requirements.

Incorporate any future growth plans in your specification

Although difficult to forecast, you need to take into account likely future events when specifying a WMS. For example: are you looking to increase the number of SKUs significantly over the next few years; will your future operation require a 'kitting' operation; will you need to manage a group of warehouses; are you contemplating the use of a bonded warehouse, which systems are you likely to need to interface with, what technology are you planning to introduce? These are just some of the questions that need to be answered prior to specifying a new system.

List the benefits to your company of a WMS

The right WMS can maximize the productivity of your labour, increase both space and equipment utilization and increase accuracy. All of these need to be quantified and presented alongside the ROI report.

Approach a select number of vendors; visit reference sites

There are a plethora of WMS vendors in today's marketplace offering ERP systems that incorporate WMS, best-of-breed WMSs, stock-control systems and SaaS systems. Fortunately, there is assistance out there for companies.

These include consultants, comparison websites and, not to be underestimated, the experience of your own staff.

If you are in somewhat of a niche market it is always prudent to look at the systems your competitors are operating. When we took on the warehousing and distribution operation for a publishing house we realized we needed a system that could manage royalties, etc.

Visit reference sites to look at operational effectiveness and discuss the benefits the WMS system has brought about since implementation.

Prior to a full invitation to tender, discuss your requirements with a couple of vendors and ask to visit some of their operational sites. Discussions with existing users will give you further insight into system capabilities and potentially revise your own thinking on systems.

Produce an ROI report

Having undertaken sufficient research, detail your requirements and approach a select number of companies to quote.

Having received the quotes and before making any decisions, involve your finance colleagues in calculating the potential return on investment. Together with an ROI calculation you need to be certain of the following, according to Stephen Cross (2010) from ATMS:

- the potential for a WMS to give you improved stock accuracy – by reducing errors, providing real-time information and enabling perpetual inventory;
- the potential for increased productivity and cost savings – through improved labour and equipment utilization, and better space utilization;
- the need for improved traceability – a WMS can give you two-way traceability, almost as a by-product of being in place; and
- improved customer and client service – through overall improved warehouse control, improved pick and despatch accuracy.

The cost of a WMS can be broken down into the following main components:

- Licence: the software licence needed to run the system. Typically this is charged by user, ie PC user or radio data terminal user, although different models are now being offered, including paying by transaction and/or paying monthly rather than a single outright payment.
- Professional services: the costs for project management, training and go-live support.
- Development costs: software development costs for requirements not catered for in the package, including interfaces to third-party systems.

- Support cost: this is typically an annual cost based on licence costs and often development costs; look at this cost carefully: the scope of service and cost varies significantly from supplier to supplier.

- Hardware and infrastructure costs.

Ask suppliers to indicate which prices are firm and which are variable. Watch out for hidden costs such as travel costs, travel time and project management time.

Summarize all the costs in a spreadsheet, showing the initial cost and then costs for years one to five with accumulated totals. You will find that some systems look attractive initially but when costed over a longer period they may prove a lot more expensive.

What to look for in a system

In order to be effective, a WMS needs to have the following attributes (adapted from Ruriani 2003):

Ability to interface with other systems

The ability to interface with other systems such as accounts packages, ERP and MRP systems and transport management systems, is critical. The system needs to integrate with back-office tasks such as order entry, inventory control, purchase-order modules and invoicing. The system also needs to be able to interface with automation systems, conveyors, MHE and the latest in picking technology such as voice, wearable scanners, RFID and pick- and put-to-light systems. Ensure that these WMS interfaces will not incur excessive costs.

Modular and scalable

Where possible, look for a modular system where you only pay for the functionalities you require and training and implementation can be quicker. Further modules can be added at a later date if required.

Ensure that the WMS can be expanded to accommodate growth and/or acquisitions. Ensure that it is capable of handling e-commerce transactions (if applicable) and can update web page details in real time.

A WMS needs to be able to at least meet your basic current and potential future needs. Buying a system that has functionality way beyond your requirements only leads to increased training costs, time wastage and as a consequence a poor return on your investment.

Ensure that the system can operate with the maximum number of users you are planning on having and can manage multiple sites if required.

Check with other divisions within the company to ensure that the system has the capabilities to match requirements in those areas also, should the management decide to go company-wide with the solution.

Accessible

With the mobility of staff these days it is essential that the system is accessible remotely over the web and that it is secure with access levels being password protected. The ability to retrieve data simply is a must for any system. The ability of the system to produce performance reports, cost-to-serve modelling and standard inventory interrogation are expected functionalities and should be high on the list of priorities.

Ease of operation

Select a WMS that is user friendly. Choose a system that has a point-and-click operating environment and clear, easy-to-read screens. This can lead to enhanced staff productivity and system acceptance. Ensure that the system works in real time, providing instant inventory updates.

Standard system

Ensure the system supports the widely accepted standards currently in use and isn't limited to a proprietary standard that your customers may not use. Check that you receive updates regularly at no additional or at minimal cost.

Meets specific needs

If you are involved in storing Customs and Excise goods, ensure that the system is approved or can be approved by the relevant authorities. Second, ensure that the system can undertake those tasks that are crucial to your business such as tracking lot and serial numbers (if required), managing 'best before' dates, identifying hazardous goods and being able to calculate royalties, for example.

Capable of supporting warehouse best practice

According to BASDA, to achieve best warehouse practice, systems need to be able to optimize movements within the warehouse, eg pallet put-away is coupled with pallet retrieval, known as task interleaving. Other crucial attributes include automated receipt, directed put-away, optimum pick sequences, replenishment tasks, despatch management and warehouse mapping.

Ideally the system will be able to monitor the velocity of items within the warehouse and locate them accordingly (slotting) or alternatively provide the data in a format that can be transferred to programmes that have slotting functionality.

Reporting capabilities

Ensure the system provides comprehensive reporting suites and also reports failures.

Selecting a partner

This is not the type of purchase you would make through an e-auction. As with many large service offerings such as outsourcing, the likely success of the project will ultimately come down to your relationship with the people at the software vendor. As a previous manager of mine told me, 'People buy people', therefore it is very important to meet the vendors, not only the sales staff but also the operations and support staff.

The main aspects to look for in a partner include the following:

- Experience. Look for providers that employ staff with significant operational experience as well as staff with the ability to produce best-in-class WMSs. Not only will the operational staff have had input into the WMS but they will also be able to understand your own requirements better. Choose a vendor who listens effectively and understands your organization fully.

- Longevity. Check how long the company has been in business and what their creditworthiness is like; be assured, they will certainly check yours.

- Choose a vendor who emphasizes the benefits of the software, not just the features. Furthermore, choose a provider that has already installed WMS systems with clients in your industry.

- Ensure that the vendor can supply not only the system but also the installation, training, maintenance and help-desk service.

- Verify that your prospective WMS provider is reinvesting significant capital into research and development, and future product enhancements.

- Choose a vendor you are comfortable working with. Try to find a vendor who is culturally similar to your company, is professional and well respected in the industry. Ask for a large list of customers and visit the customer sites that you decide upon.

- Choose a partner that has reasonable modification rates and is willing to set up a realistic budget based on your needs assessment, prior to formalizing the relationship. Alternatively, look to set up an agreement where your own IT staff are able to introduce certain modifications.

- Resources. Make sure that the WMS provider can fully support you during the implementation phase.

- Select a partner that has an adequately staffed help desk and that is available during your company's hours of operation. Time zones can cause innumerable problems if they are not taken into account at the outset.

- Select a partner that has established partnerships with hardware providers.

Before the final decision

Ask prospective WMS providers for case studies where they have previously interfaced with your organization's specific ERP, transport management or accounting system. Ask to visit sites where this has happened and is currently happening.

Prior to making a final selection, ask the WMS provider to share a detailed implementation plan that includes an installation timeline and resource commitment.

Implementation

The following rules need to be followed prior to implementing the new system:

- Discuss with the business a suitable time to introduce a new system. The quietest sales period is normally a good time; however, this does coincide with staff taking their holidays, so ensure all the key people are available.

- Agree a realistic implementation plan with the vendor and your project team.

- Guarantee the availability of key staff during the implementation phase.
- Propose deadlines you are confident in achieving.
- Have specific milestones in place.
- Appoint super users from amongst your staff.
- Develop a training agenda for all staff and include it in your new staff induction programme.
- Don't look to modify the system until it is in place and working as initially specified.
- Keep reviewing the timeline and act on any slippage.

Some companies will also look to continue running their existing system in parallel until the new system is fully operational, all the functionalities have been user tested and any issues have been addressed.

Software as a service

Companies that have identified a need for a WMS but do not have the capital to spend on a stand-alone system are turning to alternatives.

Software as a service (SaaS) WMS is an internet-based application that is developed, hosted and maintained by a third-party software provider on secure servers. The vendor rents out the system to a number of different clients. Those clients in turn will choose the various modules within the software they require and pay for them as they use them.

The advantages are as follows:

- lower cost of entry;
- reduced start-up costs;
- instant upgrades;
- user-driven innovation; and
- ability to turn on and off as required, eg to run a temporary warehouse operation.

Such a system will be attractive to start-up companies and small and medium size enterprises (SMEs), although it could benefit larger companies who are looking for a temporary solution.

Potential disadvantages include the possibility of poor internet links between the companies and potential worries over data security. Constant upgrades can also potentially have repercussions on your own processes.

As with most things in life, rental or leasing can work out more expensive than outright purchase, therefore calculating whole-life costs and closely examining the advantages and disadvantages are paramount before making these decisions. However, as a short-term fix they can be very advantageous.

Cloud computing

With cloud computing, your WMS vendor hosts the software application and hardware infrastructure for you. You access the WMS via a web browser and gain the functional benefits of a new WMS without the upfront software costs (**www.highjump.com**).

CASE STUDY   LPT

LPT, the Liverpool-based fresh-produce terminal, has partnered with ATMS, its WMS provider, to help to bring the ATMS GlobalTrack service to market.

The ATMS STP WMS is a key part of LPT's operation, helping to optimize the receipting, warehousing and despatching operations. LPT's warehouse is a state-of-the-art, brand new, temperature-controlled facility with 5,000 locations and caters for cross docking as well as added-value services. ATMS's system supports and optimizes all of these processes, including dock, yard and vessel management.

'LPT needed to go one step further to provide a level of service for its customers far ahead of anything in the market place,' states Andy Rickard, operations director of LPT. 'One of the reasons we selected ATMS was because of their strategy of developing their WMS to become the core of a global tracking and supply chain visibility offering – in the form of GlobalTrack; we're very pleased to be one of the first companies to work with them to prove the benefits of GlobalTrack in the real world.'

Stephen Cross, ex-managing director of ATMS plc, says: 'GlobalTrack is a hosted solution that provides improved control and visibility across the supply chain. It is designed to be exceptionally easy to use and exceptionally low cost; for instance, users can pay for system usage on a per transaction, pay as you go basis. It is fully multilingual and is supported by offices in UK, Dubai, Singapore, China and Manila.'

The system helps users improve the control of their import-tracking process. Order and fulfilment requirements can be logged onto the system. The system then allows producers and manufacturers, wherever they are in the world, to log their production and productivity against these orders and call-offs. A facility is then provided for remote labelling of cartons, pallets and unit-load devices. Labelling is carried out to the global GS1 standard, the barcode on each label is unique and identifies the carton, pallet or other item and its contents; the system records quality, traceability and other conformance information. Pack sizes, weights and dimensions can also be recorded. The system can then be used to generate and share packing lists, manifests and advanced shipping information. Information can also be provided to and from customs authorities, freight forwarders and logistics providers.

Pre-labelling and electronic advanced shipment notices help LPT receive stock accurately and swiftly. Any errors are alerted automatically.

The system not only assists the upstream operation but can be used downstream as well, from the point of despatch from LPT, through re-warehousing and cross-docking operations, to proof of delivery. GlobalTrack supports proof of delivery and has a remote warehouse control module that allows warehouses to be controlled with the use of hand-held terminals communicating over mobile phone GPRS networks.

The system is designed for in-house and third-party use – for instance, the system is designed to allow clients of third-party logistics providers to view their own stock and their own supply chain information – and only their own. Information visible across the web includes production information, receipt and despatch information, stock status, quality control status. Documentation can be downloaded remotely. Stock call-offs and other action requests can be entered remotely.

David Hughes, who heads up business development at ATMS, comments: 'We are proud to be a strategic partner of LPT. They are a highly innovative operation with a superb management team, with the dedication and focus to deliver a first-class service from a first-class facility.'

James Woodward, managing director of LPT, comments: 'LPT is in a unique position geographically to reduce customer costs whilst reducing their carbon footprint and now is in a unique position technologically to provide the highest levels of visibility, traceability and control.'

Summary and conclusion

As can be seen from the case study, today's information technology systems are no longer purely involved in stock management. They also include dock, yard and labour management. They are ultra flexible, provide remote access and visibility of stock and tasks and can be operated on a pay as you go basis.

A WMS is essential in today's fast-moving environment. Information is the key and real-time data is invaluable. The introduction of a WMS can improve speed, productivity and accuracy.

The key to a successful purchase and implementation is:

- preparation and allocating sufficient time and resource to the project;
- getting your processes right before introducing the system;
- producing a base level so that the full benefits of the system can be compared;
- getting the buy-in and involvement of senior management and warehouse staff;
- choosing the most appropriate supplier; and
- ensuring that all staff are trained to an acceptable level.

However, to embark on a WMS project you need to be certain that you are going to achieve significant business benefits.

Warehouse efficiency is key to effectively managing a supply chain and achieving best-in-class performance. Technology can be an enabler in this respect.

Warehouse layout

09

> *Giving a man space is like giving a dog a computer:*
> *the chances are he will not use it wisely.*
>
> **(BETTE-JANE RAPHAEL)**

Introduction

Today's highly competitive and constantly changing markets have a significant effect on the design of our warehouses and distribution centres. Continually evolving products and changing order profiles require our warehouses to be a great deal more flexible.

Fortna a company involved in warehouse design argue that there isn't an optimal design solution for each warehouse. The most optimal design in their view is one that fully meets today's operational requirements but has an eye to future growth by being flexible, scalable and relatively inexpensive to adapt. The idea is to design for the future whilst building for today.

A typical example is the introduction of mezzanine floors at a future date, thus fully utilizing the cubic capacity of the building.

The design of a warehouse requires attention to detail and the collection and compilation of large quantities of relevant data.

Whether a company is building a new warehouse, moving into an existing building or looking to re-design their own facility there are a number of fundamental areas that need to be addressed.

In this chapter we will look at the drivers involved in warehouse design, the alternatives available in terms of layout and suggest potential areas for cost savings through relatively simple changes to existing configurations and practices.

We do not intend to show you how to fully design a warehouse as every company will have different requirements. However, we do want to give you an understanding of how to approach design and what we believe does and doesn't work in terms of efficient space utilization. This chapter provides information on the type of storage equipment that can be utilized to improve space utilization.

The Chartered Institute of Logistics and Transport has published on this subject and provides a step-by-step guide to warehouse design (Baker *et al* 2010). Again, as in many other warehouse areas, design is all about trade-offs. Between speed, travel distances, space utilization, handling, access, safety, risk and cost.

There are also many consultants, materials-handling and racking companies who can assist you in designing the most effective warehouse layout based on the available space, your requirements and your budget. There are also simulation software packages that enable you to 'build' the warehouse on a computer and simulate the operation to see which layout is the most effective (see Figure 9.1).

When (re-)designing a warehouse there are a number of factors that need to be taken into account. These include the company's likely growth over the next 5 to 10 years, the possible change in product profile, total and types of sales during this period and the likely sales channels such as online B2B, B2C and retailer sales.

There are also a number of things that can be done to facilitate the design process. This following section will outline how to approach a warehouse (re-)design.

FIGURE 9.1   Warehouse 3D drawing (courtesy of ATMS)

The areas to concentrate on are as follows:

- Gather as much data as possible and analyse it.

- Try to imagine the business in 5–10 years' time and build in flexibility.

- Concentrate on the cubic capacity of the building.

- Ensure the design is sympathetic to the existing storage equipment and MHE (if applicable).

- Put the health and safety of staff at the forefront of the design.
  - In order to retain a conscientious and motivated workforce ensure that the facility has sufficient lighting and ventilation.
  - Provide ergonomic equipment.

- Reduce the amount of movement required within the warehouse.

- Try to standardize the packaging both for movement and storage.

- Understand the local building regulations and floor loading requirements.

- Don't forget the outside of the building.

Data collection and analysis

The item and order profiling discussed earlier in the book will provide you with an understanding of existing requirements in terms of receipt and despatch areas, storage and picking operations and, finally, areas needed for undertaking value-adding services and returns processes if applicable.

The profile needs to include the whole product range, the number of items per line, the sizes and throughput for each product code. One point to emphasize here is to ensure that you have identified non-moving and obsolete stock for disposal. There is no point in moving and making space in the new warehouse for redundant stock.

Additional data required includes the number of supplier deliveries per day and the average intake together with the number of customer deliveries and the average order size. You will also need to know the method for loading and unloading these vehicles.

A survey by Cranfield University (Baker and Perotti 2008) indicated that 52 per cent of the warehouse floor area is typically used for storage, 17 per cent for the pick/pack operation, 16 per cent for receiving and despatch, 7 per cent for value-adding services and a further 7 per cent for areas such as battery charging, empty pallet storage and other uses. This of course will very much depend on the type of operation envisaged.

The main floor-space areas within the warehouse that need to be calculated are as follows:

- receiving area;
- quarantine and inspection area;
- reserve storage area;
- carton-picking area;
- item-pick area;
- value-adding services area;
- packing area;
- despatch area;
- cross-dock area;
- empty pallet and packaging storage area;
- MHE charging areas;
- warehouse offices; and
- restrooms.

The information collected is normally current or historical and therefore future volumes and changes in product characteristics also need to be taken into account.

Furthermore, the use of averages can be misleading, and you need to decide on how you deal with peaks in the business.

An example of where the use of averages can be misleading is as follows. Within an order profile we have 100 orders with a single line item and 100 orders with three line items. In total we have 200 orders and 400 lines. If we calculate the average we end up with two lines per order which doesn't feature at all in the order profile. Although simplistic in nature we need to be aware of such possibilities on a larger scale. In these circumstances we need to determine the median and mode so that we can see the most popular line per order profile.

Very few operations have a level volume of storage and activity throughout the year. For many companies there are a number of peaks and troughs.

The question is whether we plan for and accommodate peaks in business, whether we design for the average activity or somewhere in between. According to Frazelle (2002), if the duration of the peak period is short and the ratio of peak to average is high, then it is worth considering temporary storage and labour for this overspill. If the peaks are extended and the ratio of peak to average is much smaller, the warehouse and labour requirements should be sized at or near peak requirements.

The suggestion is that you size near to average if the ratio is more than 1:5 and the peak lasts for less than half a year. You should size near the peak when the ratio is less than 1:2 and the peaks last longer.

You also need to take into account fluctuations between days of the week and not rely on weekly or monthly averages. Chapter 11 examines this in more detail.

As mentioned, there are a number of software programs on the market that can calculate the amount of space required for specific operations, and storage equipment companies are more than happy to assist you in these calculations.

In the absence of sophisticated software or if you are looking for high-level calculations at an early stage, there are some rule-of-thumb calculations that can assist you in ascertaining the amount of space required for certain operations and the number of pallets that can be stored in a specific area.

Space calculations

These calculations are based on experience and are not intended to provide definitive answers to space requirements.

Receipt and despatch areas

This area is sometimes overlooked in favour of storage space; however, this is one of the most important areas in the warehouse. The warehouse operation relies on sufficient space both inside and outside the dock bays.

Getting the right balance between the number of doors, equipment and labour is difficult to achieve and as discussed in Chapter 3 requires the coordination of arrivals and departures with available resources.

A congested dock area can result in arrival and departure delays, lost or misplaced product, incorrect despatches and damage to items.

The following rule-of-thumb formula can be used to calculate the likely space requirement for staging vehicles on arrival and departure:

$$\text{Space} = \frac{(\text{number of loads} \times \text{hours to unload})}{\text{Time of shift}} \times (\text{number of pallets} \times \text{space per pallet})$$

For example: if we receive 20 vehicles per day, 26 pallets per load with a pallet size of 1.2 metres by 1.0 metres and it takes 45 minutes per load to unload and 30 minutes per load to check and we operate an eight-hour shift:

$$
\begin{aligned}
\text{Pallet floor space} &= \{\text{round-up} ((20 \times 1.25) \div 8) \times (26 \times (1.2 \times 1))\} \\
&= 4 \times 31.2 \\
&= 124.8 \text{ square metres}
\end{aligned}
$$

In addition to this space we need to add working and travel space around the pallets. This space will be determined by the type of forklift or pallet truck used to unload and load the vehicles. Potentially this can more than double the amount of space required for the pallets themselves and depends on how much access to the pallet is required. For example, a full 360-degree access to the pallet, allowing 0.5 metres of travel corridor, requires an additional 2.2 square metres of working space per pallet.

The ability to preload trailers will reduce the amount of space required at the despatch bay. The proviso here is that there are sufficient doors and/or yard space to accommodate the number of loaded trailers. The ability to double stack pallets will reduce the space required but will also limit the type of pallet truck utilized.

There may also be a requirement for a cross-dock area where goods having been received into the warehouse but not put away are to be despatched en bloc to a customer who has yet to collect the goods. This could take anywhere between a day and a month to despatch. Under these circumstances it may be prudent to use drive-in racking in the despatch area, for example to minimize product damage.

Storage space

Calculating the amount of storage space required and the storage medium depends on a large number of factors.

Each item needs to be evaluated and a table produced to record the different item properties and as a result decide on potential storage media.

Having calculated the amount of items stored per product line and converted these into pallet quantities, we are able to calculate the total number of pallets we need to store, by product line.

Once this has been calculated, produce a chart detailing the number of pallet locations required and the height requirement for each location (Table 9.1).

Depending on the nature of the product in terms of weight, crushability, etc, it is likely that the pallet heights will vary between products and some products may only require bin or tote storage as the quantities are so low.

The next decision is the type of storage medium to use. This can include block stacking, pallet racking, automated storage, shelf and bin locations or a combination of some or all.

Table 9.2 shows the characteristics of each individual stock item and the possible storage media envisaged.

As can be seen from Table 9.2, we have recorded as much information as possible regarding the storage and order profile of the products listed. This gives us the opportunity to decide on the most suitable storage and handling

TABLE 9.1 Storage space calculation

| Item code | Total number of cartons | Dimensions | | | | Cartons per pallet | Ti (cartons per layer) | Hi (layers high) | Pallet weight inc 20 kg empty pallet | Pallet height inc height of pallet (15 cm) | Number of pallets |
		Length cm	Width cm	Height cm	Weight kg						
10779	240	25	40	20	15	48	12	4	740	95	5
30456	16	10	10	15	15	N/A	N/A	N/A	N/A	N/A	<1
77021	800	10	15	10	0.75	800	80	10	620	115	1

TABLE 9.2 Storage method options

Item code	Characteristics	Pallets in store	Fast/medium/ slow mover	Order quantity	Stackable	Storage method	Handling method	Group
010356	Standard	300	Fast	Full pallet	No	Drive through	Cbt or reach	1
010672	Standard	18	Medium	Cartons	No	Wide aisle	Reach & ppt	2.1
010779	Standard	5	Slow	Cartons	Yes	Wide aisle	Reach & ppt	2.2
030456	High value/small part	>1	Slow	Units	N/A	Carousel	Hand	4
077021	High value	1	Medium	Units	N/A	Security cage shelving	Hand	5

Cbt: counterbalance forklift truck
ppt: powered pallet truck

medium. A similar table can be produced to determine the size of the pick face location(s) for each product where we need to take into account the average and maximum amount of product despatched per day.

The idea is to make sure that we do not have to replenish these locations during picking and therefore we need to size the locations appropriately based on the number of items picked per day. The number and size of the pick locations will depend on the available ground floor locations (initially) and cubic capacity of those locations.

Having produced a rule-of-thumb formula for calculating dock space there is a formula to calculate the number of pallets that can be stored within a given cubic area when using standard adjustable pallet racking. This is as follows:

(Number of width modules × pallets in a module width) × (number of length modules × pallets in module length) × number of height modules

where:

Module width = width of aisle + 2 pallet lengths (short side) + clearance between back-to-back pallets

Module length = width of upright + 3 × clearance + 2 pallets (long side)

Module height = height of pallet + clearance above pallet plus racking beam height

For example, based on the following dimensions:

Aisle width: 3.0 metres

Pallet size: 1.20 metres × 1.00 metre

Width of upright: 0.12 metre

Clearance (sides): 0.10 metre

Clearance (height): 0.15 metre

Clearance back-to-back pallets: 0.10 metre

Racking beam height: 0.14 metre

Height of goods: 1.20 metres

Height of pallet: 0.15 metre

Warehouse height: 10 metres

Storage area length: 120 metres

Storage area width: 48 metres

Module width = 3.0 + 2 + 0.1 = 5.1 metres

Module length = 0.12 + 0.3 + 2.4 = 2.82 metres

Module height = (1.2 + 0.15) + 0.15 + 0.14 = 1.64 metres

Number of width modules = 48 ÷ 5.1 = 9

Number of length modules = 120 ÷ 2.82 = 42

Number of height modules = 10 ÷ 1.64 = 6

Total pallet capacity = (9 × 2) × (42 × 2) × 6 = 9,072 pallets

Therefore in a cubic space of 120 metres by 48 metres by 10 metres we have a capacity to store 9,072 pallets based on an overall pallet dimension of 1.2 metres by 1.0 metre by 1.35 metres and utilizing a reach truck working within an aisle width of 3 metres.

The number of pallets that can be stored in this particular area is determined, in the main, by the aisle width, type of racking and the size of pallet.

As mentioned earlier, this is a rule-of-thumb calculation and other factors need to be taken into account before committing to these figures.

The calculations take into account the aisles between the racking but do not take into account aisles and gangways at the front of the racking. They do not take into account potential pallet overhang, rear walkways and fire exits.

Other factors that need to be taken into account are:

- Planned utilization within the warehouse. It is agreed that once storage utilization exceeds 85 per cent, productivity and safety decline. The operation will slow appreciably as put-away is delayed whilst space is being freed up.

- The presence and location of roof columns. Storage equipment manufacturers will take this into account when producing plans.

- The requirement for space between the backs of pallets (flue) and at the sides of pallets.

- The presence and location of sprinklers (ceiling or in rack). The overhead pipes and sprinklers will limit the height both within the warehouse and within the racking itself.

- The type of lighting utilized and any heating or cooling systems installed.

- Lift height of forklift truck. Different types of forklift truck will have different lift-height capabilities.

- Pallet orientation (short facing or long facing). How a pallet is stored within the racking has its own trade-off within the warehouse. Storing a pallet with the long face parallel to the aisle makes it easier for operators to pick, not having to stretch too far across the pallet. However, storing the pallet with the short side parallel to the aisle means greater flexibility (UK and euro pallets can be stored in the same bay) and more pallets can be stored in a length of racking.

  Number of pallets per beam (three pallets between the uprights will increase the number of pallets stored by removing a number of uprights). This can save up to 4 per cent of space. However, the maximum weight per beam needs to be adhered to.

- The requirement for cross aisles within the racking to reduce travel and the need for walkways between the end of the racking and the wall to provide escape routes for staff.

- Type of racking, for example:
  - Double-deep racking will reduce the number of aisles required.
  - Narrow aisle storage requires less aisle width.
  - Drive-in or satellite racking doesn't operate with aisles.
  - Flow racks only require two aisles depending on the length of the lane or potentially three if they are operated back to back.

If the operation is planning to have pick faces on the floor, ie underneath the reserve storage racks, we need to take into account the total number of floor locations that will be set aside for carton-pick locations and shelf locations. We also need to be aware of part-pallet receipts and part-pallet locations if we have to pick from height.

Aisle width

A crucial aspect of warehouse layout is aisle width. This is the distance between pallets in adjacent racks. To ensure safety we need to calculate the distance between the pallets once they have been put onto the racks.

The aisle width is determined by the turning circle of the forklift truck and the size of pallet being carried.

Exceptions to this are narrow aisle and turret trucks which operate in aisles which are based on the width of the truck itself whilst articulated forklift trucks calculate aisle width based on the distance diagonally across the pallet, ie from one corner to another when a pallet is being rotated in the aisle. The safety clearance of 100 mm either side (200 mm in total) of a typical pallet will need to be added to ensure fast pallet put-away and retrieval. The second

FIGURE 9.2&9.3 Aisle widths (courtesy of Carson Racking Systems Limited)

Counterbalance truck

Reach truck

dimension is the overall width of the truck chassis when travelling along the stacking aisle.

Manufacturers of forklift trucks will provide recommendations on the minimum aisle width required for their trucks.

Deciding on the optimal aisle width is a critical part of an overall storage/materials-handling strategy. Aisle width decisions need to achieve the best combination of productivity, space utilization, flexibility, safety and equipment costs for the specific application (Piasecki 2002). Other factors include the depth of the pallet on the truck and whether there is a requirement for two trucks to pass in the aisle.

The decision will also require the user to decide whether speed or storage capacity is the main driver.

The advantages and disadvantages of each type of racking system will be discussed in greater detail in the next chapter.

Other space

The amount of space set aside for packing, value-adding services and returns processing will depend on the level and type of activities envisaged within the operation, the number of staff and the type of equipment required.

An area that is regularly neglected when calculating space requirements in the warehouse is the area needed to store, recharge and change batteries or gas canisters for forklifts, a parking area for equipment when not in use, an area for storing empty pallets and packaging and an area for ancillary equipment such as stretch wrap machines, pallet inverters, etc.

Office and restroom space will be determined by the number of employees required within the warehouse.

Finally we need to ensure that we have sufficient space outside the building for the following:

- to park vehicles which are either collecting or delivering products;
- own fleet vehicles (if applicable);
- sufficient turning circle for the largest vehicle;
- waste storage and recycling areas;
- areas for weather resistant packaging;
- parking for staff and visitor cars; and
- gas or diesel storage tanks depending on the type of MHE utilized.

Warehouse layout examples

The warehouse layout will very much depend on the size and shape of the building, access to it, type of equipment utilized and the operation envisaged. As discussed in the section on picking, there is no 'silver bullet' warehouse layout; however, certain operations lend themselves to specific layouts. For example, parcel and pallet sortation centres tend to favour the through-flow warehouse as depicted in Figure 9.5.

The most popular warehouse layout tends to be the U-flow shape.

Figure 9.4 shows how receiving and despatch are on the same side of the building thus ensuring high dock utilization and facilitating cross docking. The fastest-moving items are closest to the despatch bay, thus ensuring minimum travel and the opportunity to combine put-away and retrieval. In this example reserve storage is held above the actual carton-pick locations.

The design will be heavily influenced by the type of pick operations within the warehouse, with separate areas set aside for unit pick and value-adding services. This area could, for example, be housed on a mezzanine floor above the receiving and despatch bays.

If the warehouse operation has a high incidence of picking and value-adding activities then any low height areas within the warehouses should be set aside for these activities or, as previously mentioned, mezzanine floors constructed either on one or two levels depending on the requirement and the height and cube available.

A through-flow warehouse as depicted in Figure 9.5 provides a layout where the movement is in straight lines and is more natural. Each layout has its advantages and disadvantages. The U-flow design enables greater utilization of the loading bays but can result in congestion if both areas are busy at the same time. It also makes security easier and access is via one side of the warehouse

FIGURE 9.4   U-flow warehouse (courtesy of University of Huddersfield)

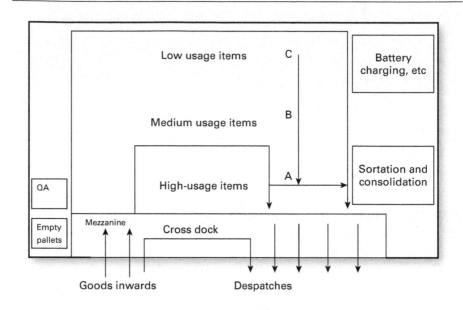

FIGURE 9.5   Through-flow warehouse (courtesy of University of Huddersfield)

FIGURE 9.6   Rail-connected warehouse (courtesy of DHL)

only. With a through-flow warehouse there are no issues with congestion but travel distances are increased and having doors on both sides of the warehouse requires increased security and access either via two separate external gates or a perimeter road around the outside of the warehouse.

Having access on more than one side of the warehouse will also restrict future expansion.

The increase in multimodal use will also have an impact on future warehouse design with access required for trainload traffic within the warehouse or at least under a canopy at one end of the warehouse.

Finding additional space

When facing a shortage of space within the warehouse there are a number of options available, namely:

- expanding the warehouse;
- renting additional space; and
- creating more space within the existing premises.

If the company is unwilling or cannot afford to rent external space and is unable to expand the existing warehouse or make significant structural changes there are ways of increasing the number of storage locations without major upheavals.

A potential solution to increasing available space within a warehouse is to reduce inventory levels. Unfortunately, this tends to be beyond the remit of the warehouse manager. However, warehouse managers can identify slow and non-moving stock with a view to disposing of it in agreement with the sales and finance departments.

Although it may sound strange to suggest looking within the existing facility, there are options that might have been overlooked. Some potential options are as follows:

- Change the type of storage medium or mechanical handling equipment used. This can include changing from single-deep to double-deep racks, utilizing drive-in racking, narrow aisle racking or introducing articulated forklift trucks which can operate in narrower aisles.

- Consolidation of stock. Unless stock items have different best-before codes, batch numbers or expiry dates it is worth checking how many part pallets there are of certain items and spending time consolidating them. This does require the use of labour but the trade-off is between the freeing up of additional space and this cost. The alternative is renting space at a third-party warehouse. Some warehouse systems allow the storage of different products in the same location. This will require careful planning and additional training.

- Reducing beam heights within the warehouse to accommodate smaller, full or part pallets. How many times have you entered a warehouse to see half metre high pallets in 2 metre high locations, not including pick locations, of course? Many warehouses prefer to have standard-height pallet locations as it is easier to manage and control and is more pleasing on the eye. However, the potential for optimum space utilization is lost.

- As the majority of warehouses operate with adjustable pallet racking the most cost-effective method of storage is to have variable height locations. These will accommodate 0.5 metre, 1 metre, 1.2 metre, 1.5 metre and 2 metre pallet heights, for example.

- Moving from fixed locations to random locations. In a warehouse with fixed locations the same product is always held in the same location, irrespective of quantity. With fixed locations if an item is out of stock you cannot use that location for anything else.

- If there is sufficient space in the yard a temporary storage structure may be the answer or the use of sea containers or trailers. Security and the potential for water damage are areas that need to be considered before embarking on such a solution.

Summary and conclusion

An efficient warehouse layout should reduce the amount of travel and labour touch points. It needs to avoid bottlenecks and cross traffic where feasible and ensure that movements take place in a logical sequence.

The whole cube of the building should be utilized and not just the floor space. The introduction of mezzanine floors and carousels provides excellent cube utilization where floor space is at a premium. The trade-off here is cubic utilization versus potentially slower retrieval times.

There are many opportunities to release additional space within the warehouse – we just need to look harder and ask more questions.

Storage and handling equipment

10

"The best handling solutions involve the least handling. Handling adds to the cost but not to the value of the product.

(LINDE MATERIALS HANDLING)

Introduction

In this chapter we examine the different types of storage systems and manual handling equipment used in warehousing today. Although warehouses should all be about throughput, the transfer of manufacturing offshore by many countries has necessitated an increase in storage requirements.

Counterbalance forklift trucks have been around for over 90 years and we are now seeing significant technological advances with laser-guided trucks, articulated trucks, hybrid trucks and high-lift, very narrow aisle (VNA) trucks.

Storage equipment

There are many different forms of racking systems available on the market today. Each one performs a different role and its use will very much depend on the type of operation envisaged.

In terms of storage systems we come across another warehouse trade-off. The trade-off here is between speed, cost and capacity.

The greater the storage an operation requires, the greater the density of pallet storage needed. The potential option in these circumstances includes the introduction of drive-in, double-deep, satellite or very narrow aisle racking.

The trade-off is the fact that these systems take longer to access and deposit pallets and may require specific handling equipment or a different type of racking. Wide aisle adjustable pallet racking on the other hand takes up more floor space but products are easier and quicker to access.

There are many different types of pallet racking configurations currently in use today. These include the following:

- wide aisle adjustable pallet racking;
- double-deep pallet racking;
- narrow aisle racking;
- very narrow aisle racking;
- AS/RS racking;
- dynamic or pallet-flow racking;
- push-back racking;
- drive-in racking;
- drive-through racking;
- mobile racking;
- cantilever racking; and
- shuttle racking.

There is of course no right answer to the type of storage medium that should be used. Put five consultants in a room with stock data, ask them to come up with the optimum storage medium and you are likely to get six different answers.

The type of storage will depend on the configuration of the building, the type of MHE currently in use and the budget available.

In a 2008 UK warehousing benchmarking study by Cranfield University the types of pallet storage systems utilized by the respondents to the questionnaire were as shown in Figure 10.1.

Interestingly, even with today's modern warehouse, the most popular forms of storage recorded for this group of companies surveyed are floor storage and standard wide aisle racking.

Each storage medium has its advantages and disadvantages as shown below.

Storage options

Block stacking

In circumstances where the warehouse height is reasonably low, where products and packaging are robust and budgets are tight, this type of storage is the most

FIGURE 10.1   Pallet storage equipment used in UK warehouses (Baker and Perotti 2008)

common method of storing large quantities of single SKU products. The goods are packed in unit loads, and stacked on the floor to their maximum safe height, which is governed by the weight and stability of the stack. This method is also used where products do not lend themselves easily to palletization and pallet racking is out of the question.

Typical products stored in this way include white goods such as washing machines and refrigerators, kegs and barrels, cans and bottles.

Other storage media include metal stillages used for storing automotive parts and pallet boxes, for example. Block stacking is a cheap way to store robust products where there are a large number of units per SKU.

There are a number of disadvantages associated with block stacking. These include:

- Access. Sufficient space needs to be allocated for forklift trucks to access each stack. Also, in order to access the bottom pallet you need to move the pallets above.

- Damage. The items at the bottom can be crushed by the weight of the items above. Care needs to be taken with the number of unit loads stacked on top of each other. Items such as white goods have a maximum number indicated on the packaging.

- Stock rotation. Unless product can be accessed at both ends of the stack, items can only be despatched on a LIFO (last in, first out) basis.

- Space utilization. Utilization can be very poor if stock does not move quickly through the warehouse. Picking stock from either the front or the rear of the stack can lead to unusable storage areas being left; this is sometimes known as honeycombing. Cubic utilization also tends to be poor when block stacking items where the clear height of the warehouse is significantly higher than the stack itself as can be seen in Figure 10.2.

  The use of pallet collars and converters can reduce the potential damage to underlying pallets and increase the stack height. The wooden, plastic or steel surrounds take the weight of the stacked pallets as opposed to the product itself. Those with drop-down front gates can enable some picking activities to take place. There is also no requirement to stretch wrap these pallets.

As can be seen from Figure 10.2, the cube of the building is not used efficiently and once a stack has been picked from, you cannot put anything in front of that stack until all the cartons have been removed.

Racked storage

The terms adjustable pallet racking (APR) and wide aisle racking (WAR) are seen as interchangeable. One point to note here is that APR is also used in narrow aisle construction. In this section we will discuss the advantages and disadvantages of the types of racking used in today's warehouses.

FIGURE 10.2   Example of block stacking (courtesy of Howard Tenens)

Wide aisle or selective pallet racking

This racking is present in the majority of warehouses worldwide. It is the most versatile of any racking without the need for any specialized handling equipment. The beam heights can be configured to any height as required.

The racking can also be configured to take pallets in either long side or short side configuration. One point to note here is that storing UK/industrial pallets (1200 × 1000), short side facing the aisle, means that euro pallets (1200 × 800) can also be stored in the same location without the use of decking.

Every pallet is accessible at any time and the racking is easy to install and, if necessary, move. Access is also quick and easy compared with most other types of racking.

As the description suggests, the disadvantage is in the fact that wider aisles are required to allow the forklift trucks sufficient turning circle. The use of reach trucks in this area reduces the amount of aisle width required compared with counterbalance trucks.

The introduction of articulated forklift trucks has further reduced the requirement for wide aisles.

One point to note here is whether you require the option of having two trucks operating in the aisle at the same time. If this is the case, aisles will need to be at least the width of both trucks plus clearance.

Double-deep racking

Double-deep pallet racking, as the name implies, allows pallets to be stored two deep in the racking thus eliminating an aisle. The pallets are still accessible from the same aisle. This system does require specialist equipment in the form of extendable forks and will require slightly wider aisles. Speed of access is slower. A further point to note is that the products on the pallets need to be the same otherwise the front pallet will need to be removed to access the rear pallet. LIFO applies.

By reducing the number of access aisles and using the space saved to accommodate additional racking, a double-deep configuration provides a highly space-efficient storage system.

Narrow aisle racking

Narrow aisle racking, as the name implies, utilizes APR and provides storage for a greater concentration of pallets by reducing the aisle width to circa 1.6 metres. This type of racking configuration requires the use of narrow aisle or turret trucks to deposit and access pallets. These trucks are not required to turn in the aisles as their forks extend from the side. They are able to access pallets from both sides of the aisle.

FIGURE 10.3 Double-deep racking (courtesy of Redirack)

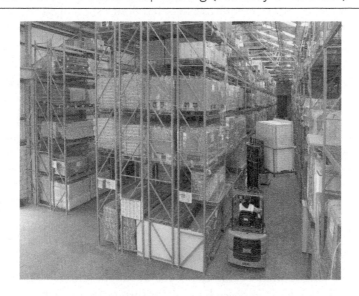

FIGURE 10.4 Narrow aisle racking (courtesy of Constructor Group)

The trucks are manoeuvred within the aisles via wire-guided systems or guide rails. Narrow aisle racking requires a very flat floor, especially if we are looking at heights in excess of 10 metres. During construction, companies will use lasers to ensure the flatness of the floor.

The use of guide rails prevents the use of powered pallet trucks in this area to pick up and deposit pallets in the pick face as they are unable to access the pallets.

Narrowing the aisles too much restricts the speeds at which a forklift can travel between picking locations.

The use of articulated trucks in narrower aisle racking means that similar aisle widths can be achieved but without the need for wire-guided systems or guide rails and a perfectly flat floor.

Drive-in/drive-through racking

Drive-in racking provides a safe and efficient equivalent to block stacking for loads that are too fragile or unstable to be stacked on top of each other. In place of the longitudinal beams that usually support the pallet and load on conventional racking, each upright of drive-through racking has an L-shaped rail for the pallets to rest on, between which there is enough space for a forklift truck to drive into the racking. The rails are carried on brackets that slot into the uprights. The pallets have to be stronger than for normal racking because they have to support the weight of the load across the gap between the rails.

With drive-in racking there is no requirement for aisles, therefore floor space is fully utilized. Cubic space utilization will depend on the lifting height capability of the forklift truck.

Drive-in racking does not allow for first in, first out (FIFO); however, drive-through racking does enable you to extract pallets from the other end of the racking. This does reduce the amount of storage space available, however, and also adds to the honeycomb effect as discussed previously.

Drive-in/drive-through racking is a high-density storage medium suitable for large quantities of single SKUs. Note that products cannot be mixed in each row and stock counting can be very difficult.

Its disadvantages are the increased potential for damage, not only to the product but also to the racking, and the low speed of put-away and retrieval.

This type of storage relies on full-pallet picks in the main as there is no scope for carton picking from the ground-floor locations.

This type of racking can be used at the despatch area to stage outgoing pallets by truck, reducing the amount of floor space required in this area.

Pallet flow/live storage

Pallet-flow racking is driven by gravity. It is perfect for fast-moving product with FIFO stock rotation. Pallets are loaded at the upper end of sloping lanes,

FIGURE 10.5   Drive-in racking (courtesy of Howard Tenens)

and move down by gravity, using heavy-duty skate wheels, when a pallet is removed from the pick face. One block of roller conveyor racking requires only two aisles: a loading face and a picking face, which means fast cycle times and high occupancy rates within your warehouse. Warehouse floor space utilization can be further maximized with fewer aisles by storing pallets back to back. Disadvantages are the potential reduction in cubic utilization and the fact that different products will require a different angle of incline based on the weight of the pallet. Each run also requires the same product to be stored in it.

Push-back racking

Push-back systems work by placing pallet loads on a series of nesting carts fed forward by gravity on rigid structural steel rails. As a pallet is loaded from the front, it pushes the pallet behind it back one position. When unloading, the front pallet is removed and the rear pallets automatically come forward to the front picking position. This allows for easily accessible LIFO inventory management.

FIGURE 10.6   Pallet-flow racking (courtesy of Constructor Group)

Operators can store product from two to five pallets deep, with front-only loading from a single aisle. Push back offers more versatile storage than drive-in rack because each lane flows independently and vertical storage operates separately from the lanes below. Multiple pick facings for a variety of SKUs can be stored and retrieved without disturbing other product above or below in a single-lane or double-lane format (Unarcomaterialhandling.com).

FIGURE 10.7   Push-back racking (courtesy of Redirack)

FIGURE 10.8   Mobile racking (courtesy of Constructor Group)

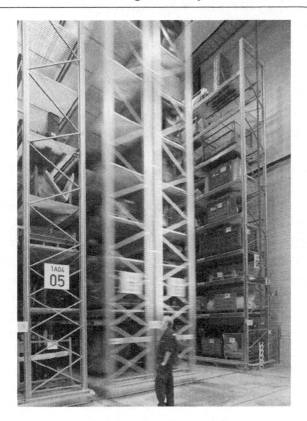

Mobile racking

Where floor space is very expensive, a warehouse can be made very compact if the units of racking are movable by being mounted on rollers. Only enough space for one access aisle is then required, as the operator can 'move' the aisle merely by moving the units (by power, by hand wheel or by pushing) to create a way through to a particular bay. But here, of course, floor space is being saved at the expense of a slowing down in the load-retrieving operation.

 www.youtube.com/watch?v=K3tPx8oPlxE

Satellite or shuttle racking

A recent entrant into the pallet storage market is satellite racking. A satellite system is similar to drive-in racking. However, it is operated by placing shuttles at the front of the racking, utilizing counterbalance, reach or narrow aisle trucks, depending on the height of the racking. The shuttles are controlled remotely via a radio frequency (RF) battery-operated control system and special channel rails. There are no aisles and therefore the cube of the warehouse is well utilized, with the use of very long lanes. The storage system can store pallets within a system that can operate to lengths of 40 metres.

The racking features guide/support rails that run the depth of the rack structure on which an automated shuttle travels. Pallets are loaded onto a shuttle at the front of the lane, which transports the pallet down to the other end. The built-in sensors on the shuttle detect the position of existing pallets and place the new load at a predetermined distance, before returning to the start face. The shuttle is easily moved between lanes by the forklift truck. Multiple shuttles can be controlled by one forklift truck.

Unlike drive-in racking, there is no necessity for the truck to enter the racking and therefore the potential for damage is minimized and the truck can carry on with other duties while the shuttle places the pallet in the correct location.

The system operates in first in, last out mode, allowing racking to be set up against a wall of a warehouse, thereby gaining space. It can also operate with FIFO, using a system that offers separate entrances and exits. This method allows for the loading to be done from one side with a forklift truck and the unloading on the opposite side with another. The system automates the placement of pallets in the storage lane, reducing loading and unloading cycle times.

Each level of racking is assigned to a specific product, unlike drive-in racking where every level has to contain the same product code.

Satellite racking can also utilize the space above the loading bays. As can be seen in Figure 10.9, the pallets are stored on a LIFO basis in this instance. This area can be used for marshalling loads prior to despatch.

FIGURE 10.9   Shuttle racking above despatch bays (courtesy of Toyota)

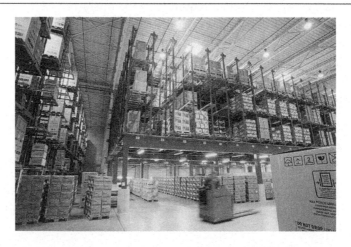

FIGURE 10.10 Example of satellite racking (courtesy of Toyota)

This racking can also provide picking areas as they do not require a forklift truck to enter the area.

Examples of shuttle racking and satellite racking are shown in Figures 10.9 and 10.10.

 www.youtube.com/watch?v=8JuQjwARtaQ

Shuttle technology with a difference

Taking shuttle technology one step further is Retrotech's Activ system.

Their patented technology works like a large sliding puzzle with multiple layers. Pallets input at one end are deposited onto cable-driven carts that slide along deep storage lanes. The software automatically places loads into optimal positions based on the order patterns. The difference being that pallets can move both horizontally and vertically thus overcoming the need to have the same product in each lane.

The ACTIV System can buffer, sort, and stage palletized unit loads in exact loading sequence. Fast movers are more accessible and slow movers are positioned out of the way, so loads can be staged and sequenced for trailer loading – 24 hours a day.

FIGURE 10.11   Activ in action (courtesy of Retrotech)

Activ users have reported the following:

- truck wait times reduced 80 per cent;
- 80 per cent reduction in warehouse space (five sites consolidated into one);
- customer service level performances of 99.5 per cent; and
- extensive flexibility to accommodate future business needs and unanticipated changes.

As can be seen in Figure 10.11 the density of storage is excellent.

As a result of its high-density capability LiDestri Foods were able to absorb 24 hours' worth of production, eliminate two outside storage facilities and consolidate all operations into their manufacturing facility.

 www.retrotech.com/resources-and-media/videos/2

Very high bay warehouses

These consist essentially of massive blocks of racking, built as an integral structure to a high degree of precision, and often acting as a support for the building's roofing and wall cladding. Warehouse heights can range from 23 metres up to 60 metres. Mast cranes built into the racking structure operate in aisles little wider than the unit load handled, under computer control, with the unit loads moving automatically into or out of the racking.

The costs are high, but so are space utilization and operating efficiency, and there is little doubt that more of these warehouses will be built to handle and provide quick access to goods where the range of products is wide and stock turnover is high.

A typical example is the Quinn Glass High Bay Warehouse constructed by Stöcklin, which is 35 metres high and has a footprint of 52,200 square metres. It has the capacity to store 280,000 industrial pallets.

Table 10.1 details each type of storage medium and compares it with its rivals, based on a number of parameters.

There are of course many variables that will impact on the price. The main one being pallet size and type and, for example with drive-in racking, there are different design options and alternative support rails available. On double-deep racking it would normally be the use of APR but some trucks require a low-level beam to accommodate reach legs which would increase the price and VNA operational costs will fluctuate depending on the guidance system used.

In terms of special MHE required we mean anything other than a counter-balance or reach truck. Comparison data is supplied by Redirack.

Figure 10.13 shows the number of euro pallets that can be stored in ground-floor locations within a given space in a warehouse based on the type of racking utilized.

FIGURE 10.12   Quinn Glass warehouse (courtesy of Stöcklin Logistik)

TABLE 10.1 Choosing a warehouse racking system

	Use of floor space	Use of cubic space	Speed of throughput	Access to individual pallets	Special MHE required	Rotation of stock	Pallets stored at Ground level in 4,636 sq. metres (50k Sq. Ft.)	Cost per location*
Adjustable pallet racking	**	**	***	****	No	FIFO	1,250	100
Very narrow aisle	***	***	***	****	Yes	FIFO	1,600	100
Drive in racking	*****	***	**	*	No	FILO	2,120	200
Double-deep racking	***	***	**	**	Yes	FILO	1,650	100
Push-back racking	***	***	**	**	No	FILO	1,950	500
Gravity fed racking	****	***	*****	*	No	FIFO	2,400	700
Mobile racking	****	***	*	****	No	FIFO	2,325	400
Satellite racking	*****	****	***	*	Yes	FILO	2,500	500

* The cost column assumes that standard adjustable pallet racking is given a base cost of 100.

FIGURE 10.13 Warehouse capacity graph: euro pallets (courtesy of Constructor Group)

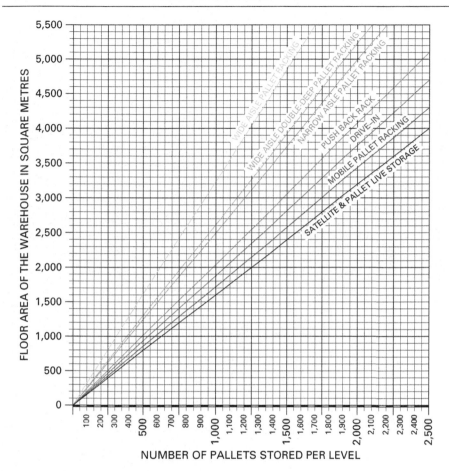

Figure 10.14 shows the number of UK pallets that can be stored in ground-floor locations within a given space in a warehouse based on the type of racking utilized.

The decision tree in Figure 10.13 enables you to decide on particular types of storage systems based on the volume of the stock, sales velocity and required access.

FIGURE 10.14   Warehouse capacity graph: UK pallets (courtesy of Constructor Group)

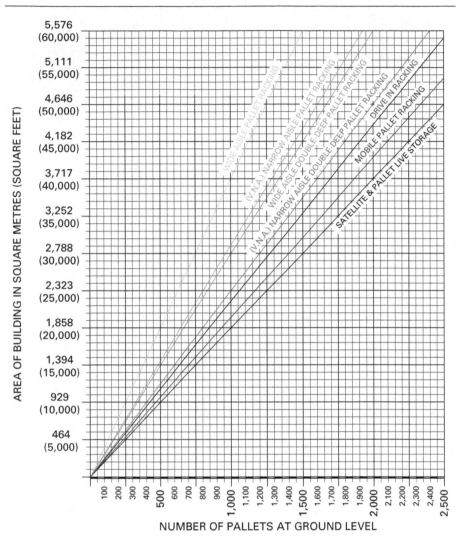

Other storage media

Cantilever racking

Cantilever racking is an ideal solution for long or heavy items such as pipe storage, timber, carpet or furniture storage.

FIGURE 10.15 Two-dimensional decision tree (courtesy of Insight Holdings)

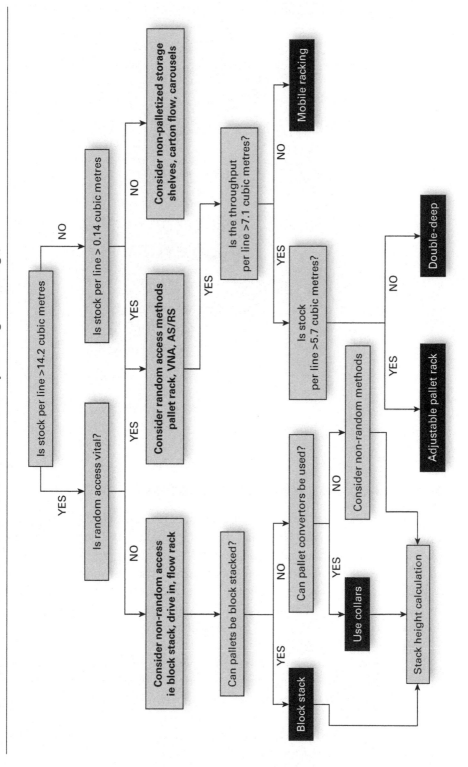

FIGURE 10.16 Cantilever racking (courtesy of 512 Sheffield)

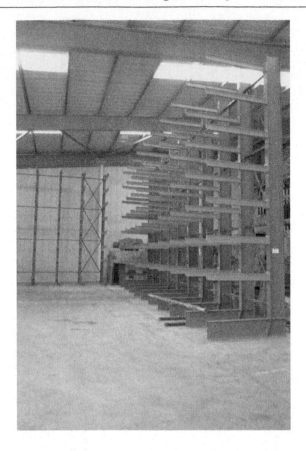

Mezzanine floors/raised storage areas

Where a warehouse has sufficient height it can be very cost effective to construct a mezzanine floor. Typical areas are above the inbound and outbound loading bays. This space can be used to construct shelving for storage and can also be used to undertake value-adding services or can be used for long-term storage.

If the mezzanine is to be used for product storage, you'll need to ensure it's properly structured to take the appropriate load, and that the supports are also properly specified. The floor that the vertical supports stand on will also need to be properly surveyed.

To gain access to your mezzanine you'll need to consider whether you need a lift, conveyor, steps and any gating or barriers that will be required. For example, if you need to load pallets on to the mezzanine, you'll need access for your forklifts.

According to Acorn Warehouse Solutions a mezzanine floor can cost approximately £5.00 per square foot to construct. This needs to be compared to moving to a larger warehouse and the costs that will incur.

Summary

The choice of storage medium very much depends on the type of operation envisaged and whether storage or throughput is the driving factor.

The decision as to which storage medium to choose also has to take into account the type of MHE required to access the racking. The different types of equipment will be discussed in the next section.

Warehouse handling equipment

The challenges of a 24/7 operations culture, together with an ageing workforce, demands for improved accuracy, shorter lead times and a reduction in cost have galvanized manufacturers into producing handling systems that require minimal manual input and provide increased throughput levels.

This section reviews equipment currently in use from the humble pallet jack through to robotic systems. It examines some of the enhancements that have taken place recently and provides comparisons between different types of handling equipment within the warehouse.

The key principles of materials handling are as follows:

- continuous movement is most economic;
- economy is directly proportional to size of load;
- standardization reduces costs;
- mechanization improves efficiency;
- gravity is cheap; and
- simplicity is the goal.

In choosing the correct equipment we are looking to:

- lower unit materials handling costs;
- reduce handling time;
- conserve floor space;
- prevent injuries to staff; and
- reduce energy consumption.

It is essential to consider all aspects of an operation in order to ensure that the most suitable equipment is specified and the best handling solution selected.

Important factors include:

- the load and the means of transfer, eg type of pallet;
- type of storage;

- type of operation;
- warehouse dimensions (height and travel distances);
- overhead obstructions;
- surfaces and gradients;
- working area; and
- environment.

To be able to decide on how to equip our warehouses with the most efficient mechanical handling equipment we need to undertake the following:

- define the functions to be performed;
- review all stock items and define their handling requirements;
- understand the travel distance and speed relationship;
- understand the limits of the building and the structures within it;
- evaluate staff capabilities; and
- evaluate vendors, equipment alternatives and relative costs.

Horizontal movement

Examples of horizontal movement equipment include the following:

- hand pallet trucks (HPTs), pallet jacks;
- powered pallet trucks (PPTs);
- tractors/tugs;
- automated guided vehicles (AGVs); and
- conveyors.

Hand pallet trucks

An HPT has a hydraulic pump to enable the operator to lift a pallet sufficiently to be able to move it across the warehouse floor. It is a cost-effective piece of equipment to move pallets across short distances. It can also be used to manoeuvre pallets within the racking or on the back of a trailer or container.

Powered pallet trucks

These are battery operated and are used for loading, unloading, picking and pallet-transfer duties to and from the receiving and despatch areas. They can be supplied as pedestrian, stand-on or seated versions.

The choice of truck will depend on pallet throughput per hour and distances travelled within the warehouse.

Tow tractors/tugs

These are utilized where distances between points within the warehouse are long and there is a requirement to move a number of pallets at the same time. Pallets can be loaded onto trailers coupled to each other and towed or trammed to the required location.

Automated guided vehicles

The use of automated guided vehicles is growing in popularity as companies struggle with a shortage of skilled labour, high labour costs and 24/7 operational requirements. Couple this with a reduction in cost and AGVs become a feasible alternative to man and machine for moving pallets horizontally throughout the warehouse and for loading and unloading palletized vehicles.

These AGVs can be wire guided, magnetic or gyroscopic. They can also use cameras to record their movements and then memorize them for the next trip.

A recent innovation has been the laser-guided truck. Using special reflective surfaces placed throughout the facility, the automated laser-guided vehicle continuously checks its position and path as it is controlled by the WMS.

By combining voice picking with laser-guided trucks, productivity increases can be up to 80 per cent, with a typical ROI of two years.

There is no requirement for the picker to collect pallets or take completed picks to the despatch area. Once a pallet is full, it automatically travels to the transfer point at the end of the aisle. While this is happening, another AGV is already bringing a new, empty pallet from the store, so that the picker's actual job – picking – is not interrupted. Automatic guided vehicles carry the full pallets to a stretch wrapper, where it is wrapped in foil, ready for despatch. The system sends all the essential despatch information to an integrated printer, which then prints this data onto a label attached to the finished pallet.

Customers using this system are reporting not only a doubling of the pick rate to some 400 packages per hour, but also a 60 per cent lower error rate. Another advantage of this solution is that the picking pallet can always be adjusted to the ergonomically optimum loading height for the picker.

Additional advantages include the automated transport of picked pallets on to despatch. Each of these factors contributes to a quick return on investment.

The advantages of automated vehicles are as follows:

- computer or hand controlled;
- more durable than people;

FIGURE 10.17   Automated guided vehicle (courtesy of Dematic)

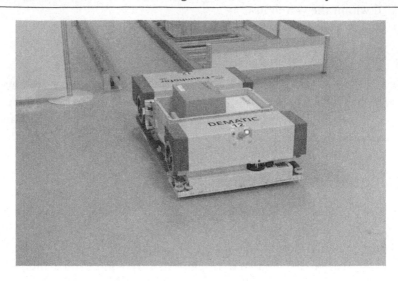

- long-distance and/or high-density traffic;
- fitted with security sensors and guards;
- limited potential for damage;
- reliable; and
- do not cause bottlenecks.

The disadvantages are that they are initially expensive, fully reliant on the RF system within the warehouse and may require a specially designed and obstruction-free floor area.

 www.youtube.com/watch?v=Zcylp1yuZCc

Vertical and horizontal movement

In order to take advantage of the cubic capacity of a building, pallets or unit loads need to be lifted into position. Forklift trucks are differentiated by their lift-height capability, weight capacity and turning circle. These trucks have become a great deal more sophisticated with onboard computer screens and cameras, as can be seen in Figure 10.18.

FIGURE 10.18   Internal view of computerized forklift truck
(courtesy of Atlet)

FIGURE 10.19   Pallet stacker (courtesy of Toyota)

Pallet or 'Walkie' stacker

These trucks are used for moving pallets around the warehouse and when required can lift pallets up to 5 metres. They can be pedestrian, ride-on, stand-in or seated.

CASE STUDY

Asda Walmart has recently introduced the pedestrian operated mini Bendi into their back of store operations.

As a business, Asda constantly looks at ways to separate pedestrians and forklift trucks in order to minimize the risk of accidental collisions. However when segregated it can often lead to cube productivity inefficiencies. With the new truck they no longer need to compromise. Simon Grass of Asda comments:

> The Mini Bendi allows us to significantly drive the use of the cube in our back of house areas as it can work in the narrow aisle format and maximise the usable height available but due to its way of working that allows us to have pedestrian pick within the same area permitting the stores to drop and fill effectively. This supports the reduction in the building footprint and thus improves the buildings selling efficiency as we can either build a smaller store or increase the selling sq ft. It also allows us to lower the height of the building as we can now store as many pallets above 'pedestrian pick' in narrow aisles, as we could in the reach truck aisles at height, which is especially welcomed by the local planning authorities in certain areas of the country.

Counterbalance forklift trucks (CBT)

CBTs are the most common trucks to be found in a warehouse. They are fast, flexible and versatile, but the major disadvantage is that in order to stack or retrieve a pallet they must approach the face of the pallet at 90° square. Thus the turning circle of the truck determines the minimum aisle width.

They are powered by diesel, battery, LPG or CNG. They can operate inside and outside the warehouse.

CBTs can carry palletized goods to and from racks up to 7 metres high and require aisles of 3.5 metres or more in width. They have been the workhorse of the warehouse for over 60 years because of their flexibility in being able to work both inside and outside the warehouse.

To increase storage capacity by making better use of the floor space available it is possible to reduce aisle widths by utilizing different types of trucks.

FIGURE 10.20 Mini-Bendi (courtesy of Bendi)

Reach trucks

These trucks are ideal for working within narrower aisles. Unlike the CBT they carry the load within the wheelbase. They are able to work in aisles of around 2.7 metres. However, most companies will increase the aisle width to 3 metres. They have a maximum lift height of up to 12 metres. They can operate in single and double-deep racking environments. As can be seen in Figure 10.21 the aisle is reasonably narrow, but not as narrow as those operated within by articulated and very narrow aisle trucks.

Narrow aisle or turret trucks

These trucks are designed to operate with little more aisle space than their own width. The normal width of a narrow aisle truck is approximately 1.6 metres. Operating this type of truck can add approximately 33 per cent to storage capacity through the adoption of narrower aisles.

FIGURE 10.21   Reach truck (courtesy of Atlet)

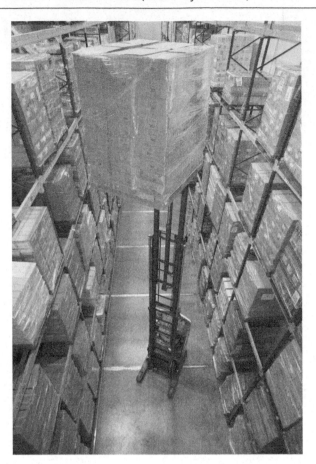

There are disadvantages, however:

- The use of man-up VNA trucks requires large transfer gangways at both ends of each aisle to allow these trucks to switch aisles – unless, of course, you have the luxury of operating one truck per aisle.

- Furthermore, there are safety issues associated with picking because reaching out from a fixed cab to pick a carton and place it on a pallet some distance away is not ergonomic or efficient.

- A man-up VNA truck operator who is working 10 metres in the air will often struggle to notice another order picker working at ground level in the same aisle, thereby compromising order-picking efficiency and health and safety within sites where there is a high degree of low-level order picking. This can be overcome by insisting that no truck is allowed in the aisle when picking is taking place, although this isn't the most efficient use of resources.

- Man-down trucks can, to a degree, overcome the safety problem; however, these aren't as efficient with no capability of picking cartons from height and retrieval, and put-away can take longer.

A recent innovation is Junheinrich's Warehouse Navigation System for Narrow Aisle Trucks. The narrow aisle truck continually feeds back its location via transponders in the floor of the warehouse. Orders received from the warehouse management system are transmitted to the truck's radio data terminal. The terminal's logistics interface translates and passes on this information directly to the truck controller (not the driver). This means the truck knows the exact destination to approach. The driver simply has to give the travel/lift command and the truck approaches the pallet location automatically in diagonal travel.

The advantages are as follows:

- efficiency increased by up to 25 per cent;
- alleviates driver stress;
- automatic responses without scanning;
- preventing incorrect put-away and retrieval; and
- less damage on the racking.

 www.youtube.com/watch?v=GXsFeX8pCKM

Articulated forklift trucks (Flexi, Bendi, Aisle Master)

The introduction of articulated trucks has overcome a number of issues, including the flexibility of being able to operate the same forklift truck inside and outside the warehouse. However, these trucks are akin to a well-known yeast extract product – you either love them or you hate them; there doesn't appear to be any centre ground. Training can potentially take longer than for an equivalent truck and put-away and retrieval times will vary depending on the ability of the driver. Bendi are confident that their trucks can produce increased productivity figures in similar aisle widths to a VNA truck.

Until the articulated truck was introduced, companies had little alternative but to operate a two-truck system with a counterbalanced truck working outside and feeding a reach truck inside the warehouse. With the arrival of articulated trucks, users can eliminate this often costly and generally inefficient arrangement. Articulated forklift trucks load and unload vehicles and deliver pallets directly to the racking in a single operation. By doing so, they increase efficiency and productivity while abolishing double handling and the costs associated with running a larger truck fleet than is necessary.

 www.bendi.co.uk/web/media/video/

FIGURE 10.22   Articulated forklift truck (courtesy of Flexi)

The truck manufacturers argue that during a typical work cycle over a one-hour period a reach truck will move 25 pallets; over the same time and doing the same job, an articulated forklift can potentially move up to 35 pallets, according to John Maguire of Narrow Aisle Flexi Limited.

CASE STUDY   Narrow Aisle Flexi

The international automotive supplier Brose has been using Flexi Euro articulated trucks in their JIS factory supplying Mercedes in Sindelfingen since August 2008. These trucks are suitable for very narrow aisles and have created more space in their existing line side warehouse.

The products produced at the Brose factory are door systems for the Mercedes S, C and E ranges.

A further order for a new Mercedes range as well as the increasing production depth urged manager Jan Francke, who is responsible for the two Brose factories in Sindelfingen and Rastatt, to react early enough. An external canopy for the factory in Sindelfingen for storing empties had already been planned when head of logistics at the Sindelfingen factory, Dana Mühlenhof, came across the concept of the Flexi articulated forklift trucks.

Narrow Aisle Flexi had recently adapted its truck for the market in Germany. The main advantages of the British-designed Flexi Euro forklift trucks are that they can work in an aisle width of only two metres at a capacity of up to two tonnes.

With two Flexis, Brose has replaced two standard forklifts whilst their tests showed they would have required at least three reach-type trucks due to the slow mast movements.

The reach truck had been dismissed because of its width and low productivity. 'If we used conventional reach trucks we would have had to increase the distance between the pallets and consequently would have lost too much space,' explains Dana Mühlenhof.

Since August 2008 Brose has been using two Flexi Euro trucks. In fact, the only disadvantage of these Flexi trucks is their comparatively lower speed compared with counterbalance forklifts. 'Due to this we have calculated additional time of 5 per cent, which is in fact much better than the reach truck tested,' says Jan Francke. This 5 per cent, however, has to be seen in relation to the longer distances which would have needed to be travelled, resulting from an expansion of the warehouse. 'By using Flexi we could keep our optimized material flow in the factory,' emphasized Mühlenhof.

The Flexi Euro is unique in that it was developed especially for customers in Germany who need to handle the Euro Alliance pallet in a 2-metre aisle without the extra cost of guidance systems or special floors and conform to the aisle security standards DIN15185 Part 2 required in Germany.

Thanks to the efficiency of the new Flexi Euro trucks, Brose could create a very compact storage layout at the factory in Sindelfingen. The remodelling of the storage racks was done simultaneously with the introduction of the new trucks. 'Instead of an aisle width of 4 metres we are now mainly working with a distance of only 2 metres,' says Francke.

Automated storage and retrieval systems (AS/RS)

This system utilizes fixed path cranes to collect pallets at the front of the racking system and transport them to empty locations within the racking. In order to improve productivity, the system collects a full pallet from the racking and deposits it at the front of the aisle prior to collecting another pallet. This dual-command system or task interleaving is very efficient. The crane can travel horizontally and vertically simultaneously, thus reducing travel time between pick up and put down.

The cranes will normally remain in one aisle. However, where storage requirements are relatively high and throughput relatively low, the cranes can be transferred from one aisle to another using transfer cars.

The racking can be one deep or potentially two deep, necessitating retractable forks. To fully automate the process, pallets are collected by AGVs and taken to the despatch area.

FIGURE 10.23   Crane system for AS/RS (courtesy of Stöcklin Logistik)

Table 10.2 provides data to enable the reader to compare the different pallet movement trucks.

The aisle width quoted is the minimum requirement. Any operation that has more than one truck operating in an aisle at the same time will require wider access.

TABLE 10.2 Comparison chart for MHE (courtesy of Toyota)

Product type	Lift height	Aisle width (mm)	Lift capacity in kg from	To	Cost from (£)	To (£)
Hand pallet, truck, pallet jack	N/A	1,800	2,300	3,000	300	1,000
Powered pallet truck	N/A	2,800	1,200	3,000	2,800	16,000
Powered pallet stacker	1,350–6,300 mm	2,200–3,000	1,000	1,600	5,000	18,000
Reach truck	4,500–12,500 mm	2,650–3,150	1,400	2,500	15,000	30,000
Counter-balance truck	3,000–7,000 mm	3,000–7,000	1,300	5,000	12,000	20,000
Low-level order picker	N/A	1,636	1,800	2,500	7,000	12,000
Medium-level order picker	2,000–4,700 mm	1,590	1,000	1,200	10,000	18,000
High-level order picker	4,700–9,500 mm	1,664	1,000	1,200	19,000	32,000
Combination truck	14,800 mm	1,600–2,300	1,000	1,500	40,000	80,000
Articulated forklift truck	Up to 12 m	1,600–2,100	1,000	2,000	29,000	35,000

Prices at July 2013 UK only

Specialized equipment

Not all unit loads can be moved or picked up by standard pallet forks. There are a number of operations and products stored within a warehouse which require specialized handling equipment.

Examples of additional equipment are as follows:

- extended forks: used for retrieval from double-deep racking and for the movement of large pallets;
- crane attachment: used for picking up heavy bags, etc;
- boom attachment: used for picking up loads with a central coil, eg tyres, carpets;
- drum grip and clamps: used for moving drums and barrels;
- load clamps: used for moving or tilting items;
- carton clamps: used for lifting or moving large boxes or white goods;
- rotating paper roll clamps: used for moving and lifting paper reels;
- double pallet handlers: ability to move two pallets at the same time;
- slip sheet attachments: load push/pull mechanism for moving product from a slip sheet onto a pallet.
- side loading trucks for longer loads (see Figure 10.24).

FIGURE 10.24   Articulated forklift truck with side-loading attachment (courtesy of Bendi)

Recent technical advances

Forklift truck manufacturers are continually looking to introduce new technology to enhance the capabilities of their forklift trucks.

Jungheinrich recently introduced a new automated pallet scanning and identification solution that is an integral part of the forklift truck and brings considerable time and efficiency advantages to the supply chain.

The new fork-based scanning process not only results in significant time savings compared with manual scanning, but reduces the forklift driver's workload and ensures low picking error rates.

With pressure from the environmental sector and a need to reduce energy consumption within the warehouse, manufacturers are also looking to alternative energy sources. These include the introduction of hybrid vehicles and fuel cells that are used to power lift trucks in high-throughput warehouse applications. Hydrogen fuel cells can offer higher productivity in electric lift trucks because they can be rapidly refuelled by operators, eliminating the need to change, store and maintain batteries. Plus, fuel cells produce constant voltage, which means there is no battery drop towards the end of a shift.

A number of trucks are also able to return charge to their batteries through regenerative lifting and braking.

FIGURE 10.25   Toyota hybrid truck (courtesy of Toyota)

Summary and conclusion

The choice of equipment very much depends on the product characteristics, the warehouse dimensions and environment, the required velocity of the product through the warehouse and the available budget.

Technology within MHE is fast moving and although the counterbalance truck remains popular even after all these years it is also being adapted to keep up with these advances.

The majority of mechanical handling and storage equipment manufacturers have sophisticated systems including simulation software that are able to assist companies with their decision as to what type of racking and MHE will efficiently suit their operation. This service is normally free and although a potential sale is the goal, so is a satisfied customer.

Resourcing a warehouse

DAVID CAIRNS AND GWYNNE RICHARDS

The devil is in the detail. **(ANONYMOUS)**

Introduction

Having examined both people and equipment within the warehouse, we now turn our attention to how much of these resources we require to operate efficiently.

The types of resource found in a warehouse are numerous and will include operatives, equipment, consumables, general supplies, etc. In this section the focus will be on the two main types generally associated with warehouse operations – labour and equipment.

These are generally acknowledged as key, as under-resourcing will usually mean failure to meet service requirements, while over-resourcing will mean failure to meet financial performance targets. However, while other resource types may appear less significant, the effects of inaccurate ordering of consumables can be equally dramatic – for example, running out of stretch-wrap may contribute to damaged goods in transit, while no labels to print can result in a loss of ability to track product through a warehouse, and potentially an inability to fulfil orders.

Resources can be categorized by the principal driver of requirements; there are two main categories: determined by level of processing activities; and determined by other factors.

Processing activities

Processing activities will generally involve handling product and will generate 'multiples' of resource, for example receiving product into a warehouse. By contrast, a good example of a resource whose level is determined by other factors is site security, where manning is likely to be determined by warehouse operating hours.

There is no absolute definition as to how to categorize resources, but a good guideline for 'processing activity' resources is one where a small change in activity level will change the level of resources employed.

For example, Figure 11.1 illustrates the activity of put-away (of pallets to racked storage). This is a processing activity: the units measured are pallets over a set time period, the work rate (productivity) is the time taken to identify and collect a pallet, transport it and lift it into its storage slot, confirm the put-away (in this case a barcode scan is assumed) and return to the start location for the next put-away task.

The time for this single put-away cycle can be expressed as pallets per hour (or as minutes per pallet) and the division of the productivity rate into the activity level generates a number of hours for the task in the given time period. See Table 11.1.

The example in Table 11.1 is based on a simple warehouse operation putting away 500 pallets per day. There are three put-away options for inbound product:

- into high-density storage (in this example drive-in racking);
- into standard wide aisle reserve slots (upper levels, above picking slots);
- into pick slots (ground-level wide aisle racking – small amount of product with no current stock).

FIGURE 11.1 Put-away time illustration

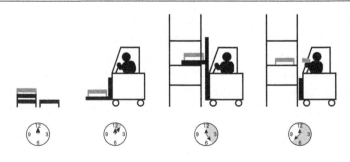

TABLE 11.1 Task breakdown

| Activity description | Daily volume (average) | | Productivity standard | Hours required | MHE type | Other equipment |
	Activity (units)	Unit of measure				
Put-away:						
Collect pallets, put-away in wide aisle racking	198	Pallets	24	8.25	Reach truck	
Collect pallets, put away in drive-in racking	300	Pallets	16	18.75	Reach truck	
Collect pallets, put-away in pick locations	2	Pallets	5	0.4	Reach truck	

Each has a different productivity standard to reflect the different nature of the task. To calculate the time for put-away into drive-in racking slots, the calculation of the workload for the day is:

$$300 \text{ pallets} \div 16 \text{ pallets per hour} = 18.75 \text{ hours}$$

This activity utilizes an operative and a reach truck and therefore generates:

- 18.75 operative hours; AND
- 18.75 reach truck hours.

For this example it is assumed that reach trucks have a truck-mounted terminal and barcode scanner. If the operative uses voice technology, 18.75 hours of voice terminal use will also be generated.

When constructing a resource model there needs to be a balance between creating task lines for every element of work and recognizing where elements are interdependent and should be considered collectively. This process is different from work study as it is driven by different considerations. For example, in the illustration above there is an element of direct put-away. This is intended for product which, when received, goes direct to the pick face for replenishment.

In this process it is assumed that the reach truck driver will include this process element in his daily work. Alternatively the driver could deliver the pallet to the front of the aisle and a second operative, using different equipment, could be employed to place product into the pick face. This is illustrated in Table 11.2.

Note that in this example a second unit of measure has been added (cartons) along with two other pieces of equipment powered pallet truck and a handheld barcode scanner).

In both approaches we can see that each additional unit to be processed generates an incremental resource requirement.

Work rates (productivity)

A key element in the resource budget is the productivity rate. There are many ways to set productivity rates. Quantitative benchmarks can provide useful comparisons; however, no two warehouses are identical.

Productivity rates are driven by multiple factors and where significant change or a new warehouse is being considered it may be difficult to establish productivity rates accurately. The following three options are regularly employed to establish budget productivity rates:

- synthesis: composite construction of productivity rates for an activity from components of each work element;

TABLE 11.2 Task breakdown, version 2

| Activity description | Daily volume (average) | | Productivity standard | Hours required | MHE type | Other equipment |
	Activity (units)	Unit of measure				
Put-away:						
Collect pallets, put-away in wide aisle racking	198	Pallets	24	8.25	Reach truck	
Collect pallets, put away in drive-in racking	300	Pallets	16	18.75	Reach truck	
Collect pallets, deliver to aisle	2	Pallets	30	0.07	Reach truck	
Load cartons to pick face	80	Cartons	240	0.33	Powered pallet truck	Handheld scanner

- work study: preferably using an approved work study engineer and work measurement techniques;
- historical comparison: identification of productivity levels in existing operations and factoring in change elements.

The last option is probably the most accessible. It relates to an existing work profile and has a number of the inherent characteristics that drive productivity (hit rates, order composition, etc). If a key driver for a new warehouse is productivity improvement, then understanding and building from the existing process can help identify improvements.

Points to bear in mind are the size of the new warehouse and the likely increase in travel time. If the new warehouse is significantly larger, performances may reduce as a result of longer travel distances within the warehouse. A change of equipment will also have an effect on productivities (for example moving from 1 to 2 pallet capacity picking trucks).

Comparison with available productivity benchmarks is useful, as is supplier data for envisaged equipment. When options have been reduced to a shortlist it is appropriate to invest time and cost by reviewing, in detail, these productivity rates to confirm assumptions and further refine and subsequently build confidence in the rates.

Techniques such as simulation may also be appropriate at this stage, and may be particularly relevant where congestion is a factor in driving change. In an established situation there are often common effects. Generally, increased activity provides opportunities to improve productivity, through increased order sizes and picking full as opposed to part cases and pallets. However, growth can also result in bottlenecks and delays occurring while operatives are obliged to wait to carry out specific tasks. These delays, and related effects can be classed as 'congestion' effects. Figure 11.2 shows the typical combined influence of scale economies and congestion on work rates.

In practice the scale economy effect is generally easier to identify than the congestion effect. As a guide the scale economy effect will progressively flatten and an 'optimum' productivity rate may be achieved – the congestion effect, however, may materialize as minor or substantial deterioration of productivity. In these circumstances you need to identify the bottleneck and consider introducing processes to improve throughput. From a picking perspective multiple pick faces for the most popular product line is an example.

For resource modelling/budgeting purposes the work (productivity) rate required is one which reflects the actual time taken – this may be different to a rate developed by a work study engineer, where the rate may be an absolute rate which will have a performance factor applied to generate an expected level. Care should also be taken to make sure that matching assumptions are made about elements such as authorized and impromptu breaks, collection of

FIGURE 11.2 Growth Factors influencing work rates

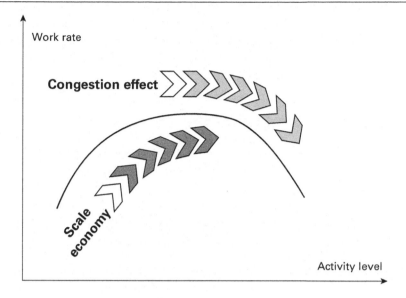

equipment, on the job training, and changes in equipment. This is particularly relevant when considering start up scenarios or introduction of significant numbers of new employees, when productivity may build progressively to target.

When constructing a resource budget the primary aim is to produce output that can be used to set resource levels and feed into the financial budget to forecast costs. However, other applications include providing a basis for managing ongoing operations, to assist in activity costing, and, for some operations, constructing charging mechanisms.

The process is subject to 'the law of diminishing returns'; the effort needed to develop and interpret detailed budget information for smaller elements may not justify the end result; for basic warehousing operations a rule of thumb would be that when more than 80 per cent of total time can be calculated by quantifiable activities then the effort required to further develop the model is unlikely to be justifiable; for costing or charging applications, a higher percentage may be required.

In basic warehouse operations there are a number of core processes: receiving, put-away, retrieval, picking, replenishment and despatch. In most warehouses these will account for over 80 per cent of the handling (touch points), and most use of mechanical handling equipment. Specific applications, notably the growth of e-commerce, may include packing and value-adding services as substantial core processes.

In a standard manual warehouse where the majority of goods are picked as cases, the largest component in the resource budget is likely to be case picking, which will often account for more than 50 per cent of direct operator hours. In e-commerce applications, where the unit of handling is likely to be a single sales item, the picking and packing elements combined will account for a higher proportion of labour hours.

Seasonality/demand variation

A fundamental characteristic of most businesses is that demand is variable. There is a need to model variations in demand to understand how the resource requirements will change.

The key to developing an effective resource plan and budget lies in understanding when specific warehousing activities are likely to occur. There are three main sources of variance in demands on a warehouse:

- Seasonal variations through the course of a year. These range from clearly recognized seasonal demands, such as barbecues in summer, to variations influenced by general purchasing behaviour.

- Variations during the course of a week. These are typically influenced by sales patterns of customers and associated buying processes; for example, there may be a surge in orders following sales at the weekend or, by contrast, a push to meet projected sales through promotions.

- Variations during the course of a day. This is most obvious when considering order placement on the warehouse. Many service businesses will seek to place orders up to close of normal trading for next-day delivery – in these instances the warehouse is unlikely to see complete scheduled orders until late afternoon for despatch by the beginning of the next working day.

Activity profiles generated during data gathering or from existing trading patterns should provide a good indication. In many operations there are predictable changes in operating profiles at peak periods – there may be larger order sizes and a tradition of a longer working day/week; in these circumstances it may be appropriate to model 'peak' activity alongside 'average'. Figure 11.3 below is drawn from a live warehousing situation and illustrates through the year variation.

The columns in Figure 11.3 represent order lines and units illustrating variations in profile composition as well as activity. In this instance there was launch (promotional) activity in February, followed by selling pushes in May and July with a more sustained peak towards the end of the year. The average is 8.3 per cent per month; even with allowances for diseconomies of scale in

FIGURE 11.3   Demand variability

productivity, resourcing this profile will need to address a substantially lower need for resource in the first half of the year.

Resource modelling

An illustrative example has been used to demonstrate typical modelling techniques. The following profile applies:

- Single stand-alone warehouse (ambient goods).
- Incoming product received on pallets (side-loaded vehicles) and containers (loose loaded).
- Storage is palletized (standard wide aisle Adjustable Pallet Rack + Drive-In Pallet rack).
- Core business is carton/pallet pick, palletized despatch on tailgate loaded vehicles.
- Additional area for support activities such as relabeling, promotional packing, export preparation (Value Add 1). (Product is processed and returned to warehouse stock).
- Additional area for e-commerce business providing unit pick-and-pack for internet customers (B2C). Despatch as parcels through carriers.

Four levels of activity are defined – average (24 weeks), low (18 weeks, including some with no working on public holidays); these 42 weeks traditionally operate as five-day weeks, while the remaining higher activity periods – high and peak (five weeks each) operate six days to meet increased demand.

In this example two profiles have been modelled – for average and peak levels of activity – and low and high levels are extrapolated from these core profiles. Usually the modelling process begins with producing either an averaged figure (say an average day or week), however an alternative option is a typical day/week – where a typical day represents what happens on most days of the year, but is not necessarily the average. This is often appropriate where there is a prolonged or pronounced peak as found with seasonal products.

The main activities within the warehouse, with associated productivities and volumes for average and peak profiles, are shown in Table 11.3.

The model generates summary information for labour and each equipment type, and includes data summarizing activity level. In this illustration the modelling will be taken forward using data summarized by area of activity and by equipment used, however there is the means to include further variation using this source, for example if modelling variable mix between intake and despatch, which would reflect a stock build ahead of a peak period.

There is an important need to establish the relationship between the data used in modelling and the total volume (measure of activity) that the resource budget covers. This will typically be one year, and at various points in the modelling process it is advisable to undertake a reconciliation, by multiplying each model activity element by the number of relevant days/weeks and summing to generate a (annual) total that the modelling caters for. This can also be achieved by including a data line that generates a common figure, eg number of cases affected by the components.

The next stage of modelling addresses the second variation category – day-to-day seasonality. In many businesses, profiles will emerge that show different levels of activity on different days of the week, with businesses serving fast-moving retail outlets likely to exhibit demand patterns that will reflect purchasing behaviour. The precise effect can vary if a business pulls stock (ie replenishes sales made) or pushes stock (pre-empting anticipated sales), with busiest days (for a warehouse) likely to occur after or before the busiest sales day, depending on method of supply. Note that for e-commerce the relationship is more directly linked to customer demand, with warehouse activity patterns closer to the pull model.

In practice, goods receipt is likely to follow a different profile from that of despatch in a stockholding operation, so it is recommended to determine different daily profiles for discrete aspects of the warehouse operation. In the example, the main warehouse operations are split into palletized receipt, loose receipt, despatch and other activities, reflecting circumstances in which palletized receipt may be determined by production running times, while loose receipt reflects shipping and container transfer constraints. Figure 11.4 shows a graphic representation of these categories. Table 11.4 shows the daily activity levels for the two value-add operations in the warehouse. In both areas it is possible that some activities may not be extended (to a sixth day) at peak.

TABLE 11.3 Example of resource model

Process	Activity Description	Daily Volume (Average) Activity (Units)	unit of measure	Productivity Standard (Units/hr)	Hours Required	MHE type	Other Equip	Peak Daily Volume Activity (Units)	unit of measure	Productivity Standard (Units/hr)	Hours Required	MHE type	Other Equip
Goods in	**Goods Receiving**												
	Prep (Veh ID, etc)/Process Documentation-Trailers	15.36	vehicles	12.0	1.3	–	–	19.97	vehicles	12.0	1.7	–	–
	Open Vehicle (Trailer-tailgate offload only)		vehicles	40	0.0	–	–		vehicles	40	0.0	–	–
	Offload Pallets (side offload, place in receipt bay)	384.0	pallets	24	16.0	B	–	499.2	pallets	24	16.0	B	–
	Inspect Pallets (inc Count, Label scan)	384.0	pallets	60	6.4	–	H	499.2	pallets	60	8.3	–	H
	Remedial work – repalletization (replace pallet)	2.9	pallets	60	0.0	C	–	3.7	pallets	60	0.1	C	–
	Remedial work – repalletization (stack cases)	230.4	cases	240	1.0	–	–	299.5	cases	240	1.2	–	–
	Prep (Veh ID, etc)/Process Documentation-Containers	3.8	vehicles	10.0	0.4	–	–	5.0	vehicles	10.0	0.5	–	–
	Open Vehicle (Container)	3.8	vehicles	30	0.1	–	–	5.0	vehicles	30	0.2	–	–
	Provide pallets for palletization of cases	96.0	pallets	160	0.6	–	–	124.8	pallets	160	0.8	–	–
	Offload Cases (from container) & palletize	7,680.0	cases	275	27.9	A	–	9,984.0	cases	275	36.3	A	–
	Label & Inspect Pallets (inc Count, Label scan)	96.0	pallets	48	2.0	–	H	124.8	pallets	48	2.6	–	H
	Receive Goods at external storage location					B2		50.0	pallets			B2	
Put Away	**Put Away**												
	Collect Pallets/Put Away in WA Reserve Slots	190.2	pallets	20.0	9.5	E	–	249.1	pallets	20.0	12.5	E	
	Collect Pallets/Put Away in Drivein Slots	288.0	pallets	16.0	18.0	E	–	374.4	pallets	16.0	23.4	E	
	Collect Pallets/Put Away in WA Pick Slots	1.8	pallets	18.0	0.1	E		0.5	pallets	18.0	0.0	A	
Retrieve	**Retrieve**												
	Extract Pallets from Drivein for FP despatch	82.1	pallets	16.0	5.1	E		142.5	pallets	16.0	8.9	A	
	Extract Pallets from WA Reserve for FP despatch	4.3	pallets	20.0	0.2	E		7.5	pallets	20.0	0.4	E	
	Extract Pallets from DI, Replenish WA pick slot	205.9	pallets	15.0	13.7	E		231.9	pallets	15.0	15.5	A	
	Extract Pallets (from WA), Replenish Pick Slot	185.9	pallets	18.0	10.3	E		241.6	pallets	18.0	13.4	E	
	Value-Add Operations (1 – Case product)												
	Extract pallets from DI, transfer to VA area (mezz)	*12*	*pallets*	*15*	*0.8*	*E*		*1.5*	*pallets*	*15*	*0.1*	*E*	
	Receive Packaging Material to area (@1 lift /job)	*1*	*(pallet)*	*15*	*0.1*	*E*		*1*	*(pallet)*	*15*	*0.1*	*E*	
	Unpack singles from cases to workstations	*14,400*	*units*	*600*	*24.0*			*1,800*	*units*	*600*	*3.0*		
	VA Process (Bundling) [** aggregate for budget]	*7,200*	*units*	*1,200*	*6.0*			*0*	*units*	*1,200*	*0.0*		
	VA Process (Labelling) [** aggregate for budget]	*7,200*	*units*	*900*	*8.0*			*1,800*	*units*	*900*	*2.0*		
	Pack product to cases, build to pallet quantities	*14,400*	*units*	*480*	*30.0*		*H*	*1,800*	*units*	*480*	*3.8*		*H*
	Remove waste packaging to recycle area	*1*	*(pallet)*	*12*	*0.1*			*1*	*(pallet)*	*12*	*0.1*		
	Return pallets from VA area to storage (Drive In)	*12*	*pallets*	*15*	*0.8*	*E*		*1.5*	*pallets*	*15*	*0.1*	*E*	
	VA area Indirect work	*12.5%*	*%(VA dir)*	*n/a*	*8.7*			*12.5%*	*%(VA dir)*	*n/a*	*1.1*		
Case Pick	**Case Picking**												
	Acquire Pick Assignment, Collect (MT) Pallet	474.2	pallets	Incl below		D		551.2	pallets	Incl below		D	
	Select Cases sequentially, place on order pallet	31,488	cases	165	190.8	D	V	37,920	cases	165	229.8	D	V
	Deposit Picked Pallet in Marshalling Area	474.2	pallets	Incl above		D		551.2	pallets	Incl above		D	
Marshalling	**Marshalling (Despatch)**												
	Consolidate pallets for despatch	394	cases	180	2.2	C	H	379	cases	180	2.1	C	H
	Detail Check (proportion of picked pallets)	13.0	pallets	1.7	7.8		H	11.0	pallets	1.7	6.6		H
	Stretch-wrap despatch pallet (picked pallets)	474.2	pallets	54.5	8.7	C	W	551.2	pallets	54.5	10.1	C	W
Despatch	**Goods Outloading (Despatch)**												
	Load Pallets (to despatch vehicles)	560.1	pallets	50	11.2	C	H	699.9	pallets	50	14.0	C	H
	Transfer Pallets to Singles Pick'n'Pack area (mezzanine)	0.50	pallets	20	0.0	E		2.3	pallets	20.0	0.1	E	
	Seal Vehicle, Issue Documentation	33.0	vehicles	10	3.3			39.0	vehicles	10	3.9		
	Value-Add Operations (2-Unit Pick & Despatch)												
	Receive Mixed Pallet of cases from main operation	*0.50*	*pallets*	*15*	*0.0*	*E*		*2.25*	*pallets*	*15*	*0.2*	*E*	
	Receive Packaging Materials (Cartons, bags, filler)	*0.50*	*pallets*	*15*	*0.0*	*E*		*2.25*	*pallets*	*15*	*0.2*	*E*	
	Case putaway to shelf slots	*40*	*cases*	*100*	*0.4*	*A*		*180*	*cases*	*100*	*1.8*	*A*	
	Unit pick (from cases), transfer to packing bench	*600*	*units*	*220*	*2.7*			*2,700*	*units*	*220*	*12.3*		
	Pack into shipping media, add docs & carrier label	*451*	*orders*	*75*	*6.0*			*2,160*	*orders*	*75*	*28.8*		
	Seal packs, scan for despatch, place on ship pallet	*451*	*packs*	*150*	*3.0*			*2,160*	*packs*	*150*	*14.4*		
	Transfer ship pallet to despatch (for collection)	*2*	*pallets*	*18*	*0.1*	*E*		*9*	*pallets*	*18*	*0.5*	*E*	
	Despatch via carrier (including package check)	*451*	*packs*	*600*	*0.8*			*2,160*	*packs*	*600*	*3.6*		
	Returns receive, examine, action	*60*	*units*	*50*	*1.2*			*270*	*units*	*50*	*5.4*		
	Indirect Work Hours (% of Direct Hours)	*10%*	*%(VA dir)*	*n/a*	*1.4*			*10%*	*%(VA dir)*	*n/a*	*6.7*		
Other	**Other Work**												
	Hygiene (Planned Cleaning)		2 person	n/a	14.334	F			2.2 person	n/a	15.767	F	
	Indirect Work Hours (% of Main WH Direct Hours)	7.5 %		n/a	25.3			7.5 %		n/a	30.6		
	– General Housekeeping		Incl above						Incl above				
	– Recoupation, Damages, (Case) Returns processing		Incl above						Incl above				
	– Physical Stock Checks, Remedial Activity		Incl above						Incl above				
	– Handling of Pallets, consumables, etc		Incl above						Incl above				
	– Other unquantified work		Incl above						Incl above				
	TOTAL				**470.6**						**538.7**		

TABLE 11.3 *continued*

Process	Activity Description	Daily Volume (Average) Activity (Units)	unit of measure	Productivity Standard (Units/hr)	Hours Required	MHE type	Other Equip	Peak Daily Volume Activity (Units)	unit of measure	Productivity Standard (Units/hr)	Hours Required	MHE type	Other Equip
	SUMMARY BY ACTIVITY												
	Goods Receiving				55.7						67.6		
	Put Away (to stock)				27.6						35.9		
	Retrieve (from stock) – FP despatch				5.3						9.3		
	Retrieve (from Stock) – Case Picking				24.1						28.9		
	Case Picking				190.8						229.8		
	Despatch – Marshalling Case Picked Product				18.7						18.8		
	Despatch – Outloading Pallets				14.5						18.0		
	Other Activities (Main Warehouse)				39.6						46.4		
	SUB TOTAL – Main Warehouse				376.4						454.7		
	Value-Add Ops 1 (Case product)				78.5						10.2		
	Value-Add Ops 2 (Unit Pick'n'Pack – e-shop)				15.7						73.8		
	TOTAL – All Operations				470.6						538.7		
	EQUIPMENT SUMMARY												
	Machine Type A: **Hand Pallet Truck**				28.3						38.1		
	Machine Type B: **Counterbalances**				16.0						16.0		
	Machine Type C: **Powered Pallet Trucks**				22.1						26.3		
	Machine Type D: **Order Picker Truck (LLOP)**				190.8						229.8		
	Machine Type E: **Reach Truck**				59.5						76.0		
	Machine Type F: **Floor Scrubber**				14.3						15.8		
	Other Equipment Type H: **Hand Held Terminal**				59.6						37.4		
	Other Equipment Type V: **Voice Terminal**				190.8						229.8		
	Other Equipment Type W: **Pallet Wrapper**				9.7						10.1		

FIGURE 11.4 Daily activity profile

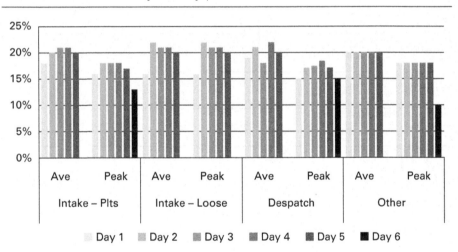

The variance factors are then applied to the core resource model to generate daily resource requirements. The primary objective here is to gain an idea of overall requirements and extract a base from which to make judgements on setting resource levels. In the example, the scope of the modelling has been extended to include resource estimates for low and high periods.

It is possible to vary profiles further, and indeed vary productivity rates for different periods. For example, there may be periods of the year when case sizes vary and it is legitimate to amend the picking rate to reflect this. Similarly

TABLE 11.4 Value-adding service volumes by day

		Day 1	Day 2	Day 3	Day 4	Day 5	Day 6
Value Add 1	Ave	22%	20%	21%	19%	18%	
	Peak	22%	20%	21%	19%	18%	0%
Value Add 2	Ave	24%	20%	16%	25%	15%	
	Peak	24%	16%	12%	22%	18%	8%

productivity differences can also occur between different shifts. In practice, such additions will increase the complexity of the resource model, and care is necessary to ensure: the resulting model(s) allows for all aspects of its use to take place subsequently, eg KPI measurement and comparison; and the model does not become so complex that it loses practical application, including visibility to others.

Table 11.5 shows the application of period and daily variations to the main warehouse elements of the model at workgroup level. Similar information is available at individual activity level, and for each day of low/high period (one day shown as illustration).

The table illustrates the varying requirement for resource through the course of the year. For the main warehousing operations the average daily requirement is 376.4 hours (direct labour), varying between 351.7 and 405.9 during the week; at peak the average daily figure rises to 454.7 hours, with a peak daily requirement of 507.0 hours. This implies peak days are around 20 per cent busier than average. However, the weekly requirement rises from 1,882 hours (average) to 2,728 hours at peak, almost 50 per cent; this statistic effectively affirms the logic of extending to a sixth day at peak and illustrates the nature of decision guidance that follows from careful resource planning.

Peaks and troughs of activity precipitate changes to the resources required in the warehouse. Just as there are times when additional resources are required and decisions need to be made on how to meet these needs (eg overtime, equipment hire, etc), there will also be occasions when there may be insufficient work to occupy core resources in the operation (idle time).

The approach can be applied to other elements of the operation, such as the value-add operations, and for equipment requirements.

In essence the model progressively reflects the key concept of variability in resource planning. The final step to introduce is to look at the process of determining the actual levels of resource required. This invokes the third source of variability – at what times during the day is resource required.

TABLE 11.5 Period and daily variations

	Low	Average					High	Peak					
	Day 3	Day 1	Day 2	Day 3	Day 4	Day 5	Day 3	Day 1	Day 2	Day 3	Day 4	Day 5	Day 6
Goods In	49.4	47.1	58.8	58.5	58.5	55.7	70.8	64.9	82.7	80.3	80.3	76.3	21.3
Put Away	24.5	24.3	28.2	29.0	29.0	27.6	35.3	34.4	40.5	40.0	40.0	37.9	22.4
Retrieve (FP Desp.)	4.0	5.1	5.6	4.8	5.9	5.3	9.1	8.4	9.5	9.7	10.2	9.5	8.4
Retrieve (Case Pick)	18.0	22.9	25.3	21.6	26.5	24.1	28.2	26.0	29.6	30.2	31.9	29.6	26.0
Case Pick	143.1	181.3	200.4	171.8	209.9	190.8	224.7	206.8	235.8	239.9	253.7	235.8	206.8
Marshalling	14.0	17.8	19.6	16.8	20.6	18.7	18.4	16.9	19.3	19.7	20.8	19.3	16.9
Despatch	10.9	13.8	15.3	13.1	16.0	14.5	17.6	16.2	18.5	18.8	19.9	18.5	16.2
Other	35.4	39.6	39.6	39.6	39.6	39.6	45.4	50.1	50.1	50.1	50.1	50.1	27.8
	299.3	351.7	392.7	355.2	405.9	376.4	449.5	423.8	486.0	488.7	507.0	477.0	345.8
ave/day	316.9			376.4			409.2			454.7			
week	1584.6			1882.0			2455.3			2728.2			

FP Desp. = full pallet despatch

As an example consider despatches, which, in turn, largely determines picking. In many warehouses it is common to find that intake is biased to mornings to allow clear use of loading areas for despatch later in the day. In turn demand is placed by customers through the (office) day, with many orders being placed or finalized by a 'cut-off' time for next-day delivery. In many cases such deliveries need to be loaded and en route by early morning to meet delivery schedules and, in essence, the warehouse window for picking and despatch is concentrated into the afternoon and evening.

UK retailer Next has recently extended its latest order cut off time to 10 pm for next-day delivery.

The total workload (in the example) justifies a two-shift operation and, whilst flexibility of labour allows manpower to switch tasks, some equipment is very specific in its use. In the example there are 191 hours/day of case pick on an average day (210 hours on busiest day) during an average week.

This activity – the only one to use low-level order picking trucks – takes place primarily on the late shift as there is limited work available in morning. Despatch must be completed by the end of the day, resulting in 80 per cent of activity occurring during the second shift.

In this example the requirement for order picking trucks (LLOPs) is four times higher in the afternoon than in the morning; the modelling needs to reflect this, as using a daily average will lead to a serious shortfall in equipment. In the example this is achieved by allocating a proportion of each task to time windows (shift) in the working day.

Shorter time windows may be more appropriate for other operations. As the critical requirement is likely to occur on the busiest day, it is usual to use this requirement to determine equipment needs. In the example this is day 4, for both average and peak weeks, but it should be noted that for some equipment types the day may vary.

Table 11.6 shows the allocation of hours to shifts, and the subsequent derived numbers for equipment – this is based on the greatest required number over each of the shifts, and assumes availability of 7.16 hours/shift (to match operators' availability after break allowances are taken into account).

The model in Table 11.6 has generated an estimate of the number of *working* pieces of equipment *at average and peak periods*. This is a guide to managers who are responsible for setting resource levels (equipment and labour) and requires full interpretation to finalize. This process should be more of a fine tuning effort and will take into account elements such as availability (after maintenance/repair), ability to obtain short-term hires and a practical perspective. For example, the requirement for two counterbalance trucks may be viewed as marginal so that no further provision for maintenance spares is needed (particularly if 'emergency' hire is readily available). However the requirement for 24 LLOPs may translate into 27 to cover repairs and maintenance based on

TABLE 11.6 Allocation of hours

	Average/Day 4			Peak/Day 4			Operational Equipment	
	Early Shift	Late Shift	Night Shift	Early Shift	Late Shift	Night Shift	Ave	Peak
Goods In	46.8	11.7	0.0	67.1	13.3	0.0		
Put Away	15.9	13.0	0.0	22.0	18.0	0.0		
Retrieve (FP Desp.)	1.2	4.7	0.0	2.0	8.2	0.0		
Retrieve (Case Pick)	5.3	21.2	0.0	6.4	25.5	0.0		
Case Pick	42.0	167.9	0.0	50.7	203.0	0.0		
Marshalling	4.1	16.5	0.0	4.2	16.6	0.0		
Despatch	3.2	12.8	0.0	4.0	15.9	0.0		
Other	19.8	19.8	0.0	25.1	25.1	0.0		
	138.4	267.6	0.0	184.1	325.5	0.0		
Value Add 1	48.5	26.1	0.0	7.6	4.1	0.0		
Value Add 2	11.8	7.9	0.0	58.4	39.0	0.0		
	198.6	301.5	0.0	247.4	368.6	0.0		
Machine Type A: Hand Pallet Trucks	29.6	0.2	0.0	47.2	1.0	0.0	5.0	7.0
Machine Type B: Counterbalances	9.2	7.6	0.0	9.5	7.8	0.0	2.0	2.0
Machine Type C: Powered Pallet Trucks	4.9	19.5	0.0	5.8	23.2	0.0	3.0	4.0
Machine Type D: Order Picker (LLOP)	42.0	167.9	0.0	50.7	203.0	0.0	24.0	29.0
Machine Type E: Reach Truck	24.2	39.6	0.0	32.3	52.4	0.0	6.0	8.0
Machine Type F: Floor Scrubber	7.2	7.2	0.0	8.5	8.5	0.0	1.0	2.0
Other Equip Type H: Hand Held Terminal	29.0	31.7	0.0	16.0	25.6	0.0	5.0	4.0
Other Equip Type V: Voice Terminal	42.0	167.9	0.0	50.7	203.0	0.0	24.0	29.0
Other Equip Type W: Pallet Wrapper	1.9	7.7	0.0	2.2	8.9	0.0	2.0	2.0
Activity by Shift Intake – Plts	55%	45%	0%	55%	45%	0%		
Intake – Loose	100%	0%	0%	100%	0%	0%		
Despatch	20%	80%	0%	20%	80%	0%		
Value Add 1	65%	35%	0%	65%	35%	0%		
Value Add 2	60%	40%	0%	60%	40%	0%		
Other	50%	50%	0%	50%	50%	0%		

experience (plus five seasonal hires). These judgements will be determined by factors such as history and availability of equipment and will generally be specific to the equipment; it should be noted that the more specialized the equipment the more likely the requirement to carry peak and maintenance cover for the full year.

When calculating the base and supplementary levels of each type of resource there are no definitive rules. However, modelling techniques can be used to compare alternative scenarios. In our example this is achieved by manual input of different core levels of resource. Table 11.7 shows this for the calculation of labour resources, where inputs are used for the number of permanent (full-time) employees and a maximum proportion of hours worked as overtime. The model structure generates paid hours (at base rate) for the full permanent workforce, available hours (after allowances for planned and unplanned absence) and then identifies any idle hours (where less work is required than base hours available), overtime hours and temporary hours (generating overtime use first until the pre-set level is achieved, then overtime is capped and temporary labour used for remaining requirement). A contingency may also be factored in for unforeseen circumstances arising during day-to-day operations (in this model a contingency is identified for review purposes as an estimate of daily FTE (full-time equivalents) required). The complexity of the modelling process is directly proportional to the complexity being modelled, so modelling multiple shift lengths for example will increase intensity.

It may be prudent to review aspects of the resource calculations separately – for example if, historically, the warehouse management team had a view that it was difficult to obtain and/or manage more than 20 temporary employees effectively then a review of each day's work content needs to take place. In this example this occurs on three days of peak week operations (over five weeks) and an appropriate strategy can be developed. This can either be formally included in the model, informally added to the model or implemented outside the model, depending on the impact. For example, if a different spread of base hours, overtime and temporary hours through the peak week solves the problem, but makes no material change to the weekly totals it may be simpler to leave the model at the simpler level.

As previously noted it is likely that there will be some idle or unused time in the quietest periods. This is estimated in the output lines. In practice, particularly for long-established operations, such idle time may effectively appear as a reduced productivity standard, ie the productivity standard has become a measure of work per attended hour. Care should be taken in understanding what the source information consists of, and therefore how it will model reality.

To assist in judging an appropriate resource level, weighted hours for the full budget are calculated. This is done by considering likely cost, and estimating this by weighting overtime and temporary hours relative to paid base hour.

TABLE 11.7 Labour hours calculations

	Low					Average					High						Peak					
	Day 1	Day 2	Day 3	Day 4	Day 5	Day 1	Day 2	Day 3	Day 4	Day 5	Day 1	Day 2	Day 3	Day 4	Day 5	Day 6	Day 1	Day 2	Day 3	Day 4	Day 5	Day 6
Daily Workload (Hrs – Main Warehouse)	296	341	299	331	317	352	393	355	406	376	398	435	450	466	427	279	424	486	489	507	477	346
FTE required (for day workload)	41.3	47.6	41.8	46.2	44.2	49.1	54.8	49.6	56.6	52.5	55.5	60.8	62.7	65.0	59.6	38.9	59.1	67.8	68.2	70.7	66.6	48.3
FTE required (inc Contingency)	42.2	48.5	42.6	47.1	45.1	50.1	55.9	50.6	57.8	53.6	56.5	62.0	64.0	66.3	60.8	39.7	60.3	69.2	69.5	72.1	67.9	49.2
Heads (main w/h)	49.0	56.4	49.5	54.7	52.4	58.1	64.9	58.7	67.1	62.2	65.8	72.0	74.3	77.0	70.6	46.1	70.0	80.3	80.8	83.8	78.8	57.2
VA1 Workload (Hrs)	72	65	69	62	59	86	78	82	75	71	12	11	12	11	10	0	14	12	13	12	11	0
FTE required (VA1)	10.0	9.1	9.6	8.7	8.2	12.0	10.9	11.5	10.4	9.9	1.7	1.6	1.6	1.5	1.4	0.0	1.9	1.7	1.8	1.6	1.5	0.0
VA2 Workload (Hrs)	16	13	10	16	10	19	16	13	20	12	96	64	48	88	72	32	106	71	53	97	80	35
FTE required (VA2)	2.2	1.8	1.5	2.3	1.4	2.6	2.2	1.8	2.7	1.6	13.4	8.9	6.7	12.3	10.1	4.5	14.8	9.9	7.4	13.6	11.1	4.9
Heads (VA2)	2.5	2.1	1.7	2.7	1.6	3.1	2.5	2.0	3.2	1.9	15.6	10.4	7.8	14.3	11.7	5.2	17.2	11.5	8.6	15.8	12.9	5.7

permanent employees: **54**
Max Overtime: 20%

Per Day (Main Warehouse)	Low					Average					High						Peak					
Idle Time	37	0	34	2	16	0	0	0	0	0	0	0	0	0	0	0	0	0	0	0	0	0
Overtime	0	8	0	0	0	18	59	22	73	43	56	56	56	56	56	1	56	56	56	56	56	68
Temp Hours	0	0	0	0	0	0	0	0	0	0	65	102	116	133	94	0	91	153	155	174	144	0
Base Hours	333	333	333	333	333	333	333	333	333	333	278	278	278	278	278	278	278	278	278	278	278	278
Paid Base Hours	387	387	387	387	387	387	387	387	387	387	323	323	323	323	323	323	323	323	323	323	323	323
Per week	paid base				1,935	paid base				1,935	paid base					1,935	paid base					1,935

Per Period (contribution to annual budget)	Low	Average	High	Peak
# weeks	18	24	5	5
base hours	29,994	39,992	8,332	8,332
Idle hours	1,612	0	0	0
Paid Hours	34,832	46,442	9,675	9,675
Overtime	142	5,176	1,395	1,729
Temp Hours	0	0	2,550	3,580

2% Contingency

99,608 REQD HOURS

86,649 BASE HOURS
1,612 IDLE HOURS
100,625 PAID BASE HOURS
8,441 O/T HOURS
6,131 TEMP HOURS
122,905 Weighted Hours

FIGURE 11.5   Weighted hours

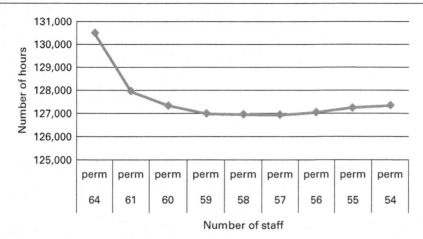

The calculation includes time paid for absence as this will be a factor in the financial budget. Figure 11.5 illustrates different levels of permanent resource in the main warehouse for our example.

The graph, although specific to the example, illustrates some common features in resource modelling. The shape is typical with a 'flat' U-shape near the optimum number – in this case the difference is negligible between 57 and 58 permanent employees. (Given these exclude contingency, which was estimated as 1–2 operatives, the model would indicate 59–60 is the optimum level in this case). The increases in hours committed on either side of the optimum reflect common phenomena:

- a higher number of permanent staff will carry a penalty of higher idle hours,
- a lower number of permanent staff generates higher costs for overtime payments and temporary staff.

There is also a potential for lower productivity if excessive overtime is worked or large numbers of temporary staff are employed.

Model outputs can be tailored to financial budget inputs, but most of the core information is contained in this model – permanent staff, hours worked, overtime hours, temporary staff hours, equipment levels, equipment hire, etc.

It may not be necessary or appropriate to use such techniques for all resource types, illustrated by the two value-add examples.

Here value-add 1 covers bundling and re-labelling work and is expected to be a series of individual jobs. The resource model provides a broad estimate, but in practice each job will be an individual cost (or price) and there is likely to be more inherent variability.

For such circumstances it may be more appropriate to have a small core of staff, supplemented by temporary labour as required for individual jobs. For value add 2 there is more consistency in work content, but as this is a more volatile business stream then it may be appropriate to consider part-time employees whose hours can be increased at peak periods then supplemented by temporary resource.

Other factors

Other resource requirements are not driven by processing activity. These include resources that are determined by time cycles. Examples are clerical, administrative and managerial staff, the equipment they use (system terminals, etc) and indirect activities for the operation as a whole, such as canteen staff and security. For these resources there may be choices between direct provision and bought-in services. The touch-labour modelling will give a forecast of activity in terms of volume and numbers employed along with timings, from which judgements of levels of such resources can be made.

For example, an operations office will require manning whilst the operation is active, but numbers of personnel may vary according to type of activity. Factors such as the number of orders, type of paperwork (eg import/export documentation) will influence choice, and a key element will be the nature of the IT systems employed and the levels of manual intervention envisaged.

A voice picking operation should require less intervention than a paper-based operation. It is also necessary to consider which functions are the responsibility of the warehouse. Security could be within the warehouse remit on a stand-alone site, but excluded if the warehouse is co-located with production or other company functions.

The scale of an operation will drive the management structure along with functional responsibility. Reference to historical arrangements can provide a good starting point as approaches vary significantly between organizations. This is particularly the case for first line management, where responsibilities can be incorporated as working supervisors or shared with team leaders.

In these cases some adjustments to the hours required for processing activity may therefore be required – in the example it is quite likely that this will apply in both value-add operations.

Resource modelling will also generate projected usage data that can be used to assist in the procurement process for new MHE, where lease/rental costs vary with use. Daily hours of use for equipment will help determine whether spare batteries are required.

Suppliers can also help advise on availability and cost of equipment hire during peak periods – in some instances this element can be incorporated into lease/long-term rental arrangements for the main fleet.

Summary and conclusion

Having built up the resource model, you are able to transfer this data into a financial budget and will be able to monitor the actual resource requirements and costs against those budgeted.

Productivity standards can also be compared with actual achievement and the resource model adjusted accordingly.

Finally, the model can assist you in estimating prices for goods and services as the model can be adapted to calculate not only the resource for the whole warehouse but specific operations or clients within it.

Warehouse costs

12

> *Every dollar of cost (or expense) that is cut falls directly to the bottom line. This makes sense because it is true.* **(ANONYMOUS)**

Introduction

The cost of operating a warehouse can average between 1 and 5 per cent of total sales depending on the type of company and the value of its goods. For example, a pallet of laptops will take up the same amount of space and the same amount of handling as a pallet of baked beans, yet the value of goods will be significantly different. Hence the variation in the percentage cost of sales. Warehousing also makes up around 22 per cent of a company's total logistics costs with inventory carrying costs at a further 23 per cent.

As a result, warehouse managers require a comprehensive knowledge of all costs and cost drivers within the warehouse as they are under significant pressure to reduce costs yet continue to produce optimum customer service with the added pressure of reduced inventory but increased numbers of SKU.

Managers are also expected to contribute data to the company budget and continually reassess the resource and cost budget in line with the actual operation.

This chapter looks at the typical costs within a warehouse and aims to assist managers in understanding these costs, enabling them to produce budgets, calculate return on investment for particular projects and use the information for decision making, evaluating performance, activity costing and, in the case of third-party logistics service providers, charging.

The chapter also compares traditional costing models with activity-based costing.

The chapter goes on to discuss the advantages and disadvantages of costing models such as open book, closed book and cost plus.

Types of costs

The costs typically associated with a warehouse operation are shown below:

Space costs:

- rent/leasing costs on building/land and building depreciation (depending on how the building and land has been acquired);
- insurance;
- rates or local government taxes;
- utility and telecoms costs;
- fixtures and fittings depreciation;
- racking depreciation;
- refrigeration plant depreciation;
- repairs and maintenance;
- cleaning, security, other building equipment depreciation;
- waste disposal.

Direct labour costs (fixed): warehouse operators:

- wages including on-costs;
- personnel insurance;
- safety wear (PPE);
- welfare;
- training.

Indirect labour costs (fixed): warehouse management including supervisors and administrators:

- wages including on-costs;
- insurance;
- safety wear (PPE);
- welfare;
- training.

Labour costs (variable):

- overtime, bonuses.

Equipment costs (fixed):

- depreciation/lease costs/rental costs.

Equipment costs (variable):

- – running costs, eg fuel, tyres, lubricants, batteries;
- – packaging, pallets, stretch wrap.

Overhead costs (management, finance, human resources, IT and administration):

- – salaries and on-costs plus benefits in kind such as mobile phones, accommodation, etc;
- – company cars and running costs;
- – office equipment and furniture depreciation/lease/rental costs;
- – information technology costs (hardware and software).

Overhead costs (sales and marketing in 3PLs):

- – salaries and on-costs plus benefits in kind such as mobile phones, accommodation, etc;
- – company cars and running costs;
- – marketing spend, eg advertising, exhibitions, brochures, etc.

Miscellaneous costs:

- – communication costs;
- – postage;
- – bank charges and interest payments;
- – funding costs/cost of finance;
- – insurance;
- – legal and professional fees;
- – audit fees.

As well as wages and salaries, total labour costs include employer's social contributions (including national insurance contributions (UK) and pensions, paid on behalf of the employee) and other non-wage costs including sickness, maternity and paternity costs, vocational training costs and recruitment costs plus any benefits in kind which might apply.

As can be seen in Figure 12.1, the costs can be built up to produce a total warehouse cost. Third-party logistics companies can add an element of profit in order to produce a costing model to charge clients. This model can be used in conjunction with the resource model in Chapter 11 to calculate activity rates such as handling costs per pallet and/or per case picked and cost per pallet stored.

FIGURE 12.1 Simple warehouse cost tree

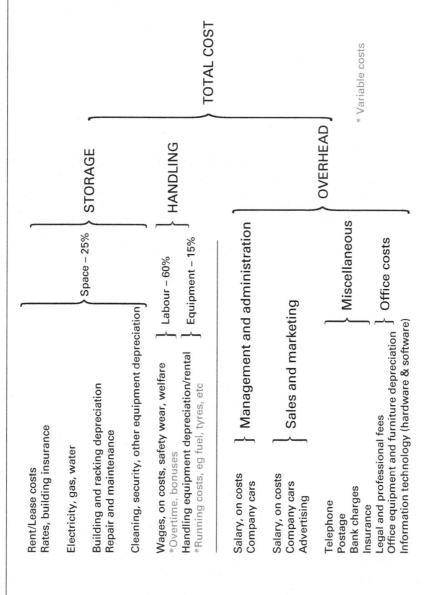

Return on investment (ROI)

This is a measure used to evaluate the efficiency of an investment or to compare a number of different investments. ROI is important to calculate because if an investment doesn't have a positive ROI or if there are other opportunities with a higher ROI, then the investment should not be made.

The calculation of ROI percentage is as follows:

$$(\text{Gain from investment (or savings)} - \text{cost of investment}) \div \\ \text{cost of investment} \times 100$$

A similar calculation is the payback period. This basically measures how long an investment takes to pay for itself. It does have drawbacks, however, as it does not properly take into account finance cost and opportunity cost, the latter being what must be given up (the next best alternative) as a result of the decision.

During a recent voice picking trial a client calculated that their ROI, by replacing barcode scan picking, was approximately 25.4 per cent in the first year with a payback period of nine and a half months.

The figures were as follows:

- pick productivity savings: £52,800;
- increased accuracy: £33,600;
- total savings: £86,400;
- investment in voice: £68,900;
- therefore (£86,400 − £68,900) ÷ £68,900 × 100 = 25.4 per cent;
- payback period = £68,900 ÷ £86,400 × 12 months = 9.6 months.

This isn't a totally accurate picture as no account is taken of extra training costs, effect on the business during the early stages of implementation, etc.

However, this does give the company a reasonably accurate picture of the potential ROI for other similar investments.

Traditional versus activity-based costing systems

According to Themido *et al* (2000), companies in the past could keep unprofitable products and customers in the hope that one day they would become profitable, because the winners would more than compensate for the losers.

In today's economy the margin for error is much smaller and pressures are increasing on companies to improve their bottom-line performance.

The knowledge of the real cost of a product or service and the cost to serve specific channels and customers is very important to a company in today's competitive market.

Christopher (1998) states that logistics costing systems 'should be capable of not only identifying the costs that result from providing customer services in the marketplace but also enabling separate cost and revenue analyses to be made by customer type and by market segment or distribution channel'.

Managers therefore need to be able to calculate the cost to serve for each customer and where possible the warehousing cost for each product.

From experience, smaller customers tend to be high maintenance. The 80/20 rule can apply in these situations. The 80 per cent of customers generating 20 per cent of the revenue tend to be the more demanding.

When I joined a third-party logistics shared-user operation I found that we had 29 clients in total. The total revenue generated from 20 of the customers came to less than 10 per cent of total sales. At the time we didn't have the systems in place to calculate the profitability of each customer, but having evaluated each one in terms of future potential we decided to terminate the agreements of 19 of the customers and as a result we ended up with an increased profit margin.

In this section we will look at two types of costing system which are relevant to warehouse operations. These are the traditional costing method and activity-based costing.

Traditional costing methods

Traditional costing models tend to allocate overhead costs arbitrarily. Table 12.1 shows a typical warehouse cost structure.

In terms of storage, let us assume that our warehouse has 10,000 × 1.5 metre high pallet locations. From a cost point of view each location costs £167.70 per annum. In order to allocate the overhead cost we need to add a further 24 per cent to this figure, which comes to a total cost of £207.95.

In terms of labour, if we assume total labour hours within the warehouse each year of 120,000 hours our labour cost is £10.00 per hour. By adding the overhead our cost comes to £12.40.

Taking this one step further, if we look at Customer A, who uses a large number of warehouse labour hours and space yet his pull on management time, for example, is low, he is penalized for the way the overhead costs have been allocated. See Table 12.2.

We will look at how shared-user warehouses can calculate storage and labour charges later in this chapter.

TABLE 12.1   Warehouse cost structure

Space cost	£1,677,000
Space as percentage of total warehouse cost	54%
Labour cost	£1,200,000
Labour as percentage of total warehouse cost	39%
Equipment cost	£215,000
Equipment as percentage of total warehouse cost	7%
Total direct cost	£3,092,000
Overhead cost	£742,000
Total cost	£3,834,000
Overhead as percentage of cost	24%

TABLE 12.2   Overhead contribution

	Number of pallet locations	Number of labour hours	Total overhead contribution %	Pull on management time %
Customer A	2,000	20,000	17.3%	5%
Customer B	200	200	1.15%	10%

With the proliferation of products and service complexity, a single overhead rate is no longer sufficient.

In most cases overhead does not reduce as labour or equipment reduces. Therefore as volumes reduce, overhead as a percentage of direct costs actually increases.

Overhead rates are also based on predicted volumes or utilization and therefore as utilization reduces the percentage allocation of overhead needs to increase.

For example, going back to our shared-user warehouse and Customer A, if he decides to reduce his stockholding and it is not replaced by another client, the charge per location needs to be increased. Based on a reduction of 500 pallets, his overhead contribution reduces by 2.7 per cent (£20,125), yet the overhead cost to the company is unlikely to reduce in the short term.

As can be seen, therefore, traditional costing methods have a number of weaknesses – which is why many companies are turning to other methods of costing. Activity-based costing is one of these methods.

Activity-based costing

According to Griful-Miquela (2001):

> Activity-based costing systems are designed so that any costs that cannot be attributed directly to a product (or service) flow into the activities that make them necessary. The cost of each activity then flows to the product(s) (or service) that makes the activity necessary based on their respective consumption of that activity.

Activity-based costing looks to allocate indirect costs to processes in a way that accurately reflects how the costs are actually incurred. This is in contrast to traditional costing methods.

When looking to introduce an ABC model, you need to have a comprehensive knowledge of the company, its operations and the roles of each of the staff members. This is normally carried out by observing the operation for a period of time and recording how long it takes for each activity.

A good guideline for selecting the cost drivers that most accurately reflect the cost of performing an activity is to ask the people who do that work what would increase or decrease the time and effort required to do their job. Table 12.3 provides an example.

Once all the operational and overhead costs have been calculated and each customer's pull on the services has been documented, companies can calculate the profitability of each client and see how they affect the cost structure of the business.

The overheads should be allocated based on the actual management time dedicated to each activity and customer. Cost of telephone calls, printing, etc should also be allocated on a usage basis for example.

This analysis of overheads is likely to be the most complicated to perform. This is the main difference between ABC and traditional methods, where in the latter overheads are allocated across all activities as a percentage of cost. With ABC it is necessary to carry out in-depth studies over a period of time in order to find the relationship between overheads, services and customers.

Once all of the activities have been evaluated and costs allocated to customers there is likely to be some unused capacity.

TABLE 12.3   Main warehouse activities and cost drivers
(adapted from Griful-Miquela 2001)

Activities	Cost drivers
Order receipt	Order volume and order source (EDI, fax, phone or post)
Unload incoming goods	Quantity and unit load (pallets or cartons)
Palletize	Quantity of cartons
Check incoming goods	Quantity and quality of supplier (including returns)
Put away incoming goods	Quantity, cubic volume
Picking	Number of visits to pick location, number of lines, number of units
Packaging and labelling	Number of orders picked
Replenishment	Unit load quantity
Load outgoing goods	Unit load quantity

For example, a warehouse with a total capacity for storage of 10,000 pallets is not going to be 100 per cent occupied. Similarly, not all of the MHE and labour hours will be allocated to individual customers in totality.

It is therefore very useful to produce a table indicating the degree of utilization for all those areas.

These costs either need to be managed out of the operation through a reduction in labour and equipment, for example, or taken into account when initially quoting the customer or allocating to a particular product, or accepted in the short term as an inevitable cost and work towards increasing utilization or throughput to allocate these costs to a new product or client.

If all the costs incurred are allocated against individual customers this will increase the charges to those customers, which could result in lower sales and a further reduction in capacity utilization.

According to Griful-Miquela (2001), whenever unused capacity appears, it is necessary to analyse the reasons leading to this situation. Depending on the reasons, the actions to be undertaken may differ. For example, the degree of unused capacity can be an indicator of how the employees are allocated among the different activities. It is possible to reallocate some of them with this information. For example, the in-handling team may have additional capacity and could therefore be allocated to replenishment or picking tasks. It is very important to analyse when a constraint appears. This might indicate the need for a new investment in the short term or risk being unable to cope with future requirements if no action is taken.

As previously discussed, a warehouse cannot operate efficiently if it is 100 per cent occupied, therefore there have to be some empty pallet locations. Similarly with labour, we have to take into account breaks during the working day.

Table 12.4 shows an example of an ABC model. We have calculated the number of pallet spaces occupied and number of labour and MHE hours allocated to each customer. We have also allocated the management time in hours per customer and allocated other overhead costs such as postage, legal expenses, insurance, etc on a percentage basis, based on the administrative hours.

The above hours can be further broken down into the individual activities within the warehouse and the costs allocated by customer. These costs can then be compared to the actual charges levied to the customer and any shortfall examined.

Having calculated all of the above, we are also able to see the amount of unused capacity within the warehouse.

The disadvantages of using ABC include the amount of work involved and difficulty in collecting accurate data. Implementation can take time and there needs to be a cost–benefit analysis in terms of the time taken and the benefits accrued.

Charging for shared-user warehouse services

A shared-user warehouse is one in which a third-party logistics provider stores on behalf of a number of different customers. They may be related in some way as suppliers to a particular retailer, for example, or competitors who have decided to come together to share resource and save on outbound distribution costs.

Examples of the latter include bicycle manufacturers in the Netherlands who saw the storage and handling of their products being specialized and potentially costly. Other warehouses can have very diverse clients. When operating a third-party warehouse in the 1990s we had three toy companies, a book publisher, a drinks manufacturer, two white goods manufacturers, a software company, a kitchen utensils manufacturer, a pet food manufacturer and a photographic film manufacturer.

TABLE 12.4 Example ABC model

	Space (no of pallets)	Labour (no of hours)	MHE No. of hours	Administration hours	Overhead A Management hours	Overhead B Other costs
Total capacity	10,000 pallets	120,000 hours	30,000 hours	10,000 hours	20,000 hours	100%
Customer A	2,000	20,000	5,000	500	1,000	5%
Customer B	200	200	100	1,000	2,000	10%
Customer C	1,400	25,000	8,000	2,000	3,500	20%
Customer D	900	18,000	4,500	2,500	5,000	25%
Customer E	2,300	21,800	3,000	1,500	1,000	15%
Customer F	1,000	12,000	1,900	1,000	500	10%
Operational leeway/ unproductive hours	1,500	18,000	5,000	1,000	4,000	0
Unused capacity	700	5,000	2,500	500	3,000	15%

Products ranged from bulk block-stacked cans and bottles of beer, bulk block-stacked washing machines, pallets of cartons containing toys, kitchen utensils, cans of pet food and books and shelves of software titles.

So how do you charge these clients for the storage, handling and despatch of their products?

Shared-user warehouse customers are normally charged on an activity basis. Typical methods of charging are as follows.

Storage charges

Storage charge examples:

- rate per pallet per week;
- rate per item per week;
- rate per square foot per week;
- rate per cubic foot per week;
- rate per tonne per week;
- rate per shelf location per week; and
- fixed rental cost per week/month.

In the first six examples the rate is based on the unit of measure (UoM). This can cover clients who are storing pallets or items such as white goods which can be bulk block stacked, clients who require racked pallet storage or those who require smaller locations such as shelving or a combination of all three.

Calculating the total number of pallets to be charged per week can be done in a number of ways:

- the highest number of pallets in store during the week;
- the average number of pallets in stock per week;
- opening stock plus intake; and
- opening stock plus intake minus despatches.

In scenario 1 (Table 12.5) the charge will be for 200 pallets, this being the highest number in stock that week.

In scenario 2 the charge will be for 125 pallets, this being the average over the week.

In scenario 3 the charge will be for 400 pallets.

In scenario 4 the charge will be for 70 pallets.

Most companies will look for a minimum charge. In this example the minimum charge is likely to be for 100 pallets.

In the case of a fixed rental cost per week or month, the client pays a fixed rate each week or month based on a previously agreed area or number of

TABLE 12.5   Pallet storage charge calculations

Number of pallets/days	Monday	Tuesday	Wednesday	Thursday	Friday	Saturday	Sunday
Number of pallets	100	175	200	190	70	70	70
Intake	100	100	50	10	20	20	0
Despatches	25	75	60	130	20	20	0

UoMs. For example, a client may require an area of 1,000 square feet in which to store product and carry out some value-adding services.

If the client does not use the whole space they will still be charged the full rate. From the client's point of view they are able to budget accurately each month. If the client exceeds the amount of space agreed they will pay an additional charge.

Handling charges

These are commonly known as RH&D charges, or receipt, handling and despatch. These are normally charged on a rate per pallet in-handled. Companies have to be careful here as this only covers full pallets handled in and handled out. If items are despatched as cartons an in-handling charge per pallet is normally used together with a rate per case despatched.

The costs are based on the amount of time calculated to undertake each movement plus the cost of the mechanical handling equipment utilized.

A typical example is shown in Table 12.6.

In terms of outhandling costs if it is the same full pallet we can use the same costs as above but in reverse. If the despatch is in cartons or individual items we need to calculate the amount of time it takes to pick and load an order.

For this rate we need to understand the customer's outbound operation in terms of number of orders, lines and units per order, packing and labelling requirements.

The cost build-up will be as follows:

- Labour – time
  - collection of order;
  - travel time to each location;
  - pick time at each location;

TABLE 12.6 In-handling cost per pallet

Activity	Labour time	Labour charge per hour	Total labour cost	Equipment cost per hour	Total equipment cost	Total cost
Unload 13.6 metre trailer (26 pallets)	0.5 hours	£17.00	£8.50	£10.00	£5.00	£13.50
Take to racking	0.5 hours	£17.00	£8.50	£10.00	£5.00	£13.50
Put away in racking	1 hour	£17.00	£17.00	£18.00	£18.00	£35.00
Total cost						£62.00
Cost per pallet in-handled excluding administration and supervisory costs, overhead and profit						£2.39

- – travel time to despatch area;
- – labelling and packing time;
- – checking time (if necessary);
- – loading time.
- • Equipment – time
  - – use of powered pallet truck;
  - – contribution to voice technology;
- • other;
  - – packing and labelling materials;
  - – supervisory and administration costs;
- • overhead;
- • profit.

Once calculated and divided by the average number of cases per order we should end up with a cost per unit outhandled.

Value-added services

These would normally be charged on an hourly basis until a cost per unit can be calculated taking into account the productivity, eg number of units labelled per hour. In this case you will also need to take into account the cost of the labels and allocate space and equipment costs to the charge. You need to factor in the cost of picking the products from their locations together with any ancillary items and the transfer to and from the value-added services area. Supervisory costs should also be taken into account.

Logistics charging methods

In both internally and externally operated warehouses, costs need to be presented to customers – whether these are external customers or internal customers who have a cost attributed to their products.

As noted earlier, many businesses look at warehousing costs as a percentage of sales or production cost. In some instances costs are applied on this basis. This can be dangerous unless there is a safety net for the supplier. As throughput and storage decline it is unlikely that the number of people required will be reduced at the same percentage rate. Also it is unlikely that the vacated space will be filled immediately. More often, though, costs are presented to the customer as an internal or external charge supported, to different degrees, by invoices and cost justifications.

The principles discussed earlier in this chapter identify the basis of justifying costs and charges for services supplied. In the case of third-party supply this will be in the form of invoices. The following sections describe how to construct those invoices or cost allocations.

Open book

An open-book contract is based on total transparency between supplier and customer. The client is able to see exactly what costs the third party is incurring and is able to discuss these costs and potential cost-reduction strategies.

It is common in these types of contract to agree a management fee that is determined by performance. A base fee will be agreed together with set targets. If the targets are achieved, the management fee will be increased; if the third party falls short due to poor performance, they will forfeit *some* of their management fee.

This type of charging allows the client to become involved in the process and identify areas where its own performance can have an effect on the overall cost. Within an internal process the product owner can identify which factors have an impact on the total product cost.

Cost-plus contracts

These contracts are similar to open book; however, in most cases the 'plus' element is based on a percentage increase on cost. This can lead to the perverse situation where the higher the costs incurred on the contract, the higher the profit earned by the third party.

Cost-plus arrangements historically evolved to counter fears that fixed and variable rates masked true costs and allowed third-party providers to extract high profits. Cost plus took the first step towards identifying cost and setting (at the time) a 'reasonable' profit.

In these types of contract there need to be stringent targets and a commitment to reduce overall costs. A gain-share agreement where both parties 'win' when costs are reduced is a potential method of ensuring focus on cost reduction.

Closed-book contracts

In these types of contract, charges are based on the activities carried out by the third party as discussed above. The charges will include an element for overhead contribution and profit margin.

As volumes increase, so will the total revenue earned by the third party. Conversely, as volumes reduce so will the third-party provider's revenue.

With closed-book contracts customers get fixed, index-linked prices for given volumes and are unable to see the actual third-party costs. Third parties will look to cushion some of the fluctuations in volume by imposing minimum storage and throughput levels.

This type of charging has its advantages and disadvantages. The main advantage is that costs are closely related to sales in terms of order throughput. Storage costs are based on the number of items stored and therefore can highlight when stock levels are higher than expected.

The main disadvantage is that it is more difficult to budget as costs will vary month by month depending on activities within the warehouse.

Secondly, rate reviews tend to occur annually and therefore do not reflect performance improvement as it occurs.

Hybrid

There are a number of different charging systems which can take elements of the above and combine them – for example, charges for fixed items such as property rental and IT assets may be paid for on an open-book basis while item throughput can be charged for on an activity basis.

Summary and conclusion

Warehouse managers require a comprehensive understanding of the costs that relate to their warehouse operation. This is not only to contribute to the company budget but also to enable the company to allocate costs to products or, in a third-party relationship, to charge for the services provided. It can also identify loss-making customers or products if we delve deeply enough into the figures.

Performance management

13

> "What you do not measure, you cannot control.
>
> **(TOM PETERS)**

Introduction

In today's economy it has been said that the customer is no longer king but dictator. With the proliferation of websites reviewing products and services it has become even more important to match or even exceed customer expectations in terms of quality and the service provided.

One example of poor service can far outweigh all of the times where deliveries were made on time and complete.

No longer can companies take an order and quote a 28-day delivery service; in most cases delivery is expected next day and in some cases even on the same day.

The next point to note is that it is far cheaper to keep an existing customer than find a new customer. Therefore satisfying your current customer base is paramount.

Well-established research by Reichheld and Teal (2001) found that, for many companies, an increase of 5 per cent in customer retention can increase profits by 25 to 95 per cent. The same study found that it costs six to seven times more to gain a new customer than to keep an existing one.

From a warehouse perspective this means that you have to ensure accuracy, quality, timeliness and cost effectiveness within the processes you control. By doing this, you are contributing to a high-performance operation and as a result, contributing to customer satisfaction and retention.

As discussed previously, the warehouse operation is crucial in ensuring that the customer gets the right product at the right time and in the right condition.

This chapter looks at why we need to measure, what we need to measure and how we can use this information to improve our overall service to our customers.

Why do we need to measure?

There are a number of reasons why we need to measure performance and productivity within the warehouse. We measure because we need to:

- ensure customer satisfaction;
- ensure that there is a culture of continuous improvement within the operation;
- discover potential issues before they become major problems;
- train staff in the right areas; and
- reward staff where appropriate.

Unless we measure our performance against our customers' expectations and continually improve on that performance, we are not only in danger of losing our customers but we will also incur additional costs.

For example, incorrect item or quantity of items sent will incur the following:

- Finance department is affected by delayed payments and possible penalties.
- Inventory department has to provide extra stock cover.
- Sales department has to handle complaints and authorize returns.
- Transport department has to effect extra deliveries and collections.
- Warehouse has to re-pick, re-pack and duplicate activities.
- Returns procedure has to take place.
- Possible product disposal/write-off.
- Review of processes needs to take place.
- Potential additional training required.
- Loss of product if client keeps the over-delivered product.
- Potential loss of customer.

What should we be measuring?

According to Ackerman (2003), we should be measuring four areas within the warehouse:

- reliability;
- flexibility;
- cost; and
- asset utilization.

Reliability includes on-time delivery, fill rates and accuracy. Order cycle time is probably the best measure of flexibility as it covers all aspects of the customer order process: how we handle the order initially, whether we have the stock available, how quickly we can process the order through the warehouse and, finally, how quickly we can deliver to the customer.

Cost measurements include cost as a percentage of sales and productivity against labour hours. Asset utilization will include efficient use of warehouse space, MHE, staff and storage equipment.

Warehouse utilization is normally measured in the amount of floor space utilized. However, it is more realistic to measure the cubic utilization of the building. Other companies will look at the number of pallet locations utilized against the total number of locations available.

Frazelle (2002) suggests that as occupancy rates exceed 86 per cent utilization, productivity and safety decline exponentially with each percentage point increase in occupancy. He goes on to say that warehouses managed in real time might be able to operate at 90 per cent occupancy, although this is wholly dependent on the accuracy of the system and the experience of the warehouse team.

Third-party logistics companies will look to increase space utilization to the maximum as this is a revenue stream for them. However, productivity reduces significantly when space is at a premium. The coordination of pallets out and pallets in (in that order) is paramount, otherwise major bottlenecks appear.

In order to ensure that you provide your customers with the service they require, you need to understand your customers' requirements both as a whole and individually and, secondly, the limitations you have within your company and operation.

Performance is a broad term that covers both overall economic and operational aspects. Slack et al (2001) offer the following description of high-performance operations that most companies strive to accomplish:

- High-quality operations don't waste time or effort having to redo things, nor are their internal customers inconvenienced by flawed service.

- Fast operations ensure a quick turnaround of orders.

- Dependable operations can be relied on to deliver exactly as planned. This eliminates wasteful disruption and allows the other micro operations to operate efficiently.

- Flexible operations adapt to changing circumstances quickly and without disrupting the rest of the operation.

- Low-cost operations lead to higher profits as well as allowing the company to sell their products at a competitive price.

FIGURE 13.1 Retailer and third-party KPIs (courtesy of Steve Whyman)

Retail Customer	Provider
• Costs as a % of sales • Fixed cost/variable cost split and YOY change • YOY cost increase versus YOY sales increase • Inventory value change versus sales value change YOY • Freight costs as a % of COGS • Costs as a % of sales – new stores versus LFL stores • Waste costs – (product/late delivery, etc) • Segmented cost to serve – eg product/store format/channel • On shelf availability/lost sales opportunity	• Logistics costs – absolute • Cost per line/order • Units/cases per man hour • Management fee/incentive won/lost • % pick accuracy • Service level – delivery to schedule • Direct/indirect hours • Lost time/cost • Cost per pallet – core/seasonal flex
Consumer/investor centric	**Operational centric**

Key
YOY – Year on year
LFL – Like for like
COGS – Cost of goods sold

One of the main things to understand is that in terms of performance measures, you need to:

- monitor performance against the criteria that are important to your customers (delivery of the perfect order);

- monitor performance against the criteria that are important to you (costs).

As can be seen in Figure 13.1, different players have different ideas as to what is important in terms of performance measurement. The figure depicts which key performance indicators (KPIs) are important to a retailer and which are important to their third-party logistics service provider.

The best measures therefore are those that are aligned to and governed by customer expectations. However, they also need to be aligned to your company's resources.

According to Rushton, Croucher and Baker (2010), there is a need to balance the level of customer service with the cost of providing that service. They go on to say that the cost of providing a given service is markedly higher the nearer it reaches the 'perfect service', that is, 100 per cent.

FIGURE 13.2   Cost of service improvement (courtesy of Rushton, Croucher and Baker 2010)

Cost of service improvement

For example, 100 per cent next day, on time, in full may only be achieved by having sufficient inventory to satisfy every customer's needs, and every order that leaves the building would need to be double or triple checked for accuracy.

They say that the cost of an increase in service from 95 per cent to 100 per cent will be far greater than an increase from 70 to 80 per cent, as can be seen in Figure 13.2. This may be anathema to certain companies and cultures where service is overriding and paramount; however, you have to be realistic and accept that 100 per cent on time in full every time is desirable but not always achievable.

Productivity is part of the overall performance umbrella: productivity output such as goods and services produced in relation to inputs that include labour, finance, material and other resources.

Warehouse managers have a number of inputs and resources under their control including labour and MHE. The key to running an efficient warehouse is to make best use of these inputs.

The essence of productivity measurement is the recording and analysis of the time it takes to perform each handling movement within the warehouse. This seems a daunting task. However, if you are to continually improve the operation you need to be able to measure it accurately. Not only do you need

TABLE 13.1   Manual record of work

Name: D Morgan
Shift No. 1
Area: zone 1
Day: Monday

Task description	Start time	Finish time	Volume	Lines per order	Equipment	Measure
Pick order 123456	08.45	09.03	50 cases	5	PPT	167 cases per hour
Pick order 123498	09.05	09.30	80 cases	6	PPT	192 cases per hour
Stretch wrap pallets	09.31	10.07	24 pallets		S/W machine	40 pallets per hour
Load trailer ab072	10.08	10.38	24 pallets		PPT	48 pallets per hour

to measure each activity but also measure it at different times of the day and undertaken by different people.

The task, of course, is much easier if you are using technology such as voice or radio data terminals, where the system can log start and finish times. As previously discussed, this technology can record all the movements and tasks performed by operators in the warehouse, providing reports that the warehouse manager can use to assess and improve performance.

The example in Table 13.1 shows a typical manual record of work.

When measuring these activities you also need to take into account the following:

- preparation time (collecting, equipment, pallet, paperwork);
- human factors (skills, motivation, fatigue);
- mechanical factors (battery changing, attachment changes, refuelling); and
- operational factors (location system, product placement, congestion).

These can be a significant percentage of the time taken to undertake the task.

If you are a third-party operator you need to know how long it takes you to undertake the different tasks associated with the warehouse in order to quote and charge your customers accordingly. Chapter 12 looks at third-party warehousing and how to cost each activity.

The crucial factor in any form of productivity or performance measurement is to ensure the cooperation of staff.

The staff need to know how the measures are derived and why they are important. They must be made aware of the reasons behind the measurements, what the information will be used for and that they will also become beneficiaries of an improved operation.

Finally, you need to decide whether the measures are individual or taken on a group basis.

To put Tom Peters' remark, quoted at the head of this chapter, another way: you can't manage what you can't measure.

There are many areas within the warehouse where performance is key to the company's well-being.

As mentioned previously, getting the right product to the right customer in the correct quantity and condition, on time and at a competitive price are key to retaining that customer.

How to choose the right performance measures

Each company will have different priorities, a different customer base and a different method of operation. In order to choose the most appropriate measure you need to undertake the following:

- Understand your business and its strategy.
- Decide on the objectives.
- Understand which KPIs are likely to assist in meeting the objectives.
- Align the KPIs to others within the company.
- Ensure that everyone works towards achieving the targets – nominate KPI owners.
- If targets aren't achieved, analyse the reasons why and introduce processes to enable achievement.
- If the target isn't realistic, replace it.

Vitasek (2004) developed a process that helps to establish department metrics that support the overall corporate objectives and links accountability to achieve

TABLE 13.2 Department metrics (courtesy of Vitasek 2010)

Department	Target
Receiving	Reduce dock to stock time
Customer service	Reduce order process time
Picking	Improve pick accuracy Increase pick productivity

goals where the work gets done. It also creates an environment where employees use their metrics to drive positive change in the business.

For example, if the company goal is to reduce order lead time and improve accuracy the targets shown in Table 13.2 can be set for specific departments.

The first task in any performance measurement system is to understand the vision of the company and how your department can assist in achieving the company's goals.

Too often department heads will produce key performance measures which they are comfortable with and which are easily achievable but are not aligned to the company's vision and are rarely of interest to senior managers. Departments end up with too many measures which detract from the day-to-day running of the operation.

The measures you choose need to be SMART. That is, they need to be:

- **Specific.** Objectives should specify what they want to achieve. Are they clear and unambiguous?
- **Measurable.** Can we put a value on the kpi? Eg How much, how long, how many?
- **Achievable.** Are the targets you set achievable and attainable?
- **Relevant.** Are the measures relevant to the overall goal and strategy of the company?
- **Timely.** Are the timescales realistic and how often do you measure?

You need to ensure that the data collected is accurate.

Moseley (2004) and Vitasek (2004) suggest that when introducing key performance indicators you should:

- use terminology that your staff understand and is meaningful to them;
- understand what your staff need to do to improve service or reduce costs as identified by the KPIs;

- try to use common industry KPIs so that you can benchmark your own operation against your peers;

- review the data regularly and look for specific trends;

- not overreact to a particular data point;

- only introduce measures you know you can implement and measure;

- only introduce cost-effective metrics, ie ensure that it doesn't cost you more to manage than the likely savings you make;

- only introduce measures you know you can change;

- not measure what you won't or can't change;

- be seen to be using the data; there is nothing more frustrating than collecting data which isn't used.

Traditional productivity measures

There are many traditional productivity measures in use in today's warehouses.

The first of these group measures are based on labour, space and equipment utilization:

Labour hours utilization

This measurement looks at the utilization of labour hours within the warehouse based on the total number of labour hours available to work over a particular shift, day or even week. These hours should not include breaks.

The calculation is:

$$(\text{Labour hours used} \times 100) \div \text{labour hours available}$$

Warehouse area utilization

This can be measured in a number of different ways. We can look at floor space utilization but more realistically we should measure the cubic capacity of the warehouse.

Alternatively we can measure the number of pallet locations utilized against the total possible locations.

The calculation is:

$$(\text{Space used} \times 100) \div \text{space available}$$

For example, space utilization = 8,600 pallet spaces occupied ÷ 10,000 pallet spaces available = 86 per cent utilization.

If your warehouse has a number of different sections with racking in some areas and floor storage in others then a number of calculations will be required.

Note that you need to measure the space that can be specifically used for storage. Areas used for goods in, despatch, value-adding services, etc should not be included in your calculations.

Although improving space utilization is an important goal for any warehouse, the key to improving overall warehouse productivity, that is space and labour, is to find the best compromise between storage utilization and handling efficiency.

MHE utilization

The calculation is:

$$(\text{MHE hours used} \times 100) \div \text{MHE hours available}$$

The next group of measures looks at cost performance.

In financial terms, measures include cost as a percentage of sales and cost per order despatched.

These are calculated as follows:

Cost as a percentage of sales

The calculation is:

$$(\text{Total warehousing cost} \times 100) \div \text{total sales revenue}$$

Cost per order despatched

The calculation is:

$$\text{Total warehouse cost} \div \text{total number of orders shipped}$$

The above performance cost measures need to be handled with care. Cheaper products despatched from the warehouse can result in a higher cost per order, which is not a reflection of increased costs in the warehouse but a strategic decision made by the company.

The third group is based on productivity measures:

Units picked per hour

The calculation is:

$$\text{Units picked} \div \text{total hours available}$$

The unit in this example can be an individual item, a carton or a pallet.

Dock-to-stock time

This is the time taken from arrival of vehicle on the receiving bay to visibility of stock on the system

The final group is based on customer service measures:

Order accuracy

The calculation is:

$$(\text{Orders picked and despatched accurately} \times 100) \div \text{total orders received}$$

On-time shipments

The calculation is:

$$\text{Orders delivered as per customers' requests} \div \text{total orders received}$$

In terms of performance measures, the 12 metrics most commonly used in distribution centres, according to a recent survey in the United States by WERC (2012), are as follows:

- on-time shipments (orders delivered as per customers' requests);
- internal order cycle time;
- dock-to-stock cycle time in hours (time from stock arrival to available to pick);
- total order cycle time;
- order-picking accuracy (correct number of lines and units delivered);
- lines picked and shipped per hour;
- lines received and put-away per hour;
- percentage of suppliers' orders received damage free;
- average warehouse capacity used;
- order fill rate (orders filled completely on first shipment);

- percentage of supplier orders received with correct documents; and
- peak warehouse capacity used.

A full list of warehouse performance measures will be included later together with actual metrics from the study.

New performance metrics

One of the most common measures in the United Kingdom today is OTIF (on time and in full).

This metric has been joined by the perfect order metric as the most popular customer service metric. This not only requires on time in full delivery but also the item has to be damage free, have the correct documentation and label and finally an accurate invoice.

In the following example all four metrics are measured individually and then multiplied together to produce the perfect order percentage:

On-time delivery = 97%

In full delivery = 98.5%

Damage free = 99.5%

Accurate documentation, labelling and invoicing = 98%

Therefore the perfect order metric is 97% × 98.5% × 99.5% × 98% = 93.2%.
In terms of OTIF, we get a result of 95.5% (97% × 98.5%).

Inventory measures

A warehouse manager is tasked with accounting for and measuring inventory but has limited influence on the level of inventory held in the warehouse. However, you may be asked to produce the following metrics.

Stock cover in days

This can be calculated by dividing the current level of stock by the total annual sales and multiplying by 365. This can be done using the actual number of units in stock or the value of the stock. This tells us how many days' cover we have of stock.

For example, in Table 13.3 we can see that product code 99172100 has two and a half year's worth of stock in the warehouse. On the other hand, product code 90152100 only has five days' stock in the warehouse.

TABLE 13.3 Stock cover calculations

Product code	Number of units in stock	Annual sales in units	Stock cover (days)
90132100	500	4,000	46
90133100	1,400	3,250	157
90133200	1,000	800	456
90152100	30	2,000	5
90153100	40	50	292
90153200	80	500	58
99172100	1,000	400	913
99173100	16	800	7

Stock turn

This can be calculated by dividing the total number of units sold by the average number of units in stock.

For example, in Table 13.3 product 90132100 has a stock turn of eight, which is reasonable, whereas product code 99172100 has a stock turn of 0.4, which means that the stock turns over less than once per annum – in fact once every 2.5 years.

These calculations can be used to determine stock ordering policy and also whether some stock should be returned to the manufacturer, disposed of, or a sales campaign organized.

The days' stock figure should be aligned with the supplier lead time, the criticality of the item and the availability of the item from other sources.

As with many aspects of logistics, a balance needs to be reached between ensuring the maximum possible service and a minimum stockholding.

Stock/inventory accuracy

Another example of inventory measures includes stock accuracy. Whether stock is counted once, twice a year or daily by cycle counting or perpetual inventory, stock accuracy is an important measure. The more accurate the stock the more likely you are to fulfil orders correctly and increase efficiency.

Measures include the following:

Location stock accuracy percentage =
(number of correct locations ÷ number of locations counted) × 100

Stock line accuracy =
(number of correct lines counted ÷ total no. of lines counted) × 100

Stock unit accuracy =
(actual quantity by SKU ÷ expected quantity by SKU) × 100

Many companies compare the value of goods in the warehouse to book stock as a measure of stock accuracy.

Reporting a 100 per cent accurate stock count because the stock value is as expected and therefore 'correct' can hide a number of sins.

Surplus obsolete stock in the warehouse amounting to £10,000 with a corresponding shortfall of £10,000 worth of popular items, although potentially acceptable from a finance department viewpoint, can significantly affect the warehouse operation.

Accuracy by line and by location is therefore paramount for an efficient warehouse.

Damaged inventory

This measures the amount of damage caused within the warehouse. It can be measured by dividing the total number of damaged items by the total number of items processed through the warehouse. It can also be measured in monetary terms:

Damaged items percentage =
items found damaged ÷ items despatched per month

Hard and soft measures

The above forms of measurement are referred to as hard measures. By this we mean they are relatively easy to measure, being quantifiable and less ambiguous.

Having been appointed customer services manager for a third-party warehouse operator, I was constantly being told by our customers how poor our service was. I decided to introduce performance measures into the operation to enable us to either refute the customer claims or improve the service in the areas where we were failing.

We looked at which measures were important to our customers.

Once the measures were in place we were able to prove to our customers that our service was in line with the Service Level Agreements and reasonably in line with their expectations. The problem in the past was that customers only remembered the times when service was below standard. Once the measures were in place this changed the customers' perceptions immediately.

Staff were tasked with producing key performance indicators for the areas which were important to our customers. These were discussed at monthly review meetings and any shortfall in service was examined in detail. This took the adversarial approach away from the meetings and both the good and bad performances were discussed and evaluated.

In contrast, soft measurements are those that deal with intangible attributes.

A typical example is customer satisfaction with accuracy of delivery when we ask the question – how are we doing? Soft measures are good at measuring perceived changes and will often provide a more complete picture of success compared with narrowly focused hard measures.

Soft measures are difficult, but not impossible, to define and measure. For example, a survey via a questionnaire can be used to assess several aspects of user satisfaction, for example on a scale of 1 to 10. The survey can be repeated at appropriate intervals to examine changes in perceived service.

Surveys can be used to improve service quality by asking customers to score service quality for the provider against a company thought to be excellent in its market.

Research by Landrum *et al* (2009) has shown reliability and responsiveness to be the most important contributing factors to service quality. Reliability factors include the following:

- providing services as promised;
- dependability in handling customers' service problems;
- performing services right the first time;
- providing services at the promised time;
- maintaining error-free records.

As can be seen, these measures relate very closely to the perfect order metric.

Integrated performance models

Integrated performance models are a mix of actual performance data and customer perception. The data is compiled from actual performance reports and from questionnaires sent to customers on a regular basis.

TABLE 13.4 Integrated performance model (adapted from and printed with permission of Tompkins Associates 1998)

Category	Target rating	Weight	Target score	Rating	Actual score
Perfect order completion	5	50	250	1 2 3 4 5	150 (R)
Inventory accuracy	5	40	200	1 2 3 4 5	200 (G)
Housekeeping/safety	5	40	200	1 2 3 4 5	160 (A)
Labour productivity	5	30	150	1 2 3 4 5	120 (A)
Space utilization	4	30	120	1 2 3 4 5	90 (A)
Labour utilization	4	30	120	1 2 3 4 5	90 (A)
Damaged items	5	30	150	1 2 3 4 5	90 (A)
Warehouse layout	4	20	80	1 2 3 4 5	100 (G)
Equipment utilization	4	10	40	1 2 3 4 5	50 (G)
Staff training	5	10	50	1 2 3 4 5	50 (G)
Environmental	4	10	40	1 2 3 4 5	20 (R)
TOTAL		300	**1400**		**1120 (R)**
Performance index					**80%**

As can be seen from Table 13.4, each category is given a target rating and a weight of importance. This produces a target score by multiplying the two together.

An actual rating is also given based on the results of the survey and the actual performance, which in turn produces an actual score.

Areas which are underperforming against target are highlighted using the red, amber and green (RAG) model. The red areas are the ones which will require attention.

As can be seen from the table, perfect order completion is given a target rating of 5 out of 5, with the highest weighting of 50, giving a target score of 250.

The categories are chosen to reflect the vision of the company and need to be SMART.

In any form of performance measurement you need to ensure that your measures are aligned with your customers' requirements and expectations. For example, 100 per cent despatch of what's available from the warehouse is not always the same as the quantities ordered by the customer. The order may have been adjusted by the sales staff before it reached the warehouse.

Secondly, 24-hour despatch from order receipt at the warehouse may not be 24 hours from the placement of the order. The order could have been delayed in customer services.

Benchmarking

This section looks at benchmarking and how it can assist you in your operation.

Benchmarking has been around since the early 19th century; however, it came to the fore in the 1980s when it was championed by Xerox Corporation.

It is a process of comparing performance with operations of other companies, or operations within the same company, identifying high-performance or best-in-class operations and learning what it is they do that allows them to achieve that high level of performance.

Why should we benchmark?

Benchmarking enables us to:

- understand our own performance;
- identify any shortcomings;
- discover what others are doing better;
- identify performance targets that can be demonstrated to be achievable;
- accelerate and manage change;
- improve processes;
- understand what is best practice.

A word of caution. Benchmarking may point to best current practice but not to best possible practice. 'As good as' is not 'better than'. It is not a substitute for creativity and innovation.

Benchmarking can be undertaken both internally and externally. There are a number of supply chain and logistics related benchmarking clubs. These include the Chartered Institute of Logistics and Transport's Logmark, Asia's Benchmarking Success, The Best Practice Club and the United States' WERC, CSCR and DLMB Consortium.

In terms of external benchmarking you need to choose your partners carefully. To this end there are also industry-specific benchmarking surveys such as those produced by the Institute of Grocery Distribution for retailers.

As in performance measurement, there are pitfalls to avoid. Benchmarking should not be considered until you have an intimate knowledge of your own processes. Secondly, do not select processes to benchmark which don't have sufficient potential for improvement.

The principles of benchmarking are as follows:

- collaboration;
- confidentiality;
- value;
- flexibility;
- honesty;
- openness; and
- reputation.

There is always likely to be a reluctance to share information with competitors. However, in order to produce meaningful results, honesty and openness are paramount.

One potential method of ensuring confidentiality and anonymity is to utilize a third party such as a benchmarking group, a consultancy or a university.

The example in Table 13.5 is from Mondelēz, who benchmark each of their distribution centres Europe-wide. All the centres work towards the same targets to enable a comparison across sites and ensure best practice is achieved.

There are eight major areas made up from 34 individual measures. Utilizing this benchmarking tool, the Mondelēz team is able to compare its own in-house operations with that of their third-party logistics providers.

TABLE 13.5 Mondelēz benchmarking model

Country and Site			
UK: 3PL A			
Category			**Units**
Warehouse	**Operational metrics**	Cases despatched (total)	Number
		Pallets despatched (total)	Number
		Case pick pallets despatched	%
		Total warehouse cost including overheads	£
	KPIs	Full pallet pick	%
		Cost per case despatched	£
		Cost per pallet despatched	£
Service	**KPIs**	Case fill (Log Ops responsible)	%
		On time in full (Log Ops responsible)	%
Transport IB	**Operational metrics**	Number of cases received	Number
		Number of pallets received	Number
		Number of loads received	Number
	KPIs	Vehicle utilization	%
Transport OB	**Operational metrics**	Number of cases despatched	Number
		Number of pallets despatched	Number
		Number of loads despatched	Number
	KPIs	Vehicle utilization	%
Inventory	**Operational metrics**	Total inventory value	Euro
		Total warehouse pallet capacity	Number
		Number of pallets in stock (month end)	Number
		Value of inventory written off (Log Ops responsibility)	Euro
	KPIs	Warehouse utilization	%

IB = Inbound
OB = Outbound

TABLE 13.5   *continued*

Category			Units
Safety	**KPIs**	LTIFR (global definition)	Number
		Total number accidents	Number
		Number of lost time accidents	Number
Quality	**Operational metrics**	Number of pallets on hold or in quarantine	Number
	KPIs	Cases damaged in transit	Number
		Cases damaged in warehouse	Number
		Transport security incidents reported	Number
Environment	**Operational metrics**	Electricity consumption	KWh
		Gas consumption	Cubic M
		Transport CO_2 emissions	Tonnes
	KPIs	Outbound CO_2 per pallet shipped	Tonnes
	KPIs	Electricity consumption per pallet shipped	KWh

LTIFR = Lost Time Injury Frequency Rates

Balanced scorecard

The balanced scorecard, developed by Kaplan and Norton (1996), is another method of recording performance.

The scorecard looks at a number of dimensions which include finance, customer satisfaction, internal processes and staff development and innovation.

Each measure will have objectives and targets which are measured against actual performance.

Introducing a balanced scorecard approach should result in better processes, a motivated team of people, increased customer satisfaction and improved communication.

As can be seen from the Mondelēz example, the warehouse operation will contribute to the overall company scorecard. The Mondelēz scorecard has specific sections on warehouse operations, inventory, quality, safety and the environment – all of which can be integrated with other departments operating within the company.

FIGURE 13.3   The balanced scorecard (adapted from Kaplan and Norton 1996)

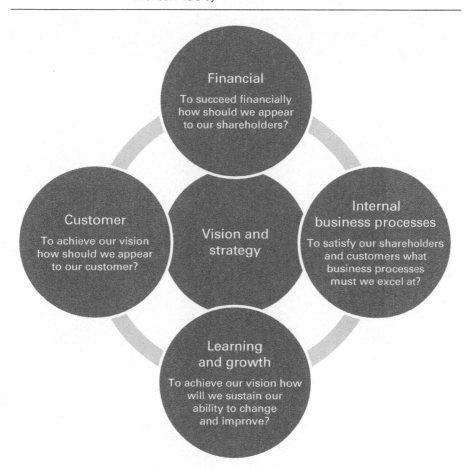

The performance metrics shown in Table 13.6 were elicited from WERC members and readers of *DC Velocity* in 2012. We have chosen our top 16 metrics with a cross section across customer satisfaction, supplier performance, accuracy, utilization, productivity and inventory measures.

The best in class figures are definitely targets to benchmark against however this will very much depend on the types of companies who replied to the survey. 92.2 per cent warehouse space utilization suggests a very slick operation with real-time technology at the forefront of operations.

Companies are able to benchmark their own activities against those in the survey including by sector by visiting **www.werc.org**

Health and safety metrics will be covered in Chapter 15.

TABLE 13.6 WERC performance metrics (2013) (courtesy of WERC, Karl Manrodt and Kate Vitasek)

Metrics	Lowest 20% of responses	Typical	Top 20% of responses	median
Perfect order index	< 81.4%	≥ 90% and < 96%	≥ 99%	95%
Order cycle time	> 72 hours	≥ 24 – < 36	< 8 hours	24 hours
Cost as a % of sales	> 10.04%	≥ 3 – < 5%	< 1.7%	3.9%
Order-picking accuracy	< 98%	≥ 99% and < 99.8%	≥ 99.9%	99.5%
On-time ready to ship	< 95.9%	≥ 98.6% and < 99.5%	> 99.9%	99%
Average warehouse capacity used	< 71.5%	≥ 80% and < 85%	> 92.2%	85%
Annual workforce turnover	> 12.2%	≥ 2.5% and < 8%	< 0.1%	5%
Labour productive hours to total hours	< 74.4%	≥ 85% and < 88%	≥ 92%	85.1%
Dock-to-stock cycle time in hours	> 24 hours	≥ 5 and < 9.6	< 2.2 hours	8 hours
Lines picked and shipped per hour	< 11.8 lines per hour	≥ 22.6 and < 43.8	≥ 74.2 lines per hour	28 lines per hour
Cases picked and shipped	<23	≥ 46.8 – < 97.2	160.6	67.5
Pallets picked and shipped per hour	< 6.2 pallets per hour	≥ 13.2 and < 20	≥ 28 pallets per hour	15 pallets per hour
Inventory shrinkage as % of total inventory	> 1.14%	≥ 0.1% and < 0.61%	< 0.01%	0.3%
Inventory count accuracy by location	< 95%	≥ 98% and < 99.3%	≥ 99.9%	99%
Days on hand, finished goods inventory	> 81 days	≥ 30 and < 40.8 days	< 13.6 days	30 days
Supplier on time delivery	< 90%	≥ 94.6 – < 97%	> 99%	95%

< Less than
> Greater than
≥ Greater than or equal to

Summary and conclusion

Measuring performance is key to running an efficient operation. However, the measures need to be SMART and aligned to the company's strategic vision.

One important point to note is that traditional KPIs report on the status of an operation or step in a process at a particular point in time. They are useful in comparing performance over time, but situations change rapidly and targets and measures need to change in unison with the changing environment.

There are a large number of performance measures related to warehouse operations. However, you should only measure those areas which are important to your customers and to your company. Don't measure just for the sake of it.

Being able to collect data is fine, but it's what happens as a result of collecting and analysing the data that is important.

These measures have to take you somewhere, as my friend Errol Matthews always says.

Outsourcing

14

BY KATE VITASEK, BILL DIBENEDETTO AND GWYNNE RICHARDS

Coming together is the beginning. Keeping together is progress. Working together is success.

(HENRY FORD (1863–1947))

Introduction

Outsourcing is generally defined as working with a supplier to provide a function or service that isn't a part of an organization's core competence. In other words, as Peter Drucker says: 'Do what you do best and outsource the rest!' The essence is to take advantage of a specialist provider's knowledge and economies of scale to improve performance and achieve the service needed, usually at a lower cost but not necessarily.

While Peter Drucker's call for action sounds logical, are companies really using outsourcing as a key strategy to drive operational efficiency and improve effectiveness of their warehouse operations? There are various studies on the topic – but in general the answer is *yes* – companies are using outsourcing to a lesser or greater degree. A survey by the Chartered Institute of Logistics and Transport (CILT) in 2012 in the UK recorded that 61 per cent of their respondents outsourced part or all of their warehousing. In a 2013 survey conducted by Cap Gemini North America recorded the same figure with mainland Europe recording 72 per cent and the Asia Pacific region 59 per cent.

Companies that decide to outsource must ensure that any outsourced processes remain seamlessly integrated with the rest of the business and furthermore improve performance.

In this chapter we discuss under what circumstances warehousing should be outsourced and examine the role of third-party operators in warehousing.

The outsourcing decision

The model by McIvor (2000), shown in Figure 14.1, provides a process companies should adopt when deciding whether to outsource.

McIvor suggests the main areas that need to be assessed are whether the activity is core to the business, whether there are political considerations, whether potential cost savings are significant enough to make outsourcing viable and, finally, whether there are capable and compatible partners in the market.

Vitasek (2010) adds the dimension of whether or not a company has expertise or core competence in this area. Specifically, Vitasek recommends if a company has internal expertise that creates value for the company beyond what the 'market' can provide – the work should remain in-house while companies that do not have the expertise should consider outsourcing as a viable option. In the Capgemini survey (2013) the five top reasons for companies not outsourcing were as follows:

- logistics is a core competence within the company;
- cost reduction would not be experienced;
- logistics is too important to consider outsourcing;
- service level commitments will not be realized; and
- corporate philosophy excludes outsourcing.

The reasons for outsourcing are many, as shown in the CILT surveys from 2011 and 2012 surveys in Table 14.1. Interestingly these are very similar to the reasons for retaining business in house – access to expertise, cost reduction and service improvement.

As seen in Table 14.1, a shift has occurred from cost the major factor for outsourcing to access to greater expertise. The top four reasons remain the same, although in a slightly different order.

The need to reduce capital expenditure is up to fourth which is indicative of the economic climate.

Any outsourcing decision should be based on the following:

- the suitability of the activity outsourced;
- the profile and culture of the potential supplier;
- impact of outsourcing on the remaining business; and
- all costs and risks.

FIGURE 14.1 The outsourcing decision (McIvor 2000)

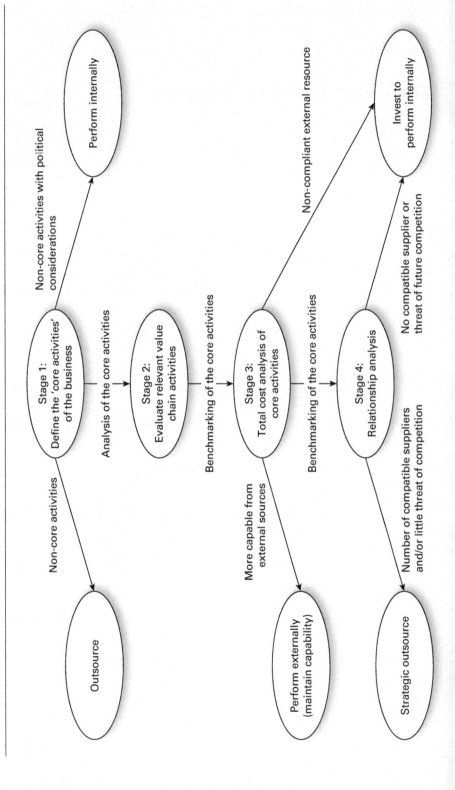

FIGURE 14.2   Outsourcing decision matrix (Vitasek 2010)

TABLE 14.1   Reasons for outsourcing (CILT UK surveys)

Advantage	Position 2012	Position 2011
Access to greater expertise	1	2
Cost reduction	2	1
Flexibility	3	4
Less capital expenditure	4	7
Service level improvement	5	4
Reduction in management time	6	–
Concentration on core competences	7	5
Cost control and visibility	8	–
Shared-user opportunity	9	–
Innovation	10	10
Resource availability	11	–
Risk reduction	12	6

Before looking at the reasons for outsourcing in more depth, consider the scale of the warehouse operation that is likely to be outsourced.

In the majority of cases where the scale of the warehouse does not warrant a dedicated operation and where the warehouse is not adjacent to a manufacturing facility, companies should seriously consider using a shared-user or public warehouse.

This enables companies to benefit from economies of scale by sharing resources and assets, increasing resource capability with no workforce increases, while benefiting from industry advances in technology.

We will now look at the main reasons cited for outsourcing warehousing operations in a bit more depth.

Core activity/core competence

There is some confusion over these phrases in relation to warehouse operations. Warehousing in the majority of companies is regarded as core to the business. However, it may not be a core competence and therefore becomes a likely candidate for outsourcing.

As discussed previously, warehouses play a major role in providing the ultimate in customer service by delivering the right product to the right place at the right time in excellent condition, and at an acceptable cost. Thus warehousing is often considered a core activity.

However, if we accept the view that core competencies differentiate one company from another and are the source of competitive advantage, then is warehousing in its basic form a core competence? Maybe not. Logistics operations can be easily imitated and the majority of companies and third parties provide similar levels of service.

According to Prahalad and Hamel (1990), 'core competencies are *the* source of competitive advantage'. They suggest three useful tests to identify a core competence:

- It provides access to a wide variety of markets.
- It contributes significantly to the end-product benefits.
- It is difficult for competitors to imitate.

Gutierrez (2003) states that 'a core competency is fundamental knowledge, ability, or expertise in a specific subject area or skill set'. This suggests more of a concentration on people skill; therefore whether a company sees logistics as a core competence may depend on the calibre of staff employed.

Companies may not have the management expertise and skills to operate a warehouse effectively and therefore outsourcing is a strong option. There can also be situations where the warehouse operation requires more management time than other areas, which can detract from the main activity of production, for example.

It is up to the company to decide whether it should bring in expertise to strengthen its management team, train existing staff or outsource.

Improvement in customer service

According to the Capgemini (2013) survey, 56 per cent of respondents said their use of third-party logistics had led to year-on-year incremental benefits.

Other surveys by Eye for Transport (in 2010) suggest that more than 80 per cent of companies outsourcing their logistics operations are pleased with the service they are receiving.

However, many companies churn frequently between third-party providers. Most often this is a result of dissatisfaction or a quest for further cost reductions. Of the companies surveyed by Eye for Transport, 47 per cent had changed service provider over the past 12 months.

Cost reduction

According to the Capgemini report those respondents who achieved incremental benefits saw a reduction of up to 15 per cent in logistics costs, 8 per cent saving in inventory costs and 26 per cent saving in logistics assets. Previous surveys such as the Aberdeen report of 2008 suggested that only 20 per cent of best-in-class companies achieved a cost reduction through outsourcing, with an average reduction of 0.3 per cent, whilst others saw a neutral to negative position on costs.

Greater cost savings can be achieved when moving from a dedicated facility to a shared-use operation where costs are incurred based on volume and fluctuate in line with sales.

Labour relations

In the early 1980s many companies outsourced warehousing operations to deal with labour relations issues and spiralling wage costs.

Those companies that did outsource for these reasons didn't always see an improvement as legislation meant that workforces had to be transferred under pretty much the same terms and conditions. Cost reduction and productivity improvements had to come from better practices, increased morale and improved working conditions.

Financial strategy

When companies decide to concentrate on improving their return on assets employed, one way of achieving this is to divest their warehouses and capital equipment. This can be achieved by moving to an existing third-party warehouse, contracting with a third party to build a warehouse for your operation, or getting the third party to buy your existing warehouse. In this situation, if the warehouse is not currently fully occupied, the third party can 'sell' the surplus space to other potential clients.

In the United Kingdom, retailers outsourced their warehouse operations but held on to the real estate and the capital equipment, which has enabled some of them to in-source without significant upheaval.

Companies also entered into back-to-back contracts on key assets employed in the service provision. Assets were either contracted from third-party suppliers in line with the period of the contract or an agreement was made to transfer the assets to the customer at the end of the contract. This not only secured specialist equipment for the customer but also ensured that the third party was not left with equipment it couldn't utilize at the end of the contract.

Under these circumstances third parties were able to base their contractual costs on the expected life of the asset, not the length of the contract period.

Flexibility

An Easter egg manufacturer I consulted for recently saw its finished goods stock move from 500 pallets to 10,000 pallets at peak. The difficulty in these circumstances is to decide on the capacity of the warehouse. The manufacturer decided to outsource the majority of the storage requirement, freeing up space for further manufacturing and putting the onus on the third party to find other clients to dovetail with the storage availability.

Changing markets can also have an effect on whether to remain in house or outsource. I'm sure that most electrical goods, computer and mobile phone manufacturers wished they had crystal balls 10 to 20 years ago to enable them to predict the significant reduction in the size of their products over time and as a result the size of the warehouse operation.

Role of third-party contractors

Third-party contractors can operate dedicated and shared-user warehousing on behalf of their clients.

Dedicated warehouses are where a company has decided to either relinquish its own warehouse operation to a third party, with the contractor taking over the building, staff and equipment or it may be a totally new operation where the client has decided to outsource rather than operate the warehouse itself. This could be a new build or the use of an existing building.

In shared-user warehousing, a third-party logistics company will acquire a warehouse and use it to provide services on behalf of a number of different clients who manufacture wide-ranging products.

The warehouses can also operate as fulfilment centres where a number of different e-commerce or mail order clients are housed in the same building and are provided with similar services.

Other shared-user warehouses may operate on behalf of companies that produce the same type of products. Although in competition, the manufacturers see the synergy advantages of their products being stored in the same warehouse and delivered through the same distribution channels.

Staff are experienced in handling the product and the cost of deliveries to retail outlets can be shared among the manufacturers.

A variation of this is the retail consolidation warehouse where a retailer's suppliers store and cross dock product destined for the retailer's DC or even direct to store. These centres can either be operated in house or by third-party companies.

Preparing to outsource

Having decided to outsource, there are a number of things to do before contacting any third- or fourth-party logistics providers:

- Ensure current processes are as efficient as possible: you should never outsource a problem – it only gets worse.
- Understand your current cost structure.
- Benchmark the operation against your peers both internally and externally.
- Determine your future strategy.
- Understand the third-party market – which third parties are operating in your market sector?
- Collect the relevant data.

Although very tempting, outsourcing a problem is not a good idea. It's much better and wiser to ensure that all processes are working efficiently prior to issuing an invitation to tender. If you do not have the resource internally then utilizing consultants is an option.

It's highly important to understand the total cost of current operations before requesting responses from potential partners. How will you compare costs and evaluate the viability of outsourcing if you do not know your own costs? Involve a number of departments in this exercise so that you understand the full cost of your logistics operation.

Furthermore, you need to know what additional costs you will incur after outsourcing. For example: do you intend to employ a contract manager; what will be the effect on the finance department regarding the checking of invoices; what will be the cost of systems integration with the third party? Take all of these costs into account.

By benchmarking your existing operation either internally or with some of your competitors you will get a better understanding of where you should be in terms of cost and performance. You can use these figures to assess the third-party bids.

One point of caution with regard to benchmarking in this situation is that you should not use the tender process to benchmark your operation unless you explain fully to the third parties what you are doing.

It costs third parties a great deal of money to put a comprehensive bid together and if they eventually realize you have no intention of outsourcing they will be very reluctant to put in the same amount of work the next time you approach them with a genuine request.

By keeping current with trade press reports, you will know about most of the third parties in the market; however, it is also prudent to take advice from other colleagues, companies or logistics consultants on which third parties are likely to provide the right service for you. It is better to target a small number of third parties rather than use a scattergun approach.

Our advice is to approach as few companies as possible to enable you to spend as much time as possible evaluating the responses. Time is valuable and inviting scores of companies wastes not only your time but also theirs.

Issuing an RFI (request for information) can assist you in shortlisting suitable candidates by asking a few pertinent questions. These could include:

- experience in and understanding of your particular market sector;
- availability of resources;
- suitable range of services;
- ability to comply with timescales;
- financial stability;

- geographic coverage;
- contract renewal success rates; and
- culture.

In order to receive accurate quotations from the third parties you should provide them with comprehensive data. This will also enable you to compare the total cost of operation and weigh up the benefits of outsourcing.

If you have decided to go out to tender and have chosen a number of third parties to respond, follow this simple advice; otherwise you are unlikely to get the most competitive and comprehensive quotation:

- Provide as much data as possible.
- Don't be too prescriptive – allow scope for 'blue sky' thinking.
- Allow the third parties to visit the existing operation.
- Share the questions and answers amongst all participants.
- Allow sufficient time for the third parties to respond.
- Ensure that key staff are available during the tender process.
- Ask for an estimate of start-up costs.
- Ensure that all responses include the third-party assumptions.
- Request a timetable for implementation.

Choosing the right partner

Bititci *et al* (2008) suggest that the following have to be taken into account when choosing the right partner:

- Strategic synergy: the potential fit of the business model and strategic priorities of the partner organization are aligned with your own.
- Operational synergy: the potential fit of the relevant business processes of the partner organization are aligned with your own.
- Commercial synergy: the nature of the commercial, risk management and service level agreements between both companies are aligned.
- Cultural synergy: the cultural fit between the two organizations at strategic and operational level is strong.

A decision table will assist you greatly in deciding on the most suitable third party. Having decided on your criteria, weigh their importance and score each company against them. Criteria will vary from company to company, as will the weighting for each criterion. Table 14.2 shows an example.

TABLE 14.2   Outsourcing decision matrix (adapted from and used with permission of Tompkins Associates 1998)

Category	Target rating	Weight	Target score	Rating 3PL (A)	Actual score
Range of services	5	40	200	**1 2 3 4 5**	120
Market experience	4	30	120	**1 2 3 4 5**	120
Quality of management	5	30	150	**1 2 3 4 5**	150
Health and safety record	5	30	150	**1 2 3 4 5**	150
Total cost	4	30	120	**1 2 3 4 5**	150
Strategy	4	20	80	**1 2 3 4 5**	60
Information technology	5	20	100	**1 2 3 4 5**	100
Financial stability	5	10	50	**1 2 3 4 5**	30
Reputation	5	10	50	**1 2 3 4 5**	50
Shared-user/public warehouses	5	10	50	**1 2 3 4 5**	50
Global coverage	5	10	50	**1 2 3 4 5**	40
TOTAL			**1120**		**1020**
Measurement index					**91.1 per cent fit**

Cottrill and Gary (2005–6) suggest that other, somewhat softer issues should also be taken into account when choosing a long-term partner, such as the following:

- Creativity and ability to innovate:
  - A supplier with a culture of creativity and innovation is normally a good problem solver, which can translate into cost-saving operations.
  - Customers look to the third party to be leading edge and challenge ways of working.

- Providers feel that they are not listened to and are boxed into a master–slave relationship.
- Need openness about what the relationship is – partnership or supplier?
- Openness and information sharing are key – you cannot innovate in a vacuum.

• Ability to communicate and collaborate. Rapid response and being able to adapt quickly to market changes are critical in today's supply chain. Communication is at the heart of this.

• Trustworthiness. A difficult area to measure. However, you can start by looking at factors such as other customers' experiences and the supplier's openness about its past performance and financial footing.

• Flexibility and operational agility. For example, can the supplier cope with a threefold increase in sales and how will he react to a sudden drop in sales? Can he react quickly to a major problem such as a product recall or a need to re-box or re-label product? How good are they at 'workarounds'?

• Cultural fit. Organizations with similar cultures tend to be more successful. Vitasek (2010) has produced a grid which shows three characteristics which are relatively easy to measure:

- Do the companies have a culture of continuous improvement?
- What are their people management styles?
- How much emphasis do they place on cross-company training?

Once suppliers are ranked on all of these soft measures you can put them together with the hard metrics and develop a matrix of criteria that compares the performance of each company.

Having decided on a shortlist of companies based on the above criteria, the next step is to visit their operations – your choice, not theirs – meet with their operations management and talk to their staff and where possible their customers.

You will of course need to respect the sensitivity of certain sites if they are operated on behalf of a competitor, and expect not to be allowed access.

Sales staff are great at selling a concept; however, it will be the operations staff who will implement and run the contract, therefore it is imperative to meet with them and also have a say in the appointment of the contract manager.

The transition

One important area that might be neglected once a contract has been signed is the transfer of staff and the potential change in culture.

Change management is an important part of the process and must be handled effectively. The third party will have expertise in this area, having taken over a number of contracts in its time. Both companies need to work together to ensure a smooth transition. The recent transfer of the ASOS fulfilment contract in the United Kingdom from Unipart to Norbert Dentressangle is a typical example.

Managing a third-party relationship

As mentioned earlier, an outsourced contract is very much like a personal relationship. During the early stages there is a great deal of communication and agreement on many things. As the relationship matures, conversation falters and new ideas become fewer. The threat of another potential relationship often will force the parties to talk in earnest again and try to come up with new ideas. Figure 14.3 shows the stages that many outsourced relationships experience, from both a user and provider perspective.

During a CILT UK seminar on insourcing versus outsourcing in 2009, Ian Stansfield of Asda Walmart said in response to a question about relationships:

> Relationships matter... but you can't take me to the races! We need to learn... we need inspiration and innovation... show me. Don't sell me what *you* want, show me what I *need*. Earn your keep.

Here the third party is seen as the expert and is expected to innovate, fully understand the client's needs and use the management fee to not only ensure the best service but introduce a culture of continuous improvement.

Why contracts fail

An Eye for Transport survey found the factors shown in Figure 14.4 as reasons why outsourced relationships fail.

In terms of improving relations, the survey suggested the following improvements needed to be made:

- Communications were cited by 67 per cent of companies surveyed as an opportunity for improvement on both sides.
- It was felt by 63 per cent that improved requirements and procedure definition would help.

FIGURE 14.3 Outsourced relationships (courtesy of Steve Whyman)

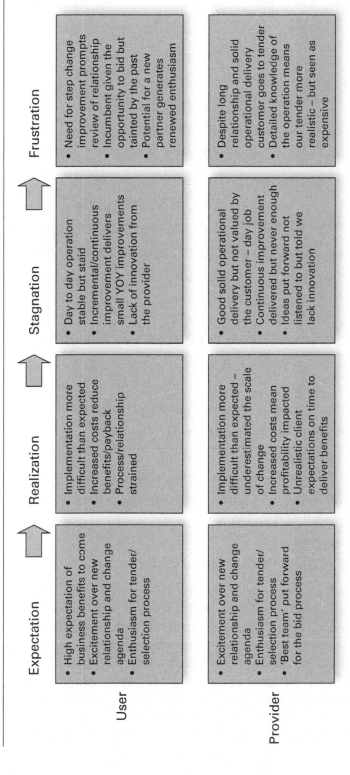

Expectation

User
- High expectation of business benefits to come
- Excitement over new relationship and change agenda
- Enthusiasm for tender/ selection process

Provider
- Excitement over new relationship and change agenda
- Enthusiasm for tender/ selection process
- 'Best team' put forward for the bid process

Realization

User
- Implementation more difficult than expected
- Increased costs reduce benefits/payback
- Process/relationship strained

Provider
- Implementation more difficult than expected – underestimated the scale of change
- Increased costs mean profitability impacted
- Unrealistic client expectations on time to deliver benefits

Stagnation

User
- Day to day operation stable but staid
- Incremental/continuous improvement delivers small YOY improvements
- Lack of innovation from the provider

Provider
- Good solid operational delivery but not valued by the customer – day job
- Continuous improvement delivered but never enough
- Ideas put forward not listened to but told we lack innovation

Frustration

User
- Need for step change improvement prompts review of relationship
- Incumbent given the opportunity to bid but tainted by the past
- Potential for a new partner generates renewed enthusiasm

Provider
- Despite long relationship and solid operational delivery customer goes to tender
- Detailed knowledge of the operation means our tender more realistic – but seen as expensive

FIGURE 14.4   Why outsourced relationships fail (courtesy of Eye for Transport)

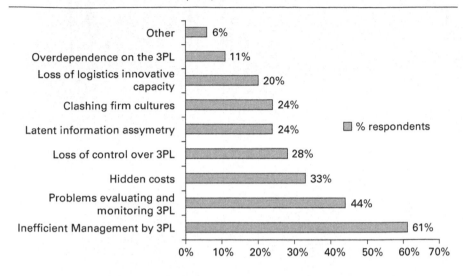

The CILT 2012 survey produced the following reasons for non-renewal of contracts:

- Loss of trust.
- Reluctance to change during contract period.
- Promised flexibility not delivered by third-party logistics.
- Poor levels of service.
- Higher cost than envisaged and rate hikes during the contract.
- Failure to deliver as contracted, charging for services they're already contracted to provide.
- Cheaper competitors.
- Lack of commitment by third-party logistics.

Arms-length management of outsourcing will foster silo behaviour, therefore relationships need to be forged at all levels within the organizations.

Outsourcing does not mean that you can walk away from responsibility for the outsourced task. The success of the outsourced relationship will depend on how well the companies work together to ensure that the initial goals are achieved. Trust and openness are key in outsourced relationships.

Outsourcing in logistics is normally based on a transactional relationship and as a result can rapidly turn adversarial. In conventional outsourcing the client looks to reduce costs and improve service levels whilst the third party is looking to increase the size of the contract and maximize profits. Cost to the company which outsources is revenue to the service provider.

The future of outsourcing

Kate Vitasek's book *Vested Outsourcing: Five Rules that Will Transform Outsourcing* (2010) offers some fascinating insights into what will likely become the future business model of outsourcing. Vitasek suggests that cost reduction, service improvement and overall profits can be increased through greater collaboration, creating and sharing value, and by forging a 'what's in it for we' (WIIFWe) relationship mindset. Her premise is that companies and suppliers/service providers should 'create a business model where both the company that outsources and the service provider are able to maximize their profits. Doing this means creating a culture where the parties work together to make the end-to-end process efficient, regardless of which party is performing activities. This means creating an approach where service providers are rewarded for reducing their revenue'. Ultimately this means moving away from the old-school transaction-based approach to outsourcing in favour of a collaborative, outcome-based structure.

This collaborative, shared-value approach is the basic premise of what Vitasek and her fellow researchers at the University of Tennessee have coined as 'vested outsourcing', or 'vested' for short.

Many cost-plus relationships are the antithesis of this approach where any increase in cost results in an increase in profits for the service provider unless there are suitable targets and rewards and margin reduction for poor performance.

Vitasek continues that the relationships and negotiations must move away from the culture of 'what's in it for me', I-win-you-lose culture to WIIFWe.

This follows the lines of Nobel laureate John Nash's Game Theory and the premise of a game show in the UK in which, at the end of each show two contestants are left with a pot of money. They have to individually decide to take the money or split the pot with the other contestant. If both decide to split they share the pot; however, if one decides to take the money and the other to split, the former gets the money. If they both decide to take the money they both lose.

In these circumstances collaboration results in a win–win situation.

This suggests a move away from transactional payments to suppliers being paid for outcomes and innovation.

The premise is that by being innovative, saving the client money whilst improving service levels, the provider will increase the client's confidence in them and as a result is likely to gain more work, thus increasing revenue and margin.

FIGURE 14.5   Performance pyramid (Vitasek 2010)

FIGURE 14.6   From confrontation to collaboration (Vitasek 2010)

Getting the supplier to meet our needs	**BECOMES**	Finding a way to meet both our needs
'It's in the contract, now it's the supplier's problem.'	**BECOMES**	Work together to achieve the performance and compensation goals
Blame and punish the supplier	**BECOMES**	Communicate the issues, jointly find solutions
Unpleasant surprises	**BECOMES**	Integrated planning and communications

The five rules set the stage of a sound outsourcing partnership, as illustrated in Figure 14.7.

Each of the five rules of vested is discussed briefly below.

Rule 1: Focus on outcomes, not transactions

Traditionally, many business and outsource models are transaction-based. Most often the transactional approach is coupled with a cost-plus or a competitively bid fixed price per transaction pricing model to ensure that the buyer is getting the lowest cost per transaction. Under this conventional method, the service provider is paid for every transaction – whether or not it is needed. The more inefficient the entire process, the more money the service provider can

FIGURE 14.7 The five rules

make. Thus, it's a perverse incentive that rewards inefficiency and unnecessary activity.

The transaction-based model can achieve lower costs; however, in an outsourcing arrangement it often does not help the company achieve what it really wants or needs. This is because the company that has outsourced gets what it contracted for – but what it actually needed was an efficient and low-cost total support solution. Vested, in contrast, operates under an outcome-based model in which the provider aligns its interests to what the company really wants (the efficient, low-cost solution).

The vested model fundamentally shifts the way a company buys services. Actually it is fairly straightforward. Instead of paying a provider for unit transactions for the various services provided – such as pallets in the warehouse, miles travelled, spare parts shipped, technical support hours, and so forth – the company and its service provider agree together upon desired performance outcomes. Desired outcomes are quantifiable, but take a different form: they can be availability, reliability, cost, revenue generation, employee or customer satisfaction, or even asset investment targets. Simply put, vested buys outcomes, not individual transactions.

Rule 2: Focus on the what, not the how

In a vested arrangement, the company specifies 'what' it wants; the service provider is responsible for determining 'how' it gets done. This is the basic reason for outsourcing: in-house operations are either too expensive or ineffective (or both) and a company looks outside for the expert who can do the job better. Once the provider is found, let them do the job! The problem that often arises, however, is something called the outsourcing paradox. By outsourcing, companies basically concede that they are not in the best position to do a specific job or jobs. Yet when they turn the work over to someone more competent, they can't resist the urge to tell the service provider how to do the job. Hence the paradox!

The most effective vested partnerships include minimal discussion of the processes the service providers must follow to meet requirements. Instead, they focus on expectations and outcomes. It's up to the service provider to figure out how to put the supporting pieces together to achieve the company's goals. The central idea is to free each company to do what they do best.

Rule 3: Agree on clearly defined and measurable outcomes

The parties must clearly define and measure desired outcomes. These outcomes are expressed in terms of a limited set (ideally, no more than five) of high-level metrics. Teams should spend time together defining how the relationship's success will be measured. Attending to this upfront helps ensure that neither time nor resources are wasted pursuing the wrong objectives.

Once the desired outcomes are agreed upon and documented, the service provider can propose a solution that will deliver the required level of performance at a pre-determined price. In the third-party logistics arena, one outcome might be orders shipped complete and on time at a 98 percent level of service. This fundamentally shifts the business model, shifting risk from the company that is outsourcing to the service provider. Under the purest form of vested, the company only pays for results (namely, orders shipped complete and on time), not transactions (picking, packing and shipping). The service provider is paid for the value delivered by its overall solution, rather than being paid for each activity performed.

Rule 4: Pricing model with incentives that optimize the business

A properly structured pricing model incorporates incentives to enable the company to achieve its desired outcomes. The pricing model is based on the type of contract – fixed price or cost reimbursement – that will be used to reward the outsource provider.

When establishing the pricing model, businesses should apply two principles:

- The pricing model must balance risk and reward for the organizations. The agreement should be structured to ensure that the service provider assumes risk only for decisions within its control. For example, a transportation service provider should never be penalized for the rising costs of fuel, and a property management service provider should never be penalized for an increase in energy prices.

- The agreement should specify that the service provider will deliver solutions, not just activities. When properly constructed, a vested agreement will provide incentives to the service provider to solve the company's problems. The better the service provider is at solving those problems, the more profits the service provider can make. Service providers are thus encouraged to develop and institute innovative and cost-effective methods of performing work to drive down total cost while maintaining or improving service.

Inherent in the vested business model is a reward for the service provider to make investments in process, service, or associated product that will generate returns in excess of contract requirements. If the service provider does a good job, it will reap the rewards of greater profitability.

When properly constructed, vested will incentivize the service provider to solve customer problems proactively.

Vested arrangements should be based on reducing the *total cost* of the process being outsourced – not simply the budget for the outsourced services. The interwoven dependencies of business and outsourcing relationships require an environment that encourages service providers to push companies to change internal processes if they are inhibiting the success of a vested partnership. Outsourcing companies also must be open-minded and accountable for driving internal process changes that drive total cost reductions that will benefit all. But properly structured Vested partnerships can – and do – create paybacks for the parties.

Rule 5: Governance structures that provide insight, not merely oversight

A vested relationship is based on insight versus oversight governance that empowers the parties to pursue improvements that will deliver better performance, higher profits, and lower total ownership cost. There are still some companies today that operate without benefit of a formal contract or any real agreement in place. Fortunately, this is a declining minority. Yet some have gone to the other extreme: they often have a small army of people, frequently referred to as 'programme managers', who micromanage the outsource provider. An effective vested partnership outsources processes to service providers that are real experts in those processes. The partnerships should be managed to create a culture of insight vs oversight.

The five key rules of a sound outsourcing partnership set the stage for companies to take their outsourcing relationships to the next level – a true vested performance partnership.

For many companies a WIIFWe, win–win approach must be learned; they have to unlearn conventional approaches and ways of thinking. In a vested relationship the organizations must work together upon a foundation of trust where there is mutual accountability for achieving the destined outcomes.

Most companies that use vested as an approach for outsourcing do not spend much time talking about how it gives their outsource providers the opportunity to make more money. Rather, they focus on how it delivers better value or better outcomes at the same or lower total cost. Nevertheless, service providers who work under vested partnerships often focus on the higher profit potential of vested and also note that such successfully designed partnerships create happier clients. Because the organizations are working together to achieve their goals, vested works as a true win–win relationship, which is what a partnership is all about.

Organizations that challenge the WIIFMe mentality are able to achieve true vested relationships that deliver outstanding results. Adopting anything less than a WIIFWe philosophy will result in less than optimal business relationships.

In order to make an outsourcing partnership work, the parties should take the following steps:

- Define why you are outsourcing and what success looks like.
- Define the value you want to create from outsourcing and test for realism.
- Tailor the selection process and understand the benefit/cost of exam-based tendering if you want a partner.
- Align the commercial structures and performance metrics to drive the right behaviours.
- Invest in the relationship and openly share information.
- Outsource for the right reasons, with total buy-in from your business.
- Make it work for both companies.
- Develop a partnership.
- Help your partner understand your business.
- Get the right people in key roles.

According to Craig Mulholland (2009) from Norbert Dentressangle:

> You need to understand that third parties work to provide excellent service to delight their customers, but are commercial organizations that need to make a profit. They exist because they are needed. Removing this cynical barrier leaves everyone free to focus on solutions.

Summary and conclusion

Outsourcing is a choice and it takes two to make it work: it's not necessarily right for all companies. Care thus needs to be taken on the decision on whether to outsource, and on the choice of partner.

Outsourcing is all about creating a relationship and crafting a framework for long-term, collaborative success. The steps can be akin to a personal relationship:

- Dating: talking prior to the contract award.
- Engagement: looking forward to a life together after the contract award.
- Marriage. contract award and early successes.
- The in-laws: parent company interventions.
- Familiarity: you don't talk anymore!
- Divorce: loss of contract.

But if the outsource partnership is crafted and nurtured correctly, those last three items need never occur!

Health and safety

15

GWYNNE RICHARDS AND TIM CULPIN

Health and safety is a fundamental part of business. Boards need someone with passion and energy to ensure it stays at the core of the organization.

(HEALTH AND SAFETY EXECUTIVE)

Introduction

During a discussion on LinkedIn, managers were asked which areas in the warehouse were high on their priority list. Safety was the most popular answer. This chapter looks to inform managers of the potential hazards found within the warehouse and how they can make the area as safe as possible for their staff. Accidents will happen; however, there are processes that can reduce the dangers significantly.

This can also be a high-cost area, not only in providing a safe environment but also the cost of not providing a safe and secure place of work.

Warehousing and storage cover a whole range of activities, all of which have their own hazards and risks. Employers need to ensure effective health and safety management, looking at the risks involved in the workplace and then putting in place effective control measures to properly manage health and safety.

In 2010/11 in the United Kingdom there was one warehouse-related fatality and over 330 major injuries.

The most recent surveys from the United States show that 16 people were killed in warehouse-related accidents in 2011. There were 31,200 non-fatal, warehouse-related occupational injuries caused by the following:

- overexertion (poor lifting, etc) – 45 per cent;
- contact with equipment – 31 per cent;
- falls and trips – 19 per cent;
- transport related – 3 per cent;
- harmful substances – 1 per cent.

Thirty-five per cent of the incidents resulted in staff being away from work for more than 31 days. 42 per cent of the injuries received were strains, sprains and muscle tears. The highest number of accidents occurred on a Monday and most accidents took place between the hours of 8 am and 12 pm. The number of incidents per 100 employees (5.3) is higher than the national average of 3.8 (US Bureau of Labour Statistics).

The main causes of major injuries in the warehouse, according to the HSE, are shown in Figure 15.1.

FIGURE 15.1 Main causes of injuries in the warehouse (**www.HSE.gov.uk**)

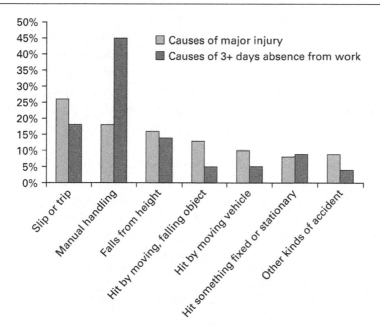

OSHA also cite the following:

- unsafe use of forklifts;
- improper stacking of products;
- failure to use proper personal protective equipment (PPE);
- failure to follow proper lockout/tagout procedures, ie prevent equipment from being accidentally energized;
- inadequate fire safety provisions; and
- repetitive motion injuries.

In terms of recording injuries received within the warehouse, OSHA require companies to record the total recordable incidence rate.

The formula is as follows:

$$\frac{(\text{Total number of injuries and illnesses} \times 200,000)}{\text{Number of hours worked by all employees}} = \text{OSHA incidence rate}$$

This can be included in the list of performance measures.

Another measure can be the number of days since a reportable accident occurred.

Depending on the workplace and specific work types, there may be other risks on site that need to be considered as well as those set out above. Warehousing is a very complex industry that exposes workers to a whole variety of risks, and therefore employers must ensure that health and safety is treated with the utmost importance at management level.

A health and safety policy is a stepping stone to ensuring health and safety in the workplace, and in the United Kingdom if a business has more than five employees (this includes directors) there must be a written policy in place. This policy should be brought to the attention of all of its employees.

Although it is not a legal requirement in the United Kingdom for companies who employ less than five staff, a written policy can improve health and safety within the business.

Each country will have its own Health and Safety legislation and therefore we will concentrate on the aspects we believe to be important and relevant. Details of the respective Health and Safety authorities by country are outlined in the list of websites.

The Health and Safety at Work Act in the United Kingdom places responsibility for health and safety into three categories:

- employer responsibilities:
  - provision of a health and safety statement policy;
  - provision of safety equipment;
  - commitment to train staff.

- employee responsibilities:
  - obligation to cooperate with their employer;
  - obligation to undertake training, report issues and not to misuse equipment.
- manufacturers' responsibilities:
  - ensure product is safe to use and fit for purpose.

Risk assessments

In today's atmosphere of increased litigation there is added pressure on managers to ensure the safety of their employees. Managers have to take appropriate steps to identify potential areas where accidents can occur and take steps to avoid them.

Note that a hazard is anything that may cause harm, such as chemicals, working from height, broken pallets, etc. The risk is the chance, high or low, that somebody could be harmed by these and other hazards, together with an indication of how serious the harm could be.

A risk assessment is an important step in protecting your workforce and your business as well as complying with the law. It helps you to focus on the risks that really matter in your workplace, ie the ones with the potential to cause harm. For most, that means simple, cheap and effective measures to ensure that the workforce is fully protected.

The law does not expect you to eliminate all risk but you are required to protect staff and visitors as far as is reasonably practicable. According to the HSE, this means that you 'have to take action on the health and safety risks in the warehouse except where the cost (in terms of time and effort as well as money) of doing so is "grossly disproportionate" to the reduction in the risk'.

A risk assessment is simply a careful examination of what can cause harm to people so that you can weigh up whether you have taken enough precautions or should do more to prevent harm. Staff and others have a right to be protected from harm caused by a failure to take reasonable control measures. You are legally required to assess the risks in your workplace, so you must put plans in place to control risks. However, don't overcomplicate the process. Most risks are easily identifiable and the necessary control measures are easy to implement.

You also need to decide whether you have the necessary experience in house to undertake the risk assessment or whether you need to employ an external health and safety expert.

A risk assessment can be broken down into five stages:

Step 1: Identify the hazards.

Step 2: Decide who might be harmed and how.

Step 3: Evaluate the risks and decide on precautions.

Step 4: Record and communicate your findings and implement them.

Step 5: Review your risk assessment regularly and update if necessary.

Identify the hazards

Walk around the warehouse, internally and externally, and look at what could reasonably be expected to cause harm.

Ask your colleagues and staff if they are aware of any potential hazards.

Check the manufacturers' instructions or data sheets for chemicals and equipment as they can be very helpful in spelling out the hazards and putting them in their true perspective. Check back on your accident records (ensure that near misses are also recorded). See Figure 15.2.

Assess potential long-term affects to health, eg high levels of noise or exposure to harmful substances.

The accident pyramid shows that for every 600 near misses there are 10 serious injuries and for every 10 serious injuries there can be one fatality. Thus every near miss needs to be recorded, investigated, actioned, staff trained and the situation reviewed regularly.

FIGURE 15.2 The accident pyramid (adapted from Bird and Germain 1996)

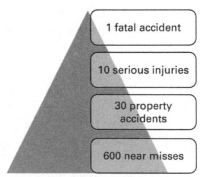

1 fatal accident

10 serious injuries

30 property accidents

600 near misses

Record, investigate, action, train, review

Decide who might be harmed and how

For each hazard you need to be clear about who might be at risk and potentially harmed; it will help you to identify the best way of managing the risk. That doesn't mean listing everyone by name, but rather identifying groups of people (eg in-handling team, visitors).

Remember:

- Some workers have particular requirements, eg new staff and people with disabilities may be at particular risk.

- Include cleaners, visitors, contractors, maintenance workers, etc who may not be in the workplace all the time.

- In each case, identify how they might be harmed, ie what type of injury or ill health might occur. For example, 'Staff stacking shelves may suffer back injury from repeated lifting of boxes.'

- Evaluate the risks and decide on precautions.

- Discuss your findings with the company's safety representative.

Having identified the hazards, you then have to decide what to do about them. The law requires you to do everything 'reasonably practicable' to protect people from harm. You can work this out for yourself, but the easiest way is to compare what you are doing with good practice.

First, look at what you're already doing. Think about what controls you have in place and how the work is organized. Compare this with good practice and see if there's more you should be doing to bring yourself up to standard. In asking yourself this, consider:

- Can I get rid of the hazard altogether?

- If not, how can I control the risks so that harm is unlikely?

- When controlling risks, apply the following principles, if possible in this order:

  - Try a less risky option (eg switch to using a less hazardous chemical).

  - Prevent access to the hazard (eg by using guardrails).

  - Organize work to reduce exposure to the hazard (eg put barriers between pedestrians and traffic).

- Issue personal protective equipment (eg clothing, footwear, goggles).

- Provide welfare facilities (eg first aid and washing facilities for removal of contamination).

Improving health and safety need not cost a great deal. For instance, placing a mirror on a dangerous blind corner to help prevent vehicle accidents is a low-cost precaution, considering the risks. Failure to take simple precautions can cost you a lot more if an accident does happen.

Involve staff, so that you can be sure that what you propose to do will work in practice and won't introduce any new hazards.

Implement your findings and record and communicate them

Putting the results of your risk assessment into practice will make a difference when looking after people and your business.

Recording the results of your risk assessment and sharing them with your staff encourage you to do this. When recording your results, keep it simple: for example 'Tripping over rubbish: bins provided, staff instructed, daily housekeeping checks', or 'Broken pallets in racking: products repalletized, daily housekeeping check'.

The HSE does not expect a risk assessment to be perfect, but it must be suitable and sufficient. You need to be able to show that:

- a proper check was made;
- you asked who might be affected;
- you dealt with all the obvious significant hazards, taking into account the number of people who could be involved;
- the precautions are reasonable, and the remaining risk is low; and
- you involved your staff or their representatives in the process.

If, like many businesses, you find that there are quite a lot of improvements that you could make, big and small, don't try to do everything at once. Make a plan of action to deal with the most important things first. Health and safety inspectors acknowledge the efforts of businesses that are clearly trying to make improvements.

A good plan of action often includes a mixture of different things such as:

- a few cheap or easy improvements that can be done quickly, perhaps as a temporary solution until more reliable controls are in place;
- long-term solutions to those risks most likely to cause accidents or ill health;
- long-term solutions to those risks with the worst potential consequences;
- arrangements for training employees on the main risks that remain and how they are to be controlled;
- regular checks to make sure that the control measures stay in place; and
- clear responsibilities – who will lead on what action and by when.

Clear signage

Remember, prioritize and tackle the most important things first. As you complete each action, tick it off your plan.

Review your assessment regularly and update if necessary

Few workplaces stay the same. Sooner or later, you will bring in new equipment, substances and procedures that could lead to new hazards. It makes sense, therefore, to review what you are doing on an ongoing basis. Every three months or after a significant incident, formally review where you are, to make sure you are still improving or at least not sliding back.

Look at your risk assessment again. Have there been any changes? Are there improvements you still need to make? Have your workers spotted a problem? Have you learnt anything from accidents or near misses? Make sure your risk assessment stays up to date.

When you are running a business it's all too easy to forget about reviewing your risk assessment – until something has gone wrong and it's too late. Set a review date for the risk assessment. Write it down and note it in your diary as a regular event.

During the year, if there is a significant change, don't wait: check your risk assessment and, where necessary, amend it. If possible, it is best to think about the risk assessment when you're planning your change – that way you leave yourself more flexibility.

Table 15.1 is an example of a warehouse risk assessment.

A Word version can be downloaded from **www.appriseconsulting.co.uk/ warehousetools**. The password is apprise1234

Layout and design

As part of a health and safety regime, steps must be taken to protect the welfare of employees and visitors, and therefore a safe and healthy environment must be ensured with proper welfare facilities being made available.

In terms of ensuring a safe environment, a warehouse should be designed and laid out to allow people to move around it safely. A well-thought-out design and layout of a warehouse will help to reduce accidents, particularly those involving vehicles and slips/trips. Points to consider when thinking about design and layout include:

- storage areas, aisles and gangways;
- pedestrian traffic routes;
- stairs and ramps; and
- emergency escape routes.

TABLE 15.1 Example risk assessment partly completed for the warehouse

Location		Date:		Assessor:		
What are the Hazards?	**Who might be harmed and how?**	**What are you already doing?**	**What further action is necessary?**	**Action by whom?**	**Action by when?**	**Completed?**
Falls from height	Staff can suffer severe or even fatal injuries if they fall whilst climbing racking	All staff are given instructions never to climb racking – monitored by supervisors	Signage put in place to reiterate the point	Warehouse Manager	01/03/20–	Yes 01/03/20–
	Staff or contractor could suffer severe or fatal injuries falling through fragile roof lights when effecting repairs	No controls in place	• Put up 'fragile roof' signs on each side of the building and at access points	Facilities Manager	01/03/20–	Yes 8/02/20–
			• Only trained contractors to access the roof	Facilities Manager	02/04/20–	No
			• Full risk assessment to be undertaken by contractor	FM/Contractor	As required	

TABLE 15.1 *continued*

			Assessor:		
Location		**Date:**			
What are the Hazards?	**Who might be harmed and how?**	**What are you already doing?**	**What further action is necessary?**	**Action by whom?**	**Action by when?**	**Completed?**
Slips, trips and falls	All staff may suffer sprains or fractures if they trip over debris or slip on spillages	• Flooring kept dry and quality maintained	• Suitable absorber to be made available for liquid spills	FM	25/02/20–	Yes 24/02/20–
		• All staff trained to maintain good housekeeping standards	• Extra bins provided for waste	FM	25/02/20–	Yes 24/02/20–
Manual handling						
Falling objects						
Operation of MHE						

TABLE 15.1 *continued*

What are the Hazards?	Who might be harmed and how?	What are you already doing?	What further action is necessary?	Action by whom?	Action by when?	Completed?
Machinery						
Traffic movements						
Portable electrical equipment						
Lighting						
Hazardous substances						
Fire						
Hygiene and Comfort						

Location

Date:

Assessor:

Included in this should be the regular inspection and maintenance of equipment within the warehouse.

Racking tends to be the largest structure within the warehouse and at times the most neglected in terms of inspection. The following racking checklist can be drawn up as an inspection sheet, and should be introduced and checked regularly:

- Is the equipment on sound, level flooring?
- Is it still installed correctly?
- Are double-sided runs connected properly?
- Are the aisles wide enough?
- Are the beam connector locks securely fastened?
- Are the racks aligned properly?
- Are the correct pallets being used?
- Are the pallets in good condition?
- Is there any visible damage?
- When was it last inspected?
- Are there signs on the end detailing weight capacities?
- Are staff trained properly?
- Are there any receptacles for rubbish, eg shrink wrap, packaging, broken bits of pallet?

A significant hazard within any warehouse is where improperly stored goods can fall and injure staff. Carrying out these checks regularly should minimize these occurrences.

Figure 15.3 shows the importance of ensuring that beam connector locks are installed for each and every beam to avoid catastrophic damage. The picture overleaf shows how damage has been minimized by correct procedures.

Fire safety

Employers need to have an emergency plan that describes what is expected of employees in the event of an emergency, including:

- provisions for emergency exit locations and evacuation procedures;
- procedures for accounting for all employees and visitors; and
- location and use of fire extinguishers and other emergency equipment.

FIGURE 15.3 Partial rack collapse (courtesy of Nene)

A fire risk assessment must be undertaken to ensure that fire safety procedures, fire prevention measures and fire precautions are all in place and correct. The five stages of fire risk assessment are:

Step 1: Identify fire hazards.

Step 2: Identify people at risk.

Step 3: Evaluate, remove, reduce and protect from risk.

Step 4: Record, plan, inform, instruct and train.

Step 5: Review and revise risk assessments as necessary.

Having an escape route at the back of the racking is an area often neglected by companies.

Slips and trips

Within the storage and warehousing industry, slips and trips are a very serious problem. They are responsible for one-third of major injuries and a fifth of over-three-days absence injuries in the United Kingdom. According to the US Department of Labor, slips, trips and falls make up the majority of general industry accidents, which account for 15 per cent of all accidental deaths, 25 per cent of all injury claims, and 95 million lost work days annually. That's 65 per cent of the total of lost workdays. Therefore a working environment must be created where they are much less likely to happen.

According to Scott Stone from Cisco Eagle companies need to:

- Enforce good housekeeping. Don't allow spills to stay on the floor. Soak up oil or greasy waste, and instantly mop up liquid spills. Be sure you have absorbent powders and other cleaning agents on hand. Also, consider purchasing spill containment systems and liquid storage cabinets.

- Don't let your aisles become cluttered. Clutter can hide spills and cause fall hazards.

- Remove or strictly control the use of cell phones. People walking in a warehouse or on a plant floor while texting or otherwise paying attention to their phone screen are asking for an accident (a slip, or worse, collision with an industrial vehicle).

- Provide anti-slip mats wherever possible, but in particular in areas known for wet or oily conditions. Install carpet mats at entrances to reduce wet shoes entering an area where polished concrete can make them into ice skates.

- Make sure workers wear appropriate footwear on your plant floor. Slippery, inadequate shoes are a major contributor to slip and fall accidents.

- Be sure handrails are installed wherever possible. Use gates and other obstructions to slow the pace of walking in critical areas.

- Be certain that lighting is adequate.

- Train for success. Make sure people understand that running isn't allowed on your floor, nor are other dangerous behaviours.

- Keep floors and traffic routes free from obstructions that may present a hazard, particularly near stairs, on emergency routes or in/near doorways.

The workplace must be regularly inspected to ensure that flooring remains adequate and repairs are undertaken wherever necessary. Any spillages must be cleaned up immediately.

Manual handling

In warehousing, manual handling can often cause work-related problems, including back pain and neck pain. If there is a risk from a manual handling task, a risk assessment must be undertaken and the potential risk should be avoided. If this risk cannot be avoided, the risk of injury occurring must be minimized as far as possible. When considering a manual handling operation, the following must be taken into account:

- the task;
- the load;
- the working environment; and
- individual capacity.

Wherever possible, you should try to use mechanical handling devices such as lift trucks, pallet trucks, trolleys or scissors lifts. Mechanical handling devices should help to avoid or reduce manual handling operations.

All employees should be trained in safe manual handling techniques, training should be specific to the tasks that they undertake and all such training should be recorded. Operators should also be encouraged to get a co-worker to assist if a product is too heavy.

Shelves and bins should also be repositioned to reduce lifts from shoulder and floor height. Popular items should be kept on the middle shelves to avoid continuous bending and stretching.

Finally, ensure that overhead lighting is adequate for the task in hand.

Working at height

Working at height can be a particular risk in the warehousing and storage industry, and any working at height must be properly planned, supervised and carried out in as safe a manner as possible. Generally, it is advisable that all work at height should be avoided; however, if this is impossible, equipment must be provided to allow such work to be carried out in as safe a way as possible. Any equipment that is provided to allow working at height must be inspected regularly to ensure that it remains safe and is being used in the correct manner.

Vehicles

A common cause of accidents in the loading bay is from vehicle creep, where a lorry either drifts slightly away from the loading dock or, in the worst-case scenario, the driver moves off before warehouse operatives have actually finished loading or unloading the vehicle. This is known as a 'drive-away' and can have serious, indeed fatal, consequences.

From a safety aspect there needs to be assurance that the vehicle cannot be driven away whilst it is in the process of being unloaded. This can be done in a number of ways:

- The vehicle keys can be held on the loading bay and handed back to the driver when the unloading operation has been completed.

- The vehicle/trailer can be immobilized in some way either by using wheel locks, clamps, chocks or trailer safety interlocks which fit to the air hose coupling and interlock with the warehouse bay door.

- A system of lights can be introduced on the loading bay indicating when it is safe for a driver to pull away from the bay.

A combination of the above is likely to be the most effective safety system. Ruth Waring of Labyrinth Logistics Consulting adds a note of warning: 'Foreign drivers with left-hand-drive vehicles operating in the UK can easily get confused by traffic light systems on bay doors, as they may be looking at the wrong set of lights and still pull away whilst loading is ongoing.'

Another thing to watch out for is drivers who deliberately carry a spare set of keys so they can listen to the radio or have the heater on while they are waiting. Placing a high 'Stop' sign right in front of the cab (this can be moved by a forklift truck if pallet mounted) makes it much harder for the driver to misinterpret any signals from the loaders and simply drive off.

Drive-away can also happen when the trailer is being loaded/unloaded from the side by forklift truck, where the driver thinks the loading has finished and drives off. If the forks are in a pallet at the time, the forklift truck can tip over 90 degrees, which has also led to fatalities.

Vehicle creep isn't the only hazard in the loading bay, according to John Meale (2010) from Thorworld:

> Most trailers are not equipped with internal lighting, so it's a good idea to fit dock lights to improve visibility. Otherwise, operatives entering the vehicle from a brightly lit warehouse can struggle to adjust to the change in conditions and may not see potential hazards, causing injury to themselves or potentially damaging goods.

Loading bays should also be fitted with safety guards to ensure that staff and trucks cannot fall from the dock when not in use.

With regard to the driver, there are a number of issues. First there is the decision whether the driver should assist in the offloading of the vehicle or at least supervise the offloading to ensure damage isn't caused to the product during this process. The driver will have to comply with the Health and Safety policy of the warehouse.

With the increase in imported goods and cross-border movements, the production of driver guidelines in different languages will assist in the communication process between drivers and the receiving team. Issuing picture guidance is also a good idea.

Moving vehicles need to be carefully managed to control and reduce the likelihood of accidents. The following points must be considered in relation to vehicles in and around the warehouse:

- managing deliveries and visitors;
- pedestrian safety: pedestrians and vehicles have to be able to circulate safely;
- traffic route: designed to minimize the need for reversing, avoiding sharp bends and blind corners;
- reversing vehicles: designed to reduce the risks from reversing vehicles wherever possible, for example a one-way system;
- coupling and uncoupling: ensure this is done safely;
- road safety: ensure that there is a safe work system in place to ensure the loading and unloading of vehicles safely;
- forklift trucks.

Forklift trucks

According to the HSE, who analysed workplace vehicle accidents over a 10-year period, there are around 2,000 forklift accidents each year in the UK, a figure that seems to remain fairly consistent.

In accidents involving forklift trucks, 87 per cent were attributed to counterbalance trucks. The highest number of accidents (48 per cent) occur when stacking/retrieving goods, and the greatest cause of accidents is being struck by a moving vehicle.

As many accidents occur when operating or when in the vicinity of forklift trucks, we have listed the following guidelines from the US National Institute for Occupational Safety and Health (NIOSH).

NIOSH recommends that employers and workers comply with OSHA regulations and consensus standards, maintain equipment and take the following measures to prevent injury when operating or working near forklifts.

The key areas are as follows:

- Make sure that workers do not operate a forklift unless they have been trained and licensed.

- Develop, implement and enforce a comprehensive written safety programme that includes worker training, operator licensing and a timetable for reviewing and revising the programme.

- Establish a vehicle inspection and maintenance programme.

- Retro fit forklifts with an operator restraint system if possible.

- Ensure that operators use only an approved lifting cage and adhere to general safety practices for elevating personnel with a forklift. Also, secure the platform to the lifting carriage or forks.

- Do not move the forklift whilst the cage is in the air.

- Provide means for personnel on the platform to shut off power to the truck whenever the truck is equipped with vertical only or vertical and horizontal controls for lifting personnel.

- Separate forklift traffic and other workers where possible.

- Limit some aisles to workers on foot only or forklifts only.

- Restrict the use of forklifts near time clocks, break rooms, cafeterias and main exits, particularly when the flow of workers on foot is at a peak (such as at the end of a shift or during breaks).

- Install physical barriers where practical to ensure that workstations are isolated from aisles travelled by forklifts.

- Evaluate intersections and other blind corners to determine whether overhead dome mirrors could improve the visibility of forklift operators or workers on foot.

- Make every effort to alert workers when a forklift is nearby. Use horns, audible reversing alarms and flashing lights to warn workers and other forklift operators in the area. Flashing lights are especially important in areas where the ambient noise level is high.

- Ensure that workplace safety inspections are routinely conducted by a person who can identify hazards and conditions that are dangerous to workers. Hazards include obstructions in the aisle, blind corners and intersections and forklifts that come too close to workers on foot. The person who conducts the inspections should have the authority to implement prompt corrective measures.

- Do not store bins, racks or other materials at corners, intersections or other locations that obstruct the view of operators or workers at workstations.

- Enforce safe driving practices such as obeying speed limits, stopping at stop signs and slowing down and blowing the horn at intersections.

- Repair and maintain cracks, crumbling edges and other defects on loading docks, aisles and other operating surfaces.

Warehouse equipment legislation

There are two major parts of legislation within the UK which relate directly to the operation of warehouse equipment: Provision and Use of Work Equipment Regulations, 1998 (PUWER 1998), and The Lifting Operations and Lifting Equipment Regulations 1998 (LOLER).

All mechanical handling and lifting equipment is classed as 'work equipment' and subject to PUWER. These regulations require:

- the inspection and maintenance of equipment;
- the provision of information, instruction and training;
- the marking of controls;
- that mobile work equipment for carrying persons is suitable;
- protection from rolling over;
- facilities to prevent unauthorized operation;
- the provision of lighting equipment where necessary;
- the provision, where necessary, of devices to improve vision.

Finally, with regard to lifting equipment used within the warehouse, LOLER states that lifting equipment needs to be inspected and thoroughly examined:

- after installation and before first use;
- if lifting people or is a lifting attachment – every six months;
- at least every 12 months for all other equipment; and
- each time the equipment has been involved in an accident.

Note that inspection has to be made by someone who is competent, sufficiently independent and impartial to make objective decisions. Serious defects should be reported to the HSE and the item taken out of service.

First aid

You should consider and plan for any accidents or emergency that could occur in which an employee or a member of the public is exposed to danger. It is recommended that procedures are in place to deal with emergencies such as serious injuries, spills or fire.

There must be some provision for first aid and the Health and Safety (First Aid) Regulations 1981 set out first aid requirements for the workplace. Assessments of first aid needs should be carried out to ensure that there are adequate and appropriate equipment and facilities in giving first aid to employees (including a first aid box and first aid room, depending on the size of the warehouse).

Businesses should have an 'appointed person' where necessary to take charge in the event of an emergency. This person does not need to be a qualified first aider, but should take charge of the first aid arrangements, whether this means just looking after a first aid box and calling the emergency services, or something more. However, qualified first aiders should be considered. Whether these are needed and the number required depends on the nature of the warehouse, number of employees and the location of the site.

First aid training must be available to any first aiders and they must be retrained before the expiration of each three-year certificate in first aid at work. In terms of how many qualified first aiders are required, an example would be that a medium-risk warehouse with fewer than 20 employees only requires at least one appointed person. However, as a general rule there must be at least one qualified first aider for every 50 people employed. Ensuring cover at different times of the day is a sensible procedure.

Summary and conclusion

Health and safety at work has become a major concern of warehouse managers. The casualty rates remain high and the increase in litigation as a result of injuries sustained in the warehouse has put added pressure on warehouse managers.

Managers need to be vigilant and undertake regular risk assessments. They need to ensure that their staff are working to the correct procedures and that equipment is maintained to the highest standards.

According to the HSE, addressing health and safety should not be seen as a regulatory burden. It offers significant opportunities. Benefits can include:

- reduced costs and reduced risks: employee absence and turnover rates are lower, accidents are fewer, the threat of legal action is lessened;
- improved standing among suppliers and partners;
- a better reputation for corporate responsibility among investors, customers and communities; and
- increased productivity: employees are healthier, happier and better motivated.

There are many excellent publications by the HSE in the UK and OSHA in the United States which provide guidance on health and safety within the warehouse. Details are given at the end of this book.

Please note: Individual managers can be prosecuted under health and safety legislation.

The warehouse and the environment

16

GWYNNE RICHARDS AND CLAIRE RIDING

> *Triple bottom line: people, planet and profit.*
>
> **(JOHN ELKINGTON)**

Introduction

In recent years, environmental and waste issues have affected us all, both at home and at work.

Recycling has become an everyday occurrence and carbon footprints are being left, but not without trace. These issues have also become ingrained into corporate social responsibility, but what does this mean for the warehousing sector?

Legislation is changing and this change is likely to result in carbon becoming a 'new currency' within a new 'carbon economy'. This new economy will make all organizations aware of their 'carbon footprints' to gain a better understanding of where their emissions come from and how they can reduce them. For all organizations reduced carbon emissions will result in reduced energy costs and increased competition (Carbon Trust 2011).

A report by the World Economic Forum (2009) suggests that humans are responsible for greenhouse gas emissions of 50,000 mega-tonnes of CO_2e. CO_2e is a measure of the amount of carbon dioxide emissions. The logistics industry contributes around 2,800 mega-tonnes of CO_2e. That is 6 per cent of total emissions with warehousing contributing 10.7 per cent of the logistics emissions. Logistics industry emissions are not only caused by fuel consumption but also packaging and the energy used in warehouses.

In 2010, according to the Carbon Trust Partnership (CTP), it was estimated that the warehousing industry in the UK represented approximately 3 per cent of the UK's CO_2 emissions.

Keith Horgan of the CTP commented that 'there are substantial opportunities within the warehousing industry to save energy, costs and reduce carbon by the simple implementation of existing, low-energy technology'. He said, 'We are not talking about high-tech solutions but pragmatic and cost-effective actions. For example, lighting and heating are the core areas for energy- and carbon-saving focus. The UK warehousing industry could save in excess of £150 million in energy costs and 1.5 million tonnes of carbon by making simple changes' (United Kingdom Warehousing Association, 2010).

According to a market report by Eye for Transport (North American 3PL Market Report, 2010), 96 per cent of third parties, 100 per cent of manufacturers/retailers and 91 per cent of solution providers see sustainability initiatives as a priority. Companies feel that customer pressure and confidence, company image and differentiation together with regulatory compliance are the main driving forces for the introduction of sustainability measures. This was borne out by a recent survey by American Shipper which stated the above as drivers for sustainability together with a return on investment. In terms of barriers to environmental initiatives, these include a lack of ROI, not prioritized by management, lack of or inconsistent standards and economic instability. The Material Handling Industry of America (MHIA) also released the results of a research study on 'Sustainability in Warehousing, Distribution and Manufacturing' in 2011. According to the report, 48 per cent of respondents currently have a sustainability initiative underway and 88 per cent say that sustainability will be of even greater importance over the next 18–24 months.

An overwhelming majority of respondents, 78 per cent, cite social responsibility as the driver behind sustainability initiatives while 63 per cent cite resulting efficiencies. Fifty-nine per cent indicated that sustainability initiatives were a management directive while 42 per cent said their customers were demanding it.

Other findings included:

- 92 per cent of companies believe that sustainable initiatives have the potential to save money and resources.
- Other benefits of sustainability are bringing greater awareness to the market, tax incentives, utility rebates, and a competitive edge.
- Green companies are investing in lighting fixtures/controls, recycling products and/or fans to circulate cool or warm air.

BNP Paribas Real Estate's Warehouse of the Future report highlights sustainability as being at the forefront of occupier's requirements with 86 per cent of respondents agreeing that sustainability initiatives are important to the future of warehousing. The findings also showed that over two thirds of the occupiers surveyed would pay a rental premium for a green unit if it saved on operational costs. In addition to this 76 per cent of respondents stated that they would look favourably on warehousing that was powered by some form of sustainable energy such as wind, solar, biomass or energy from waste.

In this chapter we look at how operations within the warehouse affect the environment and how the warehouse can play its part in reducing carbon emissions.

Legislation and other pressures

Emerging legislation will have an impact on many organizations and will increasingly require new approaches to the management and reduction of energy and carbon emissions.

Each country or group of countries will have their own legislation in relation to the environment.

Emerging regulations in Europe will include the requirement from 2019 that all new buildings must be zero carbon. Further legislation such as the CRC Energy Efficiency Scheme will require many organizations to trade carbon and appear in a published league table with their peers.

A range of European and UK targets to reduce emissions have been declared including the EU's 20 20 20 and The Climate Change Act (2008) which commits the UK to a reduction of 34 per cent of CO_2 emissions by 2020 and a reduction of 80 per cent by 2050.

Additionally, increasing numbers of customers are requiring their suppliers to demonstrate improvements in their green credentials in order to meet their own environmental targets. To meet this challenge the warehouse sector will need to adopt new approaches to managing and reducing carbon emissions from their buildings.

Warehouse energy usage

Figure 16.1 shows the energy usage within an average-sized warehouse of circa 15,000 square metres.

As can be seen, the main areas of energy use in UK warehouses are heating and lighting, with research showing that the sector could potentially achieve a 16 per cent reduction in emissions in these areas. In warmer climates cooling systems will be a significant factor.

FIGURE 16.1 Warehouse energy usage (courtesy of UKWA 2010 and the CTP)

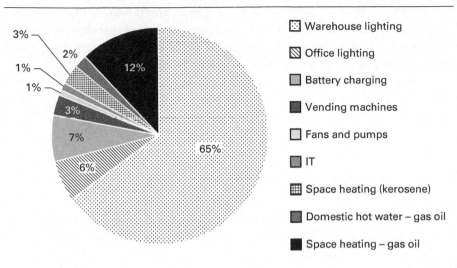

Table 16.1 outlines the key areas and low-capital-cost actions to reduce energy consumption and carbon dioxide emissions within warehouses. These opportunities were observed during a series of energy audits of UKWA members' sites under an initiative between the Carbon Trust and UKWA.

The following list provides warehouse managers with ideas on how to reduce their impact on the environment and thus help companies achieve their CSR targets.

1 Lighting in a non-automated warehouse can be up to 70 per cent of the total energy costs. Ways to reduce lighting costs are as follows:

- introduce energy efficient lighting;
- switch off all non-essential lighting out of business hours;
- install movement sensors and timers
- introduce and regularly clean skylights and clerestory windows to increase the use of natural light;
- switch off lights when daylight is sufficient;
- turn off external lights when daylight is sufficient; and
- switch off office lights on exit or introduce motion sensors.

2 Introduce solar panels where feasible.

3 Use of alternative energy production methods:

- wind turbine;
- biomass boilers.

TABLE 16.1 Potential warehouse energy savings

Key carbon reduction areas	Typical savings based on 10 fittings unless stated otherwise		
	£	CO$_2$ tonnes	Based upon
Turn lights off in warehouse when an area is unoccupied	£700	4.26	50% reduction in lighting
Turn lights off in warehouse when daylight is sufficient	£300	4.92	18% reduction in lighting
Replace 250W and 400W sodium or 400W metal halide lights	£550	3	
Install lighting controls	£70	0.4	T8 having controls added
Clean or replace roof lights	£300	4.92	18% reduction in lighting
Turn off external lights used for loading/unloading when daylight is sufficient	£420	2.5	50% reduction in lighting over 12 months
Control space heating systems efficiently	10–15% saving	10–15% saving	
Ensure efficient control of air conditioning	£120 based on one unit	0.72	
Ensure hot water supply is sized in relation to site occupancy	10% of site fossil fuel	10% of site fossil fuel	

Energy savings base consumption is based on 10 hours per day, five days per week

4 Heating can make up 15 per cent of a warehouse's energy costs.

- Use zoned and time-controlled thermostats which are set accurately (a 1 per cent reduction in temperature on the thermostat can reduce heating bills by 8 per cent).

- Experiment with switch on times for heating and air conditioning and switch off well before close of business.

- Ensure the hot water supply is sized in relation to site occupancy.

5 Install time controls on equipment which are not required after close of business such as vending machines.

6 Use of natural ventilation systems:

- using ventilation stacks;

- atria and automatic window openings combined with automatic control systems;

- passive cooling such as breathable walls;

- using the effective thermal mass of buildings to reduce cooling and ventilation energy.

7 Cooling the warehouse can also increase energy costs.

- Introduce sunlight reflectors.

- Use of mobile air handling units.

8 Switching off equipment when not in use.

9 Ensure all doors have sufficient seals to prevent air and water entry.

10 Rainwater collection for reuse in vehicle washing, toilets, etc.

11 Low water use in sanitary appliances.

12 Check insulation levels and increase where practical.

13 Recycle where feasible and cost effective.

14 Move to utilizing plastic totes/bins in place of cardboard.

15 Utilize plastic or aluminium pallets.

16 Use of gas, electric or hybrid forklift trucks.

17 In rack charging for narrow aisle trucks.

18 Movement reduction within the warehouse to reduce energy consumption.

Use of ABC analysis to ensure popular items are placed close to the despatch area.

19 Kinetic energy plates provision on the access road to produce power from vehicles entering and leaving the site.

20 Introduce car sharing schemes for staff.

21 Encourage staff to walk or cycle to work or take public transport.

22 Introduce training in green initiatives such as fuel-efficient MHE driving.

23 Source materials locally such as packaging, paper, MHE, etc.

24 Continually assess the situation by walking around the warehouse at various times during operating hours.

25 Plant trees and shrubs to assist with the removal of emissions.

The use of smart metres, which record the amount of electricity consumed and when it was consumed, will also assist companies in identifying where consumption is greater than expected.

Finally ensure that your warehouse is also operating effectively – no unnecessary movements, accurate picking and despatch and effective utilization of space.

At the time of writing, CTP were making £550 million of Energy Efficiency Financing (EEF) available in a partnership with Siemens to UK companies. It is likely that many governmental initiatives such as this will become available to companies to assist them to reduce their carbon emissions.

CASE STUDY   Chalmor's LifeSaver scheme (see Figure 16.2)

Chalmor's LifeSaver 'pay as you save' scheme has enabled leading self-adhesive materials manufacturer Ritrama to upgrade lighting and controls at its production centre in Eccles with no capital outlay. Instead, the lighting installation is being funded through quarterly payments, which are less than the money saved each quarter from reduced energy consumption.

'The LifeSaver scheme has enabled us to greatly improve the quality and responsiveness of our lighting, reduce our carbon footprint and save money at the same time,' explained Ritrama UK's managing director Mark Evans. 'Furthermore, there hasn't been any capital outlay, so the whole scheme makes perfect commercial sense.'

The work was carried out in an existing facility, part of which has recently been reorganized to create a self-contained finishing centre. The existing high-pressure sodium lighting was no longer meeting the needs of the space, so a total of 650 sodium fittings were replaced with 420 Chalmor Brilliance high-output long-life fittings. This enabled Ritrama to reduce its installed electrical load by 136kW.

In addition, the new lighting is linked to Chalmor AutoLux lighting controllers, providing presence detection and daylight modulation to ensure that the lighting is only used when needed. The enhanced control is expected to reduce the lighting's running hours by around 40 per cent, resulting in a reduced electrical load and an annual energy saving of 1,444,956kWh.

Further savings are achieved through reduced maintenance costs. Re-lamping was costing nearly £10,000 per annum, whereas the Brilliance fittings are unlikely to require re-lamping for seven years. The combination of reduced energy and maintenance costs is providing Ritrama with a total saving of over £90,000 per annum.

As Ritrama has adopted the LifeSaver scheme, the cost of the lighting, controls and installation has been spread over a period of three years, providing a net saving of over £12,000 a year from day one.

'We have been very pleased with the new lighting, which gives us a brighter light and makes the picking of colour vinyls easier through better colour rendering – as well as helping us to save money,' Mark Evans concluded.

FIGURE 16.2 Energy-saving warehouse (courtesy of Chalmor and Ritrama)

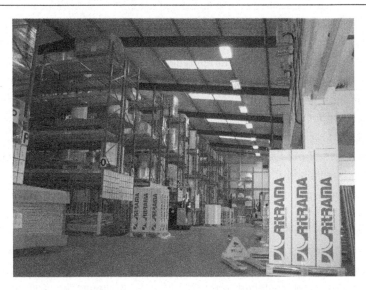

Energy production

The self-production of energy is a potential option for warehouse operators to consider when looking to offset their CO_2 usage.

Photovoltaic panels and small wind generators are still not cost efficient, but combined with subsidies and other government incentives they can have a reasonable ROI.

Wind turbines and the production of energy from biomass can also be a viable way to generate low lifecycle emissions at an acceptable cost, according to DHL's sustainability study.

Regulation plays an important role here. For example, in the UK many local authorities require businesses to generate at least 10 per cent of their energy needs onsite, using renewable energy sources.

Known as the Merton Rule, this policy is estimated to lead to a carbon saving of 350 tonnes each year for an urban town with a population of 150,000 (Energy Saving Trust, 2007).

CASE STUDY   Miniclipper Logistics Green Project 2012

How to turn a multi-building transport and warehousing organization into an environmentally friendly operation.

Miniclipper Logistics operates 180,000 square feet of third-party warehousing in the UK. Awarded ISO14001 in 2012 they embarked on making positive changes to their green policies because they wanted to prove to their customers, employees, and neighbours that they care about the consequences of their transport and warehousing operations on the environment.

Key areas to address in their warehouse operation, in addition to a company-wide change in philosophy, were:

- warehouse lighting;
- use of renewable energy; and
- waste recycling.

1 Warehouse lighting

The lighting project required an initial investment of £70,000 and has produced a return on investment within 1.5 years. This includes a tax break for the use of this technology amounting to 20 per cent of the investment in the first year.

Working with a local company – Chalmor – Miniclipper achieved the following benefits:

- 300 per cent more light in the warehouse and a reduction of 42 per cent in terms of light fittings.

- Before installation the existing individual lights were operating 70 hrs/week. After installation of new lighting and sensors they only operate for just over 13 hours per week at a much lower peak rate, producing a saving of 89 per cent in electricity consumption. Visibility is greater which has led to an increase in staff productivity.

In addition, Miniclipper decided to add:

- sensors to every warehouse fitting in the Hi-bay which aligns each light with activity, therefore varying according to productivity and business peaks;

- movement sensors for offices/toilets/canteen/packing area;

- daylight level sensors for external canopy lights and floodlit loading areas; and

- a new emergency lighting system which ensured they met health and safety legislation.

2 Solar energy

The next step was to achieve carbon neutrality and produce their own energy for the lighting. This they did by installing solar panels to the roofs of their warehouses. With the projected generation from the solar panels at >40,000 kWh, this will completely offset the energy used for the Hi-bay lighting.

See Figure 16.3 below (photograph courtesy of Miniclipper logistics).

FIGURE 16.3   Solar panels on warehouse roof (courtesy of Miniclipper)

3 Waste management

ISO14001 accreditation led to a full review of their environmental policy and communication with their employees.

An example of procedures they have introduced are as follows:

- Wood, plastic, paper, card and metal is separated and recycled and removed by three recycling companies.

- Two balers are installed (one plastic, one cardboard) and staff trained to use.

- Office paper is shredded and used as packing materials in warehouse.

- No plastic/paper cups used in office areas.

- 90 per cent of incoming cardboard boxes are reused for packing.

- No general waste goes to landfill.

In 2011 very little waste material was recycled; in 2012 over 6 tonnes of waste was certified as recycled.

Miniclipper Logistics has found that promoting and pursuing carbon reduction policies are not only good for the environment but have a positive benefit on the bottom line. A real win–win situation.

The environment and waste

Waste is something which the holder or producer discards. If something is discarded then it will remain waste until it has gone through what is known as a 'recovery operation'.

In the UK if you store, treat or dispose of another person's waste you need to hold an environmental permit, be technically competent and be regulated by the Environment Agency.

It is an offence to store, treat or dispose of waste without either an environmental permit or an exemption. There is also personal responsibility on directors and managers to ensure there is no breach of the legislation, and they can be prosecuted personally.

A holder of waste has a duty of care to ensure it is deposited or transferred to an authorized person.

Overall, to comply with the duty you must take reasonable steps to:

- prevent the escape of waste whilst you hold it;
- transfer it to an authorized (suitably licensed) person; and
- provide written information which identifies and describes the waste being transferred.

To avoid a breach of Section 33 of the Environmental Protection Act 1990 you need to prevent waste causing pollution or harm to the environment either when it is under your control or when the waste is transferred.

Other regimes for specific waste types include the Waste Electrical and Electronic Equipment (WEEE) directive. This affects, but is not limited to, importers, manufacturers, retailers and business users.

If you export WEEE you have to be approved by the Environment Agency and issue evidence notes when you receive whole WEEE appliances. You must also have systems and procedures in place to ensure you provide accurate reports to the Environment Agency. If you produce WEEE you are obliged to join a compliance scheme.

Packaging

Product packaging has a significant impact on the sustainability of the supply chain as a whole.

There are three main types of packaging, according to Envirowise, a UK government agency:

- Primary (sales) packaging. This is the packaging around a product at the point of purchase by the user/consumer. Examples include bottles, tins, plastic covers or wrapping.
- Secondary (grouped) packaging. This packaging groups a number of items together until the point of sale. Examples include an inner or outer box and strapping which binds a number of items together.
- Tertiary (transport) packaging. This packaging allows handling and transportation of a number of grouped items as a single unit load. Over recent years the mainstays of returnable transit packaging (RTP), the wooden pallet and the metal stillage, have been joined by many other forms of RTP. These include plastic pallets, tote boxes and metal cages.

There are many reasons for reducing packaging costs. These include:

- Lower packaging costs mean higher profits.
- Waste minimization benefits your own company and the environment.

By carefully segregating its waste into cardboard, plastics and general waste, one food contract packaging company reduced its waste removal costs by 45 per cent and is now recovering approximately 30 per cent of its packaging.

It is possible to significantly reduce packaging costs and cut waste levels by implementing relatively simple measures, many with low or no associated costs; or, if there is a cost, payback is relatively quick.

Taking action on waste packaging will:

- increase overall profitability;
- increase staff awareness of environmental and cost-saving issues;
- develop closer relationships with suppliers and customers through shared benefits and cost savings;
- reduce the use of finite resources;
- reduce the volume of waste going to landfill;
- reduce product damage;
- enhance environmental performance;
- promote a better company image;
- meet current and future obligations under packaging waste regulations at least possible cost.

Packaging design

Although the majority of waste initiatives begin at the design stage and are mainly the concern of the production department, the warehouse can have a significant influence on the amount of packaging used.

When designing product packaging there needs to be an input from the warehouse operation. For example, secondary packaging needs to fit the actual pallet dimensions. Any overhang on the pallet can lead to packaging damage, an increase in the amount of stretch wrap required and potential issues when the product is put away in the racking.

Pallets

Although the mainstay of transit packaging over many years, the pallet can be replaced or at least augmented by other forms of tertiary packaging.

For example, an alternative to the use of pallets where the products are lightweight in design include slip sheets and corrugated trays. Not only do they reduce the use of wooden pallets but they are lighter, take up less space in a container, for example, and are significantly cheaper, especially in circumstances where pallets are not returned.

However, if your operation necessitates the use of pallets there needs to be a process in place to track and recover pallets. A current client is spending in excess of €800,000 on wooden stillages that are left at customer premises. In such cases alternative methods of encasing and transporting the product need to be evaluated. These can include collapsible metal stillages which, although more expensive to produce initially, can be returned for reuse without significantly reducing the back-loading abilities of the delivery vehicles.

Utilizing recycled pallets can have a number of advantages over new pallets. They are likely to be cheaper and potentially stronger as a result of seasoning, which increases the strength of the wood. They are also exempt from packaging waste regulations.

Plastic pallets which are recyclable are also a potential alternative albeit they take more energy to produce, are more expensive at the outset and will require a robust system to track their whereabouts.

Stretch wrap

Suppliers can end up using excessive stretch wrap to stabilize product on a pallet. Alternatives include banding. Although a capital purchase, stretch-wrap machines can reduce the usage of wrap and make the unit load more stable.

Cartons

As with many of the topics we have discussed in relation to the warehouse operation, packaging again results in trade-offs.

A significant trade-off is the strength of the packaging and potentially less damage versus the additional cost of the packaging. A current client is having to replace packaging received from the Far East on a regular basis as a result of substandard cardboard.

When picking individual items from secondary packaging there is going to be a surplus of cartons. Where possible, cartons should be reused.

The replacement of cardboard packaging with plastic totes is possible. However, a robust system of tracking and tracing the equipment needs to be in place. Some companies are now embedding RFID chips into their reusable packaging.

Labelling

When labelling product in the warehouse it is advisable not to use paper labels that cannot be easily removed. Some plastic re-processors will not accept plastics contaminated with paper.

Product waste

Poor stock rotation can lead to waste with out-of-date items. FIFO systems must be applied to minimize out-of-life stock.

Waste disposal

If packaging cannot be reused, look to reduce disposal costs by segregating the waste correctly and, where feasible, selling it to waste recyclers or re-processors. You can also set it against the purchase of packaging recovery notes.

Hazardous waste

Something is hazardous if it is dangerous to people, animals or the environment. You should first check the goods are as stated in the consignment/transfer note and follow your own acceptance criteria. If the goods are later found to be hazardous you may become the producer of the hazardous waste and will need to comply with the legislation governing this specific waste type.

Forklift trucks

Electric lift trucks are superior to internal combustion engine models when it comes to the environment. Indoor air quality is improved by eliminating internal combustion exhaust within a facility.

If utilizing electric lift trucks, it is not necessary to vent outside air into a facility to offset internal combustion exhaust or to exchange air as frequently through heating, ventilation and air-conditioning systems, which is good for the environment and has the added benefit of reducing heating and air-conditioning costs.

If electricity is generated by renewable sources such as wind and solar power, then electric lift trucks are truly emission free. However, the environmental impact of an electric truck is more than just being emission free. Electric trucks use no engine oil, transmission fluid, radiator fluid or filters that have to be changed on a regular basis. These waste items can be very harmful to the environment if they are not handled and disposed of properly (Hyster 2010).

There is another school of thought according to Johnson (2008), however, that 'fuel carbon footprints of electric and LPG forklifts are, in principle, about equal, while in actual practice, LPG's footprint is smaller than that of electricity'.

Toyota has recently introduced a new Geneo-Hybrid forklift truck which is expected to cut CO_2 emissions and fuel consumption by 50 per cent while delivering the operational performance of an equivalent conventional diesel-powered forklift.

Summary and conclusion

A major challenge across all industry sectors today is ensuring a sustainable supply chain.

Clearly, there are solutions on the market that can help warehouses operate in a more sustainable way. By combining available technologies and solutions in terms of energy savings, heating and cooling systems, and alternative energy sources, a warehouse can be designed that emits 70 per cent less CO_2 than the typical 15-year-old warehouse (Prologis 2007).

We must also encourage staff to be responsible in terms of energy efficiency within the warehouse. Turning off lights and electronic equipment when not in use, and switching off forklift trucks when idling are only a few ways of increasing energy efficiency.

The warehouse of the future

17

The best way to predict your future is to create it.

(ABRAHAM LINCOLN)

Introduction

When I set out to write the first edition of this book I didn't think I'd be following it up with a second edition so quickly. The continuing challenges faced by companies including omni-channel retailing, significant reductions in order lead times, environmental and staffing pressures have suppliers, users and academics looking at ways to overcome these challenges. New technology is continually being introduced and, as Mark Strand says, the future is now in many respects. Concepts such as fully automated warehouses, carbon-neutral buildings, hybrid trucks, robotics, voice operations and optically guided picking are all in their various stages of development.

What of the warehouse of the future? One revolutionary product or process is 3D printing – what effect will this have on the warehouse of the future?

This section will look at the likely role of the warehouse in the supply chain in the future, what it might look like and the new technology which will potentially have a significant effect on warehouses in the future.

Context

First we need to put things into context and be aware that warehousing in the future will be affected by many factors, such as:

- Globally we have a growing but ageing population. This means that land will be at a premium but also there are likely to be labour shortages in key areas, which suggests a potential growth in automation but also the need for elder friendly workplaces.

- The growing economies of not only the BRICS countries (Brazil, Russia, India, China and South Africa) but also those of the developing world where consumerism and the growth of the internet will put even greater pressure on consumer product manufacturers and their warehouses. Consumer awareness and demand for new products and services will continue to increase.

- As economies grow and the population gets older there will be greater competition for staff. Warehousing has not been a career of choice for many people because of its image according to a recent PWC report (2012) and companies are going to have market themselves better to become more attractive to today's youth.

- Sustainability will play a significant role in supply chain operations in the future. The green lobby will look to the supply chain for initiatives in terms of alternative energy use, reduction in CO_2 emissions, reduction in waste, reduction in water usage and the use of alternative forms of transport. This will include intermodal transport initiatives as well as fuel-efficient MHE. Consumers and retailers will also be encouraged to source local products, leading to an increase in demand for neighbourhood warehouses.

- Fuel and energy costs will continue to rise as fossil fuels continue to decline. Companies will look to warehouse automation and the use of greener vehicles whilst developers and warehouse operators will be encouraged to consider solar panels, wind turbines and the use of waste product for energy production.

- The potential introduction of government taxation initiatives to encourage companies to reduce their impact on the environment.

- An increasing pressure on companies to collaborate and share resources. Many warehouses and, for that matter, transport modes are under-utilized, so pressure from the green lobby and also continued pressure to further reduce costs will encourage companies to collaborate.

- Technology will continue to improve, evolve and become more affordable. As has been proven time and again, the next big idea is likely to be just around the corner.

According to Kewill (2013) Generation Z/the post-90s generation have entered the market, as both consumers and employees. Having grown up using e-mail, social networking and communications technology such as mobile/smart phones, MP3 players, laptops/tablets and games consoles, they have never known a world without them. Adept at switching between multiple platforms, formats and devices, they expect to utilize the technology they are familiar with in the work environment, accelerating the prevalence of Bring Your Own

Device (BYOD) in industries heavily reliant on the timely transfer of data, such as logistics.

Views of the future: the landscape

Capgemini (2010), writing about the supply chain, see the characteristics of the 2016 future supply chain as follows:

- The future model will be based on multi-partner information sharing amongst key stakeholders: consumers (the originators of the demand signal, either from home or from a store), suppliers, manufacturers, logistics service providers and retailers.

- Once produced, products will be shipped to collaborative warehouses in which multiple manufacturers store their products. Collaborative transport from the collaborative warehouse will deliver to city hubs and to regional consolidation centres.

- Warehouse locations on the edge of cities will be reshaped to function as hubs where cross docking will take place for final distribution. Non-urban areas will have regional consolidation centres in which products will be cross docked for final distribution.

- Final distribution to stores, pick-up points and homes in urban and non-urban areas will take place via consolidated deliveries using efficient assets.

As we can see from Figures 17.1 and 17.2, warehouses will remain a vital cog in the supply chain, becoming consolidation centres, regional hubs and shared-use facilities for a variety of manufacturers and products.

Although there are many shared-user operations currently in place, including retail consolidation centres, Capgemini's vision of collaborative warehousing takes it to another level.

They see the key point being that both retailers and manufacturers collaborate even more closely by extending the consolidation centre premise to cover multiple retailers, thus ensuring greater warehouse utilization and full truck-load deliveries in all directions. This is borne out by recent surveys such as those by Kewill, Savills and others who cite collaboration and shared user warehouses as being one of the future solutions for cost reduction and the shortage of labour.

To succeed, this concept will require high levels of trust and commitment among manufacturers, retailers and logistics service providers, but it is a crucial enabler for realizing integrated sustainability improvements.

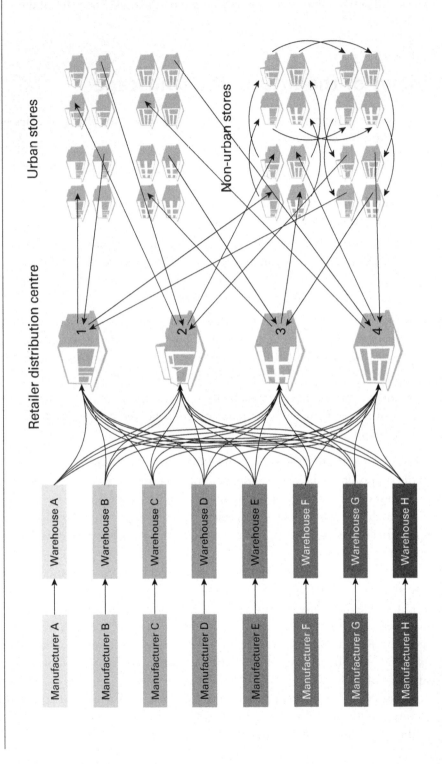

FIGURE 17.1 Current retail warehouse map (© The Consumer Goods Forum, Capgemini; reprinted with permission)

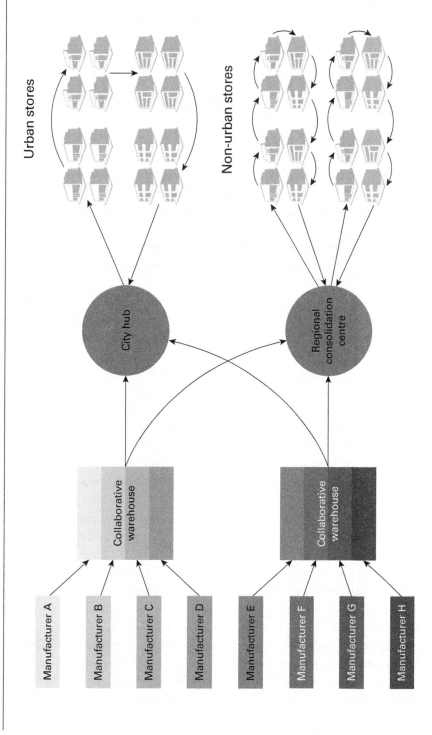

FIGURE 17.2 Collaborative warehousing (© The Consumer Goods Forum, Capgemini; reprinted with permission)

This is likely to be one of the main stumbling blocks and it will require third-party logistics companies to play a greater role by being more proactive and brokering agreements between all three parties and also taking some of the risk.

Views of the future: the warehouse

What of the warehouse itself?

I'm certain that those of us who grew up in the sixties and seventies would not have predicted that mobile phones and computers, although I use the terms loosely in this context, would have had the impact on communications that they have today. Nor that such powerful devices could be packaged into such small units.

The other phenomenon has been the internet and the effect it has on the way we do business today. This leads me on to the role of the warehouse in the future.

Some would argue that there won't be a requirement for stocked warehouses as companies will manage their supply chains so well that cross docking or transhipment will be the norm and therefore warehouses will become transit sheds, parcel and pallet hubs.

Secondly, with the growth in e-retailing there will be more fulfilment and returns centres as opposed to warehouses. In addition, with the increase in fuel costs there may be an argument for production becoming more localized and therefore warehouses will become an extension of the production plant once again. This should lead to a more just-in-time method of order fulfilment.

For those of us who subscribe to the view that warehouses will still exist some time into the future, what function will they perform and what will they look like?

The current trend seems to be towards greater centralization of warehousing, with retailers building bigger sheds with more automation, replacing smaller regional centres.

Others argue that the rising cost of fuel and customer demand for shorter lead times will result in a greater number of local warehouses.

These centres will act as replenishment centres for stores, and continued growth in e-retailing will increase home delivery significantly.

On this point, orders to the warehouse will grow appreciably but the number of lines and items per order will be small. Thus where individual items are ordered by consumers over the internet there will be a greater need for technological solutions and quicker, more accurate methods of order picking and despatch.

Automation will play a big part in the warehouse of the future and it is likely that we will have many types of robots criss-crossing the floor, collecting and depositing pallets, cartons and totes to wherever they are needed, with very few humans in sight.

Conveyors will abound and robots will move both horizontally and vertically, making full use of the cube of the warehouse. Radio frequency sensors will be placed strategically throughout the warehouse to ensure that there aren't any breaks in transmission and to guide the various automated equipment.

We humans will no doubt still be involved in some capacity but mainly as IT and equipment service engineers. Skilled pickers will still have a place on the warehouse floor where goods-to-picker systems will continue to play their part. Staff will also be required for various value-added tasks such as re-packing, kimballing and kitting.

In order for this to work efficiently, everything will need to be uniform. Pallets will need to be the same size – no combinations of UK, US, euro or print pallets, for example. Cartons will also need to be standardized. Alternatively, goods will be moved in plastic, returnable and recyclable totes.

As for the building itself it is likely to be built with sustainability in mind.

The warehouses will operate 24 hours per day. From an environmental standpoint, the warehouse roofs will have solar panels and the yards will be full of wind turbines, not only to run the warehouse but also to produce energy to recharge the electric vehicles which make the deliveries.

The equipment will be regenerative and all operations will benefit from energy-efficient lighting and heating.

The majority of warehouses are likely to be high bay (at least 12 metre eaves according to the BNP Paribas report) with some lower height warehouses or sections of warehouses to act as cross docking operations. The continued growth in third-party logistics and shared-user warehousing is also likely to see larger warehouses with the potential for sub-division.

The increase in product lines could also see greater use of mezzanine floors.

As for location, port-centric logistics is increasing in popularity together with the increased use of rail transportation which suggests coastal locations or those linked by inland waterways and rail.

Finally there will be a requirement for greater flexibility with shorter lease terms.

The following are potential scenarios for the future of warehousing. Scenario one looks at the use of technology to its utmost whilst Scenario two suggests that we humans will continue to play a significant role in warehouse operations.

Scenario one

As a vehicle arrives on site its RFID tag will be read and the vehicle guided to the relevant loading bay. On reaching the bay its roller shutter door will open, as will the loading bay door, and the rails within the trailer will connect to rails within the warehouse. The conveyor will be activated and the pallets will be unloaded. Each pallet will move through a portal where each pallet and item tag will be read and the data sent direct to the WMS. An AGV will take the pallet to its relevant location, be it the despatch bay for cross docking or into deep storage. If the products are destined for the pick section they will be de-layered robotically and each layer of product placed into a tote for onward delivery to the mini-load AS/RS storage area. Suppliers will be informed of any discrepancies and their payments adjusted accordingly.

The system will control all of the movements within the warehouse with no requirement to print pick lists, communicate with PDAs or send voice instructions to us humans. The paperless warehouse should become a reality (unlike the paperless office which has been much heralded but never achieved).

All items are RFID tagged and are tracked throughout the warehouse.

Once an order is received the mini-load system will send the tote containing the product(s) to a pick station and a robot with suction pads will read the RFID chip or compare its image with that of the order, pick up the item and place it into another tote or carton for despatch. This task may be done by a human if the robot's dexterity is called into question.

The tote will be placed on a conveyor, a lid fitted together with a destination label and it will be loaded onto a waiting vehicle.

The problem will be how to manage complexity. The requirement for individual items to be picked from cartons will continue to pose problems for a fully automated warehouse. The growth of internet shopping and orders for individual items will continue to pose challenges to warehouse operators, so human intervention will still be a fundamental requirement.

Robot dexterity may be improved but this could be at the risk of slowing down the operation as a whole.

It may be that robots, conveyors and AGVs will bring the products to the operator but the actual act of picking and packing could well remain with the operator.

Scenario two

There is an argument that people will continue to be used for specific operations within the warehouse. For example, people are currently able to pick individual items faster and more cost effectively than a fully automated system.

The following is an example of how the present and the future are coming together with most of this technology in place individually but not yet combined into a single operation.

This is a concept system called Aria put forward by LXE, a leading manufacturer of mobile computers.

We have also incorporated Jungheinrich's RFID warehouse navigation system.

The concept covers both inbound and outbound operations and is heavily reliant on the introduction of RFID technology.

The arrival of a delivery at the security gate triggers a message to the warehouse operator from the WMS via their headset, which is attached to a mobile computer worn on their arm, belt or installed on their lift truck, to 'Go to dock door 34'.

The door opens and the RFID reader on the lift truck automatically reads the RFID transponders in the floor and takes the truck and driver to the correct location. A tag on the dock door confirms that they are at the correct location.

The RFID reader then automatically reads the pallet tag which contains a unique EPC code associated with the pallet and the shipper. The WMS retrieves the electronic ASN referenced by the RFID tag.

Based on the ASN data, the WMS issues any QC instructions (damage checks, case counts, etc) to the operator via either the mobile computer screen or headset.

After the operator validates that any QC tasks are complete, the WMS does an auto-receive of the pallet.

The WMS then tells the operator via voice to take the pallet to aisle 07 and deposit it at the pick and drop location. This repetitive movement can be replaced by an AGV.

A message is sent to the very narrow aisle truck operator that there is a pallet awaiting put-away. The RFID reader on the truck follows a particular path set out by the WMS to arrive at the correct location. Upon arriving at the pick and drop point in aisle 07 the RFID reader on the operator's truck auto-confirms the operator's location by reading an RFID tag embedded in the rack.

When the pallet is deposited in the location, the RFID reader notifies the WMS that the task has been completed correctly. The WMS completes the transaction and updates the inventory location record.

Once completed, a further message is sent to the operator to retrieve a pallet from aisle 07 location 0105 and take it to pick location 012101.

A member of the picking team receives a message via their headset to go to pick location 012101.

A laser-guided truck is despatched from the outbound bay, having collected an empty pallet, to meet the picker at location 012101. On arrival at location 012101, the RFID reader on the operator's arm and on the truck auto-confirms the truck and operator's location by reading an RFID tag embedded in the floor or on the rack.

The operator is instructed to pick three cases. The warehouse operator then places three boxes on the pallet. The RFID system confirms that the correct product has been picked in the correct quantity.

If the wrong product or quantity is picked, the system immediately communicates appropriate corrective action at the pick location where the problem can be resolved with minimal disruption and expense.

The picker and the truck continue to the remaining locations on the pick list. Once completed, the truck departs for the despatch bay while the picker awaits the next instruction.

The advantages of such a system include the following:

- high levels of accuracy;
- driving to wrong location is eliminated;
- reduction in order-picking mistakes;
- greater operator comfort;
- less stress for the driver;
- up to 25 per cent higher pick rate;
- higher order-picking quality;
- distance and time optimization;
- saves energy;
- distance optimization means energy optimization; and
- reduction in lighting within aisles is possible ('pick by light on truck').

Other advances

Technology that is just around the corner includes Knapp's optically guided picking system. The picker wears a camera and is guided by the system to each required pick location using superimposed arrow symbols directly in the field of vision of the operator via a head-mounted display. There is a countdown in terms of the metres left to travel. At the pick location the goods to be picked are identified for the picker and the camera reads barcodes, lot numbers and serial numbers to confirm the pick without any further human intervention. A digital display will show the number of items to be picked.

Once established, it is thought that the system will prove even more accurate than voice, and the head-mounted equipment will be the same weight and design as a normal pair of glasses.

As with voice-directed picking, training is quick and allows operators to keep both hands free for picking.

 www.youtube.com/watch?v=BWY8uFltelM

One other piece of technology I want to share with you is 3D printing or additive manufacturing.

3D Printing was originally developed as an automated method of producing prototypes. Although there are several competing technologies, most work on the basis of building up layers of material (sometimes plastic, ceramics or even metal powders) using a computer aided design. Hence, it is referred to as an 'additive' process; each layer is 'printed' until a three dimensional product is created.

A report by Transport Intelligence suggests that 3D printing 'is already very good at producing products (even with moving parts) which previously would have required the assembly of multiple components', and that by 'eliminating the assembly phase there will be huge savings for the manufacturer in terms of labor costs'. 3D printing-based production could also reduce or eliminate storage, handling and distribution costs.

People will be able to print a required item at home providing they have the scanned image or the blueprints of the product itself.

The report goes on to say that 'A major new sector of the logistics industry will emerge dealing with the storage and movement of the raw materials which "feed" the 3D printers. As 3D printers become more affordable to the general public, the home delivery market of these materials will increase.'

Global and national parts warehouses as well as forward stock locations will become unnecessary. At present billions are spent on holding stock to supply parts to products as diverse as cars and x-ray machines. In some cases a huge amount of redundancy is built into supply chains to enable parts to be dispatched in a very short timescale to get machines up and running again as fast as possible.

The Service Parts Logistics industry will be either transformed or decimated by 3D manufacturing – or perhaps both! With small 3D Printing machines available, operations in remote locations – or even in an engineer's van – will only need electronic libraries of designs available to them on a local computer. They can then call up the design of the spare part required and immediately print it. Obsolete parts could simply be scanned in 3D, fixed in the computer's memory and the new part printed. The implications for inventory are clear.

 www.youtube.com/watch?v=X5AZzOw7FwA (PBS off book)

Summary and conclusion

Warehouses in highly developed countries will no doubt adopt the latest technology, and companies whose products can absorb the high initial capital investment will be at the forefront of warehouse automation.

However, as discussed previously, automation is not for everyone, and warehouses will continue to hold stock and employ staff to receive, put away, pick and despatch products.

It is hoped that this book has given you, the reader, an insight into warehouse operations in the 21st century. Although investment in technology will improve and speed up operations, changes in processes, attitudes and improved communication both internally and externally are the stepping stones. These need to be firmly in place and cannot be by-passed under any circumstances prior to any thoughts of automation.

The growth in e-commerce will continue to challenge warehouse managers globally and the change in profile from full-carton and full-pallet picks to individual-item picks will have equipment manufacturers seeking the holy grail of pick systems. Whatever that may be.

One thing is certain: we cannot afford to stand still. US Rear Admiral Grace Hopper (1906–92) once said, 'The most damaging phrase in the language is: "It's always been done that way."'

This is a statement I have heard many times in my career and therefore I hope this book has given you some new ideas to think about and hopefully you will be able to implement them and they will help you improve efficiency and minimize costs.

APPENDIX I
Warehouse audit checklists

Warehouse Audit						
Carried out by:				Location:		
Date:						
Item	No	Poor	Good	Excellent	N/a	Comments
External						
Comprehensive signage for delivery drivers in multiple languages						
Comprehensive signage for visitors						
Separate routes for trucks and pedestrians						
Staff cars parked away from warehouse exits						
Is there disabled access into the building?						
Perimeter fencing in good order						
Security gates/barriers in good working order						
External ground in good condition						
Exterior lighting is sufficient and in good order						
LPG Gas and diesel for MHE kept in suitably safe and secure area						
Separate area for storage of waste packaging, away from the main building						
Are broken pallets and defective equipment stored safely and away from the main building?						
Vehicle speeds are controlled						
Is there sufficient space for goods vehicle parking?						
Sufficient turning space for all types of vehicles						

Warehouse Audit						
Carried out by:				Location:		
Date:						
Item	No	Poor	Good	Excellent	N/a	Comments
Internal page 1						
Personnel Security checks on entry and exit						
All exits are secure						
Visitors and attendance books available for inspection and accurate						
Visitors are given safety briefing/instructions						
Visitors are escorted at all times						
Is there disabled access into the warehouse?						
Intruder alarm systems installed and inspected regularly						
Stock adequately protected from theft and pilferage						
Is the building, including the roof, wind- and watertight?						
Is the floor surface in good condition (clean and dry)?						
Is the floor capable of taking the weight of the storage medium and load in terms of point loading?						
Sufficient doors for volume of traffic entering and leaving the warehouse						
Warehouse is clean and tidy						
Documented cleaning schedule in place						
Adequate pest control in place						
Teams given responsibility for cleanliness of own areas						

Warehouse Audit						
Carried out by:				Location:		
Date:						
Item	No	Poor	Good	Excellent	N/a	Comments
Internal page 2						
Exits clearly lit, marked and obstruction free						
Adequate number of personnel exit doors						
Fire escapes, fire doors clearly marked						
Are there sufficient fire doors?						
Are fire doors obstruction free?						
Fire protection system in place, eg sprinklers						
Fire alarms are tested weekly						
Fire alarm drills are carried out periodically						
Fire extinguishers and water hoses clearly marked						
Escape routes clearly marked and obstruction free						
Doors and windows are fitted with safety glass						

Warehouse Audit						
Carried out by:				Location:		
Date:						
Item	No	Poor	Good	Excellent	N/a	Comments
Internal page 3						
Sufficient space between rack ends and external walls						
No smoking signs clearly visible						
Safety equipment regularly inspected, checked and maintained						
First aid boxes provided and fully stocked						
Eye wash facilities available						
Named and suitably trained first aiders						
At least one first aider per 50 staff						
Lighting is sufficient in each section						
Sufficient natural light available						
Eco lighting used					·	
Lights are switched off when area not in use						
Clerestory windows and roof lights cleaned regularly						
Is there sufficient emergency lighting provided in areas where staff are at risk?						
Is the air quality acceptable?						
Is there an audible alarm to detect unsafe areas with poor ventilation?						
Is the noise at an acceptable level?						
Is the temperature conducive to working?						

Warehouse Audit						
Carried out by:				Location:		
Date:						
Item	No	Poor	Good	Excellent	N/a	Comments
Internal page 4						
Are there sufficient, visible thermometers?						
Are battery-charging areas marked adequately and clear of obstruction?						
Trucks recharged in a well-ventilated and risk-free area						
Is there suitable safety information signage at the battery-charge area?						
Are tools and packing materials stored in their designated areas?						
Racking condition is checked regularly and reported						
Racking is independently inspected regularly						
Are there any broken or collapsing pallets in the racking?						
Are there any overhanging pallets in the racks?						
Weight capacity visible on the end of the racks						
Waste receptacles at the end of each aisle						
Are racking legs protected?						

Warehouse Audit						
Carried out by:				Location:		
Date:						
Item	No	Poor	Good	Excellent	N/a	Comments
Internal page 5						
Weight capacity is visible on the end of the racks						
Waste receptacles at the end of each aisle						
Are racking legs protected?						
Aisles are sufficiently wide for MHE						
Aisles are obstruction free						
Are there handrails and guards on stairways?						
Are office areas, canteens and rest areas clean and tidy?						
Washing facilities available for all staff						
Offices well lit, adequately furnished and well spaced						
Drinking water available and signposted						
Suitable areas provided for food consumption						
Accommodation for work clothing made available						
Is every workstation arranged in a suitable manner for staff to work at?						
Is 5S (see page 46) utilized within the warehouse?						
Are sufficient security measures in place for high value items?						
Are sufficient safety measures in place for hazardous items?						
All electrical items tested (UK PAT test)						

Warehouse Audit						
Carried out by:	Location:					
Date:						
Item	No	Poor	Good	Excellent	N/a	Comments
Systems and equipment						
Warehouse IT systems						
Is there a Warehouse Management System in place?						
Is the system adequate for the current operation?						
Are data backups taken daily and stored off-site?						
Are Display Equipment Regulations adhered to?						
Mechanical handling equipment						
Staff have correct licence for type of truck operated						
Responsible staff trained to operate MHE						
Record of safety training kept up to date						
MHE is appropriate for the tasks						
MHE is serviced regularly						
A service chart is visible for all MHE						
Service and repair records are kept up to date						
Pre-operational daily, weekly and monthly checks are carried out on the equipment and recorded						
Inspections carried out on lifting equipment every six months						

Warehouse Audit						
Carried out by:	Location:					
Date:						
Item	No	Poor	Good	Excellent	N/a	Comments
All defects reported to the employer immediately						
Safe working load limits clearly marked						
Audible signals used when trucks reversing and turning corners						
Do forklifts travel at safe speeds?						
Is equipment parked in designated areas when not in use, keys removed and forks lowered?						
Contingency planning						
Documented Contingency Plan in place for:						
Equipment downtime						
System downtime						
Labour issues						
Supplier issues						
Other emergencies						
List of emergency contact numbers held and updated						

Warehouse Audit						
Carried out by:				Location:		
Date:						
Item	No	Poor	Good	Excellent	N/a	Comments
Inbound operation						
Inbound processes manual available						
Vehicle booking-in system utilized						
Scheduling of vehicle arrivals						
Pre-notification of goods to be received						
Vehicle immobilized during unloading						
Delivery drivers given instructions on what to do whilst on site						
Drivers' instructions in multiple languages						
Instructions for inbound goods handling provided						
Is the dock area clear of stored materials and obstructions?						
Sufficient stock of empty pallets available						
Sufficient space for empty pallet storage						
Sufficient space to lay out goods for checking						
Recording of number of pallets received						
Pallet exchange system in place						
Product quantity and condition check						
Log of supplier non-conformance kept, eg incorrect paperwork, quantities, products, condition of goods, condition of packaging, TiHi met, pallet overhang.						
Sufficient handling equipment provided						
Recording of unloading times (dock to stock time)						
Quarantine area for non-compliance						
Quality control area provided						
All non-conforming stock dealt with quickly						
Are returned items dealt with immediately?						

Warehouse Audit						
Carried out by:				Location:		
Date:						
Item	No	Poor	Good	Excellent	N/a	Comments
Put-away and storage						
System/management directed put-away						
FIFO stock rotation is followed correctly						
Best-before-date stock is managed						
ABC analysis (see page 80) used for product location						
Location IDs are marked clearly						
Accurate recording of stock location						
Task-interleaving/dual cycling undertaken – One pallet in, one pallet out)						
Is slotting used effectively (see page 85)?						
Random location system used						
Stock transferred between locations based on ABC analysis						
Is the cube utilization of locations efficient?						
Is location utilization between 80% and 90%?						
Is space usage monitored and action taken to minimize wasted or excess space?						
Are part pallets consolidated where feasible?						
Product tracking in place						
Are damaged items promptly identified and dealt with appropriately?						
Items do not overhang pallets						

Warehouse Audit						
Carried out by:				Location:		
Date:						
Item	No	Poor	Good	Excellent	N/a	Comments
Stock control						
FIFO rotation is adhered to						
Are items stored in the correct location?						
Are high-value goods stored securely?						
Are hazardous items stored under the correct conditions?						
Are non-moving items regularly reviewed, eg FISH (first in still here)?						
Perpetual inventory counting takes place						
Stock counting accuracy is measured						
Stock counts use the 'blind' count method (quantity not revealed to counter)						
Errors are investigated thoroughly						

Warehouse Audit						
Carried out by:				Location:		
Date:						
Item	No	Poor	Good	Excellent	N/a	Comments
Picking						
Forward pick areas are close to despatch						
Pick locations are replenished efficiently						
Replenishment does not take place during picking						
Sufficient stock held in each location for each shift						
Items that sell together are located next to each other						
Very similar items are separated						
Fast-moving items are in the most accessible locations						
Stock is arranged with consideration to product size and weight						
Fast-moving items are on middle shelves						
The pick list provides an efficient pick path						
Heavier items are picked first						
Pick instructions are clear and concise						
Sufficient scanners/voice units available for the team						
Pyramid picking is evident						
Pick accuracy is measured and monitored						
Despatch						
Departure times are planned						
Sufficient space to lay out despatches						
Products are packed securely and safely						
Load optimization is apparent						
Products are packed to minimize transport costs						
Outbound pallets are recorded						

Warehouse Audit						
Carried out by:				Location:		
Date:						
Item	No	Poor	Good	Excellent	N/a	Comments
Other areas						
Staff and housekeeping						
Does daily and weekly resource planning take place?						
Are daily work tasks balanced and prioritized?						
Are tasks checked from an ergonomic point of view?						
Are resources maximized to avoid idle time?						
Are activities timed and compared against target?						
Are activities reviewed regularly?						
Are staff trained regularly?						
Are staff encouraged to suggest improvements?						
Are staff uniformed and smart?						
Are staff issued with PPE?						
Is PPE adequate for the tasks required?						
Warehouse – performance management						
Is performance measured?						
Is there a suite of relevant performance measures?						
Are performance measures shared with staff and visible in the warehouse?						
Is staff productivity measured?						
Is productivity data shared with staff?						

Warehouse Audit						
Carried out by:				Location:		
Date:						
Item	No	Poor	Good	Excellent	N/a	Comments
Legislative & Health and Safety requirements						
Warehouse Safety Policy Document available for inspection/displayed						
Risk assessments carried out						
Risk assessments available for inspection						
Near miss record book kept						
Accident book kept						
Accident book kept up to date						
Manual handling assessment available for inspection						
COSHH assessment carried out						
Equipment statutory Inspection Certificates available for inspection						
Waste disposal arrangements in place						
*Following notices displayed:						
Employer's Liability and Public Liability Certificate						
Health and Safety Information for Employee Regulations 1999						
Health and Safety Policy						
COSHH information signage						
Electric shock signage						

Warehouse Audit						
Carried out by:				Location:		
Date:						
Item	No	Poor	Good	Excellent	N/a	Comments
*Staff awareness of following regulations:						
Aware of HSE requirements (UK)						
Aware of OSHA requirements (USA)						
Health and Safety (Signs & Signals) Regs 1996						
Health & Safety (First Aid) Regulations 1981						
Provision and Use at Work Equipment Regulations (1998)						
Lifting Operations and Lifting Equipment Regulations 1998						
Display Screen Equipment Regulations (1992)						
Regulatory Reform (Fire Safety) Order 2005						
The Pollution Prevention and Control Act 1999						
The Environmental Protection Act 1990						
The Hazardous Waste Regulations						
Producer Responsibility Obligations (Packaging Waste) Regulations						
Waste Electrical & Electronic Equipment Regulations 2007						

* Note that different countries will have different requirements and legislation

Further information

Suggested reading to ensure safe and legal practices

UK HSE: **www.hse.gov.uk**
UK COMAH: **www.hse.gov.uk/comah/index.htm**
UK SEMA: **www.sema.org.uk/**
USA OSHA: **www.osha.gov/**
Europe EPA: **www.epa.gov/lawsregs/regulations/**
Risk: **www.ioshroutefinder.co.uk**

References

United Kingdom Warehousing Association: www.ukwa.org.uk

Ackerman K, (2003) *Auditing Warehouse Performance*, Ackerman Publications, Ohio

APPENDIX 2

The following is a list of the different types of barcodes and their typical applications.

EAN – 1 3. Character Set: Numeric only; Character Size: 13 fixed-length; Fault Tolerance: High; Application: International retail and grocery standard (Europe)

UP C – A; Character Set: Numeric only; Character Size: 12 fixed-length; Fault Tolerance: High; Application: Retail and grocery standard (United States)

A N – 8; Character Set: Numeric only; Character Size: 8 fixed-length; Fault Tolerance: High; Application: Small packages in retail (Europe)

UPC – E; Character Set: Numeric only; Character Size: 6 fixed-length; Fault Tolerance: High; Application: Small packages in retail (United States)

Code 128; Character Set: Alphanumeric (uppercase/lowercase), punctuation, controls; Character Size: Any; Fault Tolerance: High; Application: Best for full ASCII character set

Code 39; Character Set: Alphanumeric (uppercase only), punctuation; Character Size: Limited by reader; Fault Tolerance: High; Application: Military, government

GS1 DataBar Omnidirectional; Character Set: Numeric only; Character Size: 14 fixed-length; Fault Tolerance: High; Application: GTIN in small format

GS1 DataBar Expanded: Character Set: Numeric only; Character Size: Variable-length; Fault Tolerance: High; Application: GTIN, applications in ID fields

GS1 – 128; Character Set: Alphanumeric Character Size: Variable-length; Fault Tolerance: High; Application: Many uses in supply chain; lots, containers, batches, retail.

M S I / Plessey; Character Set: Numeric only; Character Size: 3 to 16 fixed-length; Fault Tolerance: High; Application: Grocery

Code 32; Character Set: Numeric only; Character Size: 8 digit (plus one check character) fixed-lengthFault Tolerance: High; Application: Pharmaceutical industry (Italy)

Two-Dimensional (2D) barcode symbologies contain information in both the X and Y axis of the symbol. In other words, there is different data encoded in the horizontal and vertical dimensions of the code. To properly decode the data, a scanner must read the entire symbol, in both dimensions simultaneously. This can be done by sweeping the scan line (in the case of a laser or linear imaging scanner) over the symbol, or by using a 2D array equipped scanner, which acts as a camera. Since the data can be stored in two dimensions, 2D barcode symbologies allow vast amounts of data to be stored.

There are two kinds of 2D barcode symbologies: stacked codes and matrix codes. Stacked codes consist of multiple layers of linear barcodes and matrix codes encode data using cells within a matrix.

Examples of stacked codes are:

PDF 417; Character Set: Alphanumeric (uppercase/lowercase), punctuation, controls Character Size: Variable-length; Fault Tolerance: High; Application: Driver licenses, transportation, inventory management, government

Codablock F; Character Set: Numeric only; Character Size: Up to 5,450 characters variable-length; Fault Tolerance: High; Application: Healthcare

Examples of Matrix codes are:

Data Matrix; Character Set: Alphanumeric, Uppercase/Lowercase Letters, Punctuation, Controls; Character Size: Up to 2,335 characters fixed-length; Fault Tolerance: High; Application: Marking small items, printed on labels and letters, industrial engineering for marketing components

Q R C ode; Character Set: Alphanumeric, Uppercase/Lowercase Letters, Punctuation, Controls. Includes Kanji characters; Character Size: Up to 7,000 numeric characters or 4,296 alpha characters variable length; Fault Tolerance: High; Application: Automobile manufacturing, mobile phone codes

For further information

AIM Global: **www.aimglobal.org**
GS1 The Global Language of Business: **www.gs1.org/**
Ten Steps to Bar Code Implementation:
   www.gs1.org/barcodes/implementation
Global Electronic Party Information Register (GEPIR). GEPIR is
   a distributed database that contains basic information on over
   1,000,000 companies in over 100 countries. You can search by GTIN
   (includes UPC and EAN-13), SSCC and GLN numbers or by company
   name in some countries.
http://gepir.gs1.org
Datalogic A D C White Papers
The Growing Requirements for 2D Imaging Technology
GS1 DataBar™ 2010 Sunrise – An Explanation from a Retailer's Perspective

www.idautomation.com/product-support/barcoding-for-beginners.html#
   bar-code-Accuracy

Information on RFID can be found at

www.aimglobal.org/?RFID
www.rfidjournal.com/

Reference

Reprinted by kind permission of Datalogic.
This work is licensed under the Creative Commons Attribution-
   Noncommercial-Share Alike 3.0 Unported License. To view a copy of
   this license, visit **http://creativecommons.org/licenses/by-nc-sa/3.0/**

REFERENCES

Aberdeen Group (2007) *Debunking Some Myths about Speech-based Warehousing*, Aberdeen Group, Boston, MA

Aberdeen Group (2008) *Evaluating Logistics Outsourcing: Look Before You Leap*, Aberdeen Group, Boston, MA

Aberdeen Group (2009a) *On Time and Under Budget*, Aberdeen Group, Boston, MA

Aberdeen Group (2009b) *Warehouse Operations: Increase Responsiveness through Automation*, Aberdeen Group, Boston, MA

Ackerman, K B (2000) *Warehousing Profitably*, Ackerman Publications, Ohio

Ackerman, K B (2003) *Auditing Warehouse Performance*, Ackerman Publications, Ohio

Acorn Warehouse Solutions (2013) www.awsltd.biz/2013/07/10-key-points-about-your-mezzanine-floor/

Allen, A (2010) *The retail challenge*, available at: www.supplychainstandard.com/Articles/2832/The+retail+challenge.html

American Shipper www.americanshipper.com/Uploads/Public/Documents/Reports/670%20AS-REP%20Sustainability%202012%20v4.pdf

Andress, U www.thoughtjoy.com (accessed 9 September 2013)

ARC Advisory Group (2007) Findings of survey quoted in LXE, Inc (2009) *Maximize the power of your workforce: learn how hands-free solutions can bring value in a tough economy*, available at: www.rfsmart.com/tinymce/filemanager/files/rfs_wp_hands_free_2.pdf (accessed 26 November 2010)

Avery and Associates (2010) *Innovative pick-to-light systems*, available at: http://elogistics101.com/Order_Picking/Innovative-pick-to-light-applications.htm (accessed 26 November 2010)

Baker, P and Perotti, S (2008) *UK Warehouse Benchmarking Report*, Cranfield School of Management, Cranfield

Bartholdi, J (2013) www.warehouse-science.com

BASDA (2009) *Logistics and Supply Chain Technology Best Practice Handbook*, available at: http://docs.basda.org/basda_tech.pdf (accessed 26 November 2010)

Bird, F E and Germain, G L (1996) *Practical Loss Control Leadership*, revised edn, Det Norske Veritas, US

Bititci, U S, Walls, L A, Geraghty, K and Attri, H (2008) To outsource or not to outsource! *Operations Management*, **34** (1), pp 9–16

BNP Paribas (2011) www.realestate.bnpparibas.co.uk/upload/docs/application/pdf/2011-10/warehouse_of_the_future.pdf

Capgemini (2010) *Collaborative Warehousing*, The Consumer Goods Forum

Capgemini (2013) www.capgemini.com/sites/default/files/resource/pdf/2013_Third-Party_Logistics_Study.pdf (accessed 16 September 2013)

Carbon trust (2011) www.ukwa.org.uk/_files/23-carbon-trust-23.pdf

Cert Octavian (2009) Twenty questions that will save you money, White Paper, September 2009 (accessed 1 October 2009)

Chappell, C (2009) Warehouse Staff: Manning the Backroom, *Retail Week*, available at www.allbusiness.com/company-activities-management/operations-supply/13170511-1.html (accessed September 2009)

Christopher, M (1998) *Logistics and Supply Chain Management: Strategies for Reducing Costs and Improving Service*, 2nd edn, Pitman Publishing, London

CILT (2009) Is In-sourcing the New Outsourcing? www.ciltuk.org.uk/download/Opquestion.pdf (accessed 1 September 2010)

Cisco Eagle (2010) Gravity flow vs static shelving, available at: www.cisco-eagle.com/storage/Flowracks/gravity_flow_vs_static_shelving.htm (accessed 26 November 2010)

Cobb, I, Innes, J and Mitchell, F (1992) *Activity-based Costing: Problems in Practice*, Chartered Institute of Management Accountants, London

Cottrill, K and Gary, L (2005–6) How soft metrics can make hard choices easier, *Harvard Business Review Supply Chain Strategy Newsletter*, December–January

Cross, S (2010) in *The Principles of Warehouse Design* (3rd edn), edited by Peter Baker, CILTUK Corby

Dematic Corporation (2009) *Goods to Person Order Fulfilment*, Dematic Corporation

Demirel, T *et al* (2010) Expert Systems with Applications 37 2010 3943–3952

DTZ (2013) Occupier Perspective, Global Occupancy Costs Logistics 2013 www.dtz.com/Global/Global+Occupancy+Costs+Logistics+2013+report (accessed 9 September 2013)

Drucker, P (nd) Finestquotes.com, retrieved 12 February 2010 from www.finestquotes.com/author_quotes-author-PeterDrucker-page-0.htm

Elkington, J (1998) *Cannibals with Forks: the Triple Bottom Line of 21st Century Business*, Capstone Publishers

Energy Saving Trust (2007) *Case Study: Energy in Planning and Building Control*, available at: www.energysavingtrust.org.uk/business/Publication-Download/?oid=351875&aid=1034625 (accessed 26 November 2010)

Eye for Transport (2010) *North American 3PL Market Report*

Forrester (2013) US Online Retail Forecast, 2012 To 2017 March 13, 2013 By Sucharita Mulpuru with Carrie Johnson, Douglas Roberge www.forrester.com/US+Online+Retail+Forecast+2012+To+2017/fulltext/-/E-RES93281?objectid=RES93281 (accessed 09 September 2013)

Frazelle, E H (2002) *World Class Warehousing and Material Handling*, McGraw Hill, New York, NY

Gagnon, G (1988) *Supervising on the Line: A Self-help Guide for First Line Supervisors*, Margo, Minnetonka, MN

Goldratt, E and Cox, J (1984) *The Goal*, Gower Aldershot.

Gooley, T B (2001) How to keep good people, *Logistics Management & Distribution Report*, 40 (1), pp 55–60

Gooley, T (2013) Lean your warehouse workforce DC Velocity http://dcvelocity.com/print/article/20130528-lean-your-warehouse-workforce/ (accessed 10 September 2013)

Griful-Miquela, C (2001) Activity-based costing methodology for third-party logistics companies, *International Advances in Economic Research*

Grossman, E (1993) *How to Measure Company Productivity: Handbook for Productivity, Measurement and Improvement*, Productivity Press, Cambridge, MA

Gunasekaran, A and Cecille, P (1998) Implementation of productivity improvement strategies in a small company, *Technovation*, 18 (5), May, pp 311–20

Gutierrez, R (2003) *What is core competency?*, available at: http://searchcio-midmarket. techtarget.com/sDefinition/0,,sid183_gci214621,00.html (accessed 26 November 2010)

Hewitt, M (2010) quoted in Allen, A (2010) *The retail challenge*, available at: www.supplychainstandard.com/Articles/2832/The+retail+challenge.html

Hicks, D T (1992) *Activity-based Costing for Small and Midsized Businesses*, John Wiley and Sons, New York, NY

Hill, T (1993) *Manufacturing Strategy: The Strategic Management of the Manufacturing Function*, 2nd edn, Open University/Macmillan, London

HSE (2010) 'Contains public sector information published by the Health and Safety Executive and licensed under the Open Government Licence v1.0' accessed from www.hse.gov.uk/warehousing

HSS (2010) *UKWA teams up with Carbon Trust on emissions toolkit*, available at: www.hsssearch.co.uk/stories/articles/-/newsletter_stories/2010/feb_2010/ukwa_ teams_up_with_carbon_trust_on_emissions_toolkit/ (accessed 26 November 2010)

Hyster (2010) *The Truth about Electric Lift Trucks Environmental and Economic Benefits*, Hyster

Iacocca, L with Novak, W (1984) *Iacocca: An Autobiography*, Bantam Books, New York, NY

Intermec (2012) Unlocking the hidden margin www.intermec.com/public-files/misc/ Intermec-DC-Survey-Infographic-UK.pdf (accessed 10 September 2013)

Johnson, E (2008) Disagreement over carbon footprints: a comparison of electric and LPG forklifts, *Energy Policy*, 36, p 1572

Kaplan, R S and Norton, D P (1996) *The Balanced Scorecard*, Harvard Business School Press, Cambridge, MA

Kewill (2013) http://info.kewill.com/rs/kewill/images/Kewill%20Whitepaper%20 %20Logistics%20in%202020%20-%20The%20Future%20is%20Closer%20 Than%20You%20Think.pdf?mkt_tok=3RkMMJWWfF9wsRonsqnAZKXonjH pfsX56e4vW6SzlMI%2F0ER3fOvrPUfGjI4ASMVkI%2BSLDwEYGJlv6SgFTL nDMbB63rgJXBc%3D (accessed 16 September 13)

Landrum, H, Prybutok, V, Xiaoni Zhang and Peak, D (2009) Measuring IS system service quality with SERVQUAL: users' perceptions of relative importance of the five SERVPERF dimensions, *Informing Science: the International Journal of an Emerging Transdiscipline*, 12

Linde Materials Handling (2010) *Pallet manufacturer completes new R&D facility*, available at: http://logistics.about.com/b/2010/07/26/pallet-manufacturer- completes-new-rd-facility.htm (accessed 21 August 2010)

LXE, Inc (2009) Maximize the power of your workforce: learn how hands-free solutions can bring value in a tough economy, available at: www.rfsmart.com/ tinymce/filemanager/files/rfs_wp_hands_free_2.pdf (accessed 26 November 2010)

McIvor, R (2000) A practical framework for understanding the outsourcing process, *Supply Chain Management*, 5 (1)

McMahon, D, Periatt, J, Carr, J and LeMay, S (2007) Managing the critical role of the warehouse supervisor, *Graziadio Business Review*, 10 (4), available at: http://gbr.pepperdine.edu/2010/08/managing-the-critical-role-of-the- warehouse-supervisor/ (accessed 26 November 2010)

Meale, J (2010) quoted in Prevent accidents in the loading bay with Thorworld safety aids, available at: www.thorworld.co.uk/news/item/prevent_accidents

MHIA 'Sustainability in Warehousing, Distribution and Manufacturing' in 2011 www.sustainableplant.com/2011/04/sustainability-in-warehousing-distribution-and-manufacturing-study-released/

Miller, A (2004) *Order Picking for the 21st Century. Voice vs. Scanning Technology. A White Paper*, Tompkins Associates

Min, H (2004) An examination of warehouse employee recruitment and retention practices, *USA International Journal of Logistics*, 7 (4) December 2004

Moseley, R (2004) When working with metrics – the fewer the better is the rule, *Inventory Management*, 4–10 October

Motorola (2013) From Cost Center to Growth Center: Warehousing 2018 https://secure.eloqua.com/Web/Motorola/Motorola_WarehouseVision.pdf?WT.mc_id=NA_ENT_2013_Q3_EDM_Warehouse-Vision-Report_Confirm2&WT.i_asset_id=NA_ENT_2013_Q3_EDM_Warehouse-Vision-Report_Confirm2&cid=&elqid=CMTRO000002332730&mls=EDM Accessed 16 September 2013

Mulholland (2009) accessed from www.appriseconsulting.co.uk/downloads/how-to-manage-a-3PL-relationship.pdf

Muller, R (2007) *Piece picking: which method is best?*, available at: www.distributiongroup.com/articles/piecepickingwhichmethod.pdf

NIOSH (2010) accessed August 2010 from www.cdc.gov.niosh/docs/2001-109default.html

OSHA (2010) accessed from www.osha.gov/SLTC/poweredindustrialtrucks/index.html

OPS (2009) Pick This – A compendium of piece-picking process alternatives WERC Illinois

Peerless Research Group (2012) http://mmh.com/images/site/MMH1203_SpecRptIndryOutlookEquipSurvey.pdf (accessed 10/09/2013)

Piasecki, D (2002) *The aisle width decision*, available at: www.inventoryops.com/Aisle%20Width.htm

Porter, M www.brainyquote.com/quotes/quotes/m/michaelpor381643.html#ol49fHg66DVWdMbJ.99 (accessed 10 September 2013)

Prahalad, C K and Hamel, G (1990) The core competence of the corporation, *Harvard Business Review*, May–June

Prologis (2007) *Sustainability Report 2007*, available at: http://ir.prologis.com/SustainReport 2007/index.html (accessed 27 July 2010)

Pwc (2012) www.pwc.com/en_GX/gx/transportation-logistics/pdf/pwc-tl-2030-volume-5.pdf (accessed 16 September 2013)

Reichheld, F and Teal, T A (2001) *The Loyalty Effect: The Hidden Force Behind Growth, Profits, and Lasting Value*, Harvard Business School Press, Cambridge, MA

Rodriguez, M (2003) Flexible working patterns using annualised hours, *Work Study*, 52 (3), pp 145–9

Ruriani, D C (2003) Choosing a warehouse management system, available at: www.inboundlogistics.com/articles/10tips/10tips0403.shtml

Rushton, A, Croucher, P and Baker, P (2010) *The Handbook of Logistics and Distribution Management*, Kogan Page, London

Sage Software (2005) *How to choose a warehouse management system*, available at: www.myadjutant.com/brochures/How_to_Choose_WMS.pdf (accessed 26 November 2010)

Savills (2013) E-tailing and the impact on distribution warehouses, available at
www.transportintelligence.com/white_papers.php?page=2 (accessed 1
September 2013)

Schuller, R H (nd) BrainyQuote.com. Retrieved 12 August 2013, from BrainyQuote.com
website: www.brainyquote.com/quotes/quotes/r/roberthsc120883.html

Slack, N, Chambers, S and Johnston, R (2001) *Operations Management*, 3rd edn,
Pearson Education Limited, Harlow

Stock, J R (2004) *Product returns / Reverse logistics in warehousing*, WERC, Oak
Brook, Illinois

Tangen, S (2005) Demystifying productivity and performance, *International
Journal of Productivity and Performance Management*, **54** (1), available at:
www.mis.boun.edu.tr/erdem/mis517/cases-08/Demistifying_Productivity.pdf
(accessed 26 November 2010)

Tarr, J D (2004) Activity-based costing in the information age, available at:
www.theacagroup.com/activitybasedcosting.htm (accessed 26 November 2010)

Themido, I, Arantes, A, Fernandes, C and Guedes, A P (2000) Logistic costs case
study – an ABC approach, *Journal of the Operational Research Society*,
51 (10), pp 1148–57

Tompkins, J A (1998) *The Warehouse Management Handbook*, Tompkins Press

Tracy B. www.brainyquote.com/quotes/quotes/b/briantracy452659.html#
oPHvI3IiHGgTOQmj.99

Transport Intelligence (2012) The Implications Of 3d Printing For The Global
Logistics Industry John Manners-Bell, Ceo, Transport Intelligence Ltd Ken Lyon,
Ceo, Virtual-Partners Ltd 2012

UKWA (2010) *Save energy, cut costs: energy-efficient warehouse operation*,
available at: www.ukwa.org.uk/_files/23-carbon-trust-23.pdf
(accessed 26 November 2010)

Van den Berg, J P (2012) *Highly competitive warehouse management*, Management
Outlook Publishing, Buren

Vitasek, K (2004) quoted in When working with metrics – the fewer the better is
the rule, *Inventory Management*, 4–10 October

Vitasek, K (2010) *Vested Outsourcing*, Palgrave Macmillan, New York, NY

Weetman, N (2009) quoted in *Retail Week*, 9 October 2009, available at:
www.allbusiness.com/company-activities-management/operations-supply/
13170511-1.html (accessed 26 November 2010)

WERC (2012) DC Measures 2012 by Manrodt, KB and Vitasek, KL, WERC
Watch, Spring 2012

WERC (2007) a guide for establishing Warehouse Job Descriptions, Oak Brook, Illinois

WEF 2009 www.weforum.org/pdf/ip/SupplyChainDecarbonization.pdf

Wild, T (2010) in Readers' letters, *Operations Management*, 5, p 7

World Economic Forum (2009) *Supply chain decarbonization: the role of logistics
and transport in reducing supply chain carbon emissions*, available at:
www.weforum.org/pdf/ip/SupplyChainDecarbonization.pdf (accessed
13 September 2010)

Wulfratt, M (2013) www.mwpvl.com/html/order_pick_technologies.html (accessed
13 September 2013)

USEFUL WEBSITES

http://onpallet.com
www.5-1-2.com
www.aaronandpartners.com
www.abcsoftwork.com
www.aberdeen.com
www.apics.org
www.appriseconsulting.co.uk
www.astl.org
www.atlet.com/uk
www.atmsglobal.com
www.atmsplc.com
www.awsltd.biz
www.bar.co.uk
www.basda.org
www.bastiansolutions.com/
www.bendi.co.uk
www.bestconveyors.co.uk
www.bifa.org
www.businesslink.gov.uk
www.carbontrust.co.uk
www.carsonrack.com
www.cdc.gov/niosh/
www.certoctavian.co.uk
www.chalmor.co.uk
www.ciht.org.uk/
www.ciltuk.org.uk
www.cimcorp.com/
www.cips.org
www.cisco-eagle.com
www.constructor-group.co.uk
www.cranfield.ac.uk
www.cscmp.org/
www.dcvelocity.com/
www.dematic.com
www.dft.gov.uk
www.dtz.com/uk
www.envirowise.wrap.org.uk
www.eyefortransport.com
www.flexi.co.uk
www.forkliftnet.com

www.fortna.com
www.fsdf.org.uk
www.fta.co.uk
www.highjump.com
www.hse.gov.uk
www.ics.org.uk/
www.igps.net
www.inboundlogistics.com
www.insight-holdings.com
www.inthergroup.com
www.inventoryops.com
www.iomnet.org.uk/
www.iso.org
www.joloda.com
www.kardexremstar.com
www.kewill.com
www.kivasystems.com
www.knapp.com
www.linde-mh.co.uk
www.link51.com
www.linkedin.com
www.lloydsloadinglist.com
www.logismarket.co.uk
www.logistics.about.com
www.logisticsit.com
www.logisticsmanager.com
www.logisticsmgmt.com
www.logisticsworld.com
www.miniclipper.co.uk/
www.mmdonline.com
www.mmh.com
www.motorolasolutions.com/
    warehouse
www.naw.org
www.nene.co.uk
www.nitl.org
www.norbert-dentressangle.co.uk
www.opsdesign.com
www.osha.gov
www.redirack.co.uk/

www.retrotech.com
www.rha.org.uk
www.savills.co.uk/
www.scemagazine.com
www.scmr.com
www.scvisions.com
www.shdlogistics.com
www.skillsforlogistics.org
www.ssi-schaefer.com
www.stockcountmanagement.com
www.stoecklin.com
www.supplychainbrain.com
www.supplychainplanet.com
www.supplychainstandard.com
www.swisslog.com

www.systemlogistics.it
www.tfl.gov.uk/
www.thorworld.co.uk
www.tompkinsinc.com
www.toyota.co.uk
www.transdek.com
www.ukchamberofshipping.com
www.ukwa.org.uk
www.unarcomaterialhandling.com
www.vanderlande.co.uk
www.vocollect.com
www.warehousenews.co.uk
www.warehouse-science.com
www.werc.org
www.youtube.com

GLOSSARY

5S	Japanese methodology for organizing the workplace
80/20 rule	See Pareto analysis
ABC (costing)	Activity-based costing: relating costs to activities performed
ABC analysis	See Pareto analysis
ADC	Automatic data capture
AGV	Automated guided vehicle: robot for moving material around (driverless vehicle)
AIDC	Automatic identification and data collection
Annualized hours	Flexible hours system
APR	Adjustable pallet racking
ASN	Advanced shipping notice
AS/RS	Automatic storage and retrieval system
B2B	Business to business
B2C	Business to consumer
Back order	Order for items that are not currently in stock
Brownfield site	Site on which there has been previous development, eg factory or other building
CBT	Counterbalanced forklift truck
Centre of gravity method	Method for finding the best location, taking into account volumes supplied, travel distances and transport costs
CHIP	Chemical hazards, information and packaging regulations: UK legislation
CILT	Chartered Institute of Logistics and Transport
CNG	Compressed Natural Gas
COI	cube per order index
Collation	Collecting together items for the same delivery vehicle; see also marshalling area
Consolidation	Bringing together items from different sources to go to the same destination
COSHH	Control of substances hazardous to health regulations: UK legislation
CPFR	Collaborative planning, forecasting and replenishment: www.cpfr.org
Cross dock	Mainly used for pallets, where arriving items are immediately sorted for despatch without being put into stock
Cycle counting	Counting inventory of an item once during each replenishment order cycle

DC	Distribution centre
Dynamic allocation	Mainly used in pallet warehouses; each time a pallet arrives, a location is assigned to it; in general, this location does not depend on the item type or location of pallets of similar items
EAN	European article number: www.ean.org
EAN 128	High-density barcode coding system
EAN-13 (gtin-13)	13-digit barcode
ECR	Efficient consumer response: a supply chain practice for meeting consumer demand whilst reducing cost and inventory with manufacturers and retailers working closely together
EDI	Electronic data interchange
EPC	Electronic product code: code issued by agreed authority for an individual product (enabling slap'n'ship) such that other organizations can recognize the product
EPC Global	Not-for-profit organization set up by UCC and EAN International, responsible for implementing and maintaining globally agreed RFID standard codes
EPOS	Electronic point of sale
ERP	Enterprise resource planning; claims to take MRP2 (manufacturing resource planning) further by linking planning between businesses, and enabling better integration between the production and business management systems used in a firm
Euro pallet	Pallets of size 1200 mm × 800 mm made to euro pallet-agreed specifications
FAO	The United Nations Food and Agriculture Organization
FIFO	First in, first out method of stock rotation
FILO	First in, last out
FLT	Forklift truck
FTL	Full truck load
FTP	File transfer protocol
GFR	Good-faith receiving: no/limited checks on inbound goods
Greenfield site	Site that has not been developed before and is still countryside
GTIN	Global trade item number
HACCP	Hazard analysis and critical control point
HASWA	Health and Safety at Work Act: UK legislation
HMI	Human–machine interaction
HU/HD	Hoist up/hoist down

ID	Identity or identification
ISPM 15	International Standards for Phytosanitary Measures Publication No 15 (2009): Regulation of Wood Packaging Material in International Trade
IT	Information technology
JIT	Ordering stock frequently in small quantities; for finished stock this means only ordering what will almost certainly be sold in the very near future
Kaizen	Japanese methodology for quality improvement
Kanban	Japanese card system for controlling just-in-time material flow
KPI	Key performance indicator
LIFO	Last in, first out method of stock rotation
LOLER	Lifting operations and lifting equipment regulations: UK legislation
LPG	Liquified Petroleum Gas
LTL	Less than truck load, ie partly full vehicle
LU	Logistical unit, eg pallet, case
Marshalling area	Where packages or items are grouped together for a purpose, eg grouped by delivery route; see also collation
MHE	Materials handling equipment, eg forklift truck
NDC	National distribution centre
OCR	Optical character recognition; usually characters are in a format readable by humans and machines
OMS	Order management system
OTIF	On time and in full: the order must be delivered with exactly the items and quantities as ordered and on the day requested
Pareto analysis	To identify the most important activities or items which account for 80 per cent of the value, turnover, etc; also known as the 80/20 rule and ABC analysis
PDA	Personal digital assistant: a mobile device that functions as a personal information manager
Perpetual inventory counting	Counting a proportion of the inventory each week, in order to spread the cost of counting stock through the year
Picking	The act of selecting items from stock for an order
Postponement	Deferring creating variants of a product or customization of a product until the latest possible stage of production or distribution

PPE	Personal protective equipment
PPT	Powered pallet truck
QC	Quality control
QR	Quick response: products are produced and delivered in the variety and volume that match demand; the manufacturer bases production on data from retailers – little and often
RDC	Regional distribution centre
RDT	Radio data terminal
RF	Radio frequency
RFDC	Radio frequency data capture
RFID	Radio frequency identification
RIDDOR	Reporting of injuries, diseases and dangerous occurrences regulations: UK legislation
RSI	Repetitive strain injury
RTP	Returnable transit packaging
SAP	A widely used ERP system; see ERP
SCM	Supply chain management
SKU	Stock-keeping unit; each different item to be stored is a different SKU; note that two different-sized packages of the same substance or item are considered to be different SKUs; also referred to as product lines
Slap'n'ship	Using EPC-compliant RFID tags such that other organizations can recognize those products, enabling tracking and tracing through the supply chain worldwide
Slotting strategy	Deciding where each item should be located in the warehouse
SMI	Supplier-managed inventory or VMI (vendor-managed inventory)
Sortation	Sorting a group of items into different orders or destinations
SSCC	Serial shipping container code: unique worldwide 18-digit number applied to logistical unit, incorporating the AN.UCC company prefix
Static or fixed allocation	Each item in the warehouse is given a particular location where that item type will always be found
Stock cover	Period of time that current level of stock is capable of supporting sales, using average usage values
Stock turns annual	Number of times on average that the stock is used and replenished during the year
SVL	System vehicle loop
TMS	Transport management system: software to plan vehicle loads and routing
TQM	Total quality management

Trans-shipment	Movement of goods from one set of vehicles to another for onward delivery
UoM	Unit of measurement
VDU	Visual display unit
VMI	Vendor-managed inventory
VNA	Very narrow aisle
WEEE directive	European directive for safe disposal of waste electrical and electronic equipment
WERC	An association for logistics and warehousing professionals
WIP	Work in progress
WMS	Warehouse management system

INDEX

NB: page numbers in *italic* indicate figures or tables

Also available from Kogan Page

Also available from Kogan Page

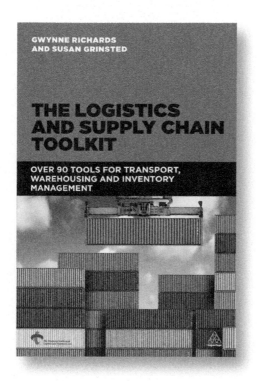

Find out more; visit www.koganpage.com and
sign up for offers and regular e-newsletters.

Also available from Kogan Page

CPSIA information can be obtained at www.ICGtesting.com
Printed in the USA
BVOW06s0941150616

452049BV00035B/297/P